Holocaust Fiction

Holocaust Fiction examines the controversies that accompany the publication of novels which represent the Holocaust. It looks at the most controversial Holocaust literature, the violently mixed receptions of these books, and what can be concluded from their reception about the ethics and practice of millennial Holocaust literature.

The novels examined, including some for the first time, are:

- *Time's Arrow* by Martin Amis
- *The White Hotel* by D.M. Thomas
- *The Painted Bird* by Jerzy Kosinski
- *Schindler's List* by Thomas Keneally
- *Sophie's Choice* by William Styron
- *The Hand that Signed the Paper* by Helen Darville
- *Perdition* by Jim Allen
- *Fragments* by Binjamin Wilkomirski

Holocaust fiction frequently elicits a polarized response from critics and readers. Although several of the novels discussed in this book won literary prizes, they were also deplored and criticized for their handling of the subject matter; as well, the issue of author 'authenticity' has been raised. By examining in detail both the critical response to these novels and the novels themselves, Sue Vice shows that Holocaust fiction is a legitimate and important genre, and argues that it is essential we engage with such literature.

In this compelling book, Sue Vice surveys the fictional, critical and theoretical territory of these novels and brings a new perspective to the key debates and issues relevant to those looking at representations of the Holocaust.

Sue Vice is Reader in English Literature at the University of Sheffield, and was involved in setting up Britain's first Holocaust Studies MA. Her publications include *Introducing Bakhtin* (1997).

Holocaust Fiction

Sue Vice

London and New York

First published 2000 by Routledge
11 New Fetter Lane, London EC4P 4EE

Simultaneously published in the USA and Canada
by Routledge
29 West 35th Street, New York, NY 10001

Routledge is an imprint of Taylor & Francis Books Ltd

Typeset in Baskerville by Taylor & Francis Books Ltd
Printed and bound in Great Britain by Clays Ltd, St Ives plc

The right of Sue Vice to be identified as the author of this Work has
been asserted by her in accordance with the Copyright, Designs and
Patents Act 1988.

British Library Cataloguing in Publication Data
A catalogue record for this book is available from the British Library

Library of Congress Cataloging in Publication Data
Vice, Sue, 1961–
Holocaust fiction/Sue Vice
Includes bibliographical references and index.
1. English fiction–20th century–History and criticism. 2. Holocaust,
Jewish (1939–1945), in literature. 3. Australian fiction–20th century–
History and criticism. 4. World War, 1939–1945–Literature and the
war. 5. Styron, William, 1925– Sophie's choice. 6. Jews in literature.
I. Title.
PR888.H6 V53 1999
823'91409358–dc21   99-054342

ISBN 0–415–18552–1 (hbk)
ISBN 0–415–18553-X (pbk)

Contents

Acknowledgements   vii

Introduction   1

1 Formal matters: Martin Amis, *Time's Arrow*   11

2 Documentary fiction: D.M. Thomas, *The White Hotel*   38

3 Autobiographical fiction: Jerzy Kosinski, *The Painted Bird*   67

4 Faction: Thomas Keneally, *Schindler's List*   90

5 Melodrama: William Styron, *Sophie's Choice*   117

6 Historical polemic: Helen Darville, *The Hand that Signed the Paper*   141

Conclusion   161

Notes   168
Bibliography   229
Index   233

Acknowledgements

I would like to thank the following people:

In Britain: Gillian Banner, Amanda Bernstein, Jeffrey Bernstein, Matt Broughton, David Burnley, Bryan Cheyette, Harriet Coles, Margaret Deith, Barbara Duke, Keith Green, John Haffenden, Sylvia Kantaris, Ruth Levin, Agnes McAuley, Moray McGowan, Deborah Marks, Julie Maylon, Ann Parry, Neil Roberts, Philip Roberts, Antony Rowland, Anthony Rudolf, Rebecca Russell, Erica Sheen, Agnes Spier, D.M. Thomas, Elizabeth Vice, John Vice, Tony Vice, Florence Vice-Coles, Rosie Waters, and the Arts and Humanities Research Board for a research grant relating to this project.

In the USA: Lawrence Douglas, Alex George and Dori Laub.

In Israel: Daphna Erdinast-Vulcan, Yehudit Kleiman and Mordechai Paldiel.

In Australia: Ian Collins, Amelia Slaytor, John Slaytor, Michael Slaytor, Petrina Slaytor and Pip Vice.

Thanks to the University of Sheffield for permission to quote from the Peter Redgrove Archive.

A much shorter verstion of material in chapter 6 appeared in the *Jewish Quarterly*, June 1998.

Introduction

Holocaust fictions are scandalous: that is, they invariably provoke controversy by inspiring repulsion and acclaim in equal measure. To judge by what many critics have to say, to write Holocaust fictions is tantamount to making a fiction of the Holocaust.

In this book I focus on scandals concerning Holocaust novels, but this phenomenon is clear, too, in the case of other genres. To take a flagrant example first, Rolf Hochhuth's 1964 play, *The Deputy*, sparked a fierce debate about its premise, the deliberate indifference of the Catholic Church and Pope Pius XII to the fate of the Jews during the war. Peter Weiss's 1966 play, *The Investigation*, based on the Auschwitz War Crimes Trial held in Germany in 1963–65, was greeted with outrage as it contrived never to name the Jews who were ostensibly its subject. In 1979 the television series based on Gerald Green's novel *Holocaust*, which was shown in the United States and Europe, provoked intense debate about the nature and purpose of Holocaust representation – a debate which was repeated with regard to Steven Spielberg's 1993 film *Schindler's List*. In 1987 Jim Allen's *Perdition* was the first play to be banned by the Royal Court Theatre in Britain, on the grounds that it was historically inaccurate. In the mid-1990s Binjamin Wilkomirski's ostensibly autobiographical *Fragments* had its authenticity called into question.[1] As these examples show, the only thing that each of these scandals has in common is the subject of the Holocaust. Apart from this shared feature, it is possible to isolate the particular theme which each debate focused on: polemic and historical accuracy in the case of Hochhuth and Allen; allegory in the case of Weiss; popular form in the case of Green and Spielberg; authenticity in the case of Wilkomirski. In other words, standard literary and cultural issues were at stake in each scandal.

Yet the common factor of the Holocaust as a subject is not easily dismissed. This is the central concern of this study: why and how fictional representations of the Holocaust are always greeted with such a mixture of acclaim and dismay. In the chapters that follow, I will trace the answers in the case of each novel – and those answers may not be the ones the dismayed critics think they are. I have limited myself to works written in English, with the consequence that all but one of the novels discussed here are by non-Jewish writers unconnected to the events of the Holocaust, the exception being Jerzy Kosinski's *The Painted Bird*. I chose English texts because this makes the analysis of their language and use of other texts a much surer task; and because these are the novels with which many readers will be familiar, although it does not follow that readers' knowledge of the events of the Holocaust will derive only from texts like these (a prevalent fear among critics). It is also true that texts written in English, because they are more likely not to be by survivors,[2] are those which provoke the most extreme responses and therefore most clearly lay bare the issues involved. The novels come from a variety of cultural contexts: Martin Amis (*Time's Arrow*, 1991, Chapter 1) and D.M. Thomas (*The White Hotel*, 1981, Chapter 2) are British; Jerzy Kosinski (*The Painted Bird*, 1965, Chapter 3) was born in Poland but became an American citizen; William Styron (*Sophie's Choice*, 1979, Chapter 5) is also an American; while Thomas Keneally (*Schindler's List*, 1982, Chapter 4) and Helen Darville (*The Hand that Signed the Paper*, 1994, Chapter 6) are Australian.

In the chapters that follow I give a summary of the critical response to each of these six novels and attempt to unravel the assumptions behind those responses. I then provide my own reading of each novel, which in most cases includes an analysis of exactly the way in which that novel has benefited from anterior sources. Indeed, if there is one method that stands out among all the others used in Holocaust fiction, it is intertextuality deployed in very specific ways. The charge of plagiarism or over-reliance on other texts, suffered by all the novels under discussion here, is far too crude for a method which is necessarily widespread, whether to back up a novelistic plot or to give an authentic, documentary aspect to the novel. The successes and failures of intertextuality are in many ways the key to the methods of Holocaust fiction, and I have been keen to investigate the precise workings of these methods.

In my view, among the novels I have investigated, Martin Amis's formal use of anterior texts works much better than William Styron's construction of a fictional autobiography in which the novel's protagonist both reads and uses historical sources. D.M. Thomas's striking temporal deformations are the novelistic result of his use of a historical source, while the unusual tenses and narrative tone in Thomas Keneally's novel are a sign of its origins in witness testimony. While the unevenness of Helen Darville's novel is partly due to unassimilated (and inaccurately deployed) historical material, Styron makes a significant but unwitting error in his use of a survivor testimony in *Sophie's Choice*. The charge of plagiarism made against Jerzy Kosinski has not been substantiated, and seems to represent fallout from critical unease about his own autobiographical fictions, which made it easy to misread his novel as a testimony.

The second most striking common feature in these novels is their treatment of time, or the relation between story and plot, to use the Russian formalist distinction between chronological events (the story) and their fictional patterning (the plot). The outcome of the Holocaust itself is well known; though in the English-speaking world in particular we are used to thinking of the Second World War in terms of a victory over Hitler, he did succeed in murdering two-thirds of

European Jewry and destroying for ever a 1,000-year-old culture. In historical and human terms, this is an irreparable tragedy; in fictional terms, it entails the loss of such novelistic staples as suspense, choosing one's ending, constructing characters with the power to alter their fate, allowing good to triumph over evil, or even the clear identification of such moral categories. A nostalgia for these fictional staples can be detected in Keneally's *Schindler's List*, which tries through its choice of story to find a crumb of comfort in universal destruction, not always to readers' satisfaction;[3] and in the final chapter of Thomas's *The White Hotel*, which is rather startlingly set in the afterlife.

On the other hand, as Michael André Bernstein has argued in his book *Foregone Conclusions* (1994), the Holocaust is often treated to a destructively teleological evaluation from the standpoint of the present.[4] In this view, although the Holocaust was unprecedented and unimaginable, its bystanders and victims should have seen it coming and taken appropriate action. In fictional terms, consciousness of such 'backshadowing' can take several forms. A return to the time when the events had not yet taken place can be effected, as in Darville's *The Hand that Signed the Paper*, where we see a recreation of perpetrators' decisions to commit mass murder; and, even more defamiliarizingly, in Amis's *Time's Arrow*. By taking on a truism of chaos theory, that the arrow of time cannot be reversed,[5] Amis's novel satirizes the logic of backshadowing by showing a world in which the Holocaust really was inevitable: but only because it had already happened. In each case, although the story – that is, the events of the Holocaust – is already known in outline, the plot – the fictional rearrangement of that chronology – attempts to reconfigure it. In Styron's *Sophie's Choice* this takes the form of delaying Sophie's horrifying revelation, hinted at in the title, until the novel's end; in *Schindler's List*, which is a story of rescue, it means that the narrative cannot help looking forward to the triumphant survival of its eponymous hero and his Jews.

The third central literary category in Holocaust fiction is that of the relation between author and narrator. In all six of the novels under consideration here, critics have invariably considered the biography of the author to be highly relevant. The exact details of Kosinski's experiences in Nazi-occupied Poland are sought out by such critics, and the reasons for Darville's masquerade under the name 'Demidenko' indignantly explored. Anxiety about a lack of authorial credentials is registered by the writers themselves: both Amis and Styron point out that they have Jewish children, as if legitimacy can work backwards.[6] Purposeful schemes and unwitting errors are ascribed to the authors of Holocaust fiction as if that figure had never died;[7] or as if the limit-case of the Holocaust shows that disregarding the author's schemes is a luxury to be reserved for other instances. In the case of Kosinski and Darville, critical outcry followed revelations that there was no direct relation between author and narrator, as there obviously is in Holocaust testimony. Kosinski may be a Holocaust survivor, but *The Painted Bird* has had a higher rating as autobiography than as a novel, precisely because in the former case a clear connection can be made between the author and the character.[8] In the other cases, the attitude of the author to the narrator has been scrutinized minutely by critics to ensure that the former is not just 'bumming a ride on the Holocaust' (to use the resonant phrase of the theatre director Peter Hall).[9]

'Authority' appears to be conferred on a writer if they can be shown to have a connection with the events they are describing; this obviously means that the writer's biography must be transparently available for all to know. This way of approaching Holocaust fiction is another result of not properly detaching it as a genre from testimony, of which one might more reasonably demand an authentic connection between the author-narrator and the events described. Even Roberto Benigni, director of the Academy Award-winning film *Life is Beautiful* (1998), felt that before the film's release he had to prove his credentials by describing the wartime imprisonment of his father in a labour camp – despite the fact that his film is so self-avowedly fabular, or 'legendary' in Erich Auerbach's term, that a literal underpinning might be thought unnecessary.[10]

There are various reasons for the expectation or even the insistence that we know as much as possible about the identity of the author of a Holocaust fiction. One is that readers are suspicious of the motives of outsiders, who might have improper reasons for choosing this subject. These reasons could range from mere sensationalism to Holocaust revisionism. The poetry of Sylvia Plath is a case in point; Plath's lack of a biographical reason for using death-camp imagery in her work opened her to the charge of appropriation, or 'subtle larceny', in George Steiner's phrase.[11] Another reason is the simple mistrust of invention in relation to the Holocaust; the more personal distance there is between the author and the subject, the more 'invented' the work must be. This is clearly a paradox if we are talking about fiction, which is by definition invented; but it is significant that on the whole fewer unsympathetic questions are raised about those with the 'right' to fictionalize the subject because of their second-generation or Jewish identity – Cynthia Ozick, Susan Fromberg Schaeffer, Diane Samuels – than about those who do not own such a right – including David Hartnett and John Hersey.[12] However, historical and ethnic authority are no guarantee of rapturous reception, as the divided response to Philip Roth's *The Ghost Writer* and Melvin Jules Bukiet's *After* suggests.[13]

The same features as in any fictional work are present in Holocaust novels: intertextuality, plot and story, author and narrator. However, because of the subject matter, all these standard features are brought to their limit, taken literally, defamiliarized or used self-consciously.[14] In this way, effective Holocaust fiction cannot help registering the shocking and unassimilable nature of its subject in formal ways, even if this does not take the extreme form of Amis's and Thomas's narrative and temporal deformations.

'... either not a novel or not about Treblinka'[15]

Inevitably, therefore, the publication of works of Holocaust fiction often meets not only a negative but an extremely polarized reception. Such works are highly praised, nominated for literary awards and become best-sellers; in equal measure they are attacked and deplored. This polarity is due to the uncertain status of imaginative texts which take the Holocaust as their subject. Critical opinion is sheerly divided about whether and in what way the Nazi genocide can be represented artistically; and what implications such representation has for the historical record. I will now briefly examine the two sides of this debate.

Theodor Adorno notoriously observed that 'After Auschwitz to write a poem is barbaric'; it is to:

> squeeze aesthetic pleasure out of artistic representation of the naked bodily pain of those who have been knocked down by rifle butts. ... Through aesthetic principles or stylization ... the unimaginable ordeal still appears as if it had some ulterior purpose. It is transfigured and stripped of some of its horror, and with this, injustice is already done to the victims.[16]

Adorno argues that it is unacceptable to gain even aesthetic or readerly pleasure from a work of art which treats the Holocaust: no aesthetic representation is appropriate.[17] Claude Lanzmann is of the same opinion: 'I deeply believe there are things that cannot and should not be represented.'[18] By this Lanzmann means that the scenes and events of the Holocaust which have not been recorded by victims or survivors should be left unimagined.[19] Lanzmann's distaste for Steven Spielberg's *Schindler's List* and its 'fabrication of archives', in particular its representation of the interior of a gas chamber, was widely quoted when the film was released.[20] By contrast, Lanzmann's documentary film *Shoah* refuses any 'direct' representation of the past, whether by fiction or archival footage.[21] Rather than attempting to recreate a past time, Lanzmann presents the bare testimony and memories of survivors, and preserves the distance between the time of the events and the time of their narration. Clearly it is not so much *representation* Lanzmann objects to, as *re-creation* of the kind that constitutes the *mise en scène* of *Schindler's List*.

Elie Wiesel has equally famously asserted that ' "The Holocaust as Literary Inspiration" is a contradiction in terms', and posed the rhetorical question that if the events of the Holocaust are exploited for literary purposes, 'Wouldn't that mean, then, that Treblinka and Belzec, Ponar and Babi Yar all ended in fantasy, in words, in beauty, that it was simply a matter of literature?'[22] It is easy to agree with Wiesel if the matter of Holocaust fiction is approached from the standpoint of a survivor (although Wiesel himself is the author of novels as well as testimony about the Holocaust). Approached the other way round, fiction is just one of several generic representations of the subject, not, despite Wiesel's eloquently expressed fears, its final resting place.[23]

Indeed, critical preference for testimony over fiction has become such a truism that it is hard to find any voices dissenting from it.[24] The bias towards testimony is often couched in formal terms: novels are said to be too self-assured and unambiguous properly to represent the Holocaust, while testimony is riven with a more fitting linguistic and narrative self-doubt. It seems that this argument is only masquerading as a formal issue, in a rhetorical move we will see time and again in the area of the reception of Holocaust fiction: apparently literary criteria slide without warning into, or cover over, moral and moralistic issues. In the case of valuing uncertain non-fiction over certain fiction, it appears that something like Erich Auerbach's distinction between history and legend is at issue. For Auerbach, this distinction rests on a structural difference which is easy to detect. The legendary

> runs too smoothly. All cross-currents, all friction, all that is casual, secondary to the main events and themes, everything unresolved, truncated and uncertain, which confuses the clear progress of the action ... has disappeared.[25]

By contrast, the 'historical event which we witness, or learn from the testimony of those who witnessed it, runs much more variously, contradictorily and confusedly'. Auerbach adds that anyone who knows of the Nazis or the First World War 'will feel how difficult it is to represent historical themes in general, and how unfit they are for legend'.[26] A moralistic slant is perceptible in Auerbach's comment even though it is expressed in structural terms; indeed, his insistence on the inappropriateness of novelistic certainty anticipates Adorno's sentiment that the realms of art and pain are entirely at odds with each other. In Auerbach's argument, it is art and history – or at least certain kinds of history – which are at odds.[27]

The critic Bryan Cheyette has likewise insisted that there is a gulf between the 'breathtaking certainties' of fiction, such as D.M. Thomas's *The White Hotel*, and the 'agonized uncertainties of those who went through the camps', such as Charlotte Delbo and Primo Levi. This argument rests on a suspicion of novelistic language – in testimony, 'words actually betray [survivors'] experiences' – and, again, of formal neatness – 'There is no sense in the [fictional] text that that act of shaping, that act of catharsis and redemption, that act of turning [the Holocaust] into a literary form, is ultimately doomed to failure.'[28] It seems that the formal objections made to legend are just other ways of saying that survivor testimony is better. Such works partake of Walter Benjamin's 'aura': we can get in touch with the reality of an extreme experience through the witness of those who were there.[29] Fiction could in any case imitate the lack of 'catharsis and redemption' which Cheyette claims characterizes testimony alone. All the same, of the six novels discussed here only *Time's Arrow* clearly does this. The others all, however 'feel-bad' their premise, end with some kind of conventional resolution: heaven in *The White Hotel*, a visit to present-day Treblinka in *The Hand that Signed the Paper*, the mourning of Oskar Schindler in *Schindler's List*, and in both *The Painted Bird* and *Sophie's Choice*, the realization by the narrators that they must write their experiences.

The preference for testimony over fiction is thoroughly understandable and probably shared by most readers. It explains the fact that it is possible to read many examples of authentic diary, testimony, memoir and novels by survivors and never tire of them; each one is a fresh experience, even if it recounts the same events as another.[30] Different factors enter into the experience of reading survivor testimony, which is a part of the imperative to remember those who survived, those who died in the middle of writing their diaries, or those who died before writing anything at all. The same is true of historical works about the Holocaust. They may exert a particular grip over the imagination by virtue of their content *and* their truth-value, as the appearance of the same texts in different novels discussed in this study suggests. Hannah Arendt's *Eichmann in Jerusalem* (1965), A. Anatoli's *Babi Yar* (1970) and Martin Gilbert's *The Holocaust* (1986) are used by several novelists, while others have been seized by less well-known works, such as *KL Auschwitz Seen by the SS* (1970) and Robert Jay Lifton's *The Nazi Doctors* (1986).[31] However, it is important to understand the view which values testimony over all fictional genres for what it is – an estimate based on non-literary criteria, and it is precisely those criteria with which I am concerned here.

'Your struggles for humanity will inspire poems'

This prediction is attributed to Zelig Kalmanovich, the Lithuanian scholar of Yiddish and editor of the pre-war *YIVO Bleter* (the newspaper of the Jewish Scientific Institute), speaking to his fellows in the Vilna Ghetto.[32] Looking forwards in such a manner, it seems appropriate to imagine the terrible struggle of resistance to the Nazis being remembered in the form of epic or lyric. Kalmanovich seems to assume that the poetry will not be written by those who fought, as he does not predict their survival; while his comment may implicitly refer to Jewish contemporaries of the resisters, it does lay open the way for non-survivors to write about these events.

The counter-argument to scepticism about the value, or even viability, of Holocaust fiction is put most pressingly – not surprisingly – by writers themselves. Joseph Skibell, author of the novel *A Blessing on the Moon* (1997), insists that a devaluation of literature is to blame for scepticism about the ability of fiction to offer insights into this subject: 'The man-made prohibition against making graven images of this event we call the Holocaust seems to derive from a suspicion of storytelling, of art and literature.'[33] Lucy Ellmann, author of *Man or Mango?* (1998), responds to the idea that writers of fiction should learn from survivors, with the remark, 'I don't believe there are any rules about who you've got to talk to before you sit down and write something.'[34] Finally, Michael André Bernstein argues against Wiesel's position by observing that 'testimonial literature' did not begin with the Holocaust – despite Wiesel's insistence that testimony is a new literary form bequeathed by Holocaust survivors to their generation – but was common, for instance, during the First World War in the form of the war memoir:

the theme of absolute trauma and the attendant impulse to grant authenticity only to those who have either endured the trauma themselves or who have, by a process of sufficiently intense identification, become its 'secondary victims', is one of our epoch's longest-lived and most influential imaginative obsessions.[35]

In other words, the example of the Holocaust just brings out in particularly stark form all kinds of habits of mind and ideology which came before, including the stock placed in authentic memoir. Bernstein's point is supported by Auerbach's link of the taboo placed on legends of the First World War with that on legends about the Nazis. Over forty years after Auerbach's study *Mimesis* was published, novels about the Great War are no longer received in anything like the scandalized fashion which greets Holocaust fiction, as the success of Pat Barker's *Regeneration* trilogy (1991, 1993, 1996) shows.[36] The trilogy was widely hailed as the recasting – the regeneration – for our time of an 80-year-old history, suggesting that proximity is a significant factor in disquiet about Holocaust fiction.

There is another way to approach the argument which places 'authentic' historical writing, particularly testimony and other works by survivors, on the acceptable side of the divide and which deems fiction to be unacceptable, particularly if it is by a writer without the 'authority' of an ethnic or historical connection to the events described. This alternative approach is the one I have used throughout this study. It involves taking for granted the notion that we cannot dismiss or outlaw Holocaust fiction, since it is simply a different genre from survivor testimony. It approaches the subject in its own way, rather than aiming to 'add' to or 'go beyond' the survivor record.[37] Any new literary perspectives on the Holocaust after the middle of the third millennium can only be written by descendants of survivors or by novelists with no connection to the event. Given that this is the case, it makes more sense to attempt to construct a typology of Holocaust fiction than to consign the genre as a whole to the status of a failed supplement. Such a typology is not concerned with prescriptive 'rules', as Lucy Ellmann puts it, but with a description of actual fictive practice.[38] Such a description is what I have aimed to provide in this study.

I will conclude this introduction by citing two examples of Holocaust fiction which seem to me *not* to push to any extreme their novelistic constituents; in other words, their content has not affected their form. The first example is Anne Michaels's novel *Fugitive Pieces* (1996), which received very favourable reviews and won several literary awards, including the Guardian Fiction Prize and the 1997 Orange Prize.[39] It concerns the rescue of Jakob Beer, a small boy whose parents and sister were killed in Poland during the war, by Athos Roussos, a Greek archaeologist; Beer's adult life in Canada; and, after Beer's death, the search for his diaries and papers by a young acolyte, himself the son of survivors. Electing not to appropriate any detailed horror, in the manner of Thomas and Darville, *Fugitive Pieces* – the first novel of a poet – infuses human loss and memory into descriptions of landscape, weather and ancient history. The novel is written in 'strange episodic images', to use its own phrase,[40] and in contrast to the materiality of the other novels I discuss, it diverts its attention to the world of the spirit and the transcendent. For instance, of slave labour: 'In the Golleschau quarry, stone-carriers were forced to haul huge blocks of limestone endlessly.... The insane task was not futile only in the sense that faith is not futile.'[41] And, of the cries of death from the gas chambers:

> At that moment of utmost degradation, in that twisted reef, is the most obscene testament of grace. For can anyone tell with absolute certainty the difference between the sounds of those who are in despair and the sounds of those who want desperately to believe?[42]

In both these examples we are reading Jakob Beer's first-person narration, so there is little sense in taking the author or the fiction to task for its idiosyncratic moves. None the less, this seems to be a way of trying to wring aesthetic and meaningful comfort from an event which offers no redemption of any kind. By contrast to the poetic option, I argue that crude narration, irony, black humour, appropriation, sensationalism, even characters who mouth antisemitic slogans, do not seem as suspect.

Throughout this book I have drawn on Mikhail Bakhtin's notion of 'double-voiced discourse': that is, novelistic language which looks seamless but is actually shot through with discourse from all kinds of sources, each of which battles for supremacy with the others. Bakhtin describes this as 'a contradiction-ridden, tension-filled unity of two embattled tendencies in the life of language'.[43] In the novel, double-voiced discourse can take several forms. At its most basic level, the clash of discourses from different walks of life ('dialogized heteroglossia', in Bakhtin's term) constructs the text's meaning. In Holocaust fiction, such a clash is likely to come about from the juxtaposition of literary with historical discourse, or that of different and opposed historical sources. At the level of characterization, Bakhtin's notion of polyphony may come into play. The narrator is constructed in just the same way as the characters, and has no superior factual or moral knowledge. (Again, meaning is constructed not by authorial fiat but by the clash of discourses.) This is an especially significant feature in Holocaust fiction, where critics and readers may precisely *not* want to read a polyphonic text, wishing rather for the clear utterance of moral certainties. I argue that, on the contrary, the polyphonic testing of such certainties is just what gives Holocaust fiction its particular representational power. Finally, Bakhtin's term for a novel which successfully frees up its constituent languages and calls on the reader – not the narrator or author – to make sense of them is 'dialogic'. Although dialogism is not a feature sufficient to make an effective Holocaust novel, it is a necessary one.

All the scandalous effects in the novels I discuss are compellingly characterized by double-voicedness, in contrast to the monologism of novels like *Fugitive*

Pieces.[44] Natasha Walter tempers her enthusiasm for Michaels's novel along similar lines by observing: 'she is putting literature on a pedestal; it would be wonderful to see her making it a little less polished'.[45] For 'pedestal', read single-voiced; for 'less polished', read double-voiced.

The same problem arises in Cynthia Ozick's *The Shawl* (1980), a novel which has been widely praised for its literary virtues. This is Ozick's description, as seen through the mother's eyes, of a young child being killed by a concentration camp guard: 'All at once Magda was swimming through the air. The whole of Magda travelled through loftiness. She looked like a butterfly touching a silver vine.'[46] Again, because this is the unbelieving viewpoint of Magda's mother, the description of a starving child as a 'butterfly', and the electrified fence as a 'silver vine', is free indirect discourse: it is the word of the character and not the narrator. But readers may none the less feel an unease at seeing the child dissolved into metaphor before their very eyes. Of course it is unnervingly hard to decide how to represent such atrocities as the gas chambers and the murder of small children. But the indirection of a deformed narrative structure, or the re-contextualizing of historical details from contemporary sources, seems altogether more challenging to the literary decorum that Michaels and Ozick feed straight back into, and so much more apt to a wretchedly recalcitrant subject.

Chapter 1

Formal matters

Martin Amis, *Time's Arrow*

Readers and critics have had notoriously polarized opinions about *Time's Arrow*'s success in representing the Holocaust, in reverse, from the point of view of a Nazi doctor. Mark Lawson describes the division as one 'between those who regard the novel as astoundingly original and those who regard it as frigid stylistic tricksiness'.[1] Novelist Simon Louvish, in the second category, describes *Time's Arrow* as simply having 'a Holocaust theme', which acknowledges the fact that it is not easy to say whether the Holocaust is central to Amis's novel.[2] The novel's title implies that it is the formal construction of the text, its backwards narration, which is central, and that the Holocaust is only an extreme instance of something which looks very strange backwards, apparently defying the principle that 'portrayal of the Holocaust cannot be subordinated to aesthetic goals';[3] but the text itself implies that the reason for the backwards narration is the 'time out of joint' of the Holocaust. Amis's own comments on his inspiration for the novel in the book's Afterword suggest that his interest in the reversed form preceded the morally reversed content, although his emphasis on the simultaneity of his perceptions is interesting. He describes reading Robert Jay Lifton's book *The Nazi Doctors*:

> It's the most extraordinary donnée I've ever had as a writer. It all fell into place at once. A doctor at Auschwitz was the absolute example of the inverted world.... German doctors went, almost overnight, from healing to killing.[4]

In *Time's Arrow*, the protagonist's years as a doctor in Auschwitz take up only twenty pages of the novel, but the repercussions of what he did during that time have a radical impact on the rest of the text. His actions inform the way the text is narrated just as they haunt his mind. It is as if this protagonist, whose real name is Odilo Unverdorben, has effected a permanent version of what Robert Jay Lifton calls an internal 'doubling'. His soul has split off from his consciousness, and this accounts for the novel's particular kind of narration, as we will see. Unverdorben lives the rest of his life with a series of new, assumed identities, under the shadow of what he did during the war years. He is unable to conduct an inner dialogue with his soul-narrator, or with anyone else who tries to get close to him.

Time's Arrow was subjected to particular critical scrutiny in Britain because it was short-listed in 1991 for the prestigious Booker Prize.[5] The process of judging the prize was fraught with scandal, as one of the judges, Nicholas Mosley, resigned in protest at the exclusion of his preferred contender, Allan Massie's *The Sins of the Father*.[6] Massie's novel is also concerned with the Holocaust, although more with its aftermath and effect on the state of Israel. Mosley notoriously described *The Sins*, in contrast to *Time's Arrow*, as a 'novel of ideas'. Most of the negative criticism focuses on the subordination of content to form in Amis's novel. The similarity of the narrator in *Time's Arrow* to the narrators in Amis's other works was noted. In his study *Doubles*, written before the publication of *Time's Arrow*, Karl Miller refers to Amis as 'the latest of Anglo-America's dualist artists', and discusses the phenomenon of 'doubling' in *Money*.[7] Mark Lawson comments, in this case in a positive vein, on Amis's novels *Money* and *London Fields*, both of which 'turn on the question of who is writing the book, with characters duped by an author-figure: this can be taken as post-modernism or a wider concern with who is in charge'. The same could be said of *Time's Arrow*: the disembodied narrator inhabiting a former Nazi doctor is simply an extreme version of how any third-person narration operates, and is used, complete with Amisian tone, for metafictional effect even in this novel. As Mark Lawson puts it, 'Its opponents are not accusing it of anti-Semitism, but of being Amisian', that is, of having excess 'technical perkiness'.[8]

Reversed narration

However, it can of course be argued that the form and content of *Time's Arrow* are inseparable. The 'counter-intuitive' nature of the Holocaust, to quote a phrase frequently on the lips of the narrator, has permeated all aspects of the text: its relation to the reader, its narrator, the narrator's choice of words and interpretation of events. In his collection of essays, *Admitting the Holocaust*, Lawrence Langer discusses the concept of backwards comprehension. He argues that the Holocaust is a stumbling block to, in particular, an American-style optimism, or any belief in improvement, forward movement or a future which will be better than the present:

> Kierkegaard wrote somewhere that life is lived forward and understood backward, and I suspect that for most of us this continues to be an attractive premise. But just the opposite is true for the Holocaust experience: we live it backward in time, and once we arrive there, we find ourselves mired in its atrocities, a kind of historical quicksand that hinders our bid to bring it forward again into a meaningful future.[9]

In *Time's Arrow*, this argument is almost literally enacted. The Holocaust is lived backward – the Nazis 'conjure a multitude from the sky above the river', as the narrator puts it – and understood forward, in the sense that effect precedes cause.[10] We read about what has happened before we read the reasons why it happened. As the narrator impishly says of one of Tod's romances, 'One thing led to another – actually it was more like the other way round' (56). The separation of cause and effect is as true of the Holocaust in this text as it is on a more local level, where 'yesterdays are always terrible, when Tod hits the tea' (31). In an amplification of Langer's argument, the narrator of *Time's Arrow* knows that 'The world is going to start making sense' at exactly the moment, '*Now*', that Unverdorben arrives at Auschwitz Central by motorbike (124). Accustomed as we are by this time to the text's logic, we know that we are 'really' reading about Unverdorben's flight from Auschwitz, and we will now see the film of his life there run past us in reverse time (16). Auschwitz only makes any sense to the narrator backwards; and this is because only seeing it in reverse can give it a moral and narrative trajectory which seems acceptable and familiar. For instance, continuing a theme of payments made with 'collar-stud'-sized gold pieces, the narrator (now much closer to Unverdorben and using the first person) observes: 'I *knew* my gold had a sacred efficacy. All those years I amassed it, and polished it with my mind: for the Jews' teeth' (130). Read the right way round, this passage loses any moral sense and becomes one of the atrocities which 'mire' attempts to understand the Holocaust, as Langer put it. We know that 'sacred efficacy' is really profane theft; the gold has not been carefully 'amassed' but hidden away and even buried by Unverdorben; and it is not 'for' but from the Jews' teeth.

Simon Louvish, an acerbic critic of *Time's Arrow*, argues that Amis's strategy of backwards narration is not a successful defamiliarization of the impossibility of bringing the Holocaust experience into any 'meaningful future', but a misguided and cynical attempt to get in on the Holocaust act. Louvish also dismisses the idea that the novel is commendable as satire:

> By inverting the morality of Auschwitz we are thereby brought to a new angle to ponder on the awfulness of it all. Or are we? After all, the Nazis saw their extermination programme as altruistic when it was the right way round.

Louvish concludes that the acceptability of non-survivors writing about the Holocaust is accompanied by a sigh of relief on the part of critics and readers, as

> the subject has been taken out of the hands of these whining victims and is now the stuff of 'mainstream' art. Jewish writers can be more effectively sidelined, their accusatory polemics quietly brushed aside, their subjects co-opted and sanitized, pain diffused, rage dissipated.

He concludes that Amis has taken up the subject of the Holocaust for modish reasons, and because 'Shoah can transform what would otherwise be an intriguing but unoriginal science fiction novel into Great Art, best seller-dom and the brink of the Booker'.[11]

Louvish's criticisms of Amis move without distinction from political arguments – this is appropriation, a 'patchy' view of the Holocaust offered by an outsider – to moral and aesthetic ones – the novel's central conceit was taken from Philip K. Dick, and it is not a very interesting one at that. It is true that 'accusatory polemics' in Holocaust texts *have* been dismissed, and expressions of rage dissipated, as the case of Elie Wiesel's *Night* shows. The English version of that work is based on the French edition, which was itself a drastically shortened translation of Wiesel's original Yiddish text, *And the World Remained Silent*. The Yiddish title was a clear signal of its polemical status. When *Night* was published in France, David Roskies argues, there was no place for such a reproach, and its central slant had to be altered; indeed, in the English translation, it seems that Eliezer, the narrator, is reproaching his own family and friends for not heeding warnings of the fate to come, not the outside world.[12]

However, it is hard to think of a recent instance of work by a survivor which has been received with the embarrassment and distaste Louvish describes and which Wiesel obviously faced.[13] There are examples to the contrary: Louis Begley's *Wartime Lies* and Ida Fink's *A Scrap of Time* have both been awarded literary prizes.[14] Louvish admits that his own agenda is partly literary envy – 'Now why didn't I think of that?' – and, revealingly, he quotes not from Amis's novel itself, but from a reviewer's quotation.

Louvish's main aesthetico-historical objection to *Time's Arrow* is to its central device of backwards representation. He argues that it presents an image of an 'altruistic Holocaust'. This is quite correct, and is the main purpose of the text's irony. The first two-thirds of Amis's novel are devoted to establishing this irony: viewed backwards, doctors destroy, but doctors *at Auschwitz* create. The narrator, momentarily turned hawker, describes the state of affairs at the New Jersey hospital where Tod works:

> If you want to get fucked up, you've got to come on over to our place. The money's reasonable. And it doesn't take that long.
>
> (53)

This is irony of the proportions of Jonathan Swift's *A Modest Proposal*, as critics have pointed out. In similar terms, the narrator chillingly describes everyday 'altruism':

> A child's breathless wailing calmed by the firm slap of the father's hand, a dead ant revived by the careless press of a passing sole, a wounded finger healed and sealed by the knife's blade: anything like that made me flinch and veer.
>
> (34)

Not only are the actions themselves reversed, that is, run backwards, but the verbs describing them are too – they are morally as well as literally turned around: 'calmed', 'revived' and 'healed'. The cruelty or destruction involved is formally disguised, but actually highlighted. Maya Slater has argued that Amis's choice of verb does not always accurately convey backwards motion; on the contrary, it seems that the narrator has particularly chosen verbs which will act as sites of the struggle for meaning, as Volosinov puts it.[15] As the quotation above shows, the narrator sees repair and healing, but still recognizes its 'violence'.

It is this effect, of reversed verbal use, which Louvish particularly objects to in *Time's Arrow*. In pre-Nazi days, German medical student Unverdorben and his friends occasionally go out 'helping' Jews (160). This is a moment when the narrator's choice of ironic word and the Nazis' view of 'their extermination programme as altruistic when it was the right way round' come most uncomfortably close together. At Auschwitz, the narrator of *Time's Arrow* notes, 'The main Ovenroom is called *Heavenblock*, its main approach road *Heavenstreet*' (133). These details are historically accurate, taken from Lifton's study *The Nazi Doctors*.[16] Louvish would argue that this seamless movement between Nazi terminology and *Time's Arrow*'s reversed world terminology is the problem; for supporters of Amis, this is the point. It is as if Amis has placed instances of the Nazis' damage to language in the one context where it makes sense: a backwards narrative. The slogan 'Arbeit Macht Frei' only has any true meaning, as opposed to its mendaciously altruistic one, in a reversed world:

> The men, of course, walk a different path to recovery. *Arbeit Macht Frei*, says the sign on the gate, with typically gruff and undesigning eloquence. The men work for their freedom.
>
> (131)

We understand from the form of the narrative that the men have in fact been worked to death. Seen backwards, work returns to them their life, and their freedom, as we also see them leave (that is, enter) the camp. In later life – that is, earlier on in the novel – the narrator describes the working week:

> Work liberates: Friday evenings, as they move off towards it, how they laugh and shout and roll their shoulders.
>
> (57)

This translated version of the 'Arbeit' slogan appears before we know that the infamous German original has any relevance to Tod Friendly. Yet again this is an example of reversed cause and effect, but one which has designs on the reader. There are 'triggers' which particularly disturb Tod in his post-war life, the narrator points out, like the smell of burning fingernails, and the recurring 'bomb baby' dream; these may be narrative triggers for us as readers too, if we

try to guess what Tod's secret might be. More obvious hints at what is to come –
which we recognize *because for us it has already been* – are individual words. In his
review, Frank Kermode quotes G.J. Whitrow's *The Natural Philosophy of Time* on
the impossibility of a reversed world except in the imagination, as if we needed
reassurance on this point: 'By definition, an event which leaves a "trace" of its
occurrence is in the past ... there is no such thing as a future analogue of a
trace.'[17] Yet Amis provides exactly this, the future analogue of a trace.

Lawrence Langer writes of the 'associative despair' accompanying certain
words or tropes, which, 'if they do not deplete available vocabulary, they
certainly limit the writer's control of their use'. He gives a list of such words,
which include 'train', 'track', 'smoke', 'roundup', 'deport', 'gas', 'shower', and in
illustration quotes a line of Eugenio Montale's verse, which he argues cannot be
read innocently: 'I've sniffed on the wind the burnt fragrance/ of sweet rolls from
the ovens.'[18] In Amis's case, rather than performing a 'depletion', the double-
voicedness of such words offers increased, multiple meaning. For one thing, each
occurrence is the site not just of reversed time, but of circular or even palindro-
mic time. We only recognize these terms because we know where they come
from; in the universe of the text, these events have not yet happened, but,
therefore, everyone knows about them. Tod dreams of things he has not yet
done, and after he has done them enjoys innocent sleep; even more paradoxically, the narrator, whose knowledge of what things mean and what he/Tod has
done fluctuates, as Slater points out, transcribes these signifiers as if innocent of
their charged meaning.[19]

The list of 'trigger' words and phrases in *Time's Arrow* includes mentions of
Jews, for instance that observant ones read the right way round (51); the words
'traumatize' and 'select'; such phrases as the 'devil isn't just following orders'
(17), 'the local frauleins' (22), 'the pleasant land – the green, the promised' (31),
the 'insane have been taken off the street; we don't ask where they've disappeared to' (57), 'I will know the nature of the offence' (73); Tod's desire for
women's heads as well as their bodies because 'the head wears the face, and
supplies the hair' (87). Obviously, the way these triggers work is varied. A phrase
like 'just following orders' has become a cliché in the post-Holocaust world, but
is used here with real as well as clichéd meaning. The same is true of 'local
frauleins', a jocular, man-of-the-world phrase, yet containing a forward-looking
trace of Tod's German background.

The use of 'select' is perhaps the most interesting instance of the triggering
phenomenon:

> Eating is unattractive too. First I stack the clean plates in the dishwasher,
> which works okay, I guess, like all my other labour-saving devices, until
> some fat bastard shows up in his jumpsuit and traumatizes them with his
> tools. So far so good: then you select a soiled dish, collect some scraps from
> the garbage, and settle down for a short wait. Various items get gulped up

into my mouth, and after skilful massage with tongue and teeth I transfer
them to the plate for additional sculpture with knife and fork and spoon.

(19)

Maya Slater argues that this language is 'idiosyncratic, over-technical, obsessional', and that 'reversed narrative imposes this kind of language'. She also suggests that in the description of eating quoted above, the reversed process of putting plates into the dishwasher is 'wrongly described'. She says,

> The word 'select' is wrong here. If he really were performing his actions
> backwards, Tod would not choose the plate from the dishwasher, but would
> lay his hand straight on it. (Imagine the normal, not reversed, everyday
> gesture of putting a dirty plate in a dishwasher: you remove your hand from
> it cleanly, without standing over it and deselecting it so that it blends with
> the other dirty dishes.) It is as if the Narrator has simply tried too hard here,
> used too meticulous a verb for a casual process.[20]

Slater's analysis fits with the almost complete lack of discussion of the Holocaust-related aspects of *Time's Arrow* in her article, and its interest rather in the novel's formal aspects; this is in contrast to Neil Easterbrook, for instance, who takes the Holocaust to be the text's centre.[21] Slater is not alone in ignoring or downgrading the importance of the Holocaust in Amis's novel. Although he does discuss the Holocaust-related implications of the novel – 'Amis turns the story of the concentration camps into a Utopian narrative' – James Wood observes, '*Most* remarkably, Amis has created a world in which the smallest human action is grotesquely difficult' (my italics). Kermode performs the same rhetorical move: 'In Odilo's regress we can recognise *more* than a new account of the vileness of an insane regime' (my italics), he claims, and goes on to back this up with what I take to be a misreading of the 'terrible baby' in *Time's Arrow*. This figure may, in its backwards context, tangentially suggest that an 'impotent baby has a potential of evil so dreadful that one can think of it as a bomb', but actually the 'bomb baby' is related to a specific memory from Tod's Nazi past: a baby's crying gives away the hiding place of some Jews, and Unverdorben is the one to open the door. To see *Time's Arrow* as about 'more' than the Holocaust explains why Kermode should prefer the general to the specific reading of the 'terrible baby'.[22] In Slater's case, not acknowledging the role of the Holocaust in *Time's Arrow* means that she overlooks the real force of 'select', which is a trigger word, even if on a small scale at this point. Of course, when the moment for real selection comes about, on the infamous train ramp at Auschwitz-Birkenau, it is not described as such, but in reverse:

> As matchmakers, we didn't know the meaning of the word *failure*; on the
> ramp, stunning successes were as cheap as spit. When the families coalesced,

how their hands and eyes would plead for each other, under our indulgent gaze.

$$(132)^{23}$$

It is a common trope in Holocaust writing to make an implicit, bitter comparison between the Jewish idea of having been chosen as God's people, and the kind of choosing to which they were subjected at Umschlagplatzes or in the Lagers. Here, however, Amis puts a different spin on the matter by reversing chosenness temporally as well as morally. Randomness looks like necessity when 'choosing' is reversed, and it is this effect to which Slater objects in criticizing the use of a 'meticulous' verb for a 'casual' process.

The transformation of contingency (defined by Leo Tolstoy in *War and Peace* as an event which happens 'for some reason')[24] into necessity is another well-known effect of narrative deformation. In *Time's Arrow*, the translation of the contingent into the necessary occurs frequently as part of its backwards movement. The culmination of the process of eating is a reversed trip to the shops:

> Next you face the laborious business of cooling, of reassembly, of storage, before the return of these foodstuffs to the Superette, where, admittedly, I am promptly and generously reimbursed for my pains. Then you tool down the aisles with trolley or basket, returning each can or packet to its rightful place.

> (19)

The phrase 'rightful place' repeats the process Slater objected to, of reversal transforming the casual (you take a can from a shelf) into the meticulous (you replace the can in *the only place it can go*). As the narrator drily puts it, he and Tod are 'fatalistic' (47). Elsewhere, weeding has the same look: the earth 'snatches at' nettles in reverse motion as Tod performs his 'meticulous vandalism' (26). In general, reversal changes what once was an action or object 'freely' chosen from among many, into the only action possible.

A satire on backshadowing

If we see the long post-war section of *Time's Arrow* as our preparation for the Auschwitz section, then this particular feature of reversed narrative – its rendering of free will into destiny – is extremely significant. To use Michael André Bernstein's terminology for two different views of time, it shows us the openness of *sideshadowing* as it turns into the fixity of *backshadowing*. Bernstein describes sideshadowing as 'a gesturing to the side, to a present dense with multiple, and mutually exclusive possibilities for what is to come'.[25] In his related book, *Narrative and Freedom*, Gary Saul Morson defines sideshadowing as 'an open sense of time' which conveys that 'there were real alternatives to the present we know now'.[26] Its opposite is *foreshadowing*, a category which falls between side- and backshadowing, and which values 'the present, not for itself, but as the harbinger of an already determined future'; sideshadowing can, by its 'attention to the unfulfilled or unrealized possibilities of the past', disrupt the 'affirmations' of foreshadowing. According to Morson, the distinctive tropes of sideshadowing are conditional or subjunctive phrases: 'what if, if only, had it not been, were it not for'.[27] It is interesting that these phrases imply regret; more positive sideshadowing tropes would be, 'thank goodness for ...', 'if we hadn't done X, then...'; 'imagine what would have happened if'.

Foreshadowing takes for granted a 'unidirectional view of history in which whatever has perished is condemned because it has been found wanting by some irresistible historico-logical dynamic'. It involves looking at the future from the present, usually in the light of a particular determinism, and seeing it as already fixed. Foreshadowing is a more specialized, and usually more literary, view of temporality than either side- or backshadowing.[28] Morson's example of its workings is Sophocles' play *Oedipus*, 'which relies heavily on foreshadowing', as an element of the special kind of fatalism evident in the play. However, as he points out, most narratives have a predisposition to fatalism and closed time: they work towards a predetermined ending, and everything makes sense in the light of that ending. The characteristic trope of foreshadowing is 'what *will* be *must* be'.[29]

There is, as Bernstein points out, a strong urge to 'the most extreme fore- shadowing' in the face of historical catastrophe, 'as the climax of a bitter trajectory whose outcome [the catastrophe] must be', and the Holocaust is a prime example. The view that it was the *inevitable* consequence of, for instance, Europe's racialized heritage, or Jewish vulnerability and assimilation in the Diaspora, is a very stark instance of extreme foreshadowing, complete with implicit apportionings of blame.[30] In fact, this extreme foreshadowing is more aptly labelled 'backshadowing'. According to Bernstein, any effective mourning for victims of the Holocaust can only partake of sideshadowing, not foreshad- owing, by recognizing the waste, rather than the inevitability, of the tragedy, for instance in the case of 'the obliterated futures of the murdered infants'.[31] At the heart of this foreshadowing lurks a historical paradox, as Bernstein shows: the Holocaust is supposed to be both inevitable *and* unimaginable. Only under foreshadowing's 'unidirectional' historical logic can it make sense to condemn the victims of Nazism in Austro-Germany (as Bernstein argues Aharon Appelfeld's novel *Badenheim 1939* (1980) does), for not predicting a fate which was *not yet set* in 1939. Even the perpetrators did not yet know that, or how, they would proceed to the 'factory of death' mode of mass murder.[32] It is possible to imagine all kinds of sideshadowing alternatives which might have stopped them or altered what we now know to have happened, such as different actions by the Pope, or the welcoming of more refugees by Allied and neutral countries after the Evian Conference of 1938, or the Allied bombing of the rail-tracks to Auschwitz.[33]

Bernstein describes *backshadowing* as a particularly pervasive and pernicious variant of foreshadowing. In fact, of the three 'shadows of time', it is the most common; its central trope, both literary and everyday, is, 'He should have known', and even, 'I told you so'. Bernstein says it is

> a kind of retroactive foreshadowing in which the shared knowledge of the outcome of a series of events by narrator and listener is used to judge the participants in those events *as though they too should have known what was to come*.[34]

Morson argues that backshadowing derives from *chronocentrism*, the 'egotism of taking one's own time as special'.[35] Past events only exist as precursors to a particular present.

Time's Arrow is beset by the same problem that Bernstein describes in relation to Robert Musil's series of novels, *The Man Without Qualities*, which is set in 1913, and Aharon Appelfeld's *Badenheim 1939*: 'how to tell a story that is set, like Appelfeld's [and Musil's], at the prelude to a universally known catastrophe'.[36] Telling the Holocaust backwards solves various narrative problems, including the absence of suspense when the outcome is already broadly known; paradoxically, *Time's Arrow* also gives the reader a reason for wanting to read this particular story, which might seem too straightforwardly unpleasurable the right way round. If 'aesthetic gratification' is involved here, of a kind which critics including Theodor Adorno, Leo Bersani and others have argued is inappropriate in Holocaust representation,[37] it serves the purpose of inducing the reader to think again about the event; in particular about the lack of distance between Unverdorben the perpetrator and the reader him- or herself, as the narrator puts it:

> I've come to the conclusion that Odilo Unverdorben, as a moral being, is absolutely unexceptional, liable to do what everybody else does, good or bad, with no limit, once under the cover of numbers.

(164)

Because we see Tod, secretive and fearful, at the end of his life, progressively unravel into the 'innocence' of pre-war Unverdorben, no longer plagued by bad dreams, we see the necessity of Nazi evil dissolve into a troubling contingency. This would not happen if Tod were narrated the right way round; then, the accumulation of circumstantial detail would form an apparently inevitable chain of cause and effect. The only flaw in this use of backwards narration to 'implicate' readers in the crime, as Easterbrook puts it,[38] by making backshadowing give up its sideshadows, is that *Time's Arrow* never presents a convincing plethora of alternative routes Unverdorben might have taken. Given the times, his profession and his lack of 'conscientious objections', perhaps the route from medical-school horseplay through killing the disabled at Schloss Hartheim to

Auschwitz *is* more or less inevitable.[39] However, representing roads not taken would have given an even greater sense of the accidental division of human subjects into victim, bystander or perpetrator. In a review in the *New Humanist*, Peter Faulkner argues that the preponderance of space given to Tod's life in the US means that 'the psychology of Nazism' is never really treated, and no attempt made to trace Odilo's attitudes back to his early life'.[40] In *Time's Arrow*, the narrator refers to Unverdorben as 'the worst man in the worst place at the worst time' (12),[41] and the first use of the adjective is not a moral one: it just means that given Unverdorben's remarkably unexceptional nature, in common with thousands of others, it was – horrifyingly – not surprising that he ended up doing what he did at Auschwitz.

Bernstein argues that the point of Musil's novels being set at such an over-determined historical moment, one year before the First World War, is to satirize readerly weddedness to fore- and backshadowing.[42] (Of course, putting it like this begs exactly the question we have been asking about *Time's Arrow*: did the formal issue – the satire – precede that of content – the war – in Musil's case?) The multiple voices and possibilities which Musil's text offers, instead of the single knowing voice and absence of options characteristic of backshadowing, serve to 'make the assumption of a superior, because subsequent, vantage point impossible'.[43] Musil's text is an example of a kind of historically based polyphony, to use Mikhail Bakhtin's term. Polyphony refers to the construction of characters' and narrators' voices in certain kinds of novel which witness the disruption of one of the tenets of classical realism: the 'hierarchy of discourses' through which realism 'offers the reader a position of knowingness which is also a position of identification with the narrative voice'.[44] In the polyphonic novel, such as Dostoevsky's *Crime and Punishment*, the narrator 'retains for himself no essential "surplus" of meaning and enters on an equal footing with Raskolnikov into the great dialogue of the novel as a whole', as Bakhtin describes it.[45] All discourses have equal weight in the polyphonic novel, including those which are 'either literally or figuratively between inverted commas' and are for that reason usually 'subordinate' to the master narrator in a non-polyphonic text. Thus the narrative voice in Holocaust fiction can take on great importance. But in contrast to support for an omniscient, historically directive narrator (see Robert Manne's argument for such a figure in Chapter 6), Bakhtin and Bernstein argue for exactly the opposite. It is an example of extremely non-polyphonic practice to have a textual collusion between narrator and reader over the heads of the characters, yet this is usually how texts which rely on backshadowing work. Knowledge of future outcomes, shared between narrator and reader, is perhaps the highest form of conventional, non-polyphonic narrative practice. As Bernstein says, sideshadowing, by contrast, directs us away from using 'our knowledge of the future as a means of judging the decisions of those living before that (still only possible) future became actual event'. It is a 'democratic and pluralist' form.[46]

In textual terms, therefore, avoiding backshadowing must entail a polyphonic representation. The backwards narration of *Time's Arrow* perfectly avoids the Appelfeldian situation in which the narrator and readers know about 'the Shoah ... of which the characters are entirely ignorant'.[47] Morson argues that a novel will be particularly polyphonic on a first reading, when '*ignorance* of an outcome is made to correspond with *uncertainty* of outcome', experienced by both characters and 'polyphonic author' (and reader).[48] In the case of *Time's Arrow*, knowledge and certainty of outcome are still, paradoxically, compatible with polyphony, because of its backwards narration.

The problem in *Badenheim 1939*, that the characters can *only* be ignorant of what is to come, is just the one addressed in D.M. Thomas's novel *The White Hotel* (see Chapter 2). Thomas's apparent violence to chronology is one reason for the scandalized reception of his novel, yet what that text does is to signal the difficult narrative position of a Holocaust fiction, where even if the narrator shows no signs of knowing what is coming, the reader will probably guess. In the case of *The White Hotel*, the character Lisa Erdman knows more than the narrator, albeit unconsciously. Amis's solution to this problem is the simple one we have been examining. Because *Time's Arrow* is narrated backwards, its characters know all about the impending Holocaust even before the narrator and reader know. As we have seen, great ironic play is made of the fact that the narrator can only guess at Tod's terrible secret, and the reader is dependent on these guesses.

Because of its reversed form, the trigger terms and tropes in *Time's Arrow* work as a test for the reader, not a judgement on the characters. The opposite is true of Appelfeld's *Badenheim 1939*, Bernstein asserts. The hints and triggers in that novel, such as repeated references to the barbed wire appearing at the holiday resort, and the posters urging people to set off for a new future in Poland, are all miniature forward-looking instances of a vicious backshadowing: 'there is something almost cruelly manipulative about the way Appelfeld's narrator calmly registers these horror-charged images just to trigger the reader's feeling of dread.'[49] The effect in *Time's Arrow* is quite different; the trigger tropes make us rethink our response to 'horror-charged images' by situating them *before* the time of our reading about the events which inspired them.

Time's Arrow follows a different logic from that of memory, which is often used to structure retrospective accounts of the Holocaust. Fink's *A Scrap of Time* and *The Journey* work according to the non-linear logic of memory. In the title story of the former, the narrator recalls fragments of the past within the present, so that two incomplete time-scales are superimposed: 'Today, digging around in the ruins of memory, I found it fresh and untouched by forgetfulness.'[50] In *Time's Arrow*, however, Tod Friendly is circumscribed by linear time; although he is moving counter-intuitively, he cannot leap over or omit any event, and we have no access to his memory (which is itself altered by the backwardness; the narrator uses the verb 'forget' when he means 'does not yet know' (89); in his review, Kermode quotes G.J. Whitrow on a reversed world, in which 'memory would be replaced by precognition').[51] In contrast to Fink's text, it is *our* knowledge or memory which is called upon.

Backwards narration in *Time's Arrow* also retrieves it from the pitfall of melodramatic observations of the kind that 1889 was a notable year because a son was born to Aloïs and Klara Hitler in Braunau, a very common kind of backshadowing.[52] Bernstein quotes a sentence from Ernst Pawel's biography of Franz Kafka, *The Nightmare of Reason*, which indulges in the same rhetorical backshadowing: at the end of his life, Kafka settled ' "not far from what was to become the infamous Terezin concentration camp, through which all three of his sisters passed on their way to the gas chambers" '. Again, this is a kind of *frisson*-production particularly common in relation to the Holocaust, where such ironies of time and place – poignant but historically meaningless – abound. [53]

In the world of *Time's Arrow*, and perhaps only there, is there a sense to such observations. The narrator sounds as if he is satirizing exactly the kind of 'negative nativity' involved in melodramatically foregrounding the day of Hitler's birth, when he comments on the birthplace of Odilo Unverdorben:

> In addition to this, modest Solingen harbours a proud secret. I'm the only one who happens to know what that secret is. It's this: Solingen is the birth-place of Adolf Eichmann. Schh ... Hush now. I'll never tell. And if I did, who would believe me?
>
> (170)

Morson quotes a moment from *War and Peace* which appears similar to this, in its effort to counteract anything like the Hitler-*frisson* and the 'distortions of memory'. In Tolstoy's novel, Pierre Bezuhov scans the landscape the day before a battle, and asks some soldiers, 'What village is that in front of us?', to which one of them replies, 'Burdino or something, isn't it?'[54] It is of course Borodino, the small village after which the Battle of Borodino, 'one of the most famous incidents in Russian history' by the time Tolstoy wrote, was named. Morson claims that Tolstoy meant the ' "fact of the event" ' to be conveyed, that is, 'the event without knowledge of what came later and with alternatives to actual subsequent events still palpably possible'. The effect of the Solingen incident in *Time's Arrow* actually works in the opposite direction: it returns us to the moment when options appeared to be open, but in a way that highlights what actually happened.

The counterpart in *Time's Arrow* to Ernst Pawel's observation about Kafka's sisters is backward-looking, rather than an instance of backshadowing. The narrator makes us perform the mental leap of imagining an 'innocent' Auschwitz (before the Germanizing of its name in the war, Auschwitz was simply a little Polish town called Oswiecim, just outside which were some deserted barracks at a rail intersection). The narrator/Unverdorben makes a 'sentimental journey' to Auschwitz on a camping trip, and sees it absent of any meaning except his own 'memory' of the future:

> Later, we filed past the site. There were about twenty brick hovels, apparently held together by their own filth (Austrian artillery barracks, for the War). ... Beyond, through the birch wood, lay birchy Birkenau, where I was in harmony with the engine of nature. Everything was miserable and innocent. All the quiddity, all the power and wonder had been washed away by time and weather.
>
> (170)

This is the opposite of what Pawel does, which is to try and make us see the impending doom in the innocent site. *Time's Arrow*'s narrator tries to make us see the overdeterminedly meaningful site before it gained those meanings.[55]

The 'doubled' narrator

The two striking narrative features of *Time's Arrow* – its backwards form, and the first-person narrator who is divided from his own body – are closely linked. As well as being narrated backwards, the novel is horizontally riven by a unique device: a first-person narrator who is within but divorced from the body he inhabits, a 'passenger or parasite', as he puts it (16). This is more than narration based on Cartesian dualist principles, as the split here is not between mind and body. The narrator has no direct access to Tod Friendly's thoughts, although he can feel his emotions and his bodily experiences. The split is rather between the soul and the rest of the subject, including his 'will' (49). Neil Easterbrook argues that the narrator of *Time's Arrow* is 'not a conscience or soul' but 'the eye-witness' or 'narratee' who replicates the reader's experience.[56] Although it is at least partly true that the narrator 'doubles' for the reader, the former's knowledge and ours about what is happening is not always symmetrical, and the narrator is often unreliable. The evidence that Easterbrook produces to suggest that the narrator is not the soul – 'in fact, as one of Tod's lovers rightly observes, Tod "has no soul" ' – seems to me to suggest exactly the opposite, that the narrator *is* the soul Tod used to have. They have become so radically divided from, and have so little contact with, each other that Tod can indeed appear soulless: '*His* isolation is complete. Because he doesn't know I'm here' (22). The narrator ironically confirms his own identity, in the continuation of the extract cited by Easterbrook: 'Irene ... tells Tod he has no soul. I used to take it personally, and I was wretched at first.'[58] Hearing praise for Tod's doctoring abilities, the narrator wonders,

> If I died, would he stop? If I am his soul, and there were soul-loss or soul-death, would that stop him? Or would it make him even freer?
>
> (96)

It is possible to chart the process of splitting which has sundered Tod from his soul. Although changes of personal pronoun throughout the text suggest fluctuations in their relationship, it is as a result of Unverdorben's time at Auschwitz that the most significant alteration takes place. During his time at the death camp, Unverdorben and his soul were united. This is the strongest evidence for the narrator's unreliability, as according to Lifton the biggest gap between perpetrators' two selves was, of necessity, in Auschwitz itself:

> I, Odilo Unverdorben, arrived at Auschwitz Central somewhat precipitately and by motorbike … shortly after the Bolsheviks had entrained their ignoble withdrawal. *Now*. Was there a secret passenger on the back seat of the bike, or in some imaginary sidecar? No. I was one. I was also in full uniform.
>
> (124)

The tone of the Auschwitz section is different from the preceding ones; now the narrator does not comment so much on the backwardness of the world, but simply describes, and even believes in it. As he predicted, in this place the world this way round makes sense, and it stops making sense when the killing ends (157). One way in which it makes *less* sense is for the reader; in contrast to the meticulous backwards realism of the earlier and later sections, it is often unclear what is going on in Auschwitz. The most likely explanation for this lack of clarity is Amis's method of composition. In this section, he is much more reliant on his intertexts, particularly Lifton and Primo Levi (Updike notes that Levi has supplied 'at the minimum, the name Unverdorben and some excremental details').[59] The details in the passage we will examine below about Mengele's medical experiments are taken verbatim from Lifton's study, and knitted together in an opaque and oddly non-realist style. As we will also see, this effect may be the result of an intertextual aesthetic; its implications, however, are that a 'knowing' reader is constructed, and that accusations of straightforward appropriation cannot be made.

After Auschwitz, while living in Portugal as Hamilton de Souza, Unverdorben and his soul are still in an uncertain state; he goes to confession, weeps, and admits that 'We lost our feeling about the human body. Children even. Tiny babies' (120). The narrator claims that 'bifurcation' occurred in 1960, when Unverdorben was temporarily known as John Young, suggesting that a hardening of internal positions took place as the war receded; including Irene, the narrator observes, 'All three of us know that John has a secret. Only one of us knows what that secret is' (98). The soul-narrator has no access to John Young's memory or thoughts, and as this insight is narrated nearly thirty pages before the Auschwitz section, although fifteen years later, he has to wait until he and his 'will' are reunited to find out what the secret is.

Neil Easterbrook points out that Unverdorben closely resembles the portrait of Nazi physicians described in Robert Jay Lifton's book *The Nazi Doctors*, which is one of the texts credited in Amis's Afterword. However, as we shall see, Easterbrook does not continue this argument to suggest that the narrator and

Tod Friendly are divided from each other in just the way Nazi doctors underwent 'doubling'. What he does say is this:

> In almost every respect, Odilo's pathology parallels the psychological profile of the Nazi doctor outlined by Lifton, who names the Nazi doctors' two [most] notable traits 'doubling' and 'psychic numbing':
> ' "Psychic numbing" is a form of dissociation characterized by the diminished capacity or inclination to feel, and usually includes separation of thought from feeling. "Doubling" carries the dissociative process still further with the formation of a functional second self, related to but more autonomous from the prior self.'[60]

Easterbrook is right to point out the importance of Lifton's study for *Time's Arrow*, but I would argue that *The Nazi Doctors* is of even greater significance for the novel than Easterbrook suggests. For one thing, it offers a resolution to the form versus content question which has troubled readers of Amis's novel. This is clear from a comparison of 'coveted' moments from the two central intertexts of *Time's Arrow*, *The Nazi Doctors* and Philip K. Dick's 1966 short story, 'Your Appointment Will be Yesterday' (later included in his novel *The Counter-Clock World*). Dick's story is not as consistently reversed as Amis's novel, but does include set-pieces of backwards action which seem to have inspired similar moments in *Time's Arrow*. In 'Your Appointment', Niehls Lehrer, an 'eradicator' at the local library, deals with food in a way not unlike the passage on the same subject we examined earlier:

> [He] walked to the kitchen and began to lay out soiled dishes. In no time at all he faced a bowl of soup, lambchops, green peas, Martian blue moss with egg sauce and a cup of coffee. These he gathered up, slid the dishes from beneath and around them ... and briskly placed the assorted foods in their proper receptacles which he placed on shelves of the cupboard and in the refrigerator.[61]

If we needed a reminder that *Time's Arrow* is not just science fiction with genocide added to it for artistic credibility, this spare, if sprightly, description of eating backwards would provide one. Similarly, Lehrer has a conversation with his girlfriend, Charise, which starts with his saying 'Goodbye' but is otherwise the right way round.[62] It is the narrator of *Time's Arrow* who notices that although 'most conversations would make much better sense if you ran them backwards, ... with this man–woman stuff you could run them any way you liked – and still get no further forward' (60). The example the narrator gives to prove this shows that it does not even matter where 'goodbye' goes in such a dialogue:

> 'Please. You can sleep over.'
> 'This is goodbye, Tod.'
> 'Beth', he'll say. Or Trudy or whatever.

'It just doesn't sit well with me any more.'
'Give me one more chance.'

(61)

Death in 'Your Appointment will be Yesterday' consists of vanishing at the opposite end of the life-cycle from usual: 'There's one killed every minute, as P.T. Barnum phrased it.' The inventor of the machine which has caused the spots of backwards time is subject to this process: ' "His Mightiness, the Anarch Peak, has become infantile and will soon shrivel up entirely into a homunculus and re-enter a nearby womb." '[63] In *Time's Arrow* the implications of this vanishing, 'the long goodbye to babies' (41), are much more sinister. Odilo Unverdorben's birth, seen in reverse, is a literal enactment of the psychoanalytic fantasy that intercourse is an act of violence committed by the father against the mother in which oneself, the child, may be killed:

> Naturally I cannot forgive my father for what he will have to do to me. He will come in and kill me with his body.

(172)

Easterbrook calls this 'a hard joke about original sin and the causes of Nazi genocide, a sort of Oedipal double reversal'.[64] In *Time's Arrow*, although the narrator knows that no one will die, nor can they commit suicide,[65] babies keep vanishing, and he wants to know where they go (47). There are echoes here of falsely naive comments by bystanders who lived through the Holocaust, as the narrator's comments on the vanishing of other groups of people suggest. In Claude Lanzmann's film *Shoah*, for instance, Mrs Pietyra, a non-Jewish Polish woman who had lived in Oswiecim since 1940, said in 1985, '[The Jews of Auschwitz] were expelled and resettled, I don't know where.' In *Time's Arrow*, at the same time as industry 'arrives' in New Jersey, '[t]he insane have been taken off the street; we don't ask where they've disappeared to' (57).[66]

Perhaps the most distinctive difference between Dick's story and Amis's novel is the light-heartedness of the former. Although Lehrer knows that the Anarch, Sebastian Peak, emerged as a saviour out of 'mid-twentieth century race violence', about which he has read in the library,[67] the story's tone is more playful than satirical. Kurt Vonnegut's novel *Slaughterhouse 5*, which Amis implicitly acknowledges in his Afterword, is more obviously the tonal intertext of *Time's Arrow*. The 'ironic realism'[68] and bathetic detachment of Vonnegut's novel are clearly due to the narrator's reaction to the Second World War, especially the carpet-bombing of Dresden, which took place while he was a prisoner of war there, as this extract from the novel's preface shows:

> I really *did* go back to Dresden with Guggenheim money (God love it) in 1967. It looked a lot like Dayton, Ohio, more open spaces than Dayton has. There must be tons of human bone meal in the ground.[69]

The narration of *Slaughterhouse 5* is divided, as it is in *Time's Arrow*; the first chapter, from which this extract is taken, is in the first person, but the rest of the text is in the third person. The first-person narrator, whose story we imagine we are really reading, reappears on a couple of occasions in the rest of the text, where he speaks as if he is indeed the protagonist, Billy Pilgrim: 'That was I. That was me. That was the author of this book.' *Slaughterhouse 5* also has a 'Martian' feel to it, much more literally than *Time's Arrow*; Billy Pilgrim claims he has been kidnapped by aliens, whose different sense of time he adopts to help himself deal with the trauma of war. It turns out, of course, that it is really the narrator who imagines he has visited the planet Tralfamadore, as his reference to the characters in the text as 'Earthlings' reveals.[70]

Billy Pilgrim, according to the narrator, 'came unstuck in time' in 1944. The phrase sounds similar to one used by the narrator of *Time's Arrow*, that everything is 'wrong in time' until he reaches Auschwitz. This marks a difference between the two texts: *Time's Arrow* has gone one step further than *Slaughterhouse 5*, as in the latter morality stays on track however much the narrative may move backwards and forwards. The episode in *Slaughterhouse 5* where this is least the case, and where it most resembles *Time's Arrow*, is that 'certain paragraph – a famous one', as Amis puts it (175), where Billy gets unstuck in time and sees the late-night war movie backwards:

> The formation flew backwards over a German city that was in flames. The bombers opened their bomb bay doors, exerted a miraculous magnetism which shrunk the fires, gathered them into cylindrical steel containers, and lifted the containers into the bellies of the planes. The containers were stored neatly in racks. The Germans below had miraculous devices of their own, which were long steel tubes. They used them to suck more fragments from the crewmen and planes. But there were still a few wounded Americans, though, and some of the bombers were in bad repair. Over France, though, German fighters came up again, made everything and everybody as good as new.[71]

The narrator's description of Billy's experience, of watching a film literally 'running backwards' (16), to which the narrator of *Time's Arrow* likens his plot, turns reverse destruction into something 'miraculous'; both novels use the same device of making formal reversal entail moral reversal. This is even clearer in the next paragraph about Billy's night in front of the television: the bomb cylinders are dismantled in special factories, and,

> Touchingly, it was mainly women who did this work. The minerals [inside the cylinders] were shipped to specialists in remote areas. It was their business to put them into the ground, to hide them cleverly, so they would never hurt anybody ever again.

Vonnegut's backwards paragraph, like Amis's Auschwitz section, satirizes war and destruction by showing that it is its polar opposite that makes perfect sense – 'so they would never hurt anybody ever again'. Moral reversal is not a sustained effect in *Slaughterhouse 5*, however, as its chronological disruption usually takes the form of time travel rather than strictly linear reversal. Within a few lines, for instance, Billy Pilgrim moves from 1965 to 1958 to 1961 and elsewhere is simultaneously in 1967 and 1944.[72] Neither free movement within time nor being in two times at once is an option for Tod Friendly in *Time's Arrow*. Ironically, Morson's observation about time's linearity is true of Tod too, even though his trajectory goes backwards: 'Regardless of our most strenuous efforts, we move through time relentlessly and in only one direction.'[73] Time is still a 'directed arrow', and the end of the book implies, chillingly, that the arrow turns around and starts going the other way, the *right* way, as the narrator hints at Odilo Unverdorben's deathly birth:

> When Odilo closes his eyes I see an arrow fly – but wrongly. Point-first. Oh, no but then …
>
> (173)

The effect of the 'unstuck' temporal movement in *Slaughterhouse 5* is to parody foreshadowing, although it looks as if it is an instance of it. Morson calls this effect 'pseudo-foreshadowing'.[74] The Tralfamadorians who are in touch with Billy have a conception of time as already determined and unchangeable, as one of them puts it to Billy:

> 'Earthlings are great explainers, explaining why this event is structured as it is, telling how other events may be achieved or avoided. I am a Tralfama-dorian, seeing all time as you might see a stretch of Rocky Mountains. All time is all time. It does not change. It does not lend itself to warnings or explanations. It simply *is*. Take it moment by moment, and you will find that we are all, as I have said before, bugs in amber.'[75]

This sounds like a description of 'monumental' time, as viewed by the pract-itioners of foreshadowing. The only difference is that the present is not privileged as a vantage-point on the past, *pace* the chronocentrist's view; as Billy's temporal dartings around and the image of the Rocky Mountains suggest, the whole of time is open to view from any point within it. There are two particular moments in *Slaughterhouse 5* which appear to be archetypal instances of foreshadowing, but in the context of the text's 'unstuck' time are actually ironic versions of it. The first is the narrator's comment on the writer Kilgore Trout: 'Billy would meet him by and by.'[76] This sounds like a version of one of foreshadowing's defining tropes, according to Michael André Bernstein: '*little did they know that…*'.[77] However, as time in *Slaughterhouse 5* is not progressive, and Billy's time travel reveals events, including his own death, before they have happened, here it is rather a trope of *pseudo*-foreshadowing. The second incident which looks like not just foreshadowing but backshadowing is the letter to his wife imagined by captured American officer Edgar Derby while he is being sent to Dresden in January 1945 as conscripted labour:

> Dear Margaret – We are leaving for Dresden today. Don't worry. It will never be bombed. It is an open city.[78]

As readers of *Slaughterhouse 5* and post-war subjects, we already know that Dresden was bombed a month later. Billy knows this too, even as Edgar Derby is comforting himself, as he has 'memories of the future'.[79] This is not vicious backshadowing at the expense of complacent people who should have predicted the destruction of Dresden and its civilian inhabitants, as it may appear, but an incident in a text narrated by someone with a 'Tralfamadorian' sense of time, in which all of history resembles a view of the Rockies. The satire on foreshadowing suggests that it is as foolish to adhere to it as to the Tralfamodorian view, but a self-protective Tralfamadorian vision is understandable when logic is reversed and 'open cities' without troops or war industries are chosen for bombing.[80] In his essay on Vonnegut, Amis points out that the popularity of *Slaughterhouse 5* in the US has partly been due to its adoption as an anti-Vietnam War novel, which raises interesting questions about the interchangeability of historical events: if the bombing of Dresden can become a metaphor for the American war in Vietnam, is the Holocaust also a metaphor, or at least a flexible signifier, in *Time's Arrow*?[81]

Intertextuality: Robert Jay Lifton's *The Nazi Doctors*

Slaughterhouse 5 is a shadowy influence on *Time's Arrow*. Its distinctive narrative tone and representation of distorted time as a way of dealing with trauma mark it out as a precursor of Amis's novel, although in the latter distorted time figures distorted morality in a much more direct fashion. By contrast, Robert Jay Lifton's book *The Nazi Doctors: Medical Killing and the Psychology of Genocide*, without which, Amis says, his novel 'could not have been written' (175), provides the main formal *and* thematic focus of *Time's Arrow*, starting with Lifton's identification of the centrality of physicians to the whole killing process at Auschwitz, and of the 'killing–healing paradox' which characterized their behaviour there. Nazi doctors supervised the process of killing at Auschwitz 'from beginning to end', Lifton observes, yet 'did no direct medical work'.[82] The 'medicalization of killing' was crucial to genocide, Lifton argues, and murder seen as a 'therapeutic imperative'. Lifton describes how 'therapeutic' killing took place on two levels at Auschwitz: first, at the level of the camp 'ecology', when selections on the ramp or in barracks took place to relieve overcrowding; and second, as 'part of the larger biomedical vision (curing the Nordic race by ridding it of its dangerous Jewish infection)'.[83] At both levels, it can be seen how the malign logic of the healing–killing paradox worked. On the smaller scale, killing the infirm, old and ill took place to 'save' the stronger and more healthy inmates; on the larger scale, killing certain groups of people would 'save' another group.

The omnipresence of doctors in the death camps, and the horrifying cloaking of murder with medicine, is symbolized in *Time's Arrow* by the figure who 'presides over' Tod Friendly's death, 'a male shape or essence [which] seemed to be wearing a white coat (a medic's stark white smock). And black boots' (12). This figure comes from Tod's past, and from Lifton's discussion of the pre-war 'euthanasia' project directed against the mentally and physically disabled, and the transportation of patients to killing centres:

> SS personnel manned the buses, frequently wearing white uniforms or white coats in order to appear to be doctors, nurses, or medical attendants. There were reports of 'men with white coats and SS boots', the combination that epitomized much of the 'euthanasia' project in general.[84]

Easterbrook points out the 'virulent absurdities' which are 'at the core of *Time's Arrow*', but concentrates on their presence as part of the text's content alone. What is even more striking is the effect of the 'killing–healing paradox' on the backwards form of the novel. Put simply, this is that the transformation of medicine's therapeutic role into a destructive one, 'a war against health' (103) in which 'we, we, we! – we demolish the human body' (83), happens automatically if one narrates it backwards. Of Tod's post-war days as a doctor in New York, the narrator observes,

> We'd just totalled a couple of teenage boys. … We took the stitches out and swabbed the boys with blood. I remember Witney's skilful insertion of some kind of crossbow bolt; me I was wedging shards of brown glass into the other boy's crown.
>
> (92)

Once the reader is lulled into a sense of familiarity about this way of reading, you only have to rewind what you read, and decode the narrator's archly 'Martian' comments,[85] to see their 'real' form: the crossbow and glass are, of course, being removed, and stitches put in. However, in the Auschwitz section of the book, medicine suddenly seems to be the right way round and requires no such decoding: it helps, saves and restores. This means that now everything *is* wrong, as nothing should make sense or look right in this backwards world. The satirical point is that everything in Auschwitz was the wrong way round, morally and humanly, to start with.[86]

The reversal of medicine's healing role in Auschwitz is revealing about the techniques of *Time's Arrow*, as a reversed narrative and as an example of Holocaust fiction which is dependent on prior texts. These texts are usually historical or survivor testimonies: as his Afterword shows, Amis has relied on both. What is curious about Amis's novel is that it seems almost like a fictionalized summary or shadow of Lifton's study, so accurately does it reproduce details and even phrases from it. For example, the chapters Lifton devotes to the prisoner doctors in Auschwitz, who could be in a relatively privileged position as long as they submitted to the 'ecology' of balancing slave labour and selections, turn up in *Time's Arrow* as a sentence: '*Some of the patients were doctors*' (143). The italics indicate Unverdorben's surprise at this particular turnaround, and the term 'patient' is clearly the reverse of 'prisoner'.

There is no suggestion, nor has there ever been one, of plagiarism in the relationship between Lifton's *The Nazi Doctors* and Amis's novel, and indeed such a charge would be rather odd, given the lengths to which Amis has gone to advertise the influence of Lifton's work on his own. The criticisms of *Time's Arrow* have been more honest; rather than using plagiarism as a screen accusation for 'moral' transgression, Amis's critics have gone straight for the problematic issues. The following example shows the way in which *Time's Arrow* has benefited from Lifton's book. Unverdorben, no longer split from the narrator, helps with the 'experiments' of Josef Mengele in Auschwitz:

> 'Uncle Pepi' has surpassed himself with his new laboratory: the marble table, the nickel taps, the blood-stained porcelain sinks.... In this new lab of his he can knock together a human being out of the unlikeliest odds and ends. It was not uncommon to see him slipping out of his darkroom carrying a head partly wrapped in old newspaper; evidently, we now rule Rome. ... Even the most skeletal patients thrust their chests out for medical inspection in the last block on the right: a scant fifteen minutes earlier they were flat on the floor of the *Inhalationsraum*.... A shockingly inflamed eyeball at once rectified by a single injection. Innumerable ovaries and testes seamlessly grafted into place. Women went out of that lab looking twenty years younger.
>
> (142–3)

This passage works in the same way as the Auschwitz section as a whole: details are taken from their place in Lifton's text and, by a method which seems almost akin to William Burroughs's cut-up technique, acquire a more chaotic, impressionistically violent identity in Amis's novel. They are, of course, also reversed. Lifton observes that Mengele was sometimes known as 'Uncle Pepi' by the twins he collected; as one survivor put it, ' "He could be friendly but kill." '[87] The description of Mengele's equipment is a version of Lifton's quotations from Miklos Nyiszli's *Auschwitz: A Doctor's Eyewitness Account*: for the bodies of twins he had killed, 'Mengele prepared a special dissection room, including a "dissecting table of polished marble", a basin with "nickel taps" and "three porcelain sinks" '.[88] It is interesting that the phrases which reappear in *Time's Arrow* are those Lifton specifically quotes from Nyiszli, a prisoner-doctor who survived and was a witness for the Budapest Commission for the Welfare of Deported Hungarian Jews after the war. In *Time's Arrow*, these phrases become the words of a perpetrator, leaving the text open to the kinds of accusation levelled against the episode in the Warsaw Ghetto in Helen Darville's novel, where a survivor's words were transferred to the consciousness of a perpetrator (see Chapter 6). As we have seen, however, such accusations have not been made; although one might want to question the use of irony at all, it is irony that seems to protect Amis's borrowings from looking like simple theft.

The other details in the passage from *Time's Arrow* quoted above have their roots in details from Lifton. The latter quotes a prisoner-doctor's testimony of Mengele's habit of 'killing for science': one day he brought in ' "two heads ... wrapped in newspaper ... children's heads ... smelling of phenol" '. Lifton adds: 'It was clear that Mengele had had the children killed in order to make possible their post-mortem study, and he was bringing the heads to this doctor for bacteriological examination.' Another 'interest' of Mengele's was his research into eye colour. This included the project of 'changing eye color in an Aryan direction.... Mengele actually injected methylene blue into [brown-eyed children's] eyes, causing severe pain and inflammation', and in some cases blindness and death.[89] Amis has planted in his text small and telling traces of the central areas of Mengele's work: his interest in the horrifying degenerative condition, noma, signified by the incident of the heads in newspaper; in eye colour;[90] and in sterilization.[91]

As well as the irony we have noted, *Time's Arrow* is shielded from imputations of plagiarism by the artistic remodelling of its borrowings. Darville's practice was spoken of as a clumsily executed deception, rather than the aesthetic rearrangement of intertexts. The way in which the details of Mengele's experiments appear in *Time's Arrow* is an instance of Amis's practice. The confused, feverish way in which they are narrated both allows the details to appear 'rewritten' and not simply transcribed, and to represent the mental state of a doubled Nazi subject who sees killing as a medical, therapeutic practice.

It is also possible to account for Amis's *omissions* in terms of his reliance on Lifton's text. It is clear, for instance, that Unverdorben has been a member of the Einsatzgruppen, the mobile killing squads who followed the Wehrmacht on their conquering mission into Eastern Europe and Russia, shooting (primarily) Jewish civilians. (Unverdorben has done everything a Nazi doctor might do, including pre-war 'euthanasia'; he is the archetypal Nazi perpetrator.) The process of the killing – forcing people to dig their own mass graves, to undress, to line up to be shot – would have been very striking in reverse, yet almost no detail is given of Unverdorben's career at this time:

> After my fortnight's leave I completed a five-month tour of duty in the East with a Waffen SS unit, operating downwind, as it were, of the military withdrawal from the Soviet Union. I like to think we achieved a great deal, though it was humble stuff compared to the Kat-Zet. And crude stuff. And aesthetically catastrophic stuff too, of course.

(148)

The narrator's tone here, shifty yet brazen, is consistent with unreliability and deception – he may be hiding the details of what he did. However, the lack of detail is equally consistent with the fact that the novel's intertext, as it is concerned with Nazi doctors and not the Einsatzgruppen, deals only scantily with this phenomenon (a mere seven page-references occur in the index to *The Nazi Doctors*, which is a 560-page book). It is not clear why the narrator says this work was 'aesthetically catastrophic'; seen in reverse, it would surely have its own beauty. The surprising omission is a matter of influence and intertextuality as much as the bad conscience of a 'doubled' fictional self.

Lifton describes interviewing the ex-Nazi doctors who form the basis of his study. He is struck by the clarity and candour of these men's recollections, but notes that not a single one 'arrived at a clear ethical evaluation of what he had done, of what he had been part of'. The events were described 'almost in the manner of the third person. The narrator, morally speaking, was not quite present'.[92] It is as if Amis has reproduced this insight in his narrative form. Throughout *Time's Arrow*, it is as if Tod is speaking about himself in the third person; and, like Lifton's former Nazi doctors, the not-quite-present narrator makes no overt ethical comments. Later on, Lifton observes that 'The Nazi doctors' immersion in the healing–killing paradox was crucial in setting the tone for doubling':[93] as the experience of reading *Time's Arrow* suggests, the two phenomena are inextricably interwoven.

The inability to arrive at a clear ethical evaluation is the legacy of the healing–killing paradox, which created what one of Lifton's interviewees called ' "*the schizophrenic situation*" ',[94] in which the Nazi doctor became two people, an 'Auschwitz self' and a prior self. The comment by Lifton's interviewee shows that the moral reversal of healing and killing was so closely linked to the internal splitting of the subject that one was impossible without the other. A review of the paperback edition of *Time's Arrow* makes this point in terms of the literary construction of the novel: 'simply reversing the chronology would not have been enough – in addition Amis also uses ironic detachment by narrating the history through the "conscience" of Odilo Unverdorben', with the effect, according to the reviewer, that the 'facts and figures of Auschwitz' are felt as well as known.[95] The success of *Time's Arrow*, and its immunity from charges of plagiarism, depend on just this symmetry of literary form and historical content.

In terms of Amis's novel, the reverse narration is the reason why the soul-narrator is divided from his Tod-body; but equally, the narrative's reverse form is enabled by the split subject. This follows from the logic identified by Lifton. He describes how hard it was initially for doctors to accede to the healing–killing reversal at Auschwitz, and how a process of acclimatization invariably led to the split subjectivity which allowed these men to take part in the reversed morality of the death camp. As Lifton puts it, 'Their adaptation involved the process I call "doubling", which permitted them to select for the gas chamber without seeing themselves as killers.'[96] Moral reversal was only possible for these men if they underwent doubling; but equally, the ability to double led to widespread moral reversal.

Lifton's description of the characteristics of doubling sheds light on the formal construction of Tod and the narrator in *Time's Arrow*. Three of the five features of doubling he lists are particularly relevant:

> The Auschwitz self had to be both autonomous and connected to the prior self that gave rise to it. [Another] major function of doubling, as in Auschwitz, is likely to be the avoidance of guilt: the second self tends to be the one performing the 'dirty work'. And ... doubling involves both an unconscious dimension – taking place ... largely outside of awareness – and a significant change in moral consciousness.[97]

These features correspond to the construction of the narration in *Time's Arrow* in the following ways. The narrator is inside Tod's head, and therefore 'connected' to him; but the narrator is 'autonomous' in the sense that he has no access to Tod's thoughts, and Tod does not know that the narrator is there. It seems that, despite appearances, there is only one protagonist in *Time's Arrow*, but this single entity appears to be two. The narrator is the second, 'Auschwitz self', Tod the prior self; while Tod apparently does experience guilt, as the confession scene shows, the narrator professes not to understand what is happening, nor does he label it as such. As we have seen, the narrator becomes much more closely involved with Unverdorben during the Auschwitz section of the text, yet the voice of narration does not significantly change. The only thing that does change is the narrator's admission of his own identity: he is Odilo Unverdorben, not someone separate. The narrator claims that he is a passenger in Tod's head, but he *is* Tod, his disavowed *alterego*. The narrator's apparent, and fluctuating, ignorance of this state of affairs represents Lifton's third point, about the 'unconscious' nature of the whole process of internal sundering and the inability to make moral judgements.

A very clear instance of the link between backwards narration and split narration in Amis's novel is that of the selection scene in *Time's Arrow*. The narrator represents this as a scene of reconciliation and joy, and because it is described backwards, this is how it looks, and how we are made to read it. The narrator is also capable of describing it thus because he is disavowing what selection really means morally, as well as temporally: 'The Nazi doctor knew that he selected, but did not interpret selection as murder', as Lifton puts it.[98] The reverse form of the selections in *Time's Arrow* forces the reader too to see selections as something else, to experience the split subjectivity that denies, or does not recognize, what it sees. The habit the reader has gained from the non-Auschwitz sections, of literally reading such scenes as conversations backwards, that is, the right way round, which induces 'alertness' and protects her or him from falling too far into a doubled, morally reversed subjectivity. James Wood describes *Time's Arrow*'s reliance on the reader-supposed-to-know as part of its meaning:

> As we read, we grate Amis's Utopian version against our knowledge of the
> dystopian event, and a pathos, a charge of great sadness, flickers and sparks
> off this collision ... the feeling is of glimpsing an unimaginable beauty: it
> *could* have been like this in another world, in another time.[99]

Despite his rather overblown phrases, Wood does point out something important
here. As he implies, *Time's Arrow* achieves an effect quite opposite to that of
backshadowing; far from implying that the events of the Nazi genocide were
inevitable and the victims blameworthy, its backwards form generates regret and
disbelief, suggesting that events *need not* have turned out as they did.

However, Wood's comment that 'it *could* have been like this in another
world' refers to a fantasy replenishment of what was lost in the Holocaust. He
does not mean that the form of the novel raises the poignant possibility of
turning back the clock to a time when individuals and communities still existed;
and *Time's Arrow* is not concerned with this. Although it continues backwards to
a time before the destruction of Jewry in Europe, we see none of the details of
this restoration. Instead, the wish-fulfilment it represents is an 'inverted utopian
vision of Auschwitz as the place where Nazi doctors created a new "Jewish
race" ', in Bryan Cheyette's words,[100] echoing those of the novel's narrator on
Auschwitz:

> Here there is no why. Here there is no when, no how, no where. Our
> preternatural purpose? To dream a race. To make a people from the
> weather. From thunder and from lightning. With gas, with electricity, with
> shit, with fire.
>
> (128)

Time's Arrow is concerned with the perpetrators and potential perpetrators
(such as the reader), not the victims, as an anonymous reviewer argues: '*Time's
Arrow* convincingly makes the point that the Holocaust was a tragedy for the
human spirit; on the other hand, one finds oneself thinking that it was a damn
sight more tragic for its immediate victims.'[101] As in Helen Darville's *The Hand
that Signed the Paper*, and Spielberg's film of Thomas Keneally's *Schindler's List*, the
Jewish victims of the Holocaust are at best a shadowy presence in *Time's Arrow*,
because, like the other two texts, its focus is on a perpetrator or bystander turned
righteous gentile. As Amis's comment to Mark Lawson suggested, his starting-
point was the Nazi doctors, not their victims.

This analysis does not suggest that a close knowledge of Lifton's text is
necessary in order to understand or appreciate Amis's novel, but *Time's Arrow*
does presuppose just the figure we will encounter again in relation to several
other novels, the reader-supposed-to-know. The structure of *Time's Arrow* as a
whole, with its prefiguring trigger-tropes and traces of an anterior factual text,
depends on, and implies, a reader attuned to the discourse and facts of the Nazi
genocide. Aviva Kipen, writing in the *Jewish Quarterly*, presupposes a very

knowing, even 'Jewish', reader, which is an interesting counter-argument to Louvish's one that novels like *Time's Arrow* represent a de-semitizing of the Holocaust.[102] In fact, the reader of Amis's novel is constructed, in a non-essential way, as Jewish.[103] Kipen says of 'the medical experiments carried out in Auschwitz' that the alert, 'Jewish' reader 'knows [they] are approaching with every passing page'. Frank Kermode, in the *London Review of Books*, argues that the structure of *Time's Arrow* is paradoxically conventional: 'the progress of the tale is fairly orthodox, it heads towards a recognition: that is, the supply of information is maximised in quite the usual way'.[104] This is only true if we discount the possibility that the reader might guess what is coming, in a way s/he could not when reading, say, George Eliot's *Mill on the Floss*. An attentive literary analysis can amply substitute for the detailed background Lifton's text gives to throwaway references in Amis's novel – for instance, the significance of phenol killings, and vans painted with a red cross but used for gassings.

The reader of Amis's novel, paradoxically, given its reliance on Lifton's history, need only be receptive to the workings of the novel's form. Various reviewers singled out the passage about the inflamed eyeball quoted above without mentioning its origin in Lifton's text. Mark Lawson, for instance, comments instead on the fact that 'Amis' somersault structure' in this image in particular 'forces reflection on what took place', as an antidote to the 'image-fatigue' that may result from representations of Auschwitz.[105] A *Sunday Times* reviewer says of the same passage that this is 'a horrible image when one realises what's really happening': knowing even more about what is 'really' happening by reading Lifton's study is illuminating but not essential.[106]

Chapter 2

Documentary fiction

D.M. Thomas, *The White Hotel*

Although different in many respects from Martin Amis's *Time's Arrow*, D.M. Thomas's *The White Hotel* has several complementary features. Like Amis's, Thomas's novel has a central Holocaust-related intertext – Anatoli Kuznetsov's 'historical novel' *Babi Yar*, and other intertexts as well – Freud's case histories, letters and journals.[1] Most strikingly, its narrative is affected by a particular view of time and history, just as the narrative form of *Time's Arrow* was (de)formed by its allegiance to an anti-backshadowing perception of time. As well as repeating motifs and incidents, *The White Hotel* looks forward rather than backward, making it another narrative satire on backshadowing. The novel consists of a prologue – letters between the fictional Freud and his contemporaries about the fantasies of one of his women patients, written between the staves of Mozart's opera *Don Giovanni* – and six sections. '*Don Giovanni*' is a first-person account of a woman's sexual fantasies, in poetic form. 'The Gastein Journal' is the fantasied prose version of the same scenario of sexual love and disaster at a white hotel, in the third person but written from the woman's point of view; it later emerges that this is Lisa Erdman's diary.[2] 'Frau Anna G.' is the case history of Lisa Erdman, written and narrated by Thomas's Freud, including details of her puzzling physical symptoms. 'The Health Resort' is the third-person account of the vagaries of Lisa's life after her analysis. In 'The Sleeping Carriage', which takes place some years later, the last few days of Lisa's life are narrated: she lives in a poor part of Nazi-occupied Kiev, and is killed in the Babi Yar massacre. Her 'hysterical' symptoms turn out to be real injuries. 'The Camp' is an after-life fantasy in which wounds begin to heal, told by a third-person narrator.

Like *Time's Arrow*, *The White Hotel* had a very polarized reception from critics and readers, which Thomas himself described as 'astonishing extremes of response'.[3] It was received enthusiastically in some quarters in Britain, where it was nominated for the Booker and Cheltenham Prizes, and had an even more enthusiastic reception in the States which prompted further plaudits in Britain. Sylvia Kantaris relates a story of New Yorkers seen wearing an 'I've stayed at the White Hotel' T-shirt, and in the early 1980s there were plans for a film version of the novel.[4] *The White Hotel* at first attracted mutedly critical notices because of a content which was Holocaust-related but also judged by some to be pornographic.

When a letter to the *Times Literary Supplement* in March 1982 unleashed a plagiarism debate concerning Thomas's reliance on Anatoly Kuznetsov's *Babi Yar*, all the literary failings of his novel instantly became much clearer, as part of the usual slide between content- and form-based criticism. As Hana Wirth-Nesher points out, Thomas has been accused of appropriating both someone else's efforts (*Babi Yar*) and someone else's pain (the eyewitness account by Dina Pronicheva from that book).[5] This is a paradoxical accusation, as the latter 'appropriation' is there to guard against, not add to, the former. As Thomas puts it in *Memories and Hallucinations*, it would have been 'immoral' if he, 'a comfortable Briton, fictionalized the holocaust'.[6]

A striking instance of scandalized reception is the accusation of narrating the Holocaust to give readers a sadomasochistic thrill. Susanne Kappeler discusses *The White Hotel* at some length in her study *The Pornography of Representation*, and argues that the Holocaust is exploited as part of the novel's pornographic agenda. She states that Thomas's use of the literary – the association with Kuznetsov and Freud, and the status conferred by his literary reputation – 'neutralizes' and 'redeems' the 'acknowledged' pornographic '*Don Giovanni*' and 'Gastein Journal' sections, even though the pornographic actually strays into the literary in the form of Thomas's changes to Kuznetsov's material.[7] These two sections are:

> in the received mould of pornographic literature, a picture of male-defined sexuality, not to mention a picture of male-defined female sexual hysteria – a more refined minority genre. They are about fucking. Violence is an integral part.[8]

Kappeler's comments are somewhat tautologous; although the two sections she discusses are indeed about 'fucking' and, to a lesser extent, 'violence', it is not clear that they conform to pornography's pattern of eroticized power relations. Wirth-Nesher says that 'The charge of pornographic sensationalism is not hard to refute superficially; for Lisa Erdman is depicted overall with dignity and subjective empathy rather than reduced to an object from start to finish'; and Linda Hutcheon argues, at a different level, that Lisa is 'presented as the "read" subject of her own and others' interpretations and inscriptions of her. She is literally the female product of readings'.[9] For Kappeler, however, Freud's patriarchal practices in, for example, his case history of Dora, are simply continued in Thomas's novel. Lisa Erdman is just 'a mention in a letter, a case study, a victim of the slaughter, an aside'. The fact that the two 'pornographic' sections in *The White Hotel* are written from Lisa's point of view, unlike Freud's case study of Dora, makes this scenario worse, according to Kappeler. 'It is indeed one of the well-tried pornographic devices to fake the female's, the victim's, point of view and many pornographic books are published under a female author-pseudonym.'[10] I will return to the debate over the representation of women in Thomas's novel below.

Anatoly Kuznetsov, *Babi Yar*

Thomas argues in *Memories and Hallucinations* that the apparent disparity in the paperback edition of *The White Hotel* between his fulsome acknowledgement of Freud, and scant reference in tiny print to Kuznetsov, is not due to a hierarchy of intertexts but to the publishers, Penguin, changing the format of the acknowledgements from the original hardback edition. Indeed, in a revealing reversal, Thomas noted in a letter to the *Times Literary Supplement* that *Babi Yar* was being reissued as a result of interest engendered by his novel, with *The White Hotel* quoted in advertisements for Kuznetsov's book. Thomas's reliance on *Babi Yar* can be seen as a recourse to documentary sources rather than crude plagiarism, which requires an act of theft.[11]

Kuznetsov's documentary text consists of three layers: the original text; the text censored by the Soviet authorities which was published in the USSR in 1966; and the 1970 translation, published in Britain, in which Kuznetsov restored the missing material and added further comments in square brackets. It is a fascinating book on several levels: as a portrait of Nazi-occupied Kiev seen through the eyes of a 14-year-old boy; as a collection of contemporary documents; and for its evidence of Soviet habits of close reading. The material in bold cut out by the censor ranges from criticisms of the Bolsheviks (Grandpa was **'the most ordinary**, the smallest, **the most hungry** and the most intimidated citizen **of the Land of the Soviets'**); emotive or metaphorical material (the narrator describes himself 'twisting and turning **like a young animal'**, and of his mother, **'I was all she had'**; Motya, who survives the Babi Yar massacre along with Dina Pronicheva, was **'a good-looking child with lovely eyes which looked at Dina as though she was his saviour'**); evidence of Ukrainian collaboration with the Nazis or references to the Ukrainian famine; any religious reference (a subheading is amended: 'A Beautiful, Spacious, **Blessed** Land'); any detail that might offend prudish Soviet sensibilities, even in the midst of horrific murder (of mobile gas chambers at Babi Yar: 'The bodies inside would still be warm, dripping with sweat, **practically all of them with excreta and urine over them**, and some of them might be not quite dead'); any knowingness on the part of the young narrator ('I touched the patches [of coins], heavy as stones. **I knew what he meant!** He wanted someone to appreciate his wealth'); and seems oblivious to the double-voicedness of irony ('GERMAN humanism, **the most noble, intelligent and purposeful of all possible humanisms'**).[12]

Thomas has based much of his account of Lisa's final days, 'The Sleeping Carriage' section, on Kuznetsov's text which relies particularly on Dina Pronicheva's testimony, because of the 'emotional impact' he claims it had on him,[13] but also grafts together a collage of incidents from elsewhere in *Babi Yar*. As we will see, using Kuznetsov's words verbatim is bad enough in the eyes of those who would accuse the author of plagiarism, but changing them to fit the rest of a novelistic scheme seems even worse. This method of altering the intertext is used by Thomas for many small details in 'The Sleeping Carriage', for instance that of the soldier who removes Lisa's coat as if she were at the opera (Dina's coat in the original is simply taken as a piece of 'warm clothing'), and another soldier's offer of escape in exchange for sex (made to a young woman in Lisa's hearing, because in *The White Hotel* Lisa is to be seen as an old woman; but made to Dina herself in *Babi Yar*).[14]

The most obvious changes Thomas makes are to the details of Dina's testimony about her narrow escape from death in the Yar. The first-person female viewpoint of which Kappeler speaks is abandoned during this altered scene, partly because Lisa dies, and partly because Kuznetsov's narrative is in the third person. This makes the scene a contrast to, not a continuation of, the first-person and third-person subjective sections of *The White Hotel* which concern Lisa. The changes Thomas makes to Kuznetsov's rendering of Dina Pronicheva's account of the Babi Yar massacre effectively blot out female subjectivity as well as female life. Clearly, Pronicheva's story is only known because she survived and related her experiences to Kuznetsov; but because there is an omniscient narrator in Thomas's novel, the fictional subject of Pronicheva's experiences can be snuffed out, and we can still learn what happened to her.

Some critics argue that 'the death of the feminine' in general is exactly what Thomas is conveying here; he is writing its elegy. This theory explains why he links the confessional 'pornographic' sections of *The White Hotel* with Holocaust atrocities – feminine sexual subjectivity is transformed into deathly sadomasochism; and why he makes the particular change he does to Pronicheva's testimony. Seeing this rewritten scene as 'the death of the feminine' can even explain why the Babi Yar material was particularly interesting to Thomas, as the name of the ravine where the massacre took place means 'old woman'.[15] While both Darville's and Amis's novels treat male perpetrators, Thomas has chosen to represent one of the female victims, whose voices are notoriously much harder to find. This is Kuznetsov's version of the scene at Babi Yar (the bold type is the material which was originally deleted by the Soviet censor):

A few minutes later she heard a voice calling from above:
    '**Demidenko!** Come on, start shovelling!'
    There was a clatter of spades and then heavy thuds as the earth and sand landed on the bodies, coming closer and closer until it started falling on Dina herself.
    Her whole body was buried under the sand but she did not move until it began to cover her mouth. She was lying face upwards, breathed in some sand and started to choke, and then, scarcely realizing what she was doing, she started to struggle in a state of uncontrollable panic, quite prepared now to be shot rather than be buried alive.
    With her left hand, the good one, she started scraping the sand off herself, scarcely daring to breathe lest she should start coughing; she used what

strength she had left to hold the cough back. She began to feel a little easier. Finally she got herself out from under the earth.

The Ukrainian policemen up above **were apparently tired after a hard day's work**, too lazy to shovel the earth in properly, and once they had scattered a little in they dropped their shovels and went away.[16]

Thomas's version is remarkable for what it keeps as much as for what it adds:

> In the stillness of the ravine a voice shouted from above: 'Demidenko! Come on, start shovelling!'
>
> There was a clatter of spades and then heavy thuds as the earth and sand landed on the bodies, coming closer and closer to the old woman who still lived. Earth started to fall on her. The unbearable thing was to be buried alive. She cried with a terrible and powerful voice: 'I'm alive. Shoot me, please!' It came out only as a choking whisper, but Demidenko heard it. He scraped some of the earth off her face. 'Hey, Semashko!' he shouted. 'This one's still alive!' Semashko, moving lightly for a man of his bulk, came across. He looked down and recognized the old woman who had tried to bribe her way out [by offering sex]. 'Then give her a fuck', he chuckled.
>
> (219)

Demidenko turns out to be impotent, but rapes Lisa with his bayonet. Eventually 'she seemed to have stopped breathing' and 'Semashko grumbled at their wasting time. Demidenko twisted the blade and thrust it in deep' (220). This passage begins as a verbatim quotation from Kuznetsov, which serves to heighten the tangent it then takes. In Thomas's additional material, the narrative voice moves disconcertingly between Lisa's viewpoint, which we are accustomed to – 'The unbearable thing was to be buried alive' – and the alien viewpoint of the Ukrainian policemen – 'the old woman ... seemed to have stopped breathing'. It is clear where Thomas got the idea for this particular defilement and death of the feminine. After Dina Pronicheva and the small boy, Motya, have escaped from the ravine, Kuznetsov relates a scene they witnessed (again, the bold type indicates that the whole of this passage was deleted by the Soviet censor in the Russian edition of *Babi Yar*):

> **Then, on the far side of the ravine, six or seven Germans appeared leading two young women. They went down into the ravine, selected a level place, and proceeded one after the other to violate the women. Having satisfied their desires they stabbed the women to death with their bayonets so that they shouldn't cry out, and left the bodies there as they were.[17]**

Thomas has conflated these horrifying details and united them in the person of Lisa. Instead of the witness Dina, nameless victims and Kuznetsov the narrator, in *The White Hotel* we have a witness who becomes a victim through the violence done to her, related by a third-person narrator. Thomas has made even more obvious the links between sex and death in the scenes Dina witnessed.

Thomas also borrows incidents from the history of the Yar in 1943 from another testimony quoted by Kuznetsov, that of his friend Davydov, a prisoner in the camp at Babi Yar who was forced to help with the attempted cover-up of mass murder by digging up the bodies and burning them. Thomas takes material extensively from this rendering of Davydov's words and reproduces the black humour of categorizing the slave labourers engaged in this terrible task as cloakroom attendants, stokers and gardeners; and an incident about the death of waitresses from Kiev in a gas-van.[18]

It is as if Thomas has gone backwards in time to the turn of the century, where his novel begins, to construct a female subject so that he can turn her into an object during the Holocaust years. Wirth-Nesher has commented that the point of this is to 'impress upon us the magnitude of the loss at Babi Yar by recreating imaginatively the *lives* of those who died, not their deaths'.[19] Such a method needs a particular temporal structure, and although Amis's backwards narration could have done just this, as we saw, the lives of individual Jews are not represented at all in *Time's Arrow*. This is what Thomas says of his method:

> [In 'The Sleeping Carriage'] my heroine, Lisa Erdman, changes from being Lisa an individual to Lisa in history – an anonymous victim. It is this transition, reflected in style as well as content, which has moved and disturbed many readers. From individual self-expression she moves to the common fate. From the infinitely varied world of narrative fiction we move to a world in which fiction is not only severely constrained but irrelevant.[20]

Although, as in *Time's Arrow*, the number of pages in *The White Hotel* devoted to the Holocaust is relatively small, the rest of the text is profoundly affected by this event, whether in retrospect (*Time's Arrow*) or in prospect (*The White Hotel*), and indeed both novels centre on it. It is as if Thomas has gone back in order to look forward, although with dread, not anticipation, to this particular moment in 1941, when the poetic and unconscious fantasies of turbulent sex and flying wombs (55) are stripped of their 'feminine' associations and therefore turn murderous. It is not metaphorical thought which is the villain in this scenario, as critics have suggested, but the lack of it.

Kappeler sees the additions Thomas makes to Pronicheva's testimony in a rather different light. She claims that 'It is inconceivable ... that [Thomas] should believe that linking sexual violence with the holocaust was a profound, original artistic achievement', as Nazi sadism is a commonplace and marketable element of everyday pornography. The role of a historical event in *The White Hotel* is to make the pornography even more realistic. Thomas 'has become the snuff artist of the literary establishment.... [Lisa] must be a true woman, and she must be truly dead to trigger the literary climax'.[21] In this reading, the issue of plagiarism, although it does not interest Kappeler in itself, is inextricably bound up with the issue of pornography. The former not only makes the latter acceptable but makes it work better. Kappeler is echoing Adorno, and adds to his comments an element of gender. Adorno followed his infamous remark about the impossibility of lyric poetry after Auschwitz by saying, 'the so-called artistic representation of naked bodily pain, of victims felled by rifle butts, contains, however remote, the potentiality of wringing pleasure from it'.[22] The rape and murder of Lisa at Babi Yar is almost a test case for this problem, and in Kappeler's eyes it is exactly to wring out pleasure that her 'naked bodily pain' is represented in *The White Hotel*.[23]

As evidence for her thesis, Kappeler discusses an interview with Thomas in which he discusses how he came to write *The White Hotel*. It started life as the poem of section 1 of '*Don Giovanni*', which was originally published separately.[24] 'The novel *The White Hotel* was provided to accommodate' the poem, Kappeler observes darkly, and quotes what Thomas has to say about this 'accommodation':

> It was only when I read Kuznetsov's *Babi Yar* that it clicked and I realised that the poems were, in fact, beginning a novel which would end in Babi Yar.... Well, that seemed to be a very exciting idea.... So, from the poem I then wrote the prose expansion, taking each part of it and re-framing it as narrative. Then it went into realism.[25]

Kappeler sees this statement as confirmation of Thomas's bad faith, and paraphrases it in the following way: 'It was only when he read the account of one of history's most violent and sadistic massacres, abounding in gratuitous brutality, that he saw an "end" to which his pornographic poems could lead.'[26] In his autobiographical *Memories and Hallucinations*, by contrast, Thomas speaks of the 'extraordinary' formal connections he recognized between Dina Pronicheva's testimony in *Babi Yar* and his own monologue, 'The Woman to Sigmund Freud': 'I couldn't escape the conviction that the woman of my poem was Dina Pronicheva: or someone very like her.'[27] Again, the overlap of accusations of pornography and plagiarism is clear: one could rephrase Kappeler's comment and say that it was the prospect of plagiarizing that excited Thomas.

History versus poetry

The American counterpart to the scandalized British reception of *The White Hotel* is to read it as a polemic in favour of one of its constituent discourses. In her book *Intimate Violence*, Laura E. Tanner devotes a chapter to the problematically hybrid nature of *The White Hotel*. Rather than criticizing the novel itself, she reads its satire of backshadowing as an attack on Freudian thought. Tanner gives a different slant to Thomas's juxtaposition of the first and second halves of *The White Hotel* – she gives them the binary titles 'symbolic' and 'realist', in contrast to Kappeler's 'pornographic' and 'historical'. Tanner gives a more positive reading of Thomas's comment that the addition of the Babi Yar material to his poems made the text 'go into realism'; her argument is that '*The White Hotel* uses its explosive subject matter to expose the contingent nature of its own claim to authority'.[28] Tanner suggests that the profoundly metaphorical early sections of Thomas's novel – Lisa's poem, her journal, and her third-person account of herself – are thrown into negative relief by the historical realism of the later sections, 'The Health Resort' and 'The Sleeping Carriage'. She asserts that psychoanalysis' reliance on metaphor inspires Lisa to produce narratives which are similarly structured, and that this reliance explains Freud's 'misdiagnosis' of Lisa's symptoms and Lisa's own transformation of real facts into the symbols of memory. It is true that hysteria is a condition which presupposes a symbolic model. Trauma from the past which is not consciously acknowledged is symbolized bodily in the present; the repressed memory is a signified whose signifier is the symptom. A classic example of this is one of Dora's symptoms, recounted in Freud's case history: she suffers from a limp which has no apparent organic cause. Freud diagnoses the limp as a metaphor. It represents the 'false step' Dora took in rejecting the advances of Herr K., the elderly, cigar-smoking family friend who approached her on two occasions, once when she was only fourteen. Freud's colleague Josef Breuer described hysteria as 'the product of a physical trauma which had been forgotten by the patient';[29] it is clear that Lisa's symptoms are the product of a physical trauma which *has not yet happened* to the patient.

Tanner argues persuasively that the poem '*Don Giovanni*' in *The White Hotel* juxtaposes 'public suffering and personal pain', which 'reflects [Lisa's] willingness to level the distinctions between violence and sexuality'.[30] Throughout the poem, the fantasized love-making between Lisa and Freud's son is counterpointed by a series of external disasters, including a boating accident, a landslide and, in this extract, a fire:

> So, pulling me on him without warning,
> your son impaled me, it was so sweet I screamed
> but no one heard me for the other screams as body after body fell or leapt
> from upper storeys of the white hotel.
> I jerked and jerked until his prick released
> its cool soft flood. Charred bodies hung from trees,
> he grew erect again ...
>
> (23)

Both Tanner and Kappeler quote this section from '*Don Giovanni*'. Kappeler argues that although Lisa is grammatically the subject here, and of the poem as a whole, agency still belongs to the man, for she is just 'the passive, receiving, suffering counter-part to this aggressive and violent actor and his action'. Tanner does ascribe agency to Lisa, who is 'willing to level' distinctions between personal and public pain, and argues that both she and her lover 'exploit the pain of others by employing that pain as a means of heightening their own pleasure', particularly in the extract quoted above. According to Tanner, Thomas's text makes out that this is the fault of Freud and the kind of psychoanalytic discourse which Lisa and her lover literalize: it 'subsumes' violence into mere metaphor by stressing 'the primacy of sexuality'.[31] Mary F. Robertson, in a similar argument, cites approvingly Robert Jay Lifton's belief that 'it is essential to amend the Freudian model of the psyche from one of repression of sexual urges to anesthesia from historical trauma'. It is not made clear why these two discourses are opposed, although their difference is often called upon in cases of Holocaust scandal.[32] As Tanner goes on to argue, the construction of the sentences makes the violence and death – 'Charred bodies hung from trees' – seem causally related to sexual pleasure – 'he grew erect again'. Not only that, but the 'violence of the sexual impalement', which is 'implicitly equated with the violence occurring around the lovers', of course prefigures the horrifying 'impalement' that Lisa undergoes in Babi Yar.[33] In Tanner's eyes, the act of prefiguring is not an experiment in temporal representation, but part of a polemic against a psychoanalytically inflected reliance on metaphors like that of impalement.[34]

Tanner argues that the prefigurative impaling shows that a purely metaphorical engagement with human pain is inadequate preparation for confronting, unmediated, the horror of what happens to Lisa in the Holocaust years. The reader remembers the details at Babi Yar from the 'safe' context of Lisa's poem – although Kappeler would hardly call them safe even the first time around. Other details, as Tanner points out, begin as metaphors in the first two sections of *The White Hotel*, and end up as realist facts in the final sections.[35] Robertson argues that 'Surely the readers of the chapter on Babi Yar in *The White Hotel* will agree that it portrays a "reality that drives out the [psychoanalytic] theory" which dominates the first part of the book', and that 'psychoanalytic sleuthing' seems at least 'morally frivolous', at worst 'somehow more directly responsible for history's nightmare'.[36]

However, the conclusion Tanner draws – that 'the inability of Freud's forms to account for the immediate horror of that violence points to the need to reevaluate the conventional frameworks within which violence is understood and communicated'[37] – seems to obscure what the real differences are between the early and the later sections of *The White Hotel*. It goes against the 'precognitive' chronology of the novel, as David Wingrove calls it,[38] to argue that material at the beginning is polemically superseded by material at the end. The effect of the premonitory details is precisely to *disrupt* the sense of being falsely drawn into a fictional world and then encouraged to abandon it after further reading, which Tanner describes thus: 'the novel draws back from its self-created universe to reveal the extent to which the reader has been entrapped by the subtle persuasions of literary form.'[39] This seems inaccurate. Rather, all kinds of details the reader may have understood on one level – the poetic or symbolic – have extra layers of meaning, including the historical, added to them when they are considered from the vantage point of the book's end. This is of course true of any narrative, but is a feature which is made into a particular repository of meaning in *The White Hotel*, and part of its satire on readerly 'weddedness' to fore- and backshadowing in the face of a well-known historical event.[40] The reader might expect to be able to 'foreshadow' the Holocaust in a novel set in Europe of the 1920s, but not in the way one can in *The White Hotel*.

An especially striking notion of Freud's, that of *Nachträglichkeit*, or 'belatedness', is developed in the case history of the Wolf Man. Lisa shows herself familiar with this case history – she has read the case history, and even passes the patient on the stairs at Freud's offices (113).[41] Freud argues that due to the operations of *Nachträglichkeit*, cause and effect may appear to have changed places when an analyst tries to make sense of the role of trauma in a child's life and its continued effect on the adult. In the case of the Wolf Man, witnessing his parents' love-making at a young age, around 18 months, was given significance and revivified only later, when he had a dream at the age of four: the dream 'brought into deferred operation his observation of intercourse'.[42] Sexualized knowledge was put back into the scene; in *The White Hotel*, historical knowledge is belatedly put back into earlier scenes. Cause and effect are reversed for the novel's reader, or causes are 'retranscribed' by their effects, as Freud puts it,[43] in the sense that the first event depends on the second for its meaning. Freud argues that in the operation of *Nachträglichkeit* chronology may be disrupted even more radically than this, as we cannot be sure the first event ever really took place. It could be a mental construction of the patient's, forged from fragments of later, analogously structured events, which s/he places in the past. If the Wolf Man did not really see his parents having intercourse, then the explanation, according to Freud, for his recalling the scene may be that the scene was constructed from a collage of other memories and experiences, or was a kind of 'racial' memory.[44]

We see this 'belated' logic throughout *The White Hotel*; events, like the happenings in the White Hotel and Lisa's pains, are placed in the past, but only make full sense belatedly, in terms of what is to come. As Neil Easterbrook asserts, belatedness may appear to make more sense in a backwards narrative like *Time's Arrow* in which cause and effect are necessarily reversed:

> [*Time's Arrow's*] treatment of psychic time make it a parable of what Freud called *Nachträglichkeit*, the revisionary retroactivity that belatedly recasts the past as a repetition of the present. ... It is *Nachträglichkeit* which directly structures the sort of revisionary history that would obscure or deny the Holocaust.[45]

Easterbrook emphasizes the constructed aspect of the past events when seen belatedly, and the potential dangers of this view; Freud's attempt at such a diagnosis in the case of the Wolf Man has been especially controversial.

However, in their definition of *Nachträglichkeit*, Laplanche and Pontalis emphasize disruption of chronology without suggesting the original experience may never have happened: 'experiences, impressions and memory-traces may be revised at a later date to fit in with fresh experiences or with the attainment of a new stage of development'.[46] The fictional Freud in *The White Hotel* discusses *Nachträglichkeit* without naming it, in the case history of Anna G.:

> What was I to make of [Anna's] memory? It was very much an adult's view; but *this was not proof that we were dealing with a phantasy*. ... Our childhood memories show us our earlier years not as they were but as they appeared at the later periods when the memories were aroused.
>
> (99–100, my italics)

The notion of *Nachträglichkeit* can clarify the significance of the external disasters that surround the love-making of Lisa and Freud's son. They make sense most fully when we have read the details of the massacre at Babi Yar. *Nachträglichkeit* can also show that the model of one level of meaning superseding another, which Tanner adheres to, is inappropriate, as Thomas says in interview:

> Ideally I hoped someone could open the book anywhere and read a paragraph and it would make them think of some other episode in the book, some other particular image. ... I do see time as something that you're looking down on – that you can see both the future and the past.[47]

The narrative of *The White Hotel* is not cumulative in any simple way. It moves not just from symbolism to realism but from reliance on one intertextual trope (Freudian discourse) to another (eyewitness testimony). However, *The White Hotel*'s temporal deformations are not as reliant on 'time's arrow' as Amis's novel, and it is able to repeat and circle around more freely. There are clear counter-movements to the goal-oriented trajectory described by Tanner within the novel. 'The Gastein Journal', for instance, at first seems like Holocaust realism – Lisa is being pursued by soldiers through a forest (30) – but soon shows itself to be an account of a proleptic dream, and makes full sense only many pages later (220). Tanner does not discuss the novel's final section, 'The Camp', which works against the replacement of symbolism by realism for which she argues. This section works by a kind of historicized dream-logic. Thomas's comment on the reasons for following the unadorned narration of 'The Sleeping Carriage' with the wish-fulfilment of 'The Camp' goes against the grain of Tanner's argument for a narrative which culminates in the 'authoritative' discourse of history, in Bakhtin's phrase. Thomas says:

> after a very realistic description [of Babi Yar], I had to get the sense of time passing.... It wasn't until very near the end that I thought I ought to write

the last episode of the book, 'The Camp'. I couldn't leave it with those bodies in *Babi Yar*. It had to go on.[48]

The way the novel does 'go on' is through a discourse which is even more symbolic than before. Equally, Tanner ignores the fact that the novel does not begin with the excessive symbolism of '*Don Giovanni*': this section is preceded by a 'historical' prologue of letters between Freud and some colleagues, as he sends the manuscript of '*Don Giovanni*' to one of them.[49] Thomas says that he added the prologue at a late stage in the book's composition, to offset the difficulty of starting *The White Hotel* with Lisa's poem:

> And then, when I thought [the novel] was complete, I realised that it was a bit much to ask a reader to plunge right into a poem, and a fairly extreme one at that, so I wrote the prologue – the letters – which I thought worked very well.[50]

Thomas sees the succession of discourses in the novel as just the opposite of the way Tanner sees it; he says that the initial foray into poetry is 'very primitive', then develops into an 'analytical' prose version, succeeded by an increasing realism which 'drifts away', full circle, into mysticism.[51]

The White Hotel is characterized by oscillations between various kinds of discourse, which is rather different from the pattern of one being succeeded by another. The most striking instance of apparent succession turning out to be something more like ambiguity is the recourse the novel makes to eyewitness testimony; in Tanner's argument, this is its move towards the realist language of history. She claims that Thomas's

> appeal to a first-person account of Holocaust experience represents a nod toward grounding his postmodern text in an experiential framework that acknowledges rather than disguises the facts of violence.[52]

The historical element is provided by Kuznetsov's *Babi Yar*, and his rendering of Dina Pronicheva's testimony. It is significant that Thomas chose a 'documentary fiction' rather than a more clearly historical account of the massacre.[53] As James E. Young has argued, 'the operative trope underpinning the documentary character of Holocaust fiction is the *rhetorical principle* of testimony or witness, not its actuality'. Rather than imparting 'actual evidential authority' to Thomas's text, Kuznetsov's emphasizes the rhetorical importance of testimony for the 'documentary novel', as 'Kuznetsov's own novel was also based upon the verbatim transcription of another testimonial source', and is 'hardly the stuff of "authentic" or unmediated testimony'.[54] As Young observes, the effect of mixing together actual events and fictional characters in documentary fictions is that the writer 'simultaneously relieves himself of an obligation to historical accuracy (invoking poetic license), even as he imbues his fiction with the historical authority of real events'.[55] This hybridity, of generic and rhetorical levels, is not consistent with Tanner's argument that metaphor is clearly swept away by realism in *The White Hotel*.

Tanner's argument is that 'symbolic forms may be used to contain and transform violence', and she claims that the clearest instance is that Freud's interpretation of Lisa's symptoms is incorrect. Freud claims that the asthma attacks Lisa suffers, and the hallucinations of fire and disaster she experiences during sex, are the signs of forgotten knowledge of her mother's adulterous relationship with her uncle, and their death by fire while illicitly together at a hotel. As becomes clear, these symptoms are actually – or also – proleptic signs of the threat of being buried or burnt alive at Babi Yar. The fictional Freud identifies the pain in Lisa's breast and pelvis as a sign of repressed homosexuality and over-identification with her mother. However, the pains do turn out to be organic 'in some peculiar way', as Lisa predicts they will (171), and as the circumstances of her death in the ravine at Babi Yar show:

> An SS man bent over an old woman lying on her side, having seen a glint of something bright. His hand brushed her breast when he reached for the crucifix to pull it free, and he must have sensed a flicker of life. Letting go the crucifix he stood up. He drew his leg back and sent his jackboot crashing into her left breast. She moved position from the force of the blow, but uttered no sound. Still not satisfied, he swung his boot again and sent it cracking into her pelvis. Again the only sound was the clean snap of the bone. Satisfied at last, he jerked the crucifix free. He went off, picking his way across the corpses.
>
> (219)

A comparison with Kuznetsov's text is instructive:

> One SS-man caught his foot against Dina and her appearance aroused his suspicions. He shone his torch on her, picked her up and struck her with his fist. But she hung limp and gave no signs of life. He kicked her in the breast with his heavy boot and trod on her right hand so that the bones cracked, but he didn't use his gun and went off, picking his way across the corpses.[56]

Thomas has added to Kuznetsov's original the 'symbols' which fit Lisa's past, and a particular view of the Holocaust. Lisa's crucifix signifies her allegiance to her mother's rather than her father's religion, and her gesture of touching the crucifix when telling a lie was noted both by Freud and by the narrator. Its presence in the scene above alters it considerably.[57] In Kuznetsov's account, Dina Pronicheva suffers injuries to her breast and to her hand; the hand will not do for Thomas's version, as it is not associated with the femininity that is central to his account, so he substitutes the pelvis. (One can imagine Susanne Kappeler's reaction to this turning of the screw of femininity; at first glance it seems to support her argument about the exploitative linking of sexuality and the Holocaust.) Because Dina survived to tell her story to Kuznetsov, it is narrated from her point of view although it is in the third person. In Thomas's version, the third-person narration emanates from an outside observer, because Lisa does not survive her ordeal, as the phrase 'he *must have sensed* a flicker of life' indicates. Although this is not necessarily incompatible with having Lisa as the focalizer – she too might have speculated about the SS man's motives – it follows from the description of her as 'an old woman', the phrase of a distant narrator.

The effect of the distant narrator, in terms of Tanner's argument, is to establish an objectivity to contrast with Freud's subjective, transference-ridden account of Lisa. Tanner claims that 'Lisa's pain serves as the variable that generates a hermeneutical contest; the narrative documents opposing interpretations of Lisa's symptoms that vie for authority in the text'.[58] This is a very interesting interpretation of the clash of discourses which characterizes Thomas's novel; according to Bakhtin, any multiplicity of languages in a text will not settle inertly alongside one another, but battle for supremacy in the way Tanner describes. However, her argument again depends on ignoring the particular temporal configuration of *The White Hotel*. To say that Freud is proved wrong about Lisa's symptoms, because events in the future turn out to be responsible for them, is akin to Michael André Bernstein's description of how backshadowing blames people in the times immediately preceding a historical catastrophe for lack of foresight. Freud's attempt at analytic mastery in *The White Hotel* is compromised by his failure to interpret Lisa's hallucinations of falling from a great height and being buried by a landslide, and why her pains attack the left side of her body. However, this failure is not the same as Freud's failure to predict the events of the Holocaust, for which critics appear to blame him, as Tanner puts it:

> Freud's limited forms of understanding lead him to read Lisa's suffering as a symbolic manifestation (rather than a literal demarcation) of a past event (rather than a future occurrence).[59]

It is hardly surprising that Freud's understanding is limited to the past, and that he does not suspect that his analysand's symptoms might be the result of events yet to happen, because, to quote Frank Kermode on G.J. Whitrow again, there can logically be ' "no such thing as a future analogue of a trace" ' or a symptom.[60] As with *Time's Arrow*, we see exactly such a trace in *The White Hotel*, but it is unreasonable to expect the characters, in Thomas's forward-moving text, to see it that way. Even Lisa herself, when she insists on the organic nature of her pains and contests Freud's analyses ('In a way you *made* me become fascinated by my mother's sin'), could hardly be said to predict the fate in store for her. As the event approaches, she loses her telepathic gift, and delays acknowledging that she is in a group of people about to be shot until it is unavoidable:

> When Lisa tried to swallow a small piece of cheese but found it would not go
> down her throat, her mind accepted what she had known ever since they
> came through the barrier – that they were to be shot.
>
> (210)[61]

Lisa's avoidance of understanding until the last minute does not, of course, mean
that she is to blame for her fate, and no critic has suggested that she is. Again,
satire is directed at the reader's devotion to backshadowing, not at the characters' inability to predict the future. Tanner's harsh treatment of Freud is the
result of her failure to notice the double-voiced element of his fictionalized
discourse. As we will see, his analysis does allow for future events.

The paradox in Tanner's reasoning seems to be the result of confusing a
spatial conflict in *The White Hotel* – between metaphorical and realist discourse –
with a temporal conflict – between backward- and forward-looking narrative.
Tanner's description of Lisa's pain as real rather than symbolic demonstrates this
conflation: 'it is the literal mark of an event to come in the future rather than a
symbolic trace of an incident in the past'.[62] It is unusual, to say the least, to
ascribe greater reality to events which have not yet happened than to past events,
particularly if we imagine that the latter may actually construct future events.
This is particularly true if we see Lisa as embodying in some way the cost of
Nazism; the wounds of such a personification would not spring out of nowhere,
but emerge out of a complicated collection of long- and short-term factors. In
other words, her symptoms do refer backwards as much as forwards. Commentators have often pointed to moments in Freud's writings where he appears to be
prefiguring features of Nazi authoritarianism or antisemitism, but this is not
foreknowledge, of course. When Freud wrote his account of Schreber, Hitler
was, after all, still a house-painter.

Tanner's argument about the wilful blindness of psychoanalysis would fit
better the case history of Schreber. Daniel Paul Schreber, a judge, suffered from
hallucinations of bodily destruction and decay, sex-change and transformation
into a Jew, which he described in disarming detail in his *Memoirs*. Freud never
met Schreber, but analysis of his writings led Freud to the conclusion that
Schreber suffered from an incestuously homosexual attachment to an 'excellent'
father. Unfortunately, the flaw in Freud's argument is that Schreber's hallucinations of bodily disintegration seem to be the result of years of mistreatment at the
hands of his father, who was famous as a child educationalist. Schreber senior's
books were best-sellers, and feature chilling illustrations of how he thought the
young should be dealt with: their hands tied up at night to prevent masturbation,
and complicated 'head-restraining' devices used to correct their posture.[63] On
top of his curious failure to mention this fact, as Eric Santner has noted, in the
extracts Freud chooses from Schreber's *Memoirs* for the case history, none of
those concerning Schreber's fantasy of becoming a Jew is quoted or mentioned.
This gives a misleading impression, Santner argues, as one of the dogmas of the
antisemitic tradition of Freud's time, with which Freud was familiar, held that

Jewish men were effeminate, so that misogyny and antisemitism were closely intertwined.[64] Freud's counter-transference, as a father and a Jewish man, appears to have made him omit these two significant features of Schreber's case, but the study remains of interest to scholars like William Niederland as an unknowing comment on the origins of Austro-German Nazism. In *The White Hotel*, Thomas has replaced 'race' with gender, reversing Ann Pellegrini's comment on Freud's habit of displacing the scene of hysteria from 'race *and* gender wholly to gender'. Lisa is Christian, despite her Jewish father, but her femininity is supposed to make her a representative Holocaust victim. However, it seems that in the novel the common assumption that 'the Jew' is male has been made, and Jewish women, such as Dina Pronicheva, are written out of the equation.[65]

The Freud of deliberate or unconscious suppressions is not the Freud of *The White Hotel*. He does discuss Lisa's mixed parentage with her, and writes letters to her about the real version of the story of assault by a group of drunken sailors: their motives were antisemitic ones directed against her Jewish father, rather than the misogynist ones directed against her adulterous mother which she tells Freud about at first.[66] Freud even shares with her a Freudian slip made in a letter to him: an 'English correspondent' wrote to 'commiserate with me on my "troublesome jew", in place of "jaw" ' (174). It could be argued that the fictional Freud's willingness to acknowledge such issues is because he too is constructed retrospectively, in the light of post-Holocaust attitudes to Jewishness and antisemitism.[67] In interview, Thomas effectively admits that his construction of the fictional Freud partakes of ironic backshadowing, as he describes how the psychoanalytic element entered into the novel:

> That was more or less when it really clicked. Suddenly the knowledge that the patients of Freud were usually Jews, and he was a Jew; that they all had something wrong with them and that Freud always thought this was something in their childhood, whereas in fact it could just as easily have been an awareness of the terror that was approaching.[68]

This is a new and positive variant of backshadowing, one that does not blame but applauds victims for foreseeing, in however unconscious a way, their impending fate.

Women and Jews

Critics are divided on Thomas's representation of women. The popular view is probably that of the column 'Pass Notes' in the *Guardian* newspaper, prompted by the publication of Thomas's 1994 novel *Pictures at an Exhibition*, in which his novels are described as 'lurid psychodramas of rape, etc.' and his initials said to stand for 'Devilish Misogynist'.[69] The reverence Thomas claims by contrast to feel for women could be described as another kind of misogyny, which sees its literary muse as a woman and regrets the beauty of female Holocaust victims. He claims 'ironically' to have been accused of misogyny considering that he has always found it harder to make his male characters sympathetic, and writing about women more 'interesting'.[70]

In contrast to Kappeler's unflattering estimate of *The White Hotel* as 'pornographic and nonsensical',[71] a different group of critics has isolated the same elements of Thomas's novel but drawn different conclusions from them. Like Kappeler, they are not interested in the issue of plagiarism as such, nor with the Holocaust except as gender politics informs it.[72] In a letter to the *Times Literary Supplement*, Sylvia Kantaris defended Thomas after D.A. Kenrick's exposé of his debt to Kuznetsov. She describes Lisa offering a link between 'the individual human psyche and mass horrors', a feminine antenna of a 'deeply disturbed society'. Elsewhere, in correspondence with Peter Redgrove on the subject of *The White Hotel*, she observes:

> The element of titillation is also strong – *and* wrapped up in an art package so that you can get it in the guise of culture and feel virtuous in the process. Same thing with the horror, also titillating, only more so.[73]

Although her conclusion is harsher – she uses the term 'pornographic' where Kantaris uses 'titillating', 'Nazi sadism' where Kantaris uses 'horror' – and more far-reaching, Kappeler says something very similar:

> My argument is that it is due to the conjuncture of the pornographic with the literary that the novel enjoys such insistent acclaim, and that the arguments for its literariness 'in spite' of its pornographic qualities reveal the fundamental investment the literary has in the pornographic.[74]

However, Kantaris goes on to argue that *The White Hotel* represents, rather than unwittingly reveals, a 'nihilism' through 'its very lack of heart' – it is suspiciously easy to read, and does not involve the reader deeply. In other words, the novel is more self-conscious than Kappeler gives it credit for.[75] Despite her doubts about the novel's heartless and 'titillating' qualities, Kantaris sees its subject as mourning the feminine which Kappeler sees it destroying:

> The way I read *The White Hotel*, the pain in Lisa's breast and ovary links Babi-Yar with the death of eros, and the feminine. She's an outrider. Her body knows the future in advance, the whole of our culture having been a battle over the female body.[76]

In Kantaris's reading, '*Don Giovanni*' and 'The Gastein Journal' are not masculinist pornographic reveries written as if from the viewpoint of a woman for an extra thrill, but instances of the feminine 'eros' of which Nazism was the opposite. It may be unconvincing and even unhelpful to have Nazism, and the Final Solution, described as 'the death of eros, and the feminine'; it may even seem to be typical of how fiction is unequal to the task of representing the Holocaust.[77] Sidra DeKoven Ezrahi argues that some Holocaust symbols may be 'so overdetermined that they cannot enter other existential universes without being either disruptive or presumptuous', and gives as an example Thomas's use of Babi Yar as a figure for 'Freudian – or Jungian – space'.[78] However, after the scene in Babi Yar in *The White Hotel*, Thomas emphasizes the loss of any care for the unconscious, the realm which Lisa's writings represented, *and* the loss of millions of individuals, in an attempt to link the psychic with the historical. The passage would make little sense in the terms proposed by Tanner and Robertson, if the narrator's regret here for the loss of Freudian attention to the subject were specious:

> Most of the dead were poor and illiterate. But every single one of them had dreamed dreams, seen visions and had amazing experiences, even the babes in arms (perhaps especially the babes in arms). Though most of them had never lived outside the Podol slum, their lives and histories were as rich and complex as Lisa Erdman-Berenstein's. If a Sigmund Freud had been listening and taking notes from the time of Adam, he would still not fully have explored even a single group, even a single person.
>
> And this was only the first day.
>
> (220)

This extract makes clear that psychoanalytic discourse is a means of measuring the cost of genocide, not a reason for it.[79]

It is not only *The White Hotel* which links fear of the feminine with the encroachment of fascism. In an essay on women's poetry and hysteria, Clair Wills discusses Klaus Theweleit's study of a group of Freikorps officers in Weimar Germany. Theweleit argues that the unconscious of fascist identity is a repressed femininity, and it is therefore inevitable that Freud should choose to investigate the psyches of hysterical women, because,

> In the course of the repression carried out against women, those two things, the unconscious and femaleness, were so closely coupled together that they came to be seen as nearly identical.[80]

The White Hotel picks up on exactly this link between the unconscious and feminine, both of which are brutally repressed under certain conditions. The personal history of Lisa Erdman unites the psychoanalytic investigation of the unconscious with its opposite, Nazi genocide.[81] She also links the novel's intertexts, and its two central geographical and psychic locations: the case study and the Holocaust eye-witness account, Freud's Vienna and Nazi-occupied Kiev, the thriving and the destruction of the feminine. Sidra DeKoven Ezrahi's reservations about Thomas using Babi Yar as a figure for a psychoanalytic space seem to be unfounded, as the relation between the two is much more direct than she implies. Rather than the site of massacre being just a figure for an ahistorical psychoanalytic category, it is the loss of the ability to value the unconscious which actually entails the Babi Yar massacre.

Wirth-Nesher argues that the discourses of femininity and Judaism in *The White Hotel* are separate and cannot coexist; one masks the other. As we have seen, Lisa withheld from Freud two central facts which appear to have sabotaged his analysis of her: the fact that the sailors who attacked her were antisemitic, and that she divorced her husband because he was so virulently antisemitic that, she felt, he would reject her if he knew of her Jewish ancestry. Wirth-Nesher asserts that

> [Lisa's] pain in her ovary and breast, far from being the result of a nuclear family drama, are premonitions of her suffering as part of a collective identity, as a Jew, the victim of history. ... That which Freud so systematically denied in his life and in his scientific methods is the very thing that is mysteriously associated with Lisa the Jewish victim, not Lisa the hysterical female.[82]

Wirth-Nesher's comments continue the critical habit of trying to engage with *The White Hotel*'s ambiguities and hybridities by resolving its discourses into a neat binary, one term of which serves to undermine the other. (She suggests that history succeeds psychoanalysis just as Lisa's Jewishness supersedes her femininity, but, as we have seen, it is in fact the other way round: psychoanalysis is historicized, and Lisa is less Jewish than Dina.) For Kappeler the binary consists of pornography superseding history; for Robertson, history outwits psychoanalysis; for Tanner, realism undermines symbolism; for John Burt Foster, the novel dramatizes a conflict between magic-realism and nineteenth-century realism.[83] Wirth-Nesher develops her opposition of femininity and Jewishness into a more general stand-off: 'Lisa's life, as we see it in the next section, the Babi Yar chapter, is part of a moral universe, *not* a psychological one', as if the two categories must be mutually exclusive.[84]

The most notable feature of the patients Freud treated for hysteria, implicit in Thomas's remark and the narrative of *The White Hotel*, is that they were almost all women. Sander L. Gilman discusses the widespread nineteenth- and early twentieth-century notion of 'the feminine nature of the Jew' in his book *Jewish Self-Hatred*.[85] Walter Rathenau argued in the 1890s that the 'soft' feminine look of the male Jew was the result of oppression,[86] and his essay joined a 'long tradition' of perceiving female discourse as both different from the mainstream, and related to that of the Jew. Both 'women and Jews misuse language', are illogical and do not tell the truth. As Gilman points out, the conjunction of women and Jews is not a coincidence, as both had 'become more visible on the horizon of European consciousness through their articulated demands for emancipation, both legal and cultural'.[87] Gilman concludes, 'The Jew is thus a degenerate woman!'[88] In *The Case of Sigmund Freud*, Gilman discusses the problem of determining what Thomas asserts, whether 'hysteria was indeed a dominant illness among European Jews of the nineteenth century'. The argument that there was a ' "Jewish psychosis" ' was linked to East European Jews, and their particular dialect and body language.[89] In Freud's case, this was associated with his father, who came from Galicia: 'Hysteria is a potential reflex of being an eastern European Jew', or a woman, or both.[90]

It is tempting to conclude that social and legal oppression linked Jews and women, as did 'a diagnostic system rooted in the belief that external appearance was the source of knowledge about the pathological',[91] and to read their common hysterical symptoms as the product of uncomfortable cultural pressures. As we have seen, a limp was one of Dora's symptoms, on which Freud put a particular interpretive emphasis; according to Gilman, who devotes a chapter of *The Case of Sigmund Freud* to the 'degenerate' Jewish foot, the hysteric and 'the limping Jew are related in the outward manifestation of their illness'.[92]

This tradition of associating Jews and femininity, although only implicit in *The White Hotel*, underlies critical efforts to read the novel as an elegy for 'the feminine': a category which can include women and (male) Jews, personified by Lisa, a female victim of the Holocaust. The fact that Lisa identifies herself as Catholic emphasizes the importance of non-essential definition for such a category. In her final days, Lisa attempts to shift her allegiance several times. At first, it seems that Jews are being 'evacuated' as a privilege before anyone else, and it is as Jews that she and Kolya make the journey to Babi Yar (206). When Lisa realizes people are being shot, she claims to be gentile in an attempt to save herself and her son; finally, when only she, and not her son, is exempted by the Ukrainian guard from a semitic taint, she insists she is really Jewish in order to stay with Kolya (210–11). 'Proof' in these instances takes the form of external attributes, such as identity cards and a particular surname, or performative abilities, such as knowing how to recite Hebrew. Ann Pellegrini discusses the 'competing discourses' of 'religion, nation and race' which constituted turn-of-the-century thinking about Jewishness.[93] All three discourses are apparent in the scene at Babi Yar (211): Lisa's identity card states that her nationality is Ukrainian, not Jewish; when Kolya is 'racially' identified as a ' "Jew-boy" ' by his surname Berenstein, Lisa resorts to the discourse of religion to prove her own Jewishness and babbles some Hebrew. Unlike her real-life prototype, Dina Pronicheva, Lisa is a Christian victim of the Holocaust and wears a crucifix which is, as we have seen, reduced to an opportunity for looting; any other meaning it may have had, about Lisa's psychic life or cultural identity, dies along with her. Kuznetsov describes Pronicheva using a mixture of the discourses described by Pellegrini:

> Dina's husband was Russian, so she had a Russian name and moreover didn't look at all Jewish. In fact Dina looked far more like a Ukrainian woman and she spoke Ukrainian.[94]

Dina is defined according to nationality (she speaks Ukrainian) and 'race' (she 'looks' Ukrainian). Lisa also 'looks' non-Jewish on account of her crucifix.

Lisa's resistance to Freud's interpretation of her symptoms – 'I don't believe for one moment *that* [my mother's sin] had anything to do with my crippling pain' (171) – is on a different level from Tanner's resistance. Lisa does not argue that Freud is looking in the wrong place for his answer: as a character in a polyphonic text, she could hardly do this. It is not even clear that Tanner is arguing that Freud should literally have looked to the seeds of violence sown in Germany and Austria before the Second World War and predicted where they would end. Such an argument would suffer from the backshadowing paradox noted by Bernstein, that the Holocaust is both unprecedented and should have been predicted. Tanner argues that, given his time and his profession, Freud was bound to get it wrong. Robertson claims that 'Freud's larger failure to put himself in dialogue with real history is symptomatic of the failure of prominent analytic languages to make the world better by understanding what happens in history', and Phillips argues that:

> While Freud correctly intuits [Lisa's] guilt when she wishes she were the child of her safely Christian uncle and not of her Jewish father, he ignores the clues of anti-Semitic brutality – both fascist and communist, as represented by Lisa's husband and by her first lover, Alexei – which would have enabled him to predict the dual 'ranks of German soldiers and Ukrainian police' at Babi Yar.[95]

However, what Freud could have done to gain insight into real *future* history, or how he alone should have predicted genocide before the word was even coined, is not clear. Lisa argues for a forward- rather than a backward-looking view of the self, but this calls on a different, temporal polarity from the one between psychoanalysis and history:

> Is there any family without a skeleton in the cupboard? Frankly I didn't always wish to talk about the past; I was more interested in what was happening to me then, *and what might happen in the future.*

> (171, my italics)

It is true that Freud's impatient response to Jung's interest in some peat-bog bodies unearthed in northern Germany at the beginning of the novel is an uncanny triggering moment – he demands, 'Why are you so concerned with these corpses?' Freud's physical reaction seems hysterical: Ferenczi, who recounts the incident in a letter, adds that Freud then 'slipped off his chair in a faint'.[96] Robertson rightly draws a connection between these prehistoric mummified bodies and the attempts of the Soviets (she mistakenly says Nazis) to fill the ravine at Babi Yar with water to make a bog and cover over Nazi crimes. However, the reading she offers, that Freud is 'evasive of historical responsibility' here, seems again not quite right in relation to the The White Hotel's own construction of time. The irony of the Soviets trying to hide the evidence at Babi Yar, and bearing similarities with the censor-deleted material from Kuznetsov's text, was that it actually drew attention to it. The dam built at the mouth of the ravine burst, much of Kiev was buried in mud and, as the narrator of The White Hotel puts it, 'Frozen in their last postures, as at Pompeii, people were still being dug out two years later' (222). The comparison implicitly continues Freud's archaeological analogy for psychoanalysis.[97] The bog-people are a variant of Lisa's symptoms; they appear to foreshadow the cataclysm of the Holocaust, particularly the specific event with which The White Hotel is concerned, but of course are not linked to it causally. Again, the incident of the bog-people seems to be directed at the reader, whose 'weddedness to foreshadowing' may mean that s/he reads these corpses as proleptic of disaster, despite the different circumstances and 'postures'. The playing around with time and history which characterizes the novel as a whole is what is prefigured here.

In The White Hotel psychoanalysis and history are not set in an opposition which the latter must win, but shown to be implicated in each other. Because the narrator does not hint at what is to come, the polyphonic structure of The White Hotel remains intact despite the greater knowledge of the reader. It could also be argued that the succession of different discourses which forms the seven sections of the novel constitutes a kind of structural polyphony, since 'both story and mode of discourse change as we move from chapter to chapter, without any pretense of an overview'.[98]

The failure of Freud to diagnose the proleptic, historical nature of Lisa's symptoms is, pace Tanner, only to be expected. The reader's failure to do so is another matter. Does The White Hotel, like Time's Arrow, construct a reader-supposed-to-know, who recognizes the text's images of pain and violence for what they are, and predicts what is to come? It seems that Thomas's construction of narrative time is, like Amis's, a response to the historical trauma of the Holocaust. Once the latter appears in a text, the classical form of orderly narrative progression concluded by a satisfactory denouement is no longer appropriate. The way time operates in The White Hotel is an alternative to reverse narration. Rather than sliding inexorably backwards to the events of genocide, as Time's Arrow does, The White Hotel is an instance of Gary Saul Morson's category of 'pseudo-foreshadowing'. Its images of pain and violence, including Lisa's symptoms, do hint forwards to a future we can predict only too easily. Although Amis's novel is analeptic, while Thomas's is proleptic, the act of reading forwards means that it may well be true of both that the alert reader 'knows [certain events] are approaching with every passing page'.[99] Trigger-tropes, which we examined in Time's Arrow, also appear in The White Hotel, and are exactly the ones singled out by Tanner as evidence for a symbolic imagination at work within the text, which, she argues, fatally 'becomes entangled in the thorny area of violence itself'.[100] The 'entanglement' does not necessarily involve some kind of endorsement or production of violence, however, as Tanner implies, but ironic warning signs of impending violence.

Clairvoyance, Lisa's gift, is a perfect vehicle for pseudo-foreshadowing, particularly in *The White Hotel*, where future predictions are unreliable. At the moments Lisa needs it most, clairvoyance does not work; and, as in the dream Lisa has at Gastein (33) which foreshadows Dina's encounter with Motya at Babi Yar (220), it may not help anyone to foresee the future if it cannot be changed. Lisa's Gastein dream concluded with her pursuers shooting her; at Babi Yar, it is the little boy, Motya, who is shot by the Germans. Kuznetsov's text determines that the future cannot be changed, as again these events are taken from *Babi Yar*. Clairvoyance also represents the reader's likely response to a Holocaust narrative: s/he will see signs of impending doom, just as Lisa does, and of course the reader will be right, because s/he already knows what is coming. This is the force of the irony that Lisa's symptoms, dreams and hallucinations all turn out to be literal: it is a glance at the reader, not the characters. Only in a fictional work could such phenomena refer forwards as much as backwards, and there is no reason to believe even Lisa realizes this. When her symptoms 'come true', she has no moment of realization. Freud's case histories work according to such a narrative logic as well, as Peter Brooks's analysis of the Wolf Man's history has shown. Freud's narrative cannot move forward sequentially, given the nature of the material he is dealing with and his penchant for interpretive mastery. Freud speaks of two levels of discourse in his account of the Wolf Man: he says that he is

> unable to give either a purely historical or a purely thematic account of my patient's story; I can write a history neither of the treatment nor of the illness, but I shall find myself obliged to combine the two methods of presentation.[101]

Brooks argues that there are four temporal and expository layers at work in the case history: (1) the history of the neurosis; (2) the reasons for the neurosis; (3) the history of the treatment and how these events came out during analysis; and (4) the order of the case history in presenting these other three categories. That is, Freud must 'manage to tell, both "at once" and "in order", the story of a person, the story of an illness, the story of an investigation, the story of an explanation; and "meaning" must lie in the effective interrelationship of all of these'.[102] The combination of 'at once' and 'in order' is an impossible one, and *The White Hotel* also has a structure bearing witness to such an impossibility. Its tale cannot be told 'at once', as if it were all set in the realm of the unconscious; yet it also cannot all be told 'in order', as if it were unproblematically historical. Within the novel, the fictional Freud is made to utter a characteristic comment on this paradox of narration, in the section 'Frau Anna G.':

The young woman was ... disinclined to dispute my interpretation to any serious extent – except on one point, of a melancholy nature, which she did not have the heart to tell me about, and which I myself will reserve till the proper time.

(98)

Lisa's clairvoyance is often counter-transferential, as is shown by her ability to predict the death of Freud's daughter Sophie, for which he has a psychoanalytic explanation: Lisa's 'sensitive mind' discerned anxieties in Freud about his daughter 'with small children, living far away, at a time when there were many epidemics' (102). Narrated temporally rather than spatially, such 'sensitivity' becomes 'second sight' (101), as Lisa calls it.

Clairvoyance extends to the trigger-tropes in *The White Hotel*, such as mentions of the cook's 'ovens' (62), the 'mass graves' of the drowned hotel guests (66), the landslide which buries the mourners in a vast 'trench' (68) like the one at Babi Yar, a disaster of which there are few 'survivors' (69), the fact that Lisa's dentist manages to save some teeth with gold fillings (158), which are self-consciously forward-looking. On the level of the (post-war) reader, these tropes trigger knowledge of the vocabulary and geography of genocide; on the level of the characters, the triggers are part of a realm of the unconscious 'which knows no time' and can refer backwards or forwards; and intertextually, the borrowings from Freud look forward to the borrowings from Kuznetsov.[103] As we have seen, Tanner does not make clear on what level – the diagnostic or the historical – Freud is wrong about Lisa's symptoms; self-conscious uncertainty of levels is another site of pseudo-foreshadowing in the novel. For instance, in 'The Gastein Journal', Vogel, a survivor of the landslide, gives vent to antisemitic opinions: 'He was saying in a very loud voice that it might have been worse – there were a large number of Yids among the victims' (78). Vogel's remark works on several different planes: historically, such a comment would not have been uncommon in inter-war Germany, where Jews were often not allowed into hotels. Metaphorically, if we see the white hotel as a chronotopic rendering of the unconscious, or the feminine,[104] Vogel's utterance represents the strand of internalized and feminized antisemitism which Lisa experiences. Textually, the utterance points forward to the notice put up by the occupying forces preparing for the Babi Yar massacre:

The order said that all Yids living in the city of Kiev and its vicinity were to report by eight o'clock on the morning of Monday, 29 September 1941, at the corner of Melnikovsky and Dokhturov Streets (near the cemetery). They were to take with them documents, money, valuables, as well as warm clothes, underwear, etc. Any Yid not carrying out the instruction and who was found elsewhere would be shot. ... how to explain the callous, brutal tone of the proclamation? 'All Yids ... any Yids ...'.

(204–6)

In both of these extracts, the word 'Yid' is a striking and uncomfortable instance of free indirect discourse. The calm and straightforward tone of the narrator is disrupted by the direct rendition of Vogel's crude choice of noun in the earlier instance; in the second example, Lisa notes the 'chilling' interaction of the 'cold and contemptuous word "Yid" ' with the 'homely, commonplace words (warm clothes, underwear, etc.)' (205). For the reader, the shock is a double one: not only is the notice referentially disturbing, it is also structurally so, because the crude noun has penetrated the reporting voice. It goes without saying that Thomas's version of this poster is based closely on a real one cited by Kuznetsov, for which he gives a precise archival reference. The most significant difference is that Kuznetsov quotes the notice directly, so that the structural shock is minimized:

> 'All Yids living in the city of Kiev and its vicinity are to report by 8 o'clock on the morning of Monday, September 29th, 1941.'[105]

Kuznetsov reports that when he saw it, it 'made me shudder. It was written so very harshly, with a sort of cold hatred'.

The combination of timelessness, or fluid chronology, with historical detail works to make *The White Hotel* idiosyncratically polyphonic: the reader may well know what is up ahead, but at least one of the characters has privileged information about it too, through her ability to see into the future. Like the Tralfamadorians' view of time in Kurt Vonnegut's *Slaughterhouse 5*, this temporal structure acts as an effective means of satirizing foreshadowing, and Thomas speaks of it in terms similar to the Rocky Mountain analogy used in Vonnegut's novel (see Chapter 1). Time can be seen all at once, like a mountain range:

> Everything relates to everything [in *the White Hotel*]. It's a mesh. And then there are extraordinary coincidences – usually trivial things – but they're like mountain tops peeping out of the sea. They're just an indication of the range of relationships that lie under the surface.[106]

A second fictional character, Thomas's Freud, also predicts the future; he is not as blind to the meaning of Lisa's afflictions as Tanner and Robertson assert. In the novel's fictional case history, 'Frau Anna G.', he notes that '[Anna] had become convinced that for her to have a child would bring nothing but misfortune' (110) and although she had, 'by her own admission, an unusually strong maternal instinct; yet [she suffered under] an absolute edict, imposed by some autocrat, whom I could not name, against having children' (116). These words could be described as double-voiced; Freud uses them with a psychoanalytic inflection, so that 'misfortune' means 'psychic unhappiness', and 'some autocrat' refers to a superego-related force. At this point in the text, the reader may also understand Freud's words in this way; however, with hindsight, and in knowledge of Lisa's actual fate, the second sense of these words becomes clear.

'Misfortune' means death by shooting, like the death suffered by Lisa's stepson Kolya; and 'some autocrat' refers to Lisa's second sight predicting Hitler-inspired mass murder.

When she sits apart from the other victims of the massacre at Babi Yar, the narrator says, 'Now [Lisa] knew why she ought never to have had children' (216). Freud's analysis of the timing of Lisa's pains, which recurred particularly painfully after she had written to her husband hinting she would like to become pregnant during his next leave, is similarly double, although this time in a spatial way. Freud interprets these pains as the price of repressing a homosexual love – Lisa would rather bear the child of her close friend Madame R. (122–3). The reader, either with hindsight or on re-reading,[107] can see another reason for the pain: it is a warning that Lisa should not have children because they will die young. Again Lisa implicitly questions why the reason for her pains should not lie in the future:

> 'You tell me that my illness is probably connected with early events in my life that I have forgotten. But even if that is so, you can't alter those events in any way. How do you propose to help me, then?'
>
> (115)

Freud's response is one of double-voicedness, almost irony: 'much will be gained if we succeed in turning your hysterical misery into common unhappiness' (115). It is not that Freud is wrong about Lisa's symptoms, but that he tells a version of the truth without realizing it. Lisa's 'hysterical misery' does indeed evaporate in the face of the very 'common unhappiness' of the ravine at Babi Yar, although the relationship is hardly one of a cure. As he puts it, 'The symptoms were, as always with the unconscious, appropriate ... and it may be that there was a propensity to illness in the patient's left breast and ovary, which would become manifest later in life' (127). If we substitute for the words 'the unconscious' and 'illness' different ones, such as 'clairvoyance' and 'injury' respectively, we see again that Freud's diagnosis tells more than at first appears.

According to Thomas, this is also true of Freud's response to Jung's interest in the mummified peat-bog bodies unearthed in Germany. In *Memories and Hallucinations*, Thomas implies that Freud's distress at the conversation about the mummified bodies is not because he is wilfully indifferent, but because, again, he knows more than seems to be the case. Thomas puts this in the form of a sideshadowing rhetorical question:

> Who could have imagined the holocaust? Yet some of the events of that journey seemed premonitory: notably Freud's fainting fit when Jung, the Aryan, described the excavation of peat-bog corpses in North Germany.[108]

Pace Tanner and Robertson, Freud is not denying that history repeats itself, but fearful that it must.

The final section of *The White Hotel*, 'The Camp', has received its own share of polarized judgements. As we have noted, Tanner does not mention it at all, as it confounds the teleological movement she detects in the text away from metaphor to history.[109] In a review of Amis's novel, John Updike compares *The White Hotel* favourably with *Time's Arrow* as an instance of 'having the Holocaust unhappen', which he says

> was given oddly moving expression in the scene of posthumous mass healing in D.M. Thomas's *The White Hotel*; the reader did not rebel against it, be-cause it arose so spontaneously, so lightly, so organically out of the ground of grief and horror prepared by Thomas's earlier dramatization of the mass murder at Babi Yar.[110]

'The Camp' is notably metaphorical, and its symbols are taken from a variety of historical realities. The title of the section hints at a different kind of Holocaust text, in which the protagonist ends up in a concentration or death camp; but Lisa dies in a mass killing just a few miles from her home. Instead, the camp in *The White Hotel* is a transit camp, a fusion of an after-life vision and the historical reality of pre-independence Palestine. Thomas claims the logic of this is a rumour prevalent in Kiev before the massacre that Jews were to be sent to Palestine;[111] it seems that his text is attempting what Amis's does, a fantasied reparation for the Holocaust, in full knowledge that this can only be represented either through narrative deformation, as in *Time's Arrow*, or through generic experimentation, as in *The White Hotel*. It seems as if a desperate utterance from *Babi Yar* by one of the victims as their belongings are taken away suggested to Thomas, via Kuznetsov, the symbolic possibilities of linking the levelling effects of certain kinds of idealism, whether Soviet or Zionist, and the levelling of mass death, particularly as this discourse attracts the censor's pen in the extract from *Babi Yar*.

> 'How are we ever going to sort out a pile of things like that? They'll simply divide them up equally **between all of us. Then there won't be rich and poor any more**.' … Let us recall that the Jews of Kiev believed they were being sent to Palestine, and that even when they could hear the shoot-ing they went on discussing how their belongings would be 'divided up equally' when they got there. How many such Palestines has the world already been promised?[112]

Not all critics agree about the success of Thomas's move. Robertson wonders whether 'To make [horrible facts] "heroic" in any way, to attempt consolation, might be a betrayal'; 'all the burden falls on the poetic artifact *as such* to "answer" to the mistaken therapy and the Nazi massacre'.[113] While Tanner sees an earlier section, 'The Sleeping Carriage', as the site of undoing a binary opposition between metaphor and history, Robertson sees *The White Hotel*'s final section as reinstating a different opposition, one between aesthetics – its 'magical-realist' style as simply one among many in the novel – and ethics, represented by Lisa's concern to know what is good and what is evil, and the reader's knowledge that 'The Camp' is no consolation at all.[114]

Thomas describes 'The Camp' as a kind of Purgatory, where suffering is redemptive, in contrast to the Hell of Babi Yar, where it is not; in fact, he argues that *The White Hotel* is not primarily a Holocaust novel, but one about 'the journey of the soul', and 'the inextricable mix of good and evil in our white hotel'.[115] In this view, the novel's structure is Catholic, which is another reason for Lisa having a gentile mother:

> I had deliberately played down [Lisa's] Jewishness; indeed, she may not have any Jewish blood in her at all. She would know about Purgatory. It would be natural for her to imagine that existence in terms of the Holy Land. That is, if she does imagine it and it is not real.[116]

'The Camp' continues the temporal disruption of the earlier parts of the text, only now its trigger-tropes look backwards, rather than forwards. These tropes include the description of the train journey to the camp (225); the new inmates scanning lists of names (226): 'Yet it seemed you did not have to be Jewish to be here; for her mother was on the lists' (228); the 'latrines' (230); and Lisa's discovery that 'her mother had not died, she had emigrated' (234). The latter is a particularly pointed trigger in reverse: more usually, emigration was a euphemism for death during the Holocaust years. Lisa's mother observes that 'wonderful healing goes on over here' (232), a healing which is the same as time going backwards. Lisa is reunited with Kolya, her stepson, but must 'prepare the way for him to *return* to the woman who had given him birth' (231, my italics). Even more strikingly, Lisa has been 'healed' in years; she is no longer the objectified 'old woman' of Babi Yar, but an individual, a daughter: 'The young woman nodded, pleased' (233). In a final reversal, she breastfeeds her own mother (235).

The fundamental formal binary opposition, according to Thomas's critics, is that of plagiarism '*or* the deliberate fictionalizing of factual accounts'.[117] Wirth-Nesher's phrasing here implies that whichever of these actions Thomas has taken, he is culpable; however, in combining the strategies of both verbatim quotation from an anterior source and amending the source in certain ways, Thomas manages to have his cake and eat it. He is neither only plagiarizing nor making events up; and the particular emendations he makes show that the act of quotation is just as self-conscious as the alteration. Thomas claimed in his first reply to critical letters in the *Times Literary Supplement* that 'I could have changed the order of the words, but that would have been untruthful. The only person who could speak was the witness'.[118] The reader-supposed-to-know should recognize the different discourses and the boundaries between them. As Thomas also said in the letter, what is disturbing is the 'transition' between Lisa as subject and Lisa as object, a transition which represents the movement between discourses of fiction and fact. An early critic of *The White Hotel* wrote of the joining of historical events to fictional characters, 'Fact and fiction, reality and unreality, do not blend in this way',[119] but, it must be pointed out, they clearly do. *The White Hotel* is concerned with the question, 'what connection exists between collective tragedy and personal desire?', for narrative, temporal and representational reasons rather than pornographic or moral ones.[120]

Chapter 3

Autobiographical fiction

Jerzy Kosinski, *The Painted Bird*

The entry in the 1991 bibliography *The Jewish Holocaust* is typical of a scandal-free view of Kosinski's 1965 novel:

> One of the most widely read, well received, and influential novels yet published on the Holocaust.... Partly based on events in Kosinski's own life, the novel is one of the best works of literature on the Holocaust experience.[1]

This passage simplifies many issues to imply that *The Painted Bird* has been uniformly 'well received', and begs many questions to describe the novel as 'partly based' on Kosinski's experiences, or even as a novel 'on the Holocaust'. The matter of (auto)biography in this case has been the source of not one but two scandals of the sort we have become familiar with.

The debates surrounding *The Painted Bird* are of three kinds: first, concerning literary issues; second, the *Village Voice* scandal of 1982 about Kosinski's literary practice; third, the scandal of 1994 about what exactly happened to the Kosinski family in Poland during the war. It is true that as a Holocaust survivor Kosinski is in a rather different category from Amis and Thomas, but this does not mean his biography has been free from scrutiny. In particular, critics have been exercised by the question of whether the fate of the boy in *The Painted Bird* really matched Kosinski's experience during the Holocaust years, as he often claimed. In my view, the most fruitful way to approach *The Painted Bird* is as a literary text; the quest for biographical accuracy is necessarily doomed to failure, and the novel is much better seen as an autobiographical fiction.

The Painted Bird is a first-person narrative about the tribulations of a small unnamed boy, who may or may not be Jewish or a Gypsy; he is separated from his parents during the Holocaust years in a Nazi-occupied Eastern European country. The incidents he narrates involve hideous cruelties, particularly to women, animals and to the boy himself. Eventually the boy is rescued by some members of the Red Army, and after the war's end is reunited with his parents, although the novel has no 'happy ending'.[2]

Aesthetic criticisms of Kosinski's novel, which are inevitably linked to its subject and often acquire a 'moral' aspect, concentrate on its genre and use of allegory, and the graphic depiction of violence. Lawrence Langer discusses Holocaust fiction which aims 'to discover legitimate metaphors that might suggest without actually describing or even mentioning its world'. He argues that the world of *The Painted Bird* is one 'populated by creatures whose values coincide with those of Auschwitz, as if no other had ever existed'.[3] Kosinski's novel is a mixture of allegory and historical specificity, which may account for the biographical trouble it has run into. Although clearly not mimetic – it is more like a fable or fairy-tale, in which the boy is the protagonist rather than the listener – *The Painted Bird* is equally clearly set during the Second World War in an 'eastern country'.[4] Trains carrying Jews pass by the village in which the boy lives, and there are occasional encounters with Nazis; the moments where the novel's two genres coincide are disconcerting for and give a historical shock to the reader. The illusion that the novel is set in some fantasied medieval period is a rhetorical ploy. The more distant from the events of the Holocaust the novel seems, the closer it is in what Lawrence Langer calls 'translated' terms, and what Sidra DeKoven Ezrahi calls 'nonanalogous reality'.[5] Langer discusses the episode in which a miller uses a soup spoon to blind a young ploughboy he suspects of 'making eyes' at his wife,[6] witnessed by the boy, as just such a translation, of

> the loss (or destruction) of human vision into a traumatic experience of family life in which 'common' passions like suspicion and jealousy, and not an elaborate political program of racial extermination, lead to scenes of unutterable horror.[7]

This could be said of the most memorable events in the novel: the killing of Stupid Ludmila by village women; mass rape and murder by the Kalmuks, who are in turn hanged by the Red Army; the parishioners throwing the boy into a pit of excrement; and the boy's maltreatment by Garbos, who makes him hang from rafters for hours by his hands while a fierce dog prowls below. These episodes all exemplify the 'translation' of the political, bureaucratic and sadistic layers of genocide into scenes of local horror.[8] If the scene in which the miller blinds the ploughboy represents loss of vision in translated form,[9] then the other events represent, respectively, the way in which victims turn on each other; the swift, meaningless reversals of power hierarchies; the involvement of organized religion in atrocity; and disbelief in unmotivated violence and a search for its causes.[10]

Like Kosinski's other novels, *The Painted Bird* is less a causally plotted narrative than a collection of loosely linked episodes. Kosinski often spoke of his suspicion of plots; and the construction of *The Painted Bird* in this way makes it, as critics have pointed out, a picaresque novel.[11] Kosinski's biographer, James Park Sloan, suggests that the novel's structure arises from its hybrid origins, which are part-autobiographical and part-imagined. Kosinski changed the actual wartime scenario of living in exile by masquerading as gentiles with his parents and brother Henryk, to one in which he and his parents were separated; he also added movement to the static situation, and the 'magic-realist' elements of the text help account for that movement.[12] This change of scenario, never advertised as such by Kosinski, took on considerable moral and aesthetic overtones in the scandal of 1994.

Literary violence

Rather like the 'pornographic' aspects of *The White Hotel*, the violence in *The Painted Bird* has been singled out for criticism.[13] It is true that reading the novel can be a sickening experience; horrifying mutilations and murders are described in a plain, non-emotive style by the boy. Kosinski's later fiction has been taken to task for its representation of sexual violence, although, according to Cahill, the author has defended himself in terms of verisimilitude: 'nothing in his fiction cannot be substantiated in the daily national newspapers'.[14] Hans Koning denies this verisimilitude in relation to *The Painted Bird*, and says of life under German occupation: 'in my experience the violence was even more pervasive, but it was also less dramatic, less "American" ', and less sexualized: 'in reality, the German violence was all tangled up with … hunger and cold. It did not engender sadism but sexlessness'.[15] It is hard to believe that the Nazis neither practised nor inspired – the local peasants were 'ignorant and brutal, though not by choice', as the prologue to *The Painted Bird* has it – the war against women documented in numerous Holocaust sources, including of course Anatoli Kuznetsov's *Babi Yar*. As well as arguing that patriarchy no longer functions in times of hunger, Koning seems to be objecting to the fabular aspects of *The Painted Bird*. Logically speaking, the boy should have died several times during the narrative,[16] but does not. Koning likens Kosinski's heroes to unrealistic and '(joyless) James Bonds'; Eric Larsen concludes that 'the crux of what is wrong with the Kosinski novels [is that] they are, to state it most simply, not true', and, even worse, in 'extremely serious ways distorting and false'.[17] It is revealing that these comments on the novel's violence accuse it of being *both* too violent and not violent enough – that is, unrealistic either way. Any aesthetic comment or objection, acquiring moral weight as it goes, almost inevitably returns to the question of autobiography, which we will examine below.

In a 1968 interview with Lawrence Langer, Kosinski emphasized the 'translated' aspect of *The Painted Bird* and its dramatization of 'the trauma of daily life' under the Nazis; he cites an apocryphal-sounding exchange with a woman who could not continue reading the novel after the eye-gouging scene:

> And I said well, there are worse things…. Have you heard of the concentration camps? Or gas chambers? And she said, gas chambers? Certainly, this I understand very well, but gouging out someone's eyes, how can you explain something like this?[18]

The assumption behind Kosinski's comment, and Langer's analysis, is that the boy's fate in *The Painted Bird* stands for events in the death camps, and that the novel is about the Holocaust in a metaphoric sense *as well as* a mimetic one. This does not mean that specific events or practices from the Holocaust years which are not represented in *The Painted Bird* are none the less to be inferred from it, but that it reproduces the atmosphere of racial hatred, occupation, sadism and lawlessness acted out on an individual level.[19]

This reading is at odds with the biographical approach to *The Painted Bird*, which sees it as a gothic but factually based account of a life spent in hiding and on the run 'at the periphery' of genocide. The boy's fascination with lying between the tracks as trains thunder over him after the war's end suggests he is conscious of a narrow escape,[20] and, apart from the scenes where Jews throw themselves off cattle-trucks and are found by peasants, the train-track game marks the closest intersection between the allegorical and the fabular-realist plots. The fact that the boy had a narrow escape at all[21] shows the difficulties of seeing the novel as being about two things at once: an allegory about the death camps, and a fable about human evil set during the war. Of course, reading *The Painted Bird* allegorically does not imply any one-to-one correspondence between its world and the details of Auschwitz; and the boy's survival is ironic in view of his own involvement with mass murder in derailing a train, and in general assuming the traits of his oppressors.

Leslie Epstein takes issue with Langer, who praises Kosinski's novel for eschewing straightforward realism. Epstein argues that non-realist, grotesque works about the Holocaust which, in Langer's phrase, do not transfigure but 'disfigure reality', result in 'the sort of novel in which people hop from graves, dwarfs beat tin drums, giants carry alter egos on their backs, rats gnaw on corpses, and so forth and so on'.[22] Epstein has in mind the episode from *The Painted Bird* in which the boy tricks a carpenter who has enslaved him into falling into a pit of starving rats, who consume him. Epstein judges this kind of writing to be intended 'to divert us from what the actual atrocity – most unbearable in its monotony, its regularity, its unobtrusiveness – was like', and 'in no way' brings the reader 'closer to what happened to Jewish men and women and children'.[23] Epstein clearly has faith only in the strictest realism to convey – and be 'faithful to' in a more general sense – the reality of the Holocaust, which he takes to mean specifically the fate of Jews in death camps. Comparing *The Painted Bird* with Begley's *Wartime Lies* (1991) is interesting in this respect: Begley's novel is not the gothic allegory to which Epstein objects, but nor is it about 'the actual atrocity'. The same is true of Fink's *The Journey* (1992), which is almost as free of dated historical events as *The Painted Bird*, as this is not how the detail of the Holocaust years was perceived from the ground. All three novels complicate the notion of history and biography, *The Painted Bird* most of all as it is so clearly allegorical.

Epstein's implicit anxiety is that allegorizing or fabulizing the Holocaust implies that its specific historical events do not matter, and that its uniqueness may be questioned. In other words, *The Painted Bird* may not primarily be about the Holocaust, but for reasons other than its failure in realist terms. This is a common worry with regard to Holocaust fiction, and seems to be the result of any kind of generic experimentation, or ambiguity in the author's status or motives. *The Painted Bird* has been praised for exactly the reasons Epstein criticizes it: for being allegorically flexible, and not limited to representing one particular historical moment, as Neil Compton puts it:

> *The Painted Bird* deserves the status of a minor classic not because it docu-ments any particular political or social abuse, but because it dramatizes and defines the dream of violence and alienation which haunts the imagination of Communists, democrats, and peasants alike in the middle of the 20th century.[24]

Compton is calling on an implicit hierarchy of textual concern: the more numerous and non-specific the abuses and 'dreams' represented, the higher up his scale the novel is. Epstein's scale works the other way round: the more specifically detailed the actual events of the Holocaust are in a text, the more likely it is to be a 'minor classic'.

Other critics veer between praising *The Painted Bird* for being about the Holocaust itself even if it does not detail the processes of genocide, or for being about something else although it appears to be about the Holocaust. The 'something else' is often taken to be the relation between the individual and society, although even at this abstract level critics have felt impelled to bring in biographical support for their interpretation. Samuel Coale, for instance, observes in a discussion of *Being There* that Kosinski 'himself fled from Commu-nist Poland in 1957'.[25] In even more general terms, the novel has been read as the tale of any outsider; Kosinski argues that he has known adolescents see themselves as alienated 'painted birds' in contemporary 'industrial America', and adds in his collection of essays, *Passing By*, that 'members of ethnic minorities and those who felt themselves socially handicapped' identified particularly with the boy's struggle.[26] Proponents of these two views seem undecided whether historical precision limits or exalts a work, and the two sides of the debate are extremely polarized when the Holocaust is the historical period in question.

Kosinski, in the 'Afterward' to the 1976 edition of the book, claims that *The Painted Bird* was the first in a cycle of five novels which would present 'archetypal' versions of the relation between individual and society:

> The first book of the cycle was to deal with the most universally accessible of these societal metaphors: man would be portrayed in his most vulnerable state, as a child, and society in its most deadly form, in a state of war. I hoped the confrontation between the defenseless individual and overpower-ing society, between the child and war, would represent the essential anti-human condition.[27]

Kosinski's comment suggests that the debate between Langer and Epstein, and many readers' unease with the idea of making the Holocaust into a symbol, could be rephrased in terms of a different opposition. In an essay on Cynthia Ozick's *The Shawl* and Holocaust aesthetics, Joseph Alkana draws on Erich Auerbach's distinction between Homeric and biblical methods of representation. According to Auerbach, the Homeric presents 'ahistorical legend' and demands from its reader a symbolic analysis; while the biblical demands a historical interpretation.[28] This distinction might remind a Bakhtinian of the equally 'ethical and political' discussion of epic versus the novel in Bakhtin's 'Epic and Novel'. In that essay, Bakhtin writes that 'an absolute epic distance separates the epic world from contemporary reality'.[29] Bakhtin emphasizes that the epic's interest in the past does not just mean that its content is about past events, but that formal elements go to make epic's represented world inaccessible and unquestionable. It is in this double sense that epic is about the past. This distinguishes it from the novel, which faces towards the future, and is based on 'experience, knowledge and practice'.[30]

Alkana's argument is an extension of Bakhtin's: not only should the novel represent the everyday, as the latter argues, but in Holocaust aesthetics 'Holocaust experiences' themselves should be assimilated 'into the everyday' as history rather than 'universalizing myth'.[31] That such an assimilation occurs in *The Painted Bird* is clear in the shocking disjunction between the 'everyday' lives of the peasants among whom the boy in *The Painted Bird* lives, and the intrusions of the Second World War: its dates, death trains, perpetrators and victims. The peasants' lifestyles may seem timeless, and this is the realm of the Homeric, or the epic; but they are intersected by precise historical detail. For instance, the boy describes how Jews on trains headed for the death camps would throw papers and photographs out of the windows, which he and the peasants would find between the rails. The peasants particularly valued the photographs; they

> traded them, and hung them in their huts and barns. In some houses there was a picture of Our Lady on one wall, of Christ on another, a crucifix on a third, and pictures of numerous Jews on the fourth.
>
> (105)

This is a perfect image of the symbolic cut across by the historical, the Homeric by the figural; not so much because Christian imagery is juxtaposed with photographs of individual Jews[32] but because the malign fairytale world of the peasants is suddenly turned into part of a historical narrative. The boy himself resists a local death in preference for a historical one. When the peasants shout at him, ' "You Gypsy-Jew.... You'll burn yet, bastard, you will" ' and try to 'toast [his] heels', he struggles free, observing that he 'had no intention of being burned in such an ordinary campfire when others were incinerated in special and elaborate furnaces built by the Germans' (100). Thus the boy in *The Painted Bird* represents, in Alkana's phrase, 'a rejection of appeals to higher authorities and causes that diminish the quotidian world of human sociality and history'. In the tradition of 'quotidian' recastings of the biblical story of Abraham and Isaac, 'no angel arrives to save the child'.[33]

' "If you paint a bird, it won't fly" '

The literary arguments about *The Painted Bird*, questioning its representation of the Holocaust, prepare the tone for the biographically centred scandals of 1982 and 1994 which beset Kosinski and his novel.[34] As we have noted, literary judgements of Holocaust texts often shade seamlessly into the moral and *ad personam*, often based on extra-textual material about or by the author. The scandal of 1982 concerned all Kosinski's writings up to that point and his reputation as a writer. Its effects included his not writing another novel for six years and plans for a musical of *Pinball* and a tour of Germany were set aside.[35] The scandal began with an article by Geoffrey Stokes and Eliot Fremont-Smith, 'Jerzy Kosinski's Tainted Words', published in the *Village Voice*.[36] The authors develop discrepancies in Kosinski's accounts of his biography, particularly about his wartime speech-loss, into a fully-fledged charge of invention intended to cover up the fact that Kosinski's first two books (*The Future is Ours, Comrade* and *No Third Path*; two scholarly works had been published in Poland under his own name)[37] were written with the blessing and editorial assistance of the CIA; he wrote *The Painted Bird* in Polish and then had it translated; and, most contentiously, he hired other people to write his novels for him:

> [Kosinski] evidently grew used to this mode of work [seeing it as a widget to be assembled by anonymous hands] during the late 1950s when, under the pen name of Joseph Novak, he published the first of two anti-Communist tracts in which the Central Intelligence Agency apparently played a clandestine role. It is perhaps this dirty little secret that explains the fast shuffle of autobiographical tales making up the Kosinski myth.[38]

These assertions are based on some kind of fact: Kosinski did use the pseudonym Joseph Novak,[39] and did not conceal his criticisms of the Communist regime in Poland, which he left in 1957. In his biography, Sloan discusses the role of the CIA in Kosinski's first two American publications and concludes that although they probably did take a positive interest in the books, Kosinski is unlikely to have been enlisted in any formal way. The debate continued in the *New York Times*, widening into one about reactionary and progressive politics in the media and in various writers' groups with which Kosinski was associated.[40] Sally Johns points out that the question of authorship went unresolved in the furore over the CIA, and links the debate to the increasingly hostile reviews Kosinski received for the novels – *Blind Date* (1976), *Passion Play* (1979) and *Pinball* (1982) – after *The Painted Bird* (which won the French Prix du Meilleur Livre Etranger) and *Steps* (which won the National Book Award in 1968, the first time it had been awarded to a foreign-born and -educated author):

> Writers throughout history have survived charges as serious as plagiarism (and those against Kosinski fall short of this extreme), but the area of literary accomplishment is one in which he has suffered, and the decline took place before the question of authorship entered the picture.[41]

In other words, the disparity in quality between *The Painted Bird* and Kosinski's later novels contributed to the scandal. Sloan discusses the authorship issue at length, and concludes that although Kosinski did engage his own copy-editors and then deny that he had done so,[42] his novels were definitely not ghost-written.

Kosinski was accused of impersonation rather than plagiarism, a theme which returns in the scandal of 1994.[43] James Sloan quotes Thomasz Mirkowicz, who translated *The Painted Bird* into Polish, saying Kosinski admitted drawing heavily on 'a postwar Polish text, "Polish Children Accuse" ... a compilation of accounts by Polish children of their experiences under German occupation'. This remarkable text, originally published in Cracow in 1946, has been translated into English as *The Children Accuse*, and it is indeed possible to detect similarities between the experiences of the protagonist of *The Painted Bird* and details from the children's testimonies, particularly in the section entitled 'In Hiding'. For instance, several children tell of peripatetic lifestyles; imagining they are about to meet their parents; pretending to be Christian; of village cruelty and bullies who try to tear down their trousers; fear of dogs; hiding in stooks of corn, bunkers, or in the water; being thrown into water; hiding under beds; being beset by drunken farmers; having to dye dark hair blonde; the cruelty of local nationalists, the 'Banderists'; and at the end of the war, entertaining high hopes of liberation by the Red Army or having to spend time in children's homes.[44] However, nowhere does Kosinski plagiarize material from *The Children Accuse*; it seems to have acted rather as a prompt and a background for his imagination and a supplement to his own experience.

In 1982, it is as if Kosinski is accused of the opposite of plagiarism: he has lent his name to works written by others, rather than taking the works of others and incorporating them into his own. Stokes and Fremont-Smith conclude that Kosinski 'denies the notion of truth'. Barbara Tepa Lupak quotes revealingly from the *New York Times* after the Stokes and Fremont-Smith article was published: Polish newspapers felt they had been vindicated in their opinion that ' "Mr. Kosinski, an enemy of all things Polish, was a fraud" '.[45] It is interesting that two contradictory accusations are made here: Kosinski is a liar who does not write his own works, yet does manage to convey his own opinion to the extent that he can be called anti-Polish.

Paul Lilly gives a detailed analysis and refutation of each of Stokes and Fremont-Smith's charges in the Appendix to *Words in Search of Victims*. For instance, in his usual habit of addressing the immediate audience with little regard for long-term truth, Kosinski claims not to have needed editorial or linguistic assistance; he would test out his novels in other ways, such as by dialling telephone operators late at night and reading passages aloud to them.[46] Jerome Klinkowitz argues that Kosinski regularly reinvented the details of his autobiography, and made the emergence of new facts chime in with the publication of each new novel. Klinkowitz adds that Kosinski was careful to keep his self-mythologizing consistent with the changes in 'American political sensibility, from Cold War hostility through detente and back again to rambunctious anti-Communism'.[47] Sloan holds to the theory that Kosinski was constructing a 'personal myth', and ascribes metaphorical resonance to Kosinski's most controversial stories: those about his experiences in the Holocaust.[48]

Black bird

Kosinski's novel was not well received in Poland, where Thomasz Mirkowicz's translation only appeared in 1989 (it was banned under the Communist regime, Kosinski notes).[49] James Park Sloan observes that on the book's publication in 1965 certain elements of Polish society banded together in anti-Kosinski feeling; Polish journals featured attacks on the book and its author over the next few years.[50] Kosinski claimed that he was accused of writing anti-Polish propaganda for a Western audience. However, partly because *The Painted Bird* was not available in Polish until over twenty years after its publication, and because of the intemperance of journalists' attacks, Sloan observes:

> So maladroit were the Polish attacks, in fact, that Kosinski's supporters could cite them as a *defense* when Kosinski came under fire from the *Village Voice*. Such enemies, the argument went, did Kosinski honor.[51]

In 1994 an article by Joanna Siedlecka, 'Czarny ptasior' ('Black Bird'), appeared in Poland arguing that Kosinski had, contrary to the assumptions of *The Painted Bird*'s readers and anyone who had met Kosinski,[52] spent the war years in hiding with sympathetic locals, and had never been separated from his parents. Although it seems he did experience some of the novel's central events, such as being chased over a frozen lake, they did not happen exactly as he told them. The background to this scandal is worth tracing. As we have noted, *The Painted Bird* deliberately does not make clear in which country its events are supposed to have taken place. Nor is it clear whether the boy is a Gypsy or a Jew or neither; he is simply dark-haired and olive-skinned, in contrast to the fair-haired, light-skinned peasants among whom he lives, and speaks a different, urban dialect. The novel's epilogue states it is '*[b]ecause of the prewar anti-Nazi activities of the child's father*' that he and his parents had to go into hiding (1). Of course this does not mean that there is not also a 'racial' dimension to the parents' flight, but it is revealing that the peasants convert an ostensibly political issue into a racial one, for superstitious as much as for ideological reasons.[53]

However, as we have seen, it is clear that the novel is set during the Second World War, and that genocide is taking place offstage. On stage, we see the playing out of the details of cruelty and the relation between a victimized individual and his society. This mixture of lack of specificity with historical detail is at the heart of the novel's unusual hybrid genre: it is a historicized allegory.[54] Novels about the Holocaust often exhibit this hybridity. Aharon Appelfeld's *Badenheim 1939* (1980) and *To the Land of the Reeds* (1994) both depend on historical recognition by the reader, but withhold exactly the kind of realist Holocaust detail Epstein demanded of *The Painted Bird*. In *The Painted Bird*, the first thing one would expect to know of a character on the run in Nazi-occupied Eastern Europe is which ethnic group he was supposed to belong to.[55] The boy reports of the Jews, 'They were being justly punished for the shameful crimes of their ancestors',[56] but as this conforms to his habit of free indirect discourse in reporting the speech of others it is not conclusive either way that he uses the third person. Labina calls him 'her poor Gypsy, her little Jewish foundling' (171), revealing that it does not matter which he is: it is the difference itself which matters. Denying the reader such information defamiliarizes the project of categorization, and reproduces the uncomprehending view of the child. After the death of a Jewish boy found by the rail tracks, the boy-narrator thinks,

> Wouldn't it be easier to change people's eyes and hair than to build big furnaces and then catch Jews and Gypsies to burn in them?
>
> (103)

This child's logic appears to be the wrong way round – even if people's colouring were changed, some other feature would be constructed as the mark of difference – but he is right to suggest that the furnaces precede the victims; it is just a question of 'catching' someone to put in them. Such defamiliarization is similarly a feature of Binjamin Wilkomirski's novel *Fragments*, in which the small boy thinks he is a victim of a war against children, not knowing anything of the complex system of racial hatred which has actually brought him to Majdanek (see further discussion of Wilkomirski in the Conclusion, this volume).[57]

Kosinski wrote his *Notes on 'The Painted Bird'* partly as a response to Polish criticisms of his novel, which arose from disagreement among Polish and Jewish factions over how to discuss and commemorate their respective wartime fates.[58] The portrayal of the peasants in *The Painted Bird* as superstitious, vicious racists who practise bestiality and rape on a grand scale, and are servile towards whoever happens to be in power, is unambiguously severe. Kosinski removed explicit references to Poland from the drafts of *The Painted Bird*, but the country was identified in the first Houghton Mifflin edition of the novel.[59] In *Notes* Kosinski refers to the country of the novel as one in which 'most' (*sic*: they were all in Poland) of the extermination camps were located,[60] and his comments and biography make clear that Poland was the model for the country in his novel.

Sloan argues that Joanna Siedlecka's discussion of the scandal is marred by a post-war Communist-inflected attitude to Jews, particularly in her unsympathetically worded assertion that Kosinski's father, who changed his name from Moses Lewinkopf to Mieczyslaw Kosinski, was not only wealthy enough to buy protection during the war but collaborated with both the Nazis and the NKVD after the war, even denouncing to the latter some of the same Polish peasants who had saved his life.[61] Siedlecka was thought to be too receptive to such *aperçus*, garnered from the peasants she interviewed in Sandomierz and Dabrowa where the Kosinskis spent the war, so that, Sloan says, in Poland 'To side against Siedlecka is to affirm one's stance as cosmopolitan, anti-Marxist, and *anti*-anti-semitic'.[62] Sloan retraced Siedlecka's footsteps and interviewed people who claimed to have sheltered the Kosinskis during the war in the south-eastern outposts of Sandomierz and Dabrowa, close to the Polish–Ukrainian border.[63] His encounters were ambiguous and inconclusive,[64] despite a meeting with the original for Lekh the bird-fancier. However, Sloan concludes in his biography that Kosinski was not separated from his family during the war, and traces the development of Kosinski's stories about himself. (The first recorded instance occurs just after his arrival in the USA when Kosinski told Mira Michalowska, wife of the Polish delegate to the United Nations, of 'his catastrophic and *solitary* adventures during the war – the wandering from village to village, the dog that had leaped at his heels, the loss of speech, the reunion at the orphanage where he was identified by … the mark on his rib cage'.) Sloan ascribes the strange fact that Kosinski's wife and mother both supported the separation story to the writer's uncanny ability to enlist back-up, although he admits that Elzbieta Kosinska's statements, even in private correspondence, that 'You were not with us', do leave the shadow of a doubt. It seems that Kosinski's propensity to create myths about himself and the Polish villagers' testimony are the main evidence against the separation story and its attendant details. The evidence for the story is Kosinski's insistence on this version of events throughout his American years, an insistence which *preceded* his novel: that he was all alone during the war, that he was mute, that he was hung up by his arms and flung into a latrine by peasants. As well as his mother's agreement with the separation story, Sloan highlights another bizarre detail: an American doctor found medical evidence that Kosinski had suffered some injury to his arms consistent with hanging by them for extended periods.[65] Sloan conjectures there was a very early instance of trauma, dealt him by his father and never related by Kosinski, to which this mysterious bodily evidence relates, and which would account for the 'intensity of his inner response' to later events.[66]

Sloan acknowledges that even if both the Kosinskis' sons[67] were with their parents throughout the war the family underwent a considerable ordeal, living in hiding with knowledge of extermination taking place nearby, and having to put up with at least the 'banal and unremarkable thuggery of village life'. Kosinski was obviously 'both a Holocaust victim and a Holocaust survivor'.[68] Sloan wonders aloud if a novel about 'the less dramatic forms of harassment [Kosinski] had to take for granted as a Jew in the Polish countryside' would have been a best-seller, which is an interesting question about a novel published in 1965. Sara Horowitz suggests that twenty years is a long time for a survivor to wait before writing a novel about his experiences; however, Louis Begley's 1991 novel *Wartime Lies* did not appear for a further twenty-five years, yet he was able to represent, unallegorized, the 'less dramatic forms of harassment'.[69]

The second background strand to the Siedlecka controversy is the generic problem of autobiography, which also underlies the Polish reception of the novel. It is stating the obvious to say that no one reading *The Painted Bird* could take it for historical reality. However, Sloan points out that the early reception of the novel did take for granted that it had some basis in reality, because of what he calls its 'authenticity': in this respect it is like the diary of a male Anne Frank who survived.[70] Sloan quotes Elie Wiesel, writing at the time of Kosinski's suicide in 1991: ' "I thought [*The Painted Bird*] was fiction, and when he told me it was autobiography I tore up my review and wrote one a thousand times better." '[71] At other times, Kosinski was almost as insistent that the book was *not* autobiography, particularly where the strictures of publishing and marketing were concerned.[72] In *The Hermit of 69th Street*, he satirizes the whole debate by having the protagonist's father ask, with reference to the *Painted Bird* episode which Kosinski claimed to have experienced, ' "What pond of manure? What pit?" '[73]

Special weight is given in these comments to two central terms: 'authenticity' and 'autobiography'. When the Holocaust is the subject, it seems that these words cannot be used lightly, and any shifting meaning they may have in everyday critical discourse is considerably reduced because of the addition of a moral element. 'Authenticity' generally means, in the case of Holocaust fiction and in Sloan's use of the term, that the author must be writing in good faith, preferably about events they have experienced. However, as well as 'real' it can mean 'real-*seeming*'; in the latter sense, it is a comment on effective style rather than accurate content.[74] 'Autobiography' must mean that the events we read about are the events the subject experienced; in Holocaust texts, testing out ideas about faulty memory, first-person narrative, the disjunction between author and narrator and that between fact and fiction, seems only to be permissible if the writer is a survivor and if s/he admits that this is the case.[75] *The Painted Bird* is more of a hybrid of invention and autobiography than either Fink's *The Journey* or Begley's *Wartime Lies*;[76] it is as if the hybridity itself is the problem for critics and readers, either because they disapprove of it, or because they do not recognize it as such.

Kosinski's *Notes of the Author on 'The Painted Bird'* were written in English as an appendix to be translated for the German-language editions of his novel,[77] allegedly to defuse Polish chagrin (he argues that the novel's lack of specificity in terms of characters' names, geography and national characteristics means that 'no ethnic or religious group has cause to believe itself to be represented, and no chauvinistic feelings need be set on edge').[78] Kosinski discusses the issue of autobiography in such a way that his comments suggesting fact has been compromised actually have the opposite effect and imply he did base his novel on fact ('To say that *The Painted Bird* is non-fiction may be convenient for classification, but is not easily justified').[79] Nowhere does he unequivocally state what relation the novel has to his own life, and, as we have seen, the story altered according to whether the audience was Elie Wiesel or Houghton Mifflin. This is fair enough; memory and retrospection can constitute a Holocaust text's form as well as its content. Kosinski argues that 'fact and memory' form too neat a binary to categorize *The Painted Bird*, which he describes in a well-known formulation as 'rather the result of the slow unfreezing of a mind long gripped by fear, of isolated facts that have become interwoven into a tapestry';[80] that is, the boy is a device in an almost therapeutic act of narration. Kosinski uses the analogy for his novel of Albert Camus's essay *Return to Tipasa*, of which Kosinski speculates that Camus had certainly 'visited Tipasa, had once lived there and was then revisiting the town', but this visit was 'subordinate to those specific emotions which *he may have felt* in Tipasa, but which he wished to convey to the reader'. The implication is that there is no way of knowing what exactly went on in Tipasa, but, as in *The Painted Bird*, 'the literal and the symbolic approach one another so closely that from their confrontation arises the meaning'.[81] Similarly, Kosinski's discussion of the child in *The Painted Bird* as 'artist-hero' would appear as if he has made a structural rather than an autobiographical choice of focalizer:

> But, one could ask, why was this book written about childhood? ... *The Painted Bird*, then, *could be* the author's vision of himself as a child, a vision, not an examination, or a revisitation of childhood.[82]

In the 'Afterward', Kosinski adds that while he 'felt strongly' about the injustice which had permitted millions of children to die during the war while he survived,

> I did not perceive myself as a vendor of personal guilt and private reminiscences, nor as a chronicler of the disaster that befell my people and my generation, but purely as a storyteller.[83]

Several critics quote Kosinski's comments on the hybridity of memory and imagination – the patterning of 'certain fairly constant fictive realities ... will lack the hard edge of total fact'; '*The remembered event becomes a fiction, a structure made to accommodate certain feelings*'.[84] In fact, such remarks give away nothing; Kosinski is not talking about his Polish past, and does so nowhere in *Notes*. In the introduction to the 1970 Modern Library edition of *The Painted Bird*, titled 'Afterward', Kosinski insists on a separation between his life and work (which of course does not mean that there is not 'really' a strong link between them): 'I remained determined that the novel's life be independent of mine. ... The paperback version of *The Painted Bird*, which followed a year after the original, contained no biographical information at all.'[85]

In his 1994 *New Yorker* article, James Park Sloan's view of readers' expectations of *The Painted Bird* is that although Kosinski has never explicitly said the novel was autobiographical, denying that it is on these grounds is only 'accurate in some narrow, legalistic sense', and he calls Kosinski's *Notes* 'baffling' and 'tortuous'.[86] However, Sloan's reasons for seeing the novel as patently fictive, apart from the fact of the odds against a divided family surviving the occupation in Poland,[87] are internal to the novel and depend on its 'episodic intensity'. The boy always manages to be in the wrong place at the wrong time, witnessing the murder of Stupid Ludmila and the eye-plucking scene at the miller's soon after his arrival in town. 'Unless one is prepared to believe that a woman is assaulted and eyeballs plucked out at least, say, once every month or two, it follows that the experiences described in the book are heightened to some degree.'[88] As well as its shaky logic – again depending on misogyny switching off under certain circumstances – this argument ignores the fact that Kosinski would be the first to admit the structure of his book is non-mimetic, partly because it is based on the logic of memory, and partly because of the child's-eye view: 'Events to the child are immediate: discoveries are one-dimensional. This kills, that maims, this one cuffs, that one caresses. But to the adult the vision of these memories is multi-dimensional.'[89]

Barbara Foley notes of generically ambiguous texts like *The Painted Bird*, 'There is no specifically linguistic essence of fictionality that is immediately perceptible in the particulars of a text', and she quotes from Victor Lange: ' "Whether or not we are in the presence of a fictional field is ... a matter of contextual analysis." '[90] These are particularly Bakhtinian comments, aware that genre recognition, the interaction of discourses, and the context in which a text is produced and read may determine not only what label it is given but, more significantly, why an outcry follows a particular shift in context. Kosinski's writings and statements encouraged readers to assume the novel was more directly and referentially based on his own life than it now appears, particularly in view of the fact, already noted, that Kosinski's personal myth-making preceded and then fed his novel. No such scandal has accompanied Louis Begley's novel *Wartime Lies*, despite its equally ambiguous relation to 'real' events and its propensity to show Polish bystanders in an unflattering light. *Wartime Lies*'s extra twenty-five years in the making, and the different effect of its prologue, which makes the issue of truth and fiction a part of the text itself, are sufficient to alter its context of reception. Foley terms the genre 'fictional autobiography', in which 'an artist-hero ... assumes the status of a real person inhabiting an invented situation; its documentary effect derives from the assertion of the artist's claim to privileged cognition'.[91] This is a common genre – one need only think of Charles Dickens's *David Copperfield* or Sylvia Plath's *The Bell Jar*. The definition is an apt description of *The Painted Bird*, suggesting that the problem with it has been readers' failure to recognize another of the novel's generic allegiances – to the

Künstlerroman – to which its other features of hybridity and allegory are at times subsidiary.[92] It is interesting to speculate that if *The Painted Bird* had been written in the third person it would not have attracted such scandal, as the illusion of a direct link between the 'artist-hero' narrator and its author would have been more tenuous; or, as Marian Scholtmeijer hazards, the text would not exist at all without 'the all-important "I" that is subjected to continuous torture'.[93]

Foley argues that the documentary novel is 'distinguished by its insistence that it contains some kind of specific and *verifiable* link to the historical world'.[94] However, it seems that, because their subject is the Holocaust, neither Kosinski's nor Thomas's text is contained by this definition of documentary fiction. The way in which Foley argues that fictional and non-fictional discourse are distinguished – by means of a 'contract' between writer and reader, which alters in 'different social formations' – is cast into doubt. *The White Hotel*, a 'documentary novel', appeared to have an imaginative link to history; the whole point of the scandal surrounding the *Babi Yar* material was that the link turned out to be clearer than readers had suspected, so the idea of a 'contract' was thrown into question. Kosinski's novel looks as if it does 'insist' on its historical credentials, but as a 'fictional autobiography' its verisimilitude consists largely in the linguistic device of first-person narration.[95] Again, the contract itself is fictive.

Objections were made to *The Painted Bird* on factual grounds by the Poles who claimed to have known Kosinski during the war, particularly Edward Warchol, the son of the Kosinskis' landlord during 1942–5, whose story Sloan recounts:

> Young Jerzy Kosinski was attacked on the surface of the frozen pond by neighbourhood toughs, who intended to pull down his pants and inspect his penis; Warchol, who was then seventeen, skated by to save him, and he vowed to me that Kosinski, unlike the boy in the novel, was never pushed below the ice. Similarly, some informants remembered the young Kosinski serving as an altar boy in the church at nearby Wola Rzeczycka, but denied categorically, and convincingly, that his dropping a missal ever led to his being beaten or being flung into a latrine.[96]

One might ask why it is relevant to a reading of *The Painted Bird* to know of these statements. Their sociological relevance consists in their being part of a debate over Polish–Jewish relations during the war. Their literary relevance is as curiosities, and in naming the genre to which *The Painted Bird* belongs. Such an approach reductively focuses on the 'truth' of autobiography, rather than paying attention to the details of the text itself.

The text as art

Treated as a work of fiction, *The Painted Bird* looks rather different from how it does if one's criterion is accuracy. In other cases looked at in this book, a central compositional element of the text is made to take on the burden of Holocaust representation: polyphony in *The Hand that Signed the Paper*; plot in *Time's Arrow*; and a satire on backshadowing in *The White Hotel*. In *The Painted Bird*, the compositional element in which the text's Holocaust meaning becomes particularly clear is free indirect discourse. As well as being a historicized allegory, *The Painted Bird* conforms structurally to the genre of 'fictionalized autobiography', and its Holocaust-related elements are an integral part of this.[97] It appears that the book's retrospection is limited to its third-person epilogue, and that as it is written in the first person and the past tense it implies a future for the boy. *Pace* Everman, who says the boy 'doesn't speak of himself in the present', that is, during the time of writing, it seems helpful to view this autobiographical narrative in Bakhtin's terms as 'double-voiced': in each utterance there is present the representing and the represented voice.[98] The presence of double-voicedness is clearer at some moments than others. For instance, the boy describes his twice-weekly attendance at church during the period he spent with Garbos: 'I understood neither the meaning of the Mass nor the role of the priest at the altar' (126). This construction implies a position of current knowledge from which the narrator speaks, and is different from the early scene in which the boy watches the body of his protectress Marta burn: 'I stood by the door, ready to run, still waiting for Marta to move. But she sat stiffly, as though unaware of anything. The flames started to lick her dangling hands as might an affectionate dog' (11). The knowledge that Marta is really dead is shared by the represent*ing* voice and the reader, while it is the represent*ed* voice alone which is heard. In the case of the boy's ignorance of the Mass, incomprehension is registered in both voices simultaneously. However, just a few lines after declaring his incomprehension, the boy suddenly displays an extremely detailed knowledge, if not understanding, of the workings of the church, its rituals and priests:

> With awe I touched the fancifully shaped objects stored in the sacristy: the chalice with the shining, polished interior where wine changed into blood, the gilded paten on which the priest dispensed the Holy Ghost, the square, flat burse in which the corporal was kept.... I would admire the humeral veil which the priest used to slip over his head and with a nimble movement slide down his arms and loop around his neck. I would stroke my fingers voluptuously along the alb placed over the humeral, smoothing out the fringes of the alb belt, smelling the ever-fragrant maniple which the priest wore suspended from his left arm, admiring ... the infinitely beautiful patterns of the chasubles, whose varied colors, as the priest explained to me, symbolized blood, fire, hope, penance, and mourning.
>
> (126)

Sanders calls this simply 'verbal pyrotechnics', but it is a passage which stands out amidst the novel's generally 'unobtrusive' language.[99] There are, of course, various possible reasons for this flourish of ecclesiastical discourse. The boy is in the process of learning about Christian ritual. We accompany him as he learns and savours the words the priest is teaching him: the 'fanciful objects' acquire their names as we read the first sentence in the extract above. As we will see, it is the boy's habit to ventriloquize the discourse of others. The boy also contrasts the world of the church and its signifiers with that of Olga's hut, 'full of its evil-smelling frogs, rotting pus from human wounds, and cockroaches', although both represent a kind of 'magic' even if they sound different.[100] Another explanation is that the adult boy, writing in the present, has supplied the correct terms for his youthful self, who was fascinated by objects he could not name. This would make the passage an analogy for all kinds of acquisition of language, including Kosinski's own adoption of idiomatic American English at the age of 24; and strengthen the case for seeing the novel as a *Künstlerroman*, one specifically about learning to write the trauma of the Holocaust.[101] If it is true that a time-lag accounts for the distinctive style of this passage, then we have a very stark instance of the representing voice being heard over the represented voice.

The same ambiguity occurs when the boy describes visits to the blacksmith with whom he is staying by 'mysterious mounted guests, who carried rifles and revolvers'; a paragraph later, he reports: 'The armed men were partisans. ... The blacksmith explained to his wife that the partisans had become divided into factions' (69). It is clearer here that the time-lag between the boy not knowing and then learning the name of the armed guests is very short, represented by the progression of paragraphs. He has overheard the blacksmith, whose words enter into the double-voiced structure: the factions are 'the "whites", who wanted to fight both the Germans and Russians, and the "reds", who wanted to help the Red Army'.[102] Corngold argues that, as the tale of an 'artist-hero', the novel involves 'disclosure of the aesthetic vocation at the close of the fictive autobiography, the acquisition of the language which will bring it into being'; in this passage the two time-schemes, before and after the acquisition of such a language, are superimposed.[103]

Various critics have noted the boy's use of what Corngold calls the 'aggrandizing and unifying power' of *style indirect libre*, or free indirect discourse.[104] The boy's habit of merging the voices of others with his own narratorial tones is clear on the very first page of *The Painted Bird*:

> [Marta's] long hair, never combed, had knotted itself into innumerable thick braids impossible to unravel. These she called elflocks. Evil forces nested in the elflocks, twisting them and slowly inducing senility.
>
> (3)

We see the boy learn and adopt Marta's words here. It is interesting that Corngold views the boy's use of this technique as a means of asserting retrospective power over people before whom he was powerless: he argues that the use of free indirect discourse 'asserts the dominance of the narrative voice over the narrated'.[105] What is unusual about the appearance of this free indirect discourse is that it is a first-person narrator who is responsible for its presence, and not a third-person narrator.[106] Rimmon-Kenan argues that free indirect discourse combines mimesis with literariness in a text. I would add that in *The Painted Bird* its presence signals through this combination the time-lag between the boy in the past (mimesis), who had barely read a book at the time when Mitka and Gavrila introduce him to Gorky's *My Childhood,* and the boy in the present (literariness), who can deploy the devices of free indirect discourse and exact detailed description. The hinge between the two, the moment at which the boy in the past opens into the boy in the present, takes place when the latter regains his power of speech and describes words falling out of him like peas from a pod. In the case of Marta's words, free indirect discourse conveys her implicitly ironized superstition, and the boy's naïve belief in what she says: he makes no comment, and allows her voice to sound through his. The 'power' is apparently Marta's, although the very fact that her words only appear indirectly signals that this is at best a compromised power.

In other instances the boy begins free indirect narration by signalling the origin of the discourse – 'In the village I had heard a tale about a skull which tumbled out of a grave' (89) – and then continues the tale without these signals. Again this device conveys structurally the boy's understandable inability to distinguish likely from unlikely utterances or events, and draws the reader into this inability to distinguish. When he is staying with Labina and relating details of her past, the facts are clearly hers but the words are never actually identified as such: 'Laba indeed was handsome, tall as a poplar, nimble as a top' (175). In this case the boy seems to have taken over Labina's description of her dead husband, whom he never met, and made it the occasion for some virtuoso wordspinning. The boy has perfected the technique begun in the description of Marta, in which her own words were easier to detect than Labina's are here.[107]

Free indirect discourse reaches its extreme in the section where the boy is adopted by the Red Army. The technique in this instance is an economical means of conveying the boy's need for the security which the army and its ideology only appear to fulfil. This illusoriness does not rely only on the reader's post-war prejudices for its ironic effect, and this is an important point in relation to the scandals we have been examining in which consensus about the implied reader's reactions is harder to reach.[108] The following introduction of Stalin is historically ironized:

> I looked at the photographs of Stalin in his youth. He had very black, bushy hair, dark eyes, heavy eyebrows, and later even a black mustache. He looked more of a Gypsy than I did, more Jewish than the Jew killed by the German officer in the black uniform, more Jewish than the boy found by the peasants on the railroad tracks. Stalin was lucky not to have lived his youth in the villages where I stayed. If he had been beaten as a child all the time for his dark features, perhaps he would not have had so much time to help others; he might have been too busy just fending off the village boys and dogs.
>
> (199)

The childish-sounding identification of a public figure with the self – 'Stalin was lucky ...' – casts doubt on the boy's conclusions, as does his inability to think outside the categories of Nazi racial law – 'beaten as a child all the time for his dark features'. Because the latter assumption is not necessarily true, as dark-featured people are not invariably hounded for their appearance, the corollary about Stalin's philanthropy itself must automatically be questioned.[109] Although yet again the boy does not overtly name Gavrila or a particular book as his source, it is even clearer that he is quoting when he relates:

> Because Stalin lived there, Moscow was the heart of the whole country and the longed-for city of the working masses of the whole world. ... Other pictures showed the Kremlin quarters where Lenin, the late teacher of Stalin, used to live.
>
> (199)

The words the boy uses have, as Bakhtin puts it, the ' "taste" of a profession, a genre, a tendency, a party, a particular work',[110] in this case from their earlier context in an idealized Communist discourse – 'longed-for city', 'working masses of the whole world'. The reverence of such a context also sounds out in the formal phrase 'the *late* teacher', which is not characteristic of the boy and his graphic, 'transparent' accounts of death.

The metamorphosis of free indirect discourse into a means of *faux-naïf* narration reaches its height, as several critics have pointed out,[111] when the boy accompanies Mitka, the sharpshooter intent on avenging the death of some soldier friends, on a deadly mission. The technique used is a kind of free indirect visualization; Mitka will not let the boy borrow his binoculars to see the result of the shots he has fired, and the boy's account of what happens shades immediately into speculation:

> I tried to visualize what he saw there. An old woman wrapped in brown rags walking out of the house, looking at the sky, crossing herself, and at the same moment catching sight of the man's body lying on the ground.
>
> (216)

The lack of a main verb in the second sentence signals its provisional status, but the rest of the boy's account of Mitka's long-distance murder proceeds seamlessly; although he is able to report on Mitka's appearance, he can only imagine the village: 'I strained my eyes but without the glasses, could see only the dwarfed houses far below.... I closed my eyes and saw the village again.... Mitka examined the village again. There must have been no one left outside, for his inspection took some time.' The combination of reportage and imagination achieves what the 'rusty shunt' of the train derailing cannot, when the boy tries out his own species of revenge. Again, the fact that the novel is about an 'artist-hero' means that the metafictional meaning overtakes all others, even the urge during the derailing to decide 'the fate of many whom one did not even know', which, as Paul Lilly points out, sounds like the utterance of a narrator about his characters.[112]

Finally, as a counterpart to its use of free indirect discourse, which affects both the structure and the meaning of the text, *The Painted Bird* also shows signs of the Kristevan abject at both levels. In *Powers of Horror: An Essay on Abjection*, Julia Kristeva discusses the formation of the human subject as rational and self-sufficient by the suppression of its material and maternal origins. In this analysis of Cartesian dualism, Kristeva argues that reminders of these origins which surface within the symbolic realm – typically triggered by the transgression of strict rules set up to contain the abject potential of food, waste and sexual difference – threaten to plunge the subject back into organic chaos. Bodily disgust, nausea and a psychic fear of falling back into pre-subjectivity are the result.[113] The subject's notion of its own 'clean and proper' body[114] develops in a way that appears natural but is artificial; the subject is more permeable and open to change than it allows itself to recognize. The boy in *The Painted Bird* is beset throughout his wanderings[115] by abject encounters which threaten his efforts to construct a selfhood of his own, often in a shockingly literal way far removed from Kristeva's description of her domestic abject response to the skin on milk, or Little Hans's to raspberry syrup.[116] Because the boy has lost his parents and has to look after himself, his quest for selfhood is particularly fraught; and his historical moment adds to the danger he faces. The realm through which the boy wanders can no longer claim it has the 'adherence to Prohibition and Law [which] is necessary if that perverse interspace of abjection is to be hemmed in and thrust aside'[117] as it is under occupation and keen to abject the boy himself. In response to this lawlessness, the boy makes up his own explanatory rules. He works out that Garbos beats him when he has just scratched his head, so gives up scratching; when that does not work, he tries to avoid a gate which he has often climbed before one of Garbos's assaults, but that just incenses Garbos further; finally, he overhears a priest explaining that God grants indulgences for certain prayers, so he takes to saying prayers to himself for a long time before deciding that is useless too (129–31). Because he is trying to keep the abject at bay on an individual level during wartime, none of the boy's laws works, although he does sometimes understand the laws, based on various kinds of superstition, which motivate others. Garbos, for instance, does not kill the boy outright because he is afraid of St Anthony, his patron, and the boy speculates that Garbos fears that because the boy has 'counted his teeth' his death would cost Garbos 'many years of his life' (134).

Kristeva argues that the abject 'confronts us ... with those fragile states where man strays on the territories of *animal*',[118] and the close confrontation of human and animal in *The Painted Bird* represents a world on the brink of chaos. Makar rapes a favourite female rabbit, and makes his daughter Ewka copulate with a goat. The boy is a witness to the latter, and it provokes in him a moment of intense psychic abjection: 'Something collapsed inside me. My thoughts fell apart and shattered into broken fragments like a smashed jug. I felt as empty as a fish bladder punctured again and again and sinking into deep, muddy waters.' The abject concerns the collapse of boundaries and order, and the boy responds here to the transgression of a fundamental boundary (157).[119] Not only are Makar's family like animals; they merge with them.

The human subject learns to see the skin as the boundary between subject and object, between what is properly inside and what is outside the body. The act of crossing this boundary, which may remind the subject of its 'fragility',[120] is an abject danger zone. As Kristeva points out, bodily substances – blood, even excrement – are a sign of the body's health when they are inside it, yet abjectly disgusting or troubling when they are outside. The skin itself takes on this abject burden; part of the reason why Kristeva finds the skin on milk off-putting is that it resembles a live human organ. Several of the horrifying events which the boy undergoes have to do with the skin. Marta, who first looks after him, dies in her chair and the boy concludes that she 'was waiting for a change of skin and, like the snake, she could not be disturbed at such a time' (9). Although the boy sees the similarity between her eyes and those of 'dead fish', he uses the animal world, usually strictly split off from the human, to deny the fact that he is being confronted with that most abject of entities, the corpse. The dead human body is an object which was once a subject; as Kristeva puts it, the corpse,

> the most sickening of wastes, is a border that has encroached upon every-thing. It is no longer I who expel, 'I' is expelled.[121]

Later, the boy is ordered to skin Makar's favourite rabbit, but she turns out still to be alive when he does so and runs around the farmyard half-skinned and screaming until Makar deals her a death blow. This is horrifying on any terms; seen abjectly, the rabbit disrupts order in a very obvious way. A dead, skinned animal's body, or an animal pelt, are both well-known features of the symbolic order;[122] the rabbit in *The Painted Bird* disrupts this order because she is not clearly one thing or another. She is not meat or fur but a suffering subject, and thus an image for the boy of his own sufferings and fragile state.[123] As Kristeva puts it, 'The non-distinctiveness of inside and outside would thus be unnamable, a border passable in both directions by pleasure and pain.' The rabbit is a reminder that inside and outside are very distinct in the symbolic order, and seeing both at the same time is a disaster for the victim and the viewer.

The scene in which the jealous miller blinds the ploughboy can be similarly analysed; it is a scene which is, not unlike the blinding of Gloucester in *King Lear*, particularly hard for readers and critics to take. Blinding in itself is of course horrible enough; and the images that surround it in *The Painted Bird* make it horribly abject.[124] The miller blinds the ploughboy with a spoon; the boy describes the motion as like that used by women 'to gouge out the rotten spots while peeling potatoes', and observes that 'The eye sprang out of his face like a yolk from a broken egg'; the miller then crushes the eyes with his boot to a 'jelly'.

The act of blinding is violent and terrible; and once out of their proper place, the eyes themselves become abject, no longer part of a subject ('If the miller had not been there I myself would have taken them') yet not quite objects ('Surely they could still see') (37–8). All the imagery accompanying the gouging is food-related, which raises the even more abject idea that, once they are objects, eyes might be introjected.[125]

In implicit answer to Leslie Epstein's objections, Kristeva questions whether 'any realist (or socialist-literature) is up to the horrors of the Second World War';[126] and quotes Mary Douglas's idea that anxiety about the abject, particularly the margins of the body and bodily products, increases at times when the body politic is under assault. This explains why *The Painted Bird* combines its concern for lawless hinterlands that are constantly traversed by occupying or marauding forces (Nazis, Kalmuks, and finally the Red Army) with the portrayal of local cruelties and other representations of the horrifying, disgusting and ambiguous.[127] Violence against the body politic is inscribed on individual bodies. Douglas's idea also accounts for the disjunction felt by the reader between the timeless-seeming peasant world and the specific historical details which locate the action during the Second World War. The peasants act out on a local level both the collapse of boundaries and their nonsensically rigid implementation, such as the 'defilement' represented by the boy's dark looks. The boy admires the perfection of an SS-man:

> In a world of men with harrowed faces, with smashed eyes, bloody, bruised and disfigured limbs, among the fetid, broken human bodies, he seemed an example of neat perfection that could not be sullied: the smooth, polished skin of his face, the bright golden hair showing under his peaked cap, his pure metal eyes. … I thought how good it would be to have such a gleaming and hairless skull instead of my Gypsy face which was feared and disliked by decent people.
>
> (115)

The boy very clearly articulates two extremes: the abjection of injury, disease and powerlessness in contrast to the inhuman symbolic which refuses to be 'sullied' by its own organic origins.

Double-voiced discourse again produces ambiguous effects in this passage, particularly in phrases such as 'my Gypsy face' and 'decent people': both represent words repeated rather than matters of fact. The use of free indirect discourse – another instance of double-voicedness – is closely linked to the abject aspects of the novel. It allows for slippage between different times and different subjects, and is another way of representing the 'processual' nature of the Kristevan subject. As critics have argued of other authors, subjective fluidity is usually most striking when it is apparent between different characters in one text, but may equally, as is the case in *The Painted Bird*, occur within a single character at different moments.[128]

Although Kristeva argues that the abject alters historically,[129] abjection may seem inadequate to, or a way of mythicizing and dehistoricizing, representations of the Holocaust. After all, it does involve accepting that the 'universal' drives of abjection surface time after time, and just happened to take on the virulent form of genocide during the 1940s. This does not necessarily mean that the Holocaust is not unique; just that it is an extreme manifestation of a shared phenomenon. In the terms of Alkana's plea for a historicized Holocaust aesthetics, a Kristevan approach does not mean that the Holocaust is 'transcended', nor that any symbolic meaning is more important than the Holocaust itself.[130] Rather, it is the other way round; Kosinski's novel has until now been read as if it were, or should have been, a straightforwardly realist work. Recognizing its ambiguous generic identity gives the reader freedom from having to decide whether the book is fact or fiction, and marks the furthest point from biographical readings.

Chapter 4

Faction
Thomas Keneally, *Schindler's List*

Critical controversy over Thomas Keneally's novel *Schindler's List* centres on two issues. The first is to do with its genre and attendant debates over accuracy (if it is primarily fact) and adeptness (if it is fiction). The second concerns the book's choice of Oskar Schindler, Holocaust rescuer, as its subject. On the representativeness of such stories of rescue, the historian Raul Hilberg says: 'There is nothing to be taken from the Holocaust that imbues anyone with hope or any thought of redemption. But the need for heroes is so strong we'll manufacture them' – meaning that Schindler was hardly a hero.[1] Omer Bartov also sees its atypical nature as the story's weakness: 'The fact that this "actually" happened is, of course, wholly beside the point, since in most cases it did not':[2] accuracy must, apparently, include all details of a particular event including its context. In this chapter I will consider whether *Schindler's List* can be described as a Holocaust text, and how its concentration on rescue by an individual, on public rather than personal memory, and a 'happy ending', can be reconciled with such a description.

After winning the Booker Prize in Britain Thomas Keneally's book sold over a million copies, making it the highest-selling Booker Prize winner to date. Its sales increased greatly after Steven Spielberg's Oscar-winning film of the book, also called *Schindler's List*, was released in 1993. I will refer to the book throughout this chapter as *Schindler's List*, although it was first published in Britain as *Schindler's Ark*; it has always been known as the former in the United States, and has since been reissued elsewhere under the film's title. Although the book caused its own critical flurry, the film had an even more remarkable worldwide impact.[3] For various reasons, including the imminence of the fiftieth anniversary of the liberation of the camps and 'a deep anxiety' over the 'gradual disappearance of Holocaust survivors', the release of Spielberg's film added to a sense of 1993 as 'the year of the Holocaust'.[4] The film created a preoccupation with Oskar Schindler himself – 'Schindlermania', the 'Schindler effect' – and with issues of Holocaust representation, public and private memory, national history and contemporary racism.[5]

The narrative of Keneally's text follows the career of Oskar Schindler, a Sudeten German entrepreneur who came to Cracow in December 1939, three months after the German occupation of Poland. For reasons that are not entirely clear, Schindler took increasing pains to shelter the Jewish workers at his enamelware plant in Cracow, and when the ghetto was due to be liquidated in 1944 he moved all his workers – their names on the infamous 'list' – to another factory which he set up in his home-town, Brinnlitz, in Moravia. Through these means, backed up by the constant bribing and sweet-talking of Nazi officials, Schindler managed to save 1,100 Jews: the largest number saved by any individual during the Holocaust years.

'Faction, that terrible word'[6]

Thomas Keneally's book won the Booker Prize in 1982. This apparently simple fact is at the heart of the debate around the novel. Keneally insisted that his work was fact, yet the Booker Prize is awarded for fiction writing.[7] The text was subject to a related debate over the representation of its central character, Oskar Schindler: the historical record does not make clear Schindler's motives in saving Jews in occupied Poland during the Second World War, and Keneally's text does not fully substantiate either Schindler's motives or his reasons for keeping them quiet, in the way readers might expect a novel to do. However, the text's structure and style do manage to convey a rootedness in the personal memory that the film was criticized for eliding in its relentless Hollywood concern for the public.[8] Keneally's text, as a best-seller which nevertheless reveals the origins of its material, does manage to unite the public and private realms – even if the personal memories serve to represent Schindler, a famous, non-Jewish figure, rather than the witnesses' own experiences.

Schindler's Ark was advertised in Hodder and Stoughton's catalogue in Britain as non-fiction in advance of the typescript arriving at the publishers.[9] Michael Hulse traces the discussions that took place between Keneally, Hodder and Stoughton and the American publishers, Simon and Schuster, after the delivery of the typescript. The latter decided to market *Schindler's List* as a 'non-fiction novel', but this was not felt appropriate for a British readership.[10] Instead, the Hodder and Stoughton compromise was to describe *Schindler's Ark* as fiction but include in the text an 'Author's Note'.[11]

The decision at Simon and Schuster to call the novel after the list emphasizes the factual, rather than the metaphorical 'ark' of the British title.[12] The latter draws on two biblical parallels, linking Oskar most obviously with Noah, who also rescued a 'saving remnant' during a time of evil; or – as Keneally himself saw it – with the Ark of the Covenant.[13] By contrast, naming the book after the list – which, following the film's publicity, is now reproduced as an illustration on both the British and US paperback covers – singles out a particular material fact of Schindler's story. However, there are many lists in this text, most of them instruments of malign selection or oppression;[14] and even Schindler's 'good' list is managed by Marcel Goldberg, a former member of the notorious Jewish Police and 'Lord of the Lists'[15] (323) who lets it be known that payment to him in valuables is the best way to secure a place on it. There is at this point in the story a flurry of narratorial commentary designed to allay suspicions that Schindler was to blame for the site of corruption which the list became: 'the Schindler list, without any malice on Oskar's side still tantalises survivors' (323), and the narrator insists that Schindler could not be expected to monitor Goldberg, especially when he was so busy with other philanthropic activities (321–2).[16] From the metaphorical and religious associations of the ark in the title of the original British edition, which is not referred to in the text itself, we move to the materiality of the actual list which now titles the text, suggesting life miraculously yet corruptly saved.[17]

In the Author's Note prefacing his novel, Keneally explains the method he has chosen to represent this factual story:

> To use the texture and devices of a novel to tell a true story is a course which has frequently been followed in modern writing. It is the one I have chosen to follow here; both because the craft of the novelist is the only craft to which I can lay claim, and because the novel's techniques seem suited for a character of such ambiguity and magnitude as Oskar. I have attempted to avoid all fiction, though, since fiction would debase the record, and to distinguish between reality and the myths which are likely to attach themselves to a man of Oskar's stature.
>
> (13)

Keneally draws a distinction between 'the novel' and 'fiction' in this passage which supports a Bakhtinian approach to his text's double-voicedness. According to Bakhtin, the defining characteristic of the novel is not its fictionality but its inclusion of the multiple, conflicting voices of dialogism: the novel is 'multiform in style and variform in speech and voice'.[18] Keneally's distinction is especially important in relation to Schindler; when Keneally says that Oskar's character is best rendered novelistically, he does not mean that material must be invented, but that novelistic 'devices' are the most helpful approach. In the familiar pattern of the Holocaust novelist caught in a double bind, critics who do not criticize Keneally for adopting a mixed form do criticize him for not novelizing Schindler enough. Fiona Fullerton argues that 'since [Keneally] chose the form of the novel to tell the story, he could have exploited it more fully to speculate on what really went on in the enigmatic heart and mind of Oskar Schindler'; D.J. Enright, in a positive review, is of the opinion that 'only if Keneally had been writing total fiction could he have given us a total and authoritative interpretation of Schindler's behaviour'. Marion Glastonbury doubts the appropriateness of Schindler as a fictional hero and scathingly refers to Keneally's version of him as a 'whisky priest' and adds: 'In the society of mass-murderers, a racketeer passes for a man of principle.' She balks at what she sees as the implication that Schindler was a 'genuine Christian martyr' with a 'final transfiguration as "savior" of the Jews', as this is a particularly clear instance of placing his story above theirs.[19]

Keneally himself willingly enters into this double bind by admitting that, despite his comments above, he *has* invented some material for this text. Peter Quartermaine (in his book, *Thomas Keneally*) implies that 'imagination' is already implicit in the phrase 'texture and devices' in the Author's Note: only the latter of the two terms really refers to formal aspects. Keneally does not mean he has just used the structures of plot and character in telling this story, but that he has embellished the story itself. Keneally adds in the Note something which is often evident to the reader:

> Sometimes it has been necessary to attempt to reconstruct conversations of which Oskar and others have left only the briefest record. But most exchanges and conversations, and all events, are based on the detailed recollections of the *Schindlerjuden* (Schindler Jews), of Schindler himself, and of other witnesses to Oskar's acts of outrageous rescue.
>
> (14)

Contemporary reviewers offered different labels in attempts to describe the genre of *Schindler's List*. Lorna Sage, D.J. Enright and Robert Taubman called it a 'documentary novel'; Paul Bailey and Gay Firth 'faction'; Michael Hulse 'imaginative historical journalism'; David Lodge, perhaps most accurately but not very snappily, a 'narrative, anecdotal history written with literary skill'.[20] Hulse adds to his suggested term the comment that 'factual records have a long history of being set in the "texture and devices" of fiction: this does not make them fiction, does not make them novels'. However, this is to confuse the concepts of 'novel' and 'fiction' which Keneally was careful to separate in his Author's Note (but which he too conflates elsewhere in the label he puts forward for his own work, of ' "non-fiction fiction" ').[21] Despite the publishers' categorization of *Schindler's List* as fiction, it is better described as a novel, and, I think, as a factional rather than documentary novel if we assume, following the Bakhtinian model, that this can include improvisations such as reconstructions of conversations and speculations about motive and subjectivity.

'Faction' is a more useful term for Keneally's text than, in Barbara Foley's phrase, 'documentary fiction'. 'Documentary' implies an aim of moral or factual instruction, through a particular presentation of evidence.[22] It is arguable that such a form only exists theoretically, although for instance those sections of William Styron's *Sophie's Choice* in which the narrator is musing over and quoting from historical sources might constitute one instance. *Schindler's List* itself is based on literal documents, including Schindler's own testimony of the war years and over fifty survivor interviews. The same is true of *The White Hotel*, which includes 'documentary' extracts from Freud and Kusnetsov; and *Sophie's Choice*, which draws on Rudolf Höss's autobiography, and survivor testimonies. However, the aim of neither of the latter novels is primarily to 'instruct', and they do not cause the problems of classification that *Schindler's List* does due to its single-minded narrative focus and ambiguous insistence on its factual origins. Documentary material has been the trigger for imaginative fiction in the case of Thomas and Styron, whereas in Keneally's case the blend of fact and fiction is much more stable and consistent.[23] For example, the section where the narrator of *Schindler's List* gives a potted history of Jewish life in Cracow (94–6) is typical of a factional and not a documentary novel: the fictional narrator has subsumed what are clearly documentary sources into a single voice. Thus while we may be happy to call Thomas's and Styron's texts simply 'novels', Keneally's is a 'factional' hybrid throughout.

'Hell is over there'

The terms of the fiction/non-fiction debate which surrounded the publication of *Schindler's List* in Britain and the United States make realist assumptions. However, Victoria Glendinning comments interestingly in a review of his novel *A Family Madness* on Keneally's 'major preoccupations' which are 'the Australian way of life and the holocaust years in Europe'. This is especially true of Michael Hollington, as the title of his article, 'The Ned Kelly of Cracow: Keneally's *Schindler's Ark*', suggests; he claims that the text owes more to 'the mythology of the bush than to that of Central Europe'.[24] In Keneally's *A Family Madness* Europe is imported into Australia; in *Schindler's List* the mores of the outback turn up in Poland. Like Ned Kelly, Schindler is an outsider – 'He was Sudeten German, Arkansas to their Manhattan, Liverpool to their Cambridge' (6) – and an 'independent spirit'.[25]

Peter Quartermaine questions realist assumptions about *Schindler's List* further in suggesting that the Holocaust is the writer's 'big subject' in our secular age, as the relation of God to man was in Milton's time, and that as a result Schindler is constructed in an ahistorical way. Quartermaine comments,

> The story of Oskar and his ark (whether we see the latter as analogous to that of Noah or of the Jewish Covenant) is a story unique in its scale and daring, and able to stand as an emblem for the inherent divinity and corruption of humanity itself.[26]

This argument does not just acknowledge how hard it is to strike a balance between particular and general in Holocaust fiction; it also means that we are back in the fraught territory of seeing the Holocaust as allegory, or heading towards that of the play *The Diary of Anne Frank*, which suggests that even in terrible circumstances 'human goodness' shines through. It also has links with the idea, uncongenial to many, of Holocaust texts as Christian allegories.[27] Michael André Bernstein argues that it is impossible both to be true to the Holocaust and to make it a 'parable of universal suffering' because of the nature of the event: 'its very essence was a deliberate, systematic, and, if such a word can be permitted in this context, "principled" denial of even minimal humanity to those it condemned to genocidal extermination.'[28]

Although the generalizing, allegorizing tendency is acknowledged within *Schindler's List* itself, as Keneally's interest in the Talmudic verse 'He who saves a single life, saves the world entire' shows,[29] the choice of a success story amid notable failure can also make the text appear ahistorical. Keneally commented in an interview that the historical novel is one 'in which the human issues are the same as those we have now, and have always had to face', while Spielberg said of the film version that 'This movie speaks not only on the Jewish Holocaust, but of every Holocaust, by anyone's definition.'[30] Of course, these are paradoxical comments; Keneally's text is full of historical and geographical detail, and acts as a reclamation of all kinds of contemporary actions, heroic or otherwise.[31]

It is not an allegorical reading which *Schindler's List* provokes so much as general suppositions about human motive and the role of the individual in a time of crisis. History is viewed from within, and in the case of the Holocaust this means that while mass murder is constantly implied, it is not the death camps themselves which are represented. Most of the action takes place in Cracow, a few miles away from Auschwitz-Birkenau. Although the wider context of anonymous death does 'constantly obtrude' and is occasionally acknowledged, there is no equivalent in the novel to the film version's shockingly frame-breaking ending.[32] The film's ending offers that element of uncertainty for which critics often argue in discussions of the difference between survivor testimony and Holocaust fiction.[33] The representation of the Schindler Jews mourning at Schindler's grave in Jerusalem's Catholic cemetery is followed in the film by a break in the image, and the catastrophe of which they are a small part is signalled by numbers on a plain background: 'There are fewer than 4 thousand Jews remaining in Poland today, but over 6 thousand descendants of the Schindler Jews.'[34] There follows the film's dedication, to the memory of more than 6 million Jews who died during these years.

The film's break in the image and its replacement by numbers on the screen suggests the unrepresentability of these facts, at least in terms of Spielberg's film-making, although they are what the film has been about. The break conveys the fact that the story we have been watching is uncharacteristic, and the fate of the majority we do not see was quite different ('worse', as survivor Rivka Bau, who is shown in the film getting secretly married in Plaszów, put it after seeing the film).[35] The contrast between the 6,000 who live, and the 6 million others, underlines this uncharacteristicness. While Spielberg does show graphic killings and undocumented events, such as ghetto *aktions*, he signals at the film's end that all this painstakingly (re)created detail[36] is only partial. The Holocaust is 'shown' in his film, and also figured. If there is an equivalent to this startling moment of metacinema in Keneally's text it is the presence of unusual narrative devices; the mode of narrative voice, tense and speech representation all serve to disrupt the impression of a seamless fiction.

'Plausible reconstruction'

The narrative voice in Keneally's *Schindler's List* is the site of several varieties of what Bakhtin calls 'double-voicedness', a 'contradiction-ridden, tension-filled unity of two embattled tendencies in the life of language'.[37] The particular variety of double-voicedness we encounter in this text is directly related to its subject: double-voicedness both conveys the retrospective and therefore sometimes speculative cast of what we are reading, and offers a way of narrating atrocity and genocide without having 'monologically' to state the case.

To take first the related issues of time-difference and speculative reconstruction: the reader is likely to notice at once that it is characteristic of the 'factional' narrator of Keneally's *Schindler's List* to shade from professing ignorance, overtly or implicitly, to showing his actual omniscience. Having claimed unambiguously that in autumn 1943, 'It is certain that by this stage in his history ... Herr Schindler approached tonight's dinner at Commandant Goeth's more with loathing than with anticipation,' the narrator adds, 'Only he could have told us whether he had to succour himself from a flask as he passed by the mute, black village of Prokocim' (17). Omniscience here on the subject of Schindler's feelings about Goeth begs the text's main question about his motives, and this uncertainty is deflected on to the minor detail of the flask – yet the effect on the reader is that Schindler does actually take such a drink.[38] There follows a similar passage about a party held by Schindler in 1939 where the narrator begins by signalling his fallibility:

> Though it is not possible to say exactly what the members of the party talked about that night, it is possible from what Oskar said later of each of these men to make a plausible reconstruction.
>
> (72)[39]

This metacomment is soon overtaken by the assured representation of the words spoken by these men, in a preterite tense, for instance: ' "They call it," said Toffel, "*concentration*. That's the word you find in the documents. *Concentration*. I call it bloody obsession" ' (72). The only signal that all is not straightforwardly either fact or fiction is the use of free direct discourse ('Direct discourse shorn of its conventional orthographic cues'[40] – that is, no quotation marks):

> Martin Plathe agreed. [The Jews will] be cooperative for the sake of avoiding something worse, he said. It's their method, you have to understand that.
>
> (73)

The device of free direct discourse is frequently used in *Schindler's List* not as part of first-person interior monologue, its usual role, but for an effect like that of the ambiguous flask above: uncertainty is registered without disturbing verisimilitude. The uncertainty takes different forms; for instance, a Nazi tries to shoot one of Schindler's Emalia workers: 'Oskar called out. You can't do that here. I won't get work out of my people if you start shooting. I've got high priority war contracts, etc. etc.' (234). Rather disconcertingly, in the middle of this dialogue appears a signal that it is a reconstruction by the narrator: 'etc. etc.'. This is disconcerting even though one could read the latter phrase as a reference to the content of the utterance and the repetitive excuses Schindler had to give to save his workers: 'It was the standard Schindler argument.' This unsettling moment disrupts the seamlessness of reconstruction, much as overt narratorial comment also does. This is the case in a speech of Schindler's which consists of both free indirect and direct speech, of which the narrator notes, 'Oskar does not detail his performance in Rasch's office.... It is not hard to imagine though' (377).

The narrator in this text is omniscient on many counts: he admits he has had recourse to depositions and testimonies and can also provide direct speech and free direct discourse, despite the fact, as Quartermaine points out, that this is 'hardly the form in which most records tend to be kept'.[41] Keneally's invention of dialogue is seen as the cornerstone of his text's fictionality.[42] The narrator also knows such things as the dreams of ghetto-dwellers in Podgórze, Amon Goeth's thoughts about his children, and the state of Schindler's digestion (139, 176, 182). The narrator's historical knowledge is considerable, and he obviously knows at any given moment what the outcome of events will be; he says of the SS, Schindler and Jews in Poland,

> What no one knew ... and many a Party planner scarcely hoped for was that a technological answer would be found, that a disinfectant chemical compound named Zyklon B would supplant Madagascar as the solution.
>
> (66–7)

David English argues that at such moments Keneally's wish to have 'the prescience of a god' when in fact all he has is 'the privilege of being the narrator' is made clear.[43] I would argue that as well as confusing author and narrator this is a generic truism which English is using against Keneally as author; rather than the author, it is the factional *narrator* who will always be bound to a predetermined outcome by the known facts.

Sometimes the narrator shows an awareness of the problems of foreshadowing and backshadowing implicit in a factional approach. *Schindler's List* attempts paradoxically both to return to and recreate the past, using retrospective accounts, to make it look as it did when it was the present.[44] Keneally describes how his method of text-construction produced this effect: all the material he had gathered for the book 'was arranged and coded with colour markers according to the month and the year the events they dealt with occurred'.[45] Thus Michael André Bernstein's notion of foreshadowing, which sees events all leading towards a fixed future, should be as much of a possibility as backshadowing, that 'kind of retroactive foreshadowing in which the shared knowledge of the outcome of a series of events by narrator and listener is used to judge the participants in those events *as though they too should have known what was to come*.[46] However, *Schindler's List* does not remain within the past as it was at the time, and often the narrator cannot resist indicating what we already know is to come. The following is an instance of what appears to be backshadowing:

> out in the darkened Arbeitslager of Plaszów wakeful Jews stir and promise themselves that no régime, the tide set against it, can afford to do away with a plentiful source of free labour.
>
> (33)

This statement is so far from the blaming rhetoric of backshadowing that it could almost be an example of sideshadowing, emphasizing by using the present tense that alternatives which turned out to be worthless did have compelling logic on their side at the time. However, the sentence does not need to highlight for the reader the historical irony of such a sentiment, and the phrasing – 'promise themselves' – suggests a need to reassure oneself against the probable odds. For these reasons it remains an instance of backshadowing, albeit of a benign variety, as much as '[Oskar] does not know the extent of payments still to be made' (33), or

> Oskar's later history seems to call out for some set piece in his childhood. The young Oskar should defend some bullied Jewish boy on the way home from school. It is a safe bet it didn't happen, and we are happier not knowing, since the event would seem too pat.
>
> (37)

In this quotation, the structure of backshadowing 'calls out' for an event to activate it, but the narrator is wryly resigned to the event's absence.[47] (In this way it is like a benign rather than traumatic instance of *Nachträglichkeit*; see Chapter 1.) In fact, as the element of blaming the victims is always absent in this narrative, the three shadowing moods, back-, fore- and side-, are less distinct than usual. Apparent sideshadowing here has the effect of driving home the extreme improbability of the eventual outcome and thereby building up Schindler's stature. Of an incident during the liquidation of the ghetto the narrator notes, 'Wulkan … knew that what was needed was a special and startling deliverance. [He] did not believe for a moment that it would be provided' (168). What looks like sideshadowing here is really foreshadowing – something, or rather, someone 'special and startling' is exactly what delivers Wulkan, even though at the time he might have entertained more mundane sideshadowing possibilities. Again, the three modes identified by Bernstein are blurred.

The text's very subject and existence are evidence of a kind of benign backshadowing: because Schindler's gamble paid off and 1,100 Jews were saved due to his efforts, he is the subject of Keneally's book. Julius Madritsch is not the subject of a book because, although he fed and sheltered his Jewish workers at a factory near Schindler's in Cracow, he did not follow Schindler's plan for both factories to move to Moravia (305). Thus the problem of establishing Schindler's motives is the product of a backshadowing view: we see the results of actions he took, and want to project backwards to know why he acted as he did. Sceptics might argue that even Schindler's own accounts of his motives partake of this benign backshadowing, as he provides a consistent and altruistic narrative to link up his actions. In Schindler's 1945 testimony his constant use of the phrase 'my Jews' of his factory-camp workers is just one of several indications of such a consistent narrative of intention to rescue.

'Promising a future' (395)

The distinctive use of tenses in *Schindler's List* is the result of both its temporal and narratorial structure, and its factional genre. In the novel particular kinds of tense are used to convey various different meanings. The verbs are in the preterite (past) tense usual in novels but the auxiliaries (for instance, the modal will/would) indicate repeated, habitual action, and may also have a forward-looking – predictive – implication.[48] Here are some examples of distinctive, factional use of tense in the text:

(i) 'If Julius Madritsch had been asked to justify the existence of his "profitable factory within the camp [of Plaszów]", he "*would have* argued that it kept nearly four thousand prisoners employed and therefore safe from the death mills" '(20, my italics). A past predictive tense here acts formally by signalling a site for reconstructed motives or dialogue which are then not fully realized, partly because in this example the character would have been unlikely to be asked such a question or to say such a thing aloud.

(ii) Schindler is agitated while reporting on conditions in Poland to Jews in Budapest:

> He rampaged across the carpet. They *would have heard* his steps in the room below, their chandeliers *would have shaken* when he stamped his foot, miming the action of the SS man in the execution squad in Krakusa.
>
> (170, my italics)

A tense combining completed action with a predictive function is the most appropriate for faction where speculation is concerned. Here the use of a perfective and predictive tense takes on a status similar to that of the text's free direct discourse: it does not aspire to be fact, but has the status of verisimilitude. In Petersson's formulation, it is 'realistic' rather than 'real',[49] and signals this by its use of tense. We can call this 'realistic' and not 'real' because 'would have' here really means 'must have (if I had been there I could verify it)', not 'would have (had they been listening)'.

In another instance, the underlying presence of testimony is revealed through a tense inconsistent with free direct discourse: 'Herr Schindler wasn't in, said Emilie. She offered young Pfefferberg a drink but he hastily refused' (78). The change in tense from a present-time utterance – 'Herr Schindler isn't in' – to the past makes this technically indirect discourse,[50] although the rhythm of speech, suggesting direct discourse, is preserved in the contraction 'wasn't'. This is not to suggest that these are Emilie Schindler's actual words, but that the generic presence of the memory of direct speech is signalled by them.

(iii) The preterite predictive tense may also have a temporal function which follows the text's particular historical structure. *Schindler's List* does not imitate the logic of memory by situating itself in the present and looking back on the past; rather, it offers the reader ' "a ringside seat to history" ', in Quartermaine's phrase,[51] placing him or her back within the action's own time. Further, the future time in which the witnesses, narrator and reader now live is occasionally acknowledged. This gives rise to such phrases as, 'Later Danka *would not know* why she had obeyed her mother and gone so mutely into hiding' (155, my italics). This is the tense of a faction narration, whereas 'Later she *did not know*' would have been the unambiguous tense of reportage of fact suitable for a purely documentary narrative.

(iv) As well as having a fast-forward temporal function, these mixed tenses convey repetitive action; Pfefferberg witnesses the murder of a child, and the narrator notes, 'he *would always* testify that the child was two or three years of age' (204, my italics).

(v) An alternative to these kinds of tense is the much more infrequent use of the present tense, as in this example: 'There *is* another Cracow Jew who *gives* an account of meeting Schindler that autumn of 1939 as well as coming close to killing him' (55, my italics; the present tense is used very occasionally for the sake of immediacy, for instance when Oskar orders stationary cattle-trucks full of people at the height of summer to be hosed down (290)). In sense this is much the same as the more typical, 'There *was* another Cracow Jew who *would give* an account'. In the present tense example, however, narrator and character are so much on the same plane that if this tense had been used throughout the text it would have seemed like documentary and not like a novel: the testimony itself is narrated here, not used as the basis for some other, factional effect.

Thus, in general the text's reliance on witness testimony does show through, albeit in indirect ways. For instance, rather than simply announcing the appearance of another witness encountered in the present, the narrator allows the (random) encounter to look as if it possessed the necessity of narrative selection and plot and took place in the past. In most cases, the appearance of a character is dictated by Keneally's having tracked down and interviewed her or him, and the narrator then incorporating them into the plot. Although the stories of Poldek Pfefferberg, Helen Hirsch and Richard Horowitz seem exemplarily extraordinary, and as if chosen for that reason, the stories of all the Schindler Jews must have been just as remarkable. The contingency of 'plot' – factional research – masquerades as the necessity of 'story' – a factual narrative. This is the opposite of what Avisar claims of Spielberg's film: 'All the principal Jewish characters that elicit our emotional involvement manage to survive, with many demonstrating their ability to actively avert their death': in fact, we only learn anything about them *because* they survived. This logic is similar to the usual state of affairs in a novel, where characters are constructed according to what Patricia Waugh calls the 'creation-description paradox', and the contingency of invented plot looks like the necessity of a story.[52] In *Schindler's List*, the masquerade of contingency as necessity is due to the fact that the characters dictate what the narrator will write about whom. For example, we learn a detail about Oskar's pre-war life: as a teenager he owned probably the only 500cc Italian Galloni motorbike in Czechoslovakia, given to him by a doting father. The narrator adds, 'A school friend, Erwin Tragatsch, watched with unspeakable desire ...' (38). The witness Tragatsch is not a function of the anecdote. It is the other way round, and the anecdote only appears because Keneally (presumably) met Tragatsch and heard what he had to say. The factional genre of *Schindler's List* is very clear in this respect: the factual origins of novelistic characters determine their narrative construction and form.

This pattern occurs throughout *Schindler's List*. The reader first encounters Helen Hirsch, Goeth's downtrodden Jewish maid, when Schindler goes down to the kitchens to see her. Helen's free indirect discourse – 'This one's tone of voice, however, was that of ordinary social exchange' – turns into her point of view – 'It was a tone to which she was not accustomed' (29), and, more strikingly – 'She knew she would not survive Amon's house, but it wouldn't be for lack of food' (30; a perfect instance of what looks like sideshadowing but is actually benign backshadowing). We are learning more about Schindler, the text's hero, through Helen, although these details about him – that he spoke to her gently, gave her a bar of chocolate – are of course dependent on her testimony. It looks as if Schindler alone has agency in the story as a whole, but paradoxically most of the features of his character we see are those related by the Jews who were once dependent on him.[53]

In other words, the construction and the meaning of the text are not straightforwardly connected, and in the instance of Helen Hirsch the factionality of the former alters the latter. The narrator notes much later that from the moment Schindler received the gold ring made from Mr Jereth's dental bridgework at the end of the war, the balance of power shifted: 'it was the instant in which [the Jews] became themselves again, in which Oskar Schindler became dependent on the gifts of others' (403), and after the war 'Now Oskar's children had become his parents' (429).[54] In terms of the text's composition, and the visibility of that composition, this has been so all along. As with the use of preterite but predictive tenses and free direct discourse, the exigencies of faction are at the root of this particular effect; the use of testimony is not overtly signalled, but the movement of the narrative – the fact that we learn anything at all about Schindler's relationship with Helen Hirsch – reveals its presence. Elsewhere, fact pushes the faction aside and the narrator does admit that testimony is being relied upon: 'One prisoner recalls wiring installed in Oskar's office in case any SS official did demand entry to the barracks' (258); 'In a testimony in the archives of Yad Vashem in Jerusalem, Biberstein declares that at the beginning of the camp, the daily ration was in excess of two thousand calories' (364); and we learn that the card game in which Schindler won the right to have Helen Hirsch work at Emalia was reported by him to Stern, who then described it to others (304).[55] At these moments the narrator's identity alters. A journalistic narrator takes over from the factional one to report on documentary evidence, such as, 'In 1963, Dr Steinberg of Tel Aviv testifies to yet another instance of Oskar's ... largesse' (383); while the source of the evidence is historical characters, one of whom is Thomas Keneally, the 'implied' and actual author.[56]

The narrator

The narrator of *Schindler's List* takes over after the facsimile signature of 'Tom Keneally' signs off for the author at the end of the Author's Note.[57] The very presence of a narrator with a distinctive voice in this text shows the fictive side of faction. The narrator appears to have two rather contradictory characteristics: he is all-seeing and all-knowing, having omniscient insight into everything from characters' thoughts and deeds to the outcome of historical events and their moral meaning; yet he also uses indirect, double-voiced discourse when describing the most morally repugnant events.

The narrator's historical omniscience is clear. He summarizes for example the history of the Jews in Cracow from 1867 to 1943 (94–6),[58] and appears to have a panoramic temporal and spatial view of scenes from recent history:

> In the first days of the German occupation, the conquerors had been as-
> tounded by the willingness of Poles to point out Jewish households, to hold a
> prayer-locked Jew still while a German docked the orthodox beard with
> scissors – or, pinking the face flesh also, with an infantry bayonet. In March,
> 1941, therefore, the promise to protect the ghetto dwellers from the Polish
> national excess fell on the ear almost credibly.
>
> (95)

This passage shows at once the narrator's omniscient *and* partial view; some have argued that this is so notably not a gentile Pole's perspective on the German occupation that investigations into the truth of the 'promise to protect the ghetto dwellers' have been made into documents held at the Library of Congress.[59] Elsewhere, however, the narrator appears not to be identified with a Jewish viewpoint but to be seeing the text's Jewish characters from a stereotypical, if sympathetic, distance, as the frequent references to 'tribe', 'race' and 'blood' suggest, as do the use of such phrases as 'shtetl eyes' and calling Pankiewicz 'the only Pole' in the ghetto (143). Again it looks as if particular anterior documents or testimonies sway the narrator's orientation.

Peter Quartermaine has argued that the narrator turns the reader of *Schindler's List* into a 'survivor' through particular kinds of temporal and generic construction:

> Keneally's documentary method places the reader always in the position of survivor … but of course we are never really in any danger of being caught up in those events whose unfolding we follow with interest – and, yes, enjoyment. Our survival is guaranteed by our status as reader, even as we see the mesmerising randomness of death under Amon Goeth's administration.[60]

This is true to the extent that the reader becomes a kind of super-survivor, who, as Quartermaine points out, can never be touched by the events of which s/he reads. However, this fact also means that the reader's viewpoint might more easily be identified with Schindler's than with the Jews'. The panoramic view which the narrator has is shared only by Schindler, for instance in the scene – strikingly reproduced in Spielberg's film, and presented as a moral turning point – where Schindler and his girlfriend Ingrid watch the liquidation of the ghetto from a hill overlooking Krakusa Street (141–3).[61] Just as the film was criticized for treating the Jewish characters as objects while the 'good German' (not to mention Goeth, the 'bad German') was a subject, the narrative also has this effect. Although horrifying events are narrated from the point of view of those who suffered them – such as a nameless 13-year-old orphan hiding in a Plaszów latrine, or Rabbi Levartov undergoing Goeth's several failed attempts to shoot him – it is significant that the liquidation can only be seen panoramically by someone outside it, and as Schindler is the hero of this story his is the viewpoint we get.

On other occasions the voices of the narrator and Schindler merge more obviously. Of Schindler's visit to Budapest to report on the condition of the Jews in Poland, the narrator begins: 'In the past few weeks, said Oskar, some two thousand Cracow ghetto dwellers had been rounded up and sent, not to the chambers of Belzec, but to labour camps near the city.' The usual absence of quotation marks here makes it easy for Oskar's 'Report' to segue into what sounds like the narrator's voice, so that there appears to be no difference between them.[62]

> The Vernichtungslagers also used people as labour for a time, but their ultimate industry was death and its by-products – recycling of the clothes, the remaining jewellery or spectacles, the toys, and even the skin and hair of the dead.

(171)

Factual detail given in sober and compassionate tones is common to both the narrator and Schindler. It is useful to compare this lack of difference between Schindler and the narrator with a structurally similar but actually very different seguing between voices in the case of Wilhelm Kunde, 'commander of the SS guard' (176), who gives Goeth 'a deft sketch' of the ghetto:

> The portion on their left was Ghetto B, said Kunde. Its inhabitants, about two thousand of them, had escaped earlier Aktions or had been previously employed in industry.... In clearing the ghetto, it might be preferable to start on that side first, though that sort of tactical decision was entirely up to the Herr Commandant.
>
> (177)

This passage is also characterized by a lack of inverted commas and consists of a mixture of free direct and indirect discourse (the grammatical changes associated with indirect discourse occur at times: 'on *their* left', rather than 'on *your* left'; but not invariably: 'it *might be*' rather than 'it *might have been*') followed by a smooth movement into what seems to be narratorial reportage ('Its inhabitants ...'). However, here there is an ironic and disapproving gap between the representing and represented voices ('up to the Herr Commandant') which makes it distinct from the combining that takes place with Schindler. The passage is a factional construction, but more double-voiced in Kunde's case because it is closer to the kind of atrocity which elsewhere attracts such discourse.

Another instance of free direct discourse which is followed by, but is extremely distinct from, narratorial utterance is the horrifying double hanging in Plaszów of the engineer Krautwirt for letter-writing and a young boy, Haubenstock, for singing Russian songs:

> In an uneven voice [Haubenstock] reasoned with the Haupsturmführer, who stood beside the scaffold. I am not a Communist, Herr Commandant. I hate Communism. They were just songs. Ordinary songs. The hangman, a Jewish butcher of Cracow, pardoned for some earlier crime on condition that he undertake this work, stood Haubenstock on a stool and placed the noose around his neck.
>
> (237)

The changes from the boy's discourse to the narrator's and back again are so abrupt they are hard to read aright, and in the US edition the boy's words do have inverted commas (216). O'Hearn claims that the use of 'graphological markers to indicate the use of free indirect thought ... does not change the meaning of the text' in the US edition.[63] On the contrary, their appearance does change the meaning, as the graphological markers are often added to instances of free *direct*, not indirect, speech. In the case above, the closeness of the boy's voice to the narrator's in the transition 'Ordinary songs. The hangman ...' suggests a horrible proximity, temporally and spatially, appropriate to the closeness of victim and hangman as both are Jews.

The narrator's omniscience, particularly of the historical variety, has the effect of backshadowing but without its element of blame: again, it is benign backshadowing. Of the Emalia women mistakenly sent to Auschwitz instead of Schindler's Moravian factory-camp at Brinnlitz, the narrator notes,

> The women were equally unaware that they had arrived in Auschwitz at a time when the progress of the war and certain secret negotiations between Himmler and the Swedish Count Folke Bernadotte were imposing a new direction on it.
>
> (333)

Just as Wulkan's helplessness led to his hopes for 'startling delivery', so the women at Auschwitz are so little in control of their own fate that no blame can be attached to their ignorance of what was going on. However, this narratorial stance also means that everyone knows better than the women: the reader, narrator and important players at the time have privileged information. This is the opposite of Bakhtin's notion of polyphony, in which the narrator is on the same plane as all the characters (here, Schindler is the only character at all thus constructed) and does not share exclusive information with the reader over the characters' heads. The text's factional genre and avoidance of a memory-based format militate against polyphony. Its promotion of the Schindler myth[64] also tends towards the non-polyphonic; as one character, Lusia, thinks of Schindler, 'A paradise run by a friend was too fragile. To manage an enduring heaven, you needed someone both more authoritative and more mysterious than that' (223). This description does double duty as that of an Aryan rescuer whose motives remain opaque, and a non-polyphonic narrator, one who is not a 'friend' but 'like Zeus' (364), to whom the Schindler Jews can feel only 'the most basic and devout gratitude' (357) in a manner even the narrator thinks may seem 'too serf-like' (366).[65] The narrative structure mirrors the women's historical victimization. As Irving Howe has pointed out in terms which are helpful for understanding *Schindler's List* as well as William Styron's *Sophie's Choice*, a novelist will face several 'narrowly literary' problems when tackling the subject of the Holocaust because it is

> not, essentially, a dramatic subject. ... The basic minimum of freedom to choose and act that is a central postulate of drama had been taken from the victims. The Nazis indulged in a peculiarly vicious parody of this freedom when they sometimes gave Jewish parents the 'choice' of which child should be murdered.[66]

Howe's comments show why Schindler and not the Jews he saved is the focus of Keneally's book; only he possessed the ability to 'choose and act', to which we might add 'know'.[67]

'And now all that good, expensive gas has been wasted on the Jews!'[68]

The narrator of *Schindler's List* is double-voiced to significantly varying degrees in representing characters. While the gap between represented and representing voices is hard to detect in the case of Schindler himself, in the case of those disapproved of, such as Nazi characters, the gap is far clearer. Other striking instances of double-voicedness take place when the narrator has to relate an atrocity or Nazi mindset. Rather than monologically commenting on such things to draw a straightforward moral, the narrator uses a distinctive double-voiced discourse to ironic and scathing effect. In her account of the trial of Adolf Eichmann, *Eichmann in Jerusalem*, Hannah Arendt uses a similar narrative tone, which debunks its subject while not failing to recognize the enormity of his deeds. Arendt says that the taped police examination of Eichmann 'constitutes a veritable gold mine for a psychologist – provided he is wise enough to understand that the horrible can be not only ludicrous but outright funny'; and speaks of the contradiction 'between the unspeakable horror of the deeds and the undeniable ludicrousness of the man who perpetrated them'.[69] In the case of Arendt's book, such mocking and understated double-voicedness is the stylistic correlative of her theory of the 'banality' of Eichmann's evil; when she refers to his 'rather modest mental gifts', for instance, she does so not to make him into a clown-Nazi but to show precisely that he was 'terribly and terrifyingly normal' – hence the strikingly 'normal' description.[70] To the same end straightforward sarcasm is often used: Arendt refers to the 'brilliant idea' enshrined in the Nuremberg Laws of making all German Jews take 'Israel' or 'Sarah' as a middle name.[71] In Arendt's text the discourse of ordinary social interaction (in my italics) is often mixed with an unstated discourse of genocide, as in the following comment on Eichmann's visit to the local SS commander in charge of Einsatzgruppen actions:

> *The trouble was* that at Lwów they were doing the same thing they had been doing in Minsk, and [Eichmann's] *host was delighted* to *show him the sights*, although Eichmann tried *politely to excuse himself*.[72]

Arendt justifies her argument about the 'terrifyingly normal' Eichmann by using a method shared by Keneally: the use of double-voiced everyday, colloquial, clichéd, or even banal discourse. This is an example from *Eichmann in Jerusalem*, on Eichmann's efforts in Vienna in 1938 to put all the offices which encouraged Jews' emigration under one roof. Arendt describes the typical applicant, who

> would no longer have to *run from office to office* and who, *presumably*, would also be spared having some humiliating chicaneries *practiced upon him*, and *certain expenses* for bribes.[73]

Her deliberately understated, everyday language ('practiced upon him', 'certain expenses') conveys a very un-everyday 'compassion, outrage and a true sense of tragedy'[74] without using any discourse of a monologically 'outraged' kind. The resulting ironic distance works at the Nazis' expense and offers an unsentimental sympathy to the 'applicant'. The understatement also shows traces of the Nazis' own use of language to disguise murderous meaning, which is a constant theme of Arendt's work. Earlier in the section on Eichmann's job in Vienna she signals some particularly fraught struggles for meaning within the sign by threading Nazi slogans and Eichmann's own words into her own discourse for economically critical effect. For example, in the later 1930s 'the "revolutionary zeal" in Austria, greatly exceeding the early "excesses" in Germany, had resulted in the imprisonment of practically all prominent Jews'; Eichmann ' "took counsel with himself " ' and ' "gave birth to the idea which I thought would do justice to both parties" '.[75]

In *Schindler's List* the following observation holds to a similar pattern:

> Early in the career of every subcamp, senior officers from the parent Lager paid a visit to ensure that the *energy* of the slave labourers was *stimulated* in the most *radical and exemplary* manner.
>
> (234, my italics)

Just as in the example describing Eichmann's endeavours in Vienna, here we read words – those in italics – with a double 'sideward glance', both at the Nazis' own view of their actions and at the reader's knowledge that these words are deliberately inadequate.

Both *Eichmann in Jerusalem* and *Schindler's List* also use a variety of double-voiced free indirect discourse, exposing the unselfconscious moral bankruptcy of an individual or group in their own words. Arendt writes of the Nazis' surprise in discovering that Scandinavia was not especially prone to the unifying ideology of antisemitism: 'what was even more *annoying* ... was that the German "radical" variety was *appreciated* only by those peoples in the East';[76] while this is said in *Schindler's List* of carbon-monoxide murders at Belzec: 'There had been an *awful* day at Belzec, which the SS chemical officer Kurt Gerstein had witnessed, when *Kommissar* Wirth's method took three hours to finish a *party* of Jewish *males* packed into the chambers.' This is narrated from Gerstein's viewpoint; his words (in italics) resound with dehumanizing officialese and include an adjective – 'awful' – more expressive of inconvenience to himself than empathy with the victims.[77]

In *Schindler's List*, the same strategies as Arendt's remove narratorial affect and replace it with an indirect poignancy. Sometimes such double-voicedness exists simply as sarcasm; the narrator refers to billboard advertisements put up by the Nazis in Cracow, linking Jews with lice, typhus and Satan, as 'artwork' (108). At other times a double-voiced interrogation of more substantive themes takes place. Pfefferberg works on his mother's disinclination to build up a German clientele for her home-decor business; the narrator adds that 'the Germans might be the only race this season with enough confidence in the future to go in for interior design' (108). The comment employs a social discourse – 'this season', 'go in for interior design' – to contrast with the unstated vocabulary of genocide that makes this remark true. As Bakhtin says of such juxtapositions, even when one of the languages is not formally present, 'the novelistic hybrid is ... a system having as its goal the illumination of one language by means of another'.[78] In an effort to make the incomprehensible at least stylistically appreciable, the narrator notes of Mrs Dresner's decision to be found on the streets during an *aktion* that this is in defiance of 'an unwritten rule that ghetto natives must stay on quivering in their rooms until discovered [so] that anyone found moving on the stairways was somehow guilty of defiance of the system' (156). The fact of the 'quivering' is registered yet distanced from a sentimental view.

In most of these instances from *Schindler's List*, the narrator is describing events from a character's point of view so that the irony is in part theirs although no markers indicating free indirect speech are present, in keeping with the text's usual practice. The following extract describes Goeth's infliction of mass punishment on slave workers for small infringements, in this case hiding a potato in a Plaszów barracks:

> It is no fast matter to have a few hundred people drag their trousers or knickers down, their shirts or dresses up and *treat* each of them to twenty-five lashes. It was Goeth's rule that the flogged prisoner call out the numbers for the *guidance* of the Ukrainian orderlies who did the flogging. If the victim lost track of the count, it was to begin again. Commandant Goeth's rollcalls on the Appelplatz were full of just such *time-consuming trickery*.
>
> (213, my italics)[79]

This is triple-voiced discourse: it is the narrator's rendering of Madritsch's irony and understatement (it begins, 'Madritsch mentioned' (212), and the phrase 'time-consuming trickery' describes his view of the workforce being delayed) with a glance at Goeth's discourse or viewpoint: 'treat', 'guidance'. In contrast to this multi-accented description, here is psychotherapist Luitgard Wundheiler's rendering of the same scene in a manner perfectly suited to his factual concerns, that is, entirely monologic: Goeth 'detained the camp population for hours at roll call in order to harass and torture them'.[80]

In drawing this comparison between two very different texts, Arendt's and Keneally's, I am not suggesting that Keneally was actually influenced by Arendt; rather, that both have adopted a double-voiced style as the best way of dealing with intractable and horrifying material.[81] In Arendt's case the frequent use of bathos and irony is the best way of presenting a man whom the Israeli Supreme Court wanted to believe was a ' "perverted sadist" ' but of whom she concludes that, 'Except for an extraordinary diligence in looking out for his personal advancement, [Eichmann] had no motives at all'.[82] In the case of *Schindler's List*, which is faction rather than journalism – Arendt's book was originally a series of articles on the Eichmann trial written for the *New Yorker* – such a narrator may, paradoxically, appear to possess the voice of clear and impeccable moral stance and historical authority for which Robert Manne argues in relation to Helen Darville's *The Hand that Signed the Paper*,[83] as in the following example. Poldek Pfefferberg is able to circumvent a Nazi declaration which threatened to render the ghetto occupants' currency worthless: 'That was the sort of policeman Pfefferberg was. Excellent by the standards of Chairman Artur Rosenzweig, deplorable by the standards of Pomorska' (109). At first glance this seems to be a monologic comment defining Pfefferberg once and for all; but it is just as stylized, and defined by the character whose viewpoint it is representing, as is usual in this text. It is hard to see how the Mannean narrator could exist in any novel, where all kinds of dialogic contexts would unseat its monologic pretensions. Of course we always know where the narrator's moral allegiance lies: with a unified, rescuing Schindler.

However, the effect in *Schindler's List* of double-voiced discourse is not to convey the terrifying normality of either Goeth or Schindler,[84] nor to establish a fixed moral position which the reader must share in order to understand the irony and sarcasm being used. It is rather the effect of faction. Faction is a hybrid form, and in the case of *Schindler's List* it is the narrator's voice which represents the fictional side, the characters' the factual side. The unusual use of tenses and speech representation is the result of the 'balance' in which the two genres are held. As Richard Johnstone argues, faction might at first appear to be a genre which reassuringly keeps 'the unknown at bay' by dealing in the ascertainable, but most examples of factional literature have the opposite effect and emphasize 'by subject or by method or by both, the inherent strangeness and unbelievability of what is described. The facts are more likely to disrupt than to console'.[85] The tension between the reassurance of narrative tone and the troubling historical facts comes through strongly in *Schindler's List*; and this tension extends to the plot itself, which gives us a story of salvation amidst a context of irredeemable death and loss which 'persistently obtrudes into our consciousness as we read'.[86] It is true that the rescue of Abraham Bankier (in the book, Stern in the film) from a death-train is just one of many incidents of this kind; the doom of the drowned serves only to emphasize the good fortune of the saved. 'Persistent obtrusions' may only take the form of emphasizing the conventional novelistic construction of Kencally's text.

'It's the personality more than anything else that saved us'[87]

The question of Schindler's motives has been the basis of further controversy. The issues are threefold: what were Schindler's reasons for saving 1,100 Jews; how can we have any access to what his reasons might have been; how successfully does Keneally represent Schindler? The controversy is especially interesting because it begs and complicates the issue of faction. As several critics note, Keneally's decision to combine fact with fiction was an ideal opportunity to reconstruct some kind of interiority for Schindler. However, Keneally's view seems to be that Schindler was an opaque person in reality, and he has retained this image of him in the text. Keneally has written, '[Schindler] wasn't the sort of man who spent a lot of time asking himself about his reasons for doing things.'[88] Keneally's other theme in discussing Schindler is that his personality was somehow always already fictive, as he says in an interview:

> the recurrent flaws and strengths of a personality such as Schindler's give his life an artistic form of the type you have to make up for a fictional character. The most remarkable coincidence between life and art lies in that phenomenon, that lives often have what appears to be an artistic neatness to them.[89]

This is an extension of Keneally's comment in his Author's Note that only the techniques of the novel would do for 'a character of such ambiguity and magnitude as Oskar' (13).

Although Quartermaine argues that in making such observations Keneally 'blurs distinctions proper to make in the response to a work of *fiction* between the raw material of the work ... and the text we engage with', and that 'others' lives are just as amenable to fiction as Oskar's',[90] the figure of Schindler has attracted widespread interest as a metafictional symbol. David English says Schindler is one of a series of 'author-prophets' Keneally includes in his work; English focuses particularly on the episode in which Schindler watches the liquidation of the ghetto from a hillside and his viewpoint becomes narratorial. Similarly, Peter Pierce's description of Schindler – 'Disdaining the abstract (racial purity, a thousand year Reich), his allegiances are altogether personal' – makes him sound like the author Keneally.[91] Keneally himself plays upon this coincidence of his own and his subject's style, and what he says of his narrative – 'It is a *risky enterprise* to have to write of virtue' (15, my italics) – sounds like a phrase appropriate to Schindler's story used here to describe an authorial adventure.[92] In an article on Spielberg's film, Miriam Bratu Hansen convincingly argues for a metacinematic Schindler. Schindler's very opacity makes him eminently suitable as a cinematic image, a character of glamour and surfaces who is 'repeatedly identified with the aesthetics of fashion, advertising and consumption', and of whose subjectivity we know very little. In the film, Schindler has the following revealing exchange with Itzhak Stern about the first scheme we see him set up:

Stern: They [the Jewish 'investors'] put up all the money; I do all the work. What, if you don't mind my asking, would you do?

Schindler: I'd make sure it's known the company's in business. I'd see that it had a certain panache. That's what I'm good at. Not the work, not the work: the presentation![93]

As a self-styled 'presenter', Schindler sounds very like his creator,[94] and like his intertextual precursor Charles Foster Kane in Orson Welles's 1941 film *Citizen Kane*. Spielberg himself has referred to 'the rosebud question' in *Schindler's List*: 'what drove Schindler along this incredible path?'[95] However, the narrative shape of Spielberg's film is self-consciously opposite to that of Welles's: in the latter, a spirited, visionary young man becomes the victim of his own obsession with the media, while the 'break in the image' at the end of *Schindler's List* suggests that this set of 'imaginary signifiers' is based on the three-dimensionality of witness, testimony and loss.[96]

Robert Taubman argues that Keneally's text is 'dispassionate' (he also ambiguously claims that it 'de-fantasizes its subject': is this Schindler or the Holocaust?) and that it uses a 'distancing technique' in making Plaszów seem normal, while normality itself – such as the courtship of Josef Bau and Rebecca Tannenbaum – seems 'bizarre'. Not all critics agree with this estimate: either that Keneally de-fantasizes Schindler, or that he deserves fantasizing. Taubman ascribes what he sees as the narrative's distancing effect to the fact that this is a 'success story', which allows Keneally to concentrate on such out-of-the-ordinary anecdotes as the Baus' marriage, and the episode where the violin-playing Rosners drive a love-sick SS officer to suicide by their deliberately heart-rending version of 'Gloomy Sunday'.[97] According to Taubman's argument, the narratorial double-voicedness could also be the result of the novel's 'success story': a wry, distancing, ironic tone is permissible because this is comedy, albeit set within a tragedy. Gaffney also claims that *Schindler's List* works as a 'hagiographic inversion' and cites the narrator's emphasis on the absence of a formative philosemitic rescue in Schindler's early life. (As we have seen, this comment is more interestingly seen in terms of its temporal, not literal, function.) However, the narrator of *Schindler's List* can be seen as partial and biased, in his focus on Schindler and his constant insistence on the latter's impeccable credentials. The time and money spent on the Jews Schindler saved is constantly mentioned, not just because it is part of the record (and forms the substance of Schindler's 1945 'Report') but because of the distinction between rescuers who took money and those who did not.[98]

Any representation of what moved Schindler raises the spectre of backshadowing. Although it can be argued that 'the facts speak for themselves',[99] Schindler's motives are open to the narrative-imposing view of backshadowing. (From a sideshadowing perspective, Wundheiler interestingly argues that Schindler's early acts of humanity, such as sheltering Jewish workers at Emalia, developed into a self-fulfilling prophecy: because he was seen as a 'good person and a good German', Schindler acted up into the role of 'principled altruist').[100] Schindler's impulsive acts of compassion,[101] which developed into a long-term, carefully planned strategy, are not really represented in *Schindler's List*. Instead, the view taken by benign backshadowing is of a consistent campaign, not a sideshadowing one of impulsive rescue[102] which would render the question one of personality rather than motive. Benign backshadowing can constitute a critical tool in the effort to establish an internal narrative for Schindler's actions. That is, the success of what Schindler did (and the testimony of the 'listees', as Brecher calls them) allows us to look back at a 'righteous gentile' career that appears planned. For instance, Herbert Steinhouse comments on 'the rotten group [Schindler] had wined and flattered while inwardly loathing, in order to save the lives of helpless people':[103] it is certain that Schindler 'wined and flattered', and plausible but not certain that this is why. Steinhouse says his material was accumulated in the 1940s when he met Schindler in Paris, but it often bears the Keneally imprint of assuming a rescuing Schindler.[104]

Although the personal seems to take precedence over the historical in Keneally's representation of Schindler, David Thomson suggests that the events of the war must have affected Keneally's hero: a writer with a different view from Keneally could argue that Schindler's increased determination to save Jews in the summer of 1944 was evidence of 'looking to impress a new crowd'.[105] Steinhouse, like Keneally, has a backshadowing view which, in contrast to Thomson's mild scepticism, constructs a subjective moral narrative for Schindler: in the spring of 1943 he moved 'into a more active anti-fascist role'.[106] Part of the reason why neither Julius Madritsch nor Oswald Bosko has been the subject of a factional inquiry is that their motives are not as interesting, *because they did not succeed* in the way that Schindler did. His motives are of interest because of his actions. It is in this sense that Schindler's life-history is always already fictive: not because his personality was 'ambiguous' – as a renegade SS officer, Bosko's must have been equally so – but because, unlike Madritsch, Schindler made the right choices at the right times. The historical and fictional backshadowing views are indistinguishable on this point.

Again we can only conclude that Schindler is appropriate as the subject of a faction about the Holocaust because his story is atypical; paradoxically this both allows the story to be told and opens it up for negative critical response. The story is about 'water not gas', redemption not annihilation, personal rescues rather than the loss of whole peoples; it concerns a very small and specific episode of the Holocaust years. Atypicality is also bound up with backshadowing and its questionability. As well as the blaming variety of backshadowing that Bernstein discusses in relation to historical and fictional writing about the Holocaust, there is a variant of foreshadowing which emphasizes the inevitability of what happened;[107] as we saw in relation to Amis's *Time's Arrow*, foreshadowing is a category which falls between side- and backshadowing, and which values 'the present, not for itself, but as the harbinger of an already determined future'. What will be must be. Keneally's text relies heavily on such foreshadowing. As the comment quoted earlier about Helen Hirsch shows – 'She knew she would not survive Amon's house, but it wouldn't be for lack of food' (30) – the foreshadowing narrator in *Schindler's List* possesses privileged knowledge which he can barely keep to himself and, here, hints at: we are pretty sure that Helen will survive or, despite the reconstructions, we would not get this moment of free indirect discourse. Janka Feigenbaum, a character who does die early (though of natural causes), is not narrated from within like this.

Foreshadowing attempts to return to the past as if it were the present: not to acknowledge the myriad possibilities of sideshadowing but to prove the inevitability of what then happened.[108] This position is one which has its cake and eats it: we have knowledge of events even when we imaginatively return to a time before they took place. Foreshadowing thus appears to acknowledge freedom of choice at the time, but simultaneously denies that freedom through its later knowledge. We see that resistance to the Nazis did indeed take place, by Jews and other civilians of occupied countries, but the Holocaust carried on none the less. Critical views of Keneally's choice of Schindler as a narrative subject divide along time-shadowing lines. The text adopts a benignly foreshadowing mode which determines its presentation of Schindler, and indeed could not do otherwise given the fact that

> Knowing the future of the past forces the [faction-writer] to shape his account to come out as things have done. The tempo, contractions, and time scale of his narrative reflect his retrospective knowledge, for he 'must not only know something of the outcomes of the events that concern him; he must use what he knows in telling his story'.[109]

In the case of Keneally's *Schindler's List* hindsight has to turn into foreshadowing because the main 'event' he is concerned with is an internal one. His decision to view Schindler as an 'intentionalist'[110] means that benign foreshadowing is the mode of his text.

The benignly foreshadowing structure of *Schindler's List* implies that 'even within sight of the death camps, the option of hampering the Nazi murder machine never wholly disappeared' and qualifies the idea that the Holocaust was 'an inherently inevitable, fateful, unstoppable event, one over which human agency had no control'.[111] Critical backshadowing questions this view of individual agency within the Holocaust. Any blame involved in foreshadowing is attached not to the victims but to the perpetrators and bystanders, and because Schindler transcends this triad of categories he too is often exempt from criticism.[112] Many of Schindler's qualities – his ordinariness, moral compromises in everyday life, apparent lack of self-consciousness, and failure to prosper before or after the war – add to the ability of *Schindler's List* to stop readers taking refuge in a critically foreshadowing perspective, which is easier to adopt than its own benign one as we need not concern ourselves with why Schindler was such an exception to the rule.[113]

Much is made by writers on Schindler of his ambiguity, the 'light and shade' theme Keneally was attracted to, which is linked to the necessity of avoiding critical backshadowing. Wundheiler argues that the light and shade aspect of Schindler may make him seem like a reproach to ordinary mortals who cannot distance themselves from him as they might from rescuers like Raoul Wallenberg and André Trocmé who seemed 'without blemish': 'It is uncomfortable to know about Schindler because he stirs our consciences precisely because of his weaknesses.' Hulse argues that 'only because he was a man of vice could Schindler accomplish his pragmatic virtue', while Wundheiler claims that had Schindler not been a Nazi Party member – one of the 'vices' critics find it hardest to forgive – he could not have accomplished what he did.[114] However, reasons other than the 'light and shade' conundrum can be adduced for choosing Schindler as the subject of a narrative. Richard Wolin asks whether the success of the book and film relies on the fact that Schindler's 'is a story that would have patent appeal to non-Jewish audiences? Is it because Schindler himself is a figure with whom a mass audience could readily identify, even sympathize?'[115] Going further than this, and apparently forgetting a significant difference between the two parts of the Bible, Michael Hollington remarks that the Old Testament reference of the title might suggest that the book offers a 'reading in which Christianity gets a large and sympathetic hearing'.[116]

'My Jews'

Keneally has been criticized for representing Schindler too uncritically, and for not exploring his motivation; in other words, Keneally has taken for granted a consistent, planned altruistic act on Schindler's behalf. Part of the reason for this assumption is Keneally's reliance on Schindler's 'Report', written in Konstanz in July 1945. In this fascinating document, Schindler says that a rabbi suggested he should write down his story, 'giving facts and figures so that outsiders could gain an overall picture of my efforts and to prevent any risk of the facts of these efforts being belittled'.[117] What follows is an account in both senses: of Schindler's expenditure over the war years 'in [his] labour camp', and one in which each item is detailed at length to form a testimony.

   In the 'Report', Schindler outlines a plan to save Jews which began on his arrival in Poland: 'the trusteeship office … with its authorisations of the plundering of Jewish property and its business practices, was an object of hatred to me.'[118] In telling his tale, Schindler assumes a consistent, humanitarian plan of rescue. At the same time the accounts-based form of his testimony is remarkably impersonal and external. Even when making a comment such as 'My attitude to the Jewish workers helped me to overcome the difficulties that threatened', Schindler does not go on to describe that attitude. His descriptions of his own actions give little away: 'I can claim with pride that it is thanks to my initiative that these Jews remained in my factory camp, since I intervened and negotiated fearlessly with the SS officials in the respect to the Jews'; and, 'No one observing from the outside can appreciate how much work went into converting the decision to take my Jews westwards into the accomplished fact of having brought more than 1000 people to safety in the new location [at Brinnlitz].'[119] This avoidance of subjective confession is picked up by Keneally as if it were a character trait when it may simply be due to the nature of the 'Report', concerned as it is with the hard facts of expenditure.

The 'Report' is clearly meant by Schindler as proof – 'testimony' – not of his *motives*, but of his *actions*, as shown by his care to name the SS officers he came across, and by his noting several times that 'Jewish witnesses are available for all my actions';[120] the 'Report' culminates in a long list of their names. This objective style characterizes the whole 'Report', when Schindler briefly mentions incidents which feature at much greater length in Keneally's text. Schindler is keen to record what he did rather than why he did it, for instance: 'I made it possible for my faithful Rabbi Levetov [*sic*] to give the bodies of those [from Golleschau] a ritual burial, probably the only time this happened in Germany during the war.'[121] Schindler's comment that "this 'Report" on my efforts is not meant to be a balance sheet, but an overview of the tangible and intangible sacrifices made',[122] does not clarify any issue of interiority. Only in relation to another individual, his 'good friend' Raimund Titsch, does Schindler imply a motive: 'As far as I know, Titsch was the only civilian in Cracow apart from myself who through all those years remained unshakably and fearlessly true to his humanitarian goal of lessening the suffering of the Jews';[123] but even this is described from the outside, and does not concern itself with the reasons for having such a goal.

Schindler's tone in the 'Report' seems to have profoundly affected Keneally's narrative. Schindler describes the car-scam perpetrated on him by the SS officers John and Scheidt, told in detail in *Schindler's List*, and simply concludes: 'I was happy to be able to do both gentlemen a favour.'[124] This is clearly a double-voiced remark, and could have come straight out of the mouth of Keneally's Schindler: the SS may have seen it as a 'favour', but would not have guessed why Schindler was happy to do it. The same effect is gained by Schindler's use of the word ' "loans" ' (' "Darlehen" ') instead of 'bribes' or 'extortion', to describe the money and goods he gave to the SS. Schindler uses a version of free indirect discourse for ironic effect when describing the move to Brinnlitz, speaking of himself in the third person: 'The regional council, the Gestapo, the District party chief, all were mobilised to try to prevent Schindler jewifying the area, importing typhus and other diseases with his "Schindler-Gang".'[125] These are tiny instances of techniques Keneally has adopted on a much larger scale for his novel.

In sum, although it is short and rather scant on detail (in the archives at Yad Vashem it is accompanied by 100 pages of testimony by others, including Itzhak Stern), Schindler's 'Report' represents a subject who is concerned to detail his actions, not his motives, and who does not show any doubt about having had a campaign of rescue from the first. Supplemented by detail from the testimonies of others, it is this subject who appears as Oskar Schindler in Keneally's novel.

Discussing Spielberg's film, Barbie Zelizer notes that images of the Holocaust 'have come to be judged … against some absolute standard of historical truth'; and this is true of Keneally's text.[126] However, we are dealing with a representation; Keneally's *Schindler's List* is a work of faction, and the fact that it presents the individual as the protagonist of history, and survival instead of destruction, is as much to do with its humanist representational agenda and benignly backshadowing view of its protagonist than a particular historical comment on the Holocaust. Its concern with intention, the role of the individual, and private versus public memory, makes it more about the Holocaust, not less.

Similarly, Schindler's unrepresentativeness is not easily explained away: he 'spent $16 million, on bribes, ransoms and rations' in order to save his Jewish workers, and although luck and accident played a part in his success, it was not achieved without effort and will – even if Keneally is content more to observe than to analyse this literal and moral expenditure. Keneally converts the ambiguity which drew him to Schindler's story in the first place – 'Paradox is what turns novelists on. Linear valor is not as important to them as light and shade' – into opacity and thus lack of ambiguity: we know that we do not know what Schindler's motives were exactly, but we are clear about both his results and his intentions.[127] *Schindler's List* is a post-war, humanist view of the Holocaust; its uneven critical reception is due not to its being an uncomfortable read, but an easy read. While we may find the challenge of *Time's Arrow* more effective as a paradigm for third-generation writing on this subject, the *Schindler's List* mode is clearly a popular approach to Holocaust fiction.

Chapter 5

Melodrama
William Styron, *Sophie's Choice*

William Styron's novel *Sophie's Choice* was published in 1979, just after the broadcast of the television series *Holocaust* in the United States at a time when the ethics of representing the subject were making headlines. *Sophie's Choice* was greeted by a mixture of acclaim and outrage. Styron repeatedly notes in interviews that at least the critical controversy was never as fierce as that which greeted the publication of his earlier novel, *The Confessions of Nat Turner* (1966), typified by the appearance of a volume called *William Styron's Nat Turner: Ten Black Writers Respond*.[1] On the publication of *Sophie's Choice* Styron breezily observed that had he got the facts wrong about Auschwitz, 'Rabbis, Poles, ex-Nazis – they'll all be after my hide', and added that at least he never had to 'dodge the assault' of a book called 'Ten Rabbis Respond' to *Sophie's Choice*. The novel stayed on the *New York Times* best-seller list for over forty weeks and won the American Book Award for fiction in 1980.[2] However, Styron did have to 'dodge the assault' by critics incensed that he had written a novel purportedly about the Holocaust, an event with which he was not only unconnected but which focuses on a Polish Catholic and not a Jewish victim. It was pointed out that his narrator (and therefore, in several minds, Styron) inaccurately likens plantation to Nazi slavery; that all the Jewish and female characters in the novel are either sexually dysfunctional or mad; and that the novel was allegedly motivated by a literary rivalry between Southern and Jewish-American writers in which Styron was trying to prove he could engage with the subjects usually considered the province of the latter.[3]

Sophie's Choice is narrated by a nameless, middle-aged author recalling his 22-year-old self, then nicknamed Stingo. In the summer of 1947 the struggling writer Stingo meets the Polish Sophie and her lover Nathan in Brooklyn, and becomes attached to them both: he reveres Nathan and falls in love with Sophie. Sophie's relationship with Nathan is unstable and during their intermittent separations she tells her wartime tale to Stingo: she was arrested in Cracow in 1943 for smuggling and spent the next twenty months in Auschwitz. Her story emerges fitfully and painfully with retellings of salient points. When things go badly between Sophie and Nathan, after Stingo learns that Nathan is mentally ill and has lied about his job as a scientific researcher, he persuades Sophie to flee with him to his home down south. She gives him the slip and returns to Nathan in Brooklyn, where Sophie and Nathan commit suicide together.

Critics have taken issue with *Sophie's Choice* on both fictional and factional grounds. The argument about Styron's 'right' to represent the Holocaust, as a non-Jewish non-survivor, takes place at the most general level of complaint.[4] Of the novel itself, critics point out that its main Jewish character, the sadistic and insane Nathan Landau, can be seen as an embodiment of antisemitic fantasy; and he is paired with Sophie Zawistowska, a beautiful and masochistic misogynist's fantasy. Barbara Foley goes so far as to claim that the novel is 'racist' because 'it promotes sympathy for a Gentile at the expense of a Jew', Sophie at the expense of Nathan; because she thinks Nathan comes across as more brutal than Rudolf Höss himself, this amounts to 'blaming the victim for the crime'. She adds that the 'epistemological relativism' implicit in Styron's 'confusion' of myth and history is 'akin to the subjectivist attitude toward truth characteristic of the very fascist nightmare' he is describing.[5] Other critics question in moral terms the novel's narrative structure, particularly the role of Stingo as narrator since he filters Sophie's words through his own and intersperses the unravelling of her past with stories of his own failed sexual encounters.[6] Furthermore, on 'pseudofactual' grounds, to use Foley's term,[7] the appropriateness of making Rudolf Höss a character in the novel and relying on his autobiography is questioned by several commentators.

The problems here are partly generic. *Sophie's Choice* makes its own shifts between genres, seeming at first as if it is to be an autobiographical novel; as Styron put it in an interview: 'if you start out in the autobiographical mode and make that convincing on its own level, it gives you an element of credibility with the reader when you touch the part that is fictional.'[8] At other times it resembles a comic *Künstlerroman* featuring scenarios indebted to Philip Roth, while in the sections dealing with Sophie's experiences in Auschwitz the novel shows signs of becoming faction. Indeed, *Sophie's Choice* is a novel based on varied and often conflicting discourses from a number of sources which it uses in a variety of different ways. The jarring nature of certain episodes and lurches between Sophie's painful testimony and Stingo's comic escapades are partly explained by the novel's publishing history. The tale of poor Leslie Lapidus, a young woman with whom Stingo has a failed sexual encounter, was originally published separately – revealingly enough in the magazine *Esquire* – entitled 'The Seduction of Leslie'.[9]

The Auschwitz experience

Styron refers to a long-standing interest in the Holocaust which led him to write *Sophie's Choice*, as well as an encounter with the real-life version of Sophie.[10] In this sense the novel is akin to *Schindler's List*, which also isolates a particular and untypical story, but it is hard not to read either story as synecdochic of the event as a whole. None the less, critics have found fault with various aspects of the novel's representation of Auschwitz, on several different levels. Alvin Rosenfeld dislikes the fact that Styron's heroine, as a Polish Catholic, gives his representation of the Holocaust a 'white-face', 'de-Judaized' cast, by 'reducing Hitler's war against the Jews to a literary war' in which the gentile, Southern Styron implicitly insists on his right to treat this subject.[11] Styron's extra-textual comments on this novel have added to the sense that he feels it necessary to 'broaden' the relevance of the Holocaust. In an interview he mentioned that Auschwitz is the culmination 'of the titanic and sinister forces at work in history and in modern life that threaten *all* men, not only Jews'.[12]

This claim is clearly a hostage to fortune in the Holocaust-as-metaphor stakes. Styron's insistence on the factual accuracy of his story actually increases the impression that he sees the matter metaphorically. He asserts that 'it minimizes the evil of the Nazi organization and desecration of life to see it only as a fulfillment of Nazi anti-Semitism. ... To say that only Jews suffered is simply to tell a historical lie', as 'vast numbers of Gentiles shared in the same perdition visited upon the Jews' – 'For although the unparalleled tragedy of the Jews may have been its most terrible single handiwork, it [Nazi evil] transcended even this ... its ultimate depravity lay in the fact that it was anti-human. Anti-life'.[13] Styron claims that he prefers the term 'Auschwitz experience' to 'Holocaust' because 'I find the latter too parochial for what I was attempting':[14] by which he means that the term 'Holocaust' refers to the Nazis' Jewish victims alone. When the narrator requires a general term he uses one like 'The Nazi concentration camps' (288).[15] This standpoint seems self-contradictory if we consider the fact that the material Styron omitted as too unassimilable for a fictional form was precisely the experience of Jewish prisoners in Auschwitz-Birkenau. In response to Styron's argument, Cynthia Ozick blisteringly asserts that Styron risks 'muddling' historical memories 'by falling into the perils of poesy, which somehow always finds the word "humanity" more palatable than "Jew" '; she insists, too, that 'The Jews were not an instance of Nazi slaughter; they were the purpose and whole reason for it.'[16] Ozick's argument is that describing the suffering of anyone other than a Jewish character is in effect to deny the specificity of the Jewish fate under the Nazis.

Styron's argument is partly formal, as anyone other than a non-Jewish prisoner living on the outskirts of Auschwitz would have exceeded his novelistic boundaries. His conviction that the apparently limited hatred of Jews will spread to consume those who imagine they are exempt and the purveyors of hatred themselves is confirmed in the novel's plot. Sophie falsely imagines that she will be safe from the Nazis as long as they are taken up with their antisemitic activities. Her rabidly antisemitic, pro-German father is none the less taken by the Nazis to Sachsenhausen in one of their first round-ups; he is shot because he is a member of the Polish intelligentsia. The hatred he professed is visited not only upon himself but on his daughter and grandchildren (503). According to this logic of contagious evil, focusing solely on the Jewish dimension of mass murder is, in Styron's words, 'to underestimate dangerously [Nazism's] totalitarian dimension'.[17]

Styron insists that he decided to locate Sophie's Auschwitz experiences away from its 'interior' because he considered it would be an 'infringement' to 'delineate the core of the concentration camp, with its tortures and personal indignities, its unspeakable barbarities'.[18] Styron is basing his comments here about the 'core' of Auschwitz particularly on Olga Lengyel's survivor account of Auschwitz-Birkenau, as well as other texts.[19] The 'interior' and 'core' clearly have an ontological as well as a spatial significance for Styron, who 'deliberately distanced' himself by 'setting all of the action outside of the camp, in the Commandant's house, where the horrors could be registered through Sophie's consciousness as remote – albeit not too remote – sights and smells'.[20] This 'remoteness' is registered by Sophie herself, who looks out of the window of Höss's house at the ramp at Birkenau and sees

> the fragmentary and flickering apparitions which from this vantage point registered only imperfectly, like the grainy shadow-shapes in an antique silent newsreel: a rifle butt raised skyward, dead bodies being yanked from boxcar doors, a papier-mâché human being bullied to the earth.
>
> (348)

Through the narrator's version of her impressions, even for Sophie seeing such events for the first time they already have the look of the newsreel footage by which they will become known. Looking back, she feels remote temporally as well as geographically from genocide. The narrator makes Styron's aesthetic reservations a part of the narrative when he claims rather ineptly that Sophie never described her experience outside the Haus Höss in great detail, 'so I never got from her the sense of the immediacy of living in hell which one obtains from written accounts; yet she obviously had seen hell, felt it, breathed it' (313).

Distance is also added by Stingo's narration of Sophie's story, which alternates between reported speech and third-person narration.[21] This is a very interesting example of a Holocaust novel's parameters being formed by what its author considered 'decent' or possible to portray, comparable to Keneally's decision to represent a 'happy story' centred on a 'good German', and Amis's and Darville's to concentrate on perpetrators rather than victims. Ozick's *The Shawl* is a significant exception to the decision to steer clear of the 'interior' of the Holocaust, whether this means the death camps or a specifically Jewish suffering. Styron has confessed, 'I could never presume to say, "Tadius Ginoufsky woke up one morning in Auschwitz and this is what he thought …". So what I had to deal with at Auschwitz had to be done in this very roundabout way.'[22]

Styron's view of the Nazis' camp system is, like Stingo's, coloured by his southern American roots. As Rosenfeld puts it, he sees the Nazis as totalitarian capitalists who used slave labour on a vast scale rather than as creators of a racial state run according to illogic. An implicit comparison between slave labour in the Nazi camps and that in the United States runs throughout *Sophie's Choice*. However, it remains implicit, and in interviews Styron has been careful to make plain what he sees as the differences. In the text juxtaposition makes it seem that the camps and slavery are being likened, and indeed the latter is used as a yardstick against which to measure other injustices: 'wasn't it in Poland that young, harmless Jewish students were … treated worse than Negroes in Mississippi?' (438). In public utterances Styron sounds self-contradictory;[23] Rosenfeld asserts that 'since he rejects historical explanations of Christian antisemitism as causative, Styron is drawn to the view, set forth by Richard Rubenstein and others of a more Marxian persuasion, that in its essential character Auschwitz was a capitalistic slave society as much as or even more than it was an extermination center'.[24] Styron's view of the death camps as an expression of capitalism at its logical end-point is due in part to his reliance on particular sources, including the work of Bruno Bettelheim.[25] The narrator of *Sophie's Choice* notes that the kind of slavery practised at Auschwitz 'casts a benign light on the old-fashioned plantation slavery even at its most barbaric: this blood-fresh concept was based on the simple but absolute *expendability* of human life' (315).

However, the rhetorical point of such an implicit comparison is to *reduce* the very distance Styron is so keen on maintaining in relation to the details of life in Auschwitz: Stingo as narrator shows how the Holocaust sounds to American ears. (Such a reduction is clear in the narrator's comment: it was not that the Nazis' slave labour enjoyed increased efficiency because of the slaves' expendability, but that a doctrine of expendability included working the victims to death as well as exterminating them.) This is the force of Morris Fink's question, having overheard something Sophie said: ' "What's Oswitch?" ' (287); and Stingo remarks that he had never heard of Höss until he met Sophie (404). These ears can hear echoes of their own historical guilt, as does Stingo, coming from a slave-owning family and living off the belated proceeds of the sale of one of these slaves in horrifying circumstances. This moral contiguity is the counterpart to the disjunctive time-relation Stingo also muses upon when he compares what he was doing in 1943 and what Sophie was doing:

> I had attempted more or less successfully to pinpoint my own activities on the first day of April, 1943, the day when Sophie, entering Auschwitz, fell into the 'slow hands of the living damnation.' … I was able to come up with the absurd fact that on that afternoon, as Sophie first set foot on the railroad platform in Auschwitz, it was a lovely spring morning in Raleigh, North Carolina, where I was gorging myself on bananas.
>
> (290)

The effect of this remark is metafictional, even more so than the overtly extra-fictional citations from George Steiner which accompany it; if the subject of Styron's novel is the Holocaust seen from a distance and through American eyes, then this paragraph represents the efforts of that 'banana-gorging' subject to formulate a different view of history.[26] This is a more interesting way to see *Sophie's Choice*'s relation to its subject than the narrator's own remark, '*Someday I will write about Sophie's life and death, and thereby help demonstrate how absolute evil is never extinguished from the world*' (680). Added to the fact that this sentiment is at odds with the novel's ending, where the American subject enjoys a resurrection and is able to weep for the victims of 'evil', such comments suggest that the narrator is unreliable. This look backwards to revise one's own place in events, by making them part of a fictional narrative, steps right outside the patterns of foreshadowing and backshadowing which we have traced in other novels about the Holocaust in the preceding chapters.

Rudolf Höss, *Commandant of Auschwitz*

Alvin Rosenfeld is of the opinion that Styron has 'relied heavily, and unwisely, on Höss's autobiography, a self-exonerating piece of writing that Höss did in a Polish prison while awaiting execution'.[27] He claims that Styron has been taken in by this self-exoneration, and that the reader is encouraged to think that 'Höss was capable of the tenderest feelings for animals, loved his horse, and could approach loving a woman' and thus to ask, 'Could such a man have been all bad?'[28] Other critics have objected to the 'humanizing' and consequent exoneration of Höss and the novel's other Nazi character, Dr Fritz Jemand von Niemand.

In fact, not only Styron[29] *but also* the narrator have relied upon Höss's autobiography, for very different effects.[30] The narrator cites Höss's writings and both summarizes and quotes extensively from them (200–8), in the manner of a documentary novel like Anatoly Kuznetsov's *Babi Yar* which both uses primary material and identifies it. Styron, however, has picked up other details from Höss's autobiography and either woven them into his novel or used them as the basis for fictional scenes. These quotations and borrowings are not signalled as such, more in the manner of a factional novel like Keneally's *Schindler's List*. This division between narrator and author and their intertextual methods is of more interest than the idea that Styron has had to resort to overt borrowings – not only from Höss but from other texts by George Steiner, Simone Weil and Hannah Arendt with which he is 'in dialogue'[31] – because of a failure of imagination in representing Auschwitz. Rather, Stingo's dialogues allow Styron's constructions to become naturalized within the text. That is, because we read extracts from Höss's autobiography as Stingo quotes them, we are less aware of the other extracts which have been assimilated into the level of plot construction which also includes Stingo.

As for the implication that Styron has been taken in by Höss's attempt at exculpation, it seems rather that the details he has focused on are representative of Höss's 'banal evil'. Such an effect is often striking in Höss's autobiography, *Commandant of Auschwitz*: while responsible for the gassing of over a million people, Höss was able to write without irony of the 'paradise of flowers' which his wife made of her garden at Auschwitz.[32] Equally without irony, the historical Höss writes in his autobiography that if he were plagued by a particular incident – such as, perhaps, the extermination of thousands of Gypsy children in the summer of 1944 – 'I would mount my horse and ride, until I had chased the terrible picture away. Often, at night I would walk through the stables and seek relief among my beloved animals.'[33] It is true that Styron expands this small detail into a romantic portrait of Höss staring longingly out of the attic window at his horse Harlekin, whose freedom he envies (301–2). Styron seems to be drawing here on a much earlier time in Höss's life; in *Commandant of Auschwitz* Höss describes being given a 'coal-black pony' for his seventh birthday: 'my greatest joy was to take my Hans into the great Haardt Forest, where we could be entirely alone together, riding for hour after hour without meeting a soul.'[34] The use of this earlier material, which deals with the year 1907, partakes of backshadowing, as if Styron is describing the older, Auschwitz commandant Höss simply as the logical continuation of his seven-year-old self. Such a view of biography is satirized in Martin Amis's *Time's Arrow*, where notions of fore- and backshadowing are upset by the doubled and backwards narration; but the reader need not allow this to sway their opinion of the Commandant of Auschwitz.[35] Styron embellishes other details from Höss's *Commandant of Auschwitz* in ways which more obviously make Höss unsympathetic; for instance, in his autobiography Höss strongly implies that his wife knew nothing of what his work involved, yet in the novel even his young daughter Emmi not only knows very well what Auschwitz means but takes a spiteful pleasure in it. Styron's choice of this kind of detail from Höss's autobiography, rather than the material that is most painful to read, for instance Höss's objective account of the development of gassing as a method of mass murder,[36] may make it look as if he is trying to present Höss in a favourable light. However, it seems that these choices have been made again in order to preserve 'distance', an aesthetic and moral choice that Styron's critics, according to their own logic, should endorse.

None the less, it is true that the narrator's rendering of and commentary on Höss do not always seem to capture the chilling detachment with which the latter writes of his role at Auschwitz. Styron describes how he came across two Auschwitz State Museum publications when he visited the camp, one a collection of writings by the perpetrators – *KL Auschwitz Seen by the SS* – and one by the victims – *Amidst a Nightmare of Crime: Notes of Prisoners of Sonderkommando Found in Auschwitz*. The parts of Höss's autobiography describing his time at Auschwitz are included in the former, and the way Styron has used this text is very revealing about the function and construction of Auschwitz in his novel.[37] Although Rosenfeld is right to call Höss's autobiography 'self-exonerating', Jerzy Rawicz, the author of the foreword to *KL Auschwitz* and a former prisoner of Auschwitz, argues that partly for this reason the document has great historical value: 'If it were possible for [Höss] to do any good before being hanged at Auschwitz, he did so by writing his autobiography, so insolubly connected with the history of mass murder.' Höss has inadvertently revealed truths about the camp, his fellow SS and himself, and it is this aspect of Höss's writing that seems to have attracted Styron. Rawicz comments on the fact that while Höss remained unmoved by the gassing of over a million people (he actually says 'millions', and in interviews Styron has followed this old estimate), 'he was indignant' when SS men and women pilfered the belongings of the dead. Höss claims to be above such corruption but Rawicz notes that 'several freight cars were needed to transport all kinds of property accumulated by this family' when Höss was transferred to Berlin; of the Höss-house salon in *Sophie's Choice* the narrator reports, 'It's not even a museum, thought Sophie, it's a monstrous warehouse' (350).[38]

Styron was obviously also struck by another grotesque detail regarding Höss's corrupt practices which Rawicz cites:

> the prisoners employed in the commandant's house ... had special 'Canadian' underwear assigned to them. This was to make them look decent and above all clean. ... Mrs Höss received the underwear to distribute among the prisoners. But instead of doing so she kept it for herself and gave the prisoners the old, worn underwear, discarded by the family. The Höss family wore the underwear of gassed people, their children wore the clothes of those children who had been murdered by their father.[39]

In *Sophie's Choice*, this detail is the basis of an invented scene in which Wilhelmine, Höss's housekeeper, attempts to seduce Sophie by offering her 'underpants'. As is often the case with his borrowings, Styron sexualizes this historical detail:

> 'Frau Höss likes to give a lot of them to the prisoners. I know you're not issued underwear, and Lotte's been complaining that those uniforms scratch so around the bottom.' Sophie let out her breath. With no chagrin, no shock, not even with revelation, the thought flew through her mind like a sparrow: They're all from dead Jews.
>
> (350)[40]

Wilhelmine's assault also has its origin in another remark in Höss's autobiography suggesting that although corruption was rife he alone remained untainted: 'Like homosexuality among the men, an epidemic of lesbianism was rampant in the women's camp.... Time and again I received reports of intercourse of this sort between supervisors and female prisoners. This in itself indicates the low level of these supervisors.'[41]

Although Höss does not mention it himself, Rawicz reveals that the commandant had an illicit relationship with a woman prisoner, Eleonore Hodys, who became pregnant and was condemned by Höss to death by starvation. Rawicz cites this as another example of Höss's corruption and the falsity of his claim that his motives for his actions at Auschwitz were 'exclusively ideological'.[42] Styron has taken this fact as the legitimating detail for his fiction regarding Sophie, whose seduction of Höss almost succeeds. Styron even has the fictional Höss implicitly refer to the details of the Hodys case when telling Sophie why involvement with her would be impossible: ' "Also, pregnancy here would be out of the question" ' (377).

Styron picks up two particular features of Höss's tone from the autobiography: his idea that 'the victim is guilty, not the murderer',[43] and the related sense that he was a martyr to his job and surrounded by incompetents. The historical Höss writes, 'There were very few nights in Auschwitz when I could sleep undisturbed by urgent telephone calls'; 'My executive officer was a complete halfwit.... Yes, I even had to visit the farms in order to collect straw.'[44] It is hard to credit the historical Höss's own deafness to what he is saying when he complains of not being able to get decent barbed wire because of obstruction from Berlin; in the novel, Höss complains: ' "I can't think what they imagine I've done wrong. Those people in Berlin, they're impossible.... They don't know what it's like to put up with contractors who can't fulfill their schedules, lazy middlemen, suppliers who fall behind" ' (366–7).

At times Styron relies on the subtext to Höss's narrative supplied by Jerzy Rawicz for his narrative borrowings, as for instance in the case of Höss's remark on the presence of radio sets in Auschwitz: 'It was not difficult [for prisoners] to listen to these enemy broadcasts, since there were plenty of wireless sets in Auschwitz. They were listened to even in my own house.'[45] Rawicz adds a very important note that, as is his habit when writing of chances for escape or 'organizing' extra supplies, Höss exaggerates what was open to the prisoners:

> Radio sets were in the possession of the SS camp garrison. The prisoners had no chance of listening in. Only very few could do so thanks to their special circumstances, e.g. of working in the offices of private homes of SS-men, where they would sometimes be left without supervision for a while. If such prisoners dared to listen in to a non-German broadcasting station, they could transmit the acquired news to their closest friends in the utmost secrecy.[46]

The use made of the radio in *Sophie's Choice* follows Rawicz's and not Höss's version. Sophie is charged by Wanda with the task of stealing the radio in Emmi Höss's room for the camp resistance; Emmi, Höss's young daughter, sees Sophie touching the radio, and her accusations of theft are only averted because Sophie faints. The narrator emphasizes that this failure and the fact that she was always too afraid on subsequent occasions to try again constituted one source of Sophie's post-war guilt (524–34).

Styron also draws on the Appendices to *KL Auschwitz*, which are testimonies by two prisoners who worked at Höss's house: the 'Deposition of Stanislaw Dubiel' and the 'Report of Janina Szczurek'. Apparently inspiring the fictional handyman Bronek in *Sophie's Choice*, Dubiel worked as a gardener at the Höss house until the family left Auschwitz (219) – the moment at which Sophie in the novel is returned to the women's barracks at Birkenau.[47] Dubiel reports that there were two Jehovah's Witnesses employed in the house, German women who were strongly anti-Nazi; Styron makes this fact the occasion for Höss in the novel to tell Sophie he has had misgivings about his children being taught by Jehovah's Witnesses, which proved unfounded, and to place antisemitic remarks in their mouths. Dubiel also mentions the 'two Jewish dressmakers' who made clothes for the Höss family out of material taken from Jews, a detail Styron embellishes.[48] Janina Szczurek worked as a dressmaker in the Höss house. She reports an eerie incident in which the Höss children asked her to sew arm-bands for them featuring badges like those worn by the prisoners: one child was a kapo while the others had differently coloured triangles. Although Styron eschews the chance to fictionalize this telling scene, the representation of Emmi Höss in the novel partakes of just such acceptance of her circumstances, for instance when she tells Sophie she preferred Dachau to Auschwitz because it had a better swimming pool (530).[49] It seems that Styron is loath to invent too many details about the Höss's living arrangements, and he relies on the appropriate testimony to people his fictional Höss-house with servants – just as he relied on Höss's autobiography to construct a fictive Höss, and on Olga Lengyel's survivor testimony for Sophie's experience.

Styron relies on Höss's own words for the scene in which Sophie's effort to cash in on a shared antisemitism fails dismally.[50] In his autobiography, Höss declares, 'I was opposed to *Der Stürmer*, Streicher's anti-Semitic weekly, because of the disgusting sensationalism with which it played on people's basest instincts. Then, too, there was its perpetual and often savagely pornographic emphasis on sex.'[51] In *Sophie's Choice*, given a fictional Höss based on these sentiments, Sophie tries quite the wrong tack when she tells an invented story about a Jew raping her sister, prefacing it with stylized Nazi discourse – the narrator emphasizes several times that Sophie is 'lying' – that is still remarkably ugly to read:

> 'The sexual profligacy of Jews is well known, one of their ugliest traits. My father, before he met an unfortunate accident [being shot by the Nazis at Sachsenhausen!] … my father was a great admirer of Julius Streicher for this reason – he applauded the way in which Herr Streicher has satirized so instructively this degenerate trait in the Jewish character.'
>
> (370)

Styron's Höss replies angrily that this is 'hogwash': ' "I loathe Streicher's pornographic garbage." ' Much of what the fictional Höss adds in this interchange also shows Styron's reliance on the autobiography. Höss wishes Streicher had portrayed Jews 'as they really are – bent upon monopolizing and dominating the world economy, poisoning morality and culture' (372), and adds that the antisemitic pamphlet Sophie offers as her credentials proves nothing, 'Only that you despise Jews. That does not impress me, inasmuch as it seems to me a very widespread sentiment'; this echoes the historical Höss's comment that the Nazis' antisemitism is not new: 'It had always existed all over the world, but only came into the limelight when the Jews pushed themselves forward too much in their quest for power, and when their evil machinations became too much for the general public to stomach.'[52]

Styron's use of his source, Höss's *Commandant of Auschwitz*, thus does unusual double duty: it is the subject of the text's *énonciation* and its *énoncé*, that is, of both the narration and the action. Höss's autobiography is used in *Sophie's Choice* in a factional and a documentary way at different moments: the former in the sections where Höss is a fictional character, the latter where he is the author of a historical text which Stingo has been reading and quotes from. The use of Höss's autobiography has been judged as if it were straightforward by Styron's critics, but its place within the narration of *Sophie's Choice* is complex and dialogic. The older Stingo – no longer so named, but we do not learn his current one[53] – provides a chastening perspective on his former self in sexual, historical and literary ways. It is the narrator, not the character, who has extensive historical knowledge and has read widely on the Holocaust. We can even include among his reading Höss's autobiography, as the narrator recommends both *Commandant of Auschwitz* and the compilation in which an extract from the latter appears, *KL Auschwitz Seen by the SS* (200); at first sight, it looks as if this reading is the result of the narrator's knowledge of Höss through Sophie, but of course both Sophie and Höss in the novel are the *products* of the reading. Any pretensions the novel might have had to being Styron's autobiography are thus disrupted by Höss's.

In various interviews Styron has noted that Höss's was not the only eye-witness account of Auschwitz that he drew on for his 'distanced' view, and Sophie's memories are a composite of Höss's words and those of *survivors* – a fact ignored by his critics. Styron says that what he has done is

> merely to suggest the horror of the place by recording in almost documentary way certain points, some of the recorded statements made by the victims, and some of the statements and diaries of the SS men that ran the camp.[54]

However, part of the reason why the Höss component is so eagerly seized upon is that it is the only Holocaust-related text credited on the copyright page of Styron's novel. This is similar to the case of *The White Hotel*, in which D.M. Thomas credited Freud more clearly than Anatoli Kuznetsov. In Styron's case no direct quotations have been made from any text other than Höss's *Commandant of Auschwitz*, which must be the ostensible reason for this omission.

'Someone from no-one'

While the fictional Höss in Styron's novel has been criticized on account of its historical origins, the other significant Nazi character, Dr Fritz Jemand von

Niemand, has been criticized because of his fictional origins. It is therefore the narrator, rather than Styron, at whom uneasiness about this figure should be directed.[55] Critical unease focuses on the way Stingo handles his fictionalized Nazi doctor, starting with the latter's invented name, which means 'Someone from no-one'. The issue is complicated by the fact that it is the older Stingo, not the implied author, who is responsible for von Niemand's name:

> Sophie did not know his name then, nor did she ever see him again. I have christened him Fritz Jemand von Niemand because it seems as good a name as any for an SS doctor – for one who appeared to Sophie as if from nowhere and vanished likewise forever from her sight, yet who left a few interesting traces of himself behind.
>
> (639)

For instance, Alvin Rosenfeld complains that describing what von Niemand does as 'the handiwork of a Nobody' 'is all but to dismiss' it.[56] This is quite clearly based on a misreading by Rosenfeld of the narrator's emphasis: the point about the doctor is that he is not no one but *some*one, who appeared 'as if from nowhere'. In this description von Niemand resembles a principle of apparent narrative choice which is no choice at all.[57]

The split between Stingo and Styron is both affirmed and elided in the overdetermined creation of von Niemand: it can be ascribed to both the narrator and the author in differing ways. As with the Höss autobiography, the older Stingo's admission of textual intervention allows the event to be naturalized into the text.[58] The narrator's comments on von Niemand strike an uncomfortable note, as he both over-estimates von Niemand's retention of conventional morality and under-estimates his role on the ramp:

> Since Sophie told me this I have brooded often upon the enigma of Dr Jemand von Niemand. At the very least he was a maverick, a sport; surely what he made Sophie do could not have been in the SS manual of regulations.... And what, in the private misery of his heart, I think he most intensely lusted to do was to inflict upon Sophie, or someone like her – some tender and perishable Christian – a totally unpardonable sin. It is precisely because he had yearned with such passion to commit this terrible sin that I believe that the doctor was exceptional, perhaps unique, among his fellow SS automata: if he was not a good man or a bad man, he still retained a potential capacity for goodness, as well as evil, and his strivings were essentially religious.
>
> (644)[59]

It is not clear that we can ascribe this unsubstantiated musing, with its trademark meandering, overblown style and wayward analysis, to the older Stingo alone, as the novel as a whole is written this way: is it all a stylization designed to reveal narratorial self-delusion?[60] On the other hand, the critic William Heath paints such a black portrait of Stingo, as a would-be rapist with homicidal tendencies, that he finds the inappropriately humanized portraits of Höss and von Niemand to be no surprise: Stingo's 'explanations for the feelings and motivations of these two important Nazis' are 'remarkably at odds with his narrative dramatization of them', and Stingo is 'more interested in the motives of the doctor than the death of Sophie's child'.[61] While this is certainly the case, Heath's argument veers between treating Stingo as a narrative effect, who can tell a good story but not interpret it convincingly, and as a real person who should be taken to task for his egotistical narration.

It is as if the results of Styron's research into SS and survivor testimony on the subject of Nazi doctors work against the narrator's fictional needs. The same tension can be seen in the decision to have Sophie's bid to emulate Eleonore Hodys fail. To have had her succeed would have greatly strained credulity and opened Styron to the charge of exploitative writing; and would have involved Styron in precisely the area he was avoiding – the 'core' of Auschwitz – as the details of Hodys's fate show. In the same way, the bleak truth about the Nazi doctors – that, in Robert Jay Lifton's terms, they had entirely split off any religious or moral sense from their camp personae – is too much for the novel to handle, but the trace of this truth that remains is sensationalist and hard to swallow.

The narrator's speculations about the religious origins of von Niemand's ramp atrocity are misplaced and unlikely.[62] The elder Stingo continues his speculations by claiming that von Niemand's drunkenness was anomalous: 'All that we can deduce from the record indicates that in the pursuit of their jobs SS officers, including doctors, were almost monkish in their decorum, sobriety and devotion to the rules' (644). We might wonder whether it is the narrator who has misread those texts which actually state the opposite: that infringements of the rules were widespread, and drunkenness an essential part of their fitting in.[63] Wilful misreading on the elder Stingo's part seems to be the only way to account for one of the narrator's final speculations about von Niemand:

> It may be hard to believe, but the vastness and complexity of Auschwitz permitted some benign medical work as well as the unspeakable experiments which – given the assumption that Dr von Niemand was a man of some sensibility – he would have shunned.
>
> (646)

Yet it does not seem that we are meant to dismiss this humanist sentiment; this is not an implicitly double-voiced utterance with an undeclared second voice suggesting the opposite view. On the contrary, we are meant to trust the narratorial voice in order to believe Sophie's story. Such errors must be Styron's, whose different sources are misleading him. In Lengyel's *Five Chimneys* it is clear that the only restorative medicine practised was managed by prisoner-doctors,[64] whose infirmaries had woefully inadequate supplies and were constantly subject to 'selections' for the gas chambers. Lengyel goes out of her way to indicate that even increasing scientific knowledge could not be argued in support of the horrifying 'experiments' carried out at Auschwitz-Birkenau: 'But there was no scientific benefit. Human beings were sacrificed by the hundreds of thousands, and that was all.'[65] In his introduction to *KL Auschwitz* Jerzy Rawicz describes Dr Johann Kremer's habit of murdering starving prisoners in order to acquire 'fresh samples' of particular organs as 'a really striking proof of the degeneration of science in the Third Reich'.[66]

Imperfectly integrated intertextuality is at the root of all details of the inadequate commentary on von Niemand. Styron seems to have relied on some historical accounts for the fictional portrait of von Niemand, probably a composite of Kremer, whose reminiscences appear alongside Höss's in *KL Auschwitz*, and Dr Fritz Klein, the SS doctor described by Olga Lengyel in *Five Chimneys*, with whom von Niemand shares a first name.[67] Rawicz, in his introduction to the former text, describes Kremer's activities at Auschwitz, which ally him with the fictional von Niemand: 'The physician's finger pointed out those who were to be led straight to the gas chambers, and decided who was to be directed to the camp, thus cooperating in the process of extermination.'[68] However, these sources conflict with Styron's literary interests. It is as if Styron's nostalgia for earlier portrayals of evil-doing has pushed him in the transcendent direction he takes when describing von Niemand and away from anything like a banality of evil. The narrator's last word on von Niemand is: 'All of his depravity had been enacted in a vacuum of sinless and businesslike godlessness, while his soul thirsted for beatitude' (646). This is very different from and less convincing than the construction of Tod Friendly, the Nazi doctor in Amis's *Time's Arrow*, who is shown to be precisely cynical and materially minded, while his 'soul', far from 'thirsting for beatitude', is radically split from his body and affects only to have been obeying orders.

The critic Robert Franciosi suggests that Styron must have had in mind when constructing von Niemand such literary forebears as 'Milton's Satan, Goethe's Mephistopheles, Byron's Manfred, even Dostoevsky's Raskolnikov', precursors which also inform the representations of Nazi doctors in Ira Levin's *The Boys from Brazil* and Rolf Hochhuth's *The Deputy*.[69] As Stingo is reading *Crime and Punishment* in 1947, this is not surprising; though again it indicates a great contiguity between the young character and the older narrator. Franciosi argues that Styron has ignored Rubenstein's description of 'bureaucratic domination' in the book to which Styron himself wrote a foreword, *The Cunning of History: The Holocaust and the American Future*[70] (John Lang notes that the older narrator 'oddly' misquotes the book's subtitle as 'Mass Death and the American Future': given the author's sentiments about the term 'Holocaust', this may not be so odd),[71] and adds: 'Styron abets our deep-seated need to obscure such evil acts as products of passionate insanity, rather than dispassionate banality, particularly when the perpetrator represents the rational, well-educated, professional world of lawyers, scientists, teachers, or physicians.'[72] Although von Niemand is not as 'passionately insane' as Steven Spielberg's filmic Amon Goeth, implying that you must be mad to be a Nazi, he is not convincingly 'dispassionate' either.

Olga Lengyel, *Five Chimneys*

Styron notes on several occasions that his novel was affected by reading Olga Lengyel's survivor testimony, *Five Chimneys*. As she testifies, in 1944 Lengyel, her husband, parents and two sons were deported to Auschwitz from Cluj, formerly the capital of Transylvania but part of Hungary after 1940. She alone of her family group survived. Lengyel's testimony concerns the 'core' of Auschwitz which Styron has not attempted to fictionalize: imprisoned in Birkenau, she survived through luck – on several occasions missing death by a hair's-breadth – and because she enjoyed slightly better conditions due to her work as a prisoner doctor.

Although Lengyel's experiences make her text very different from the part of Sophie's Auschwitz experience we read in Styron's novel, there are some features of Lengyel's testimony which have clearly influenced Styron's construction of the fictional character. For instance, Lengyel's husband was Jewish but she was Christian. One might therefore think that this explains something of Styron's 'de-judaizing' the Holocaust, as Lengyel suffered alongside Jews without being one; but as late as 1997 Styron assumed that she *was* Jewish.[73] What is significant about this error is that it means Styron read this account of Auschwitz-Birkenau believing it to be from a Jewish perspective, although no trace of such a perspective exists.[74] Real differences between different experiences are thus elided, as confirmed by Styron's protestations that despite the 'unique' Jewish experience at Auschwitz 'others were oppressed, however, and agonizingly so'.[75] If Styron thought Lengyel's a typical account of Jewish experience in Auschwitz, that explains why he appears puzzled by critics' continued insistence on the distinctiveness of the Jewish fate, for instance Alvin Rosenfeld: 'The extent of the dying and the motives behind the deaths were not equivalent, though, and it simply makes no sense to add up all the corpses without distinction.'[76] Of course it is appropriate to have relied on a testimony by a non-Jewish woman as the basis of a fictional non-Jewish woman's experience if one knows that is what it is; Styron has unwittingly put into Sophie's mouth words about her non-Jewishness which Lengyel might well have uttered herself.

The main element Styron has taken from *Five Chimneys* is Lengyel's experience at the ramp on arrival at Auschwitz.[77] Lengyel begins her testimony with the potent Catholic incantation, '*Mea culpa*, my fault, *mea maxima culpa!*',[78] and in *Sophie's Choice* Sophie is similarly guilt personified. Sophie, as a non-Jew, was offered a choice between her children, but Lengyel unknowingly made decisions which tragically resulted in the immediate gassing of her parents and sons:

> I cannot acquit myself of the charge that I am, in part, responsible for the destruction of my own parents and my two young sons. The world

understands that I could not have known, but in my heart the terrible feeling persists that I could have, I might have, saved them.[79]

The scene of 'choosing' described by Lengyel makes clear what Styron was struck by in her testimony and what different effects he sought for his novel. Lengyel calls what happened to her at the ramp 'my second terrible error', the first having been her insistence on accompanying her husband from Cluj when he received a deportation order. Lengyel narrates the scene of 'choice' at the beginning of her account in accordance with its chronological structure; unlike Styron's narrative choices regarding Sophie, she clearly feels she must tell the most painful tale first. At the ramp, Lengyel believed the words of an SS officer who claimed that 'the old and very young would be cared for' and that that was why they were being separated off to the left – in fact they were bound for Birkenau:

> Our turn came. My mother, my sons and I stepped before the 'selectors'. … The selector waved my mother and myself to the adult group. He classed my younger son Thomas with the children and aged, which was to mean immediate extermination. He hesitated before Arvad, my older son.
>
> My heart thumped violently. This officer, a large dark man who wore glasses, seemed to be trying to act fairly. Later I learned that he was Dr. Fritz Klein, the 'Chief Selector'. 'This boy must be more than twelve,' he remarked to me.
>
> 'No,' I protested.
>
> The truth was that Arvad was not quite twelve, and I could have said so. He was big for his age, but I wanted to spare him from labours that might prove too arduous for him.
>
> 'Very well,' Klein agreed amiably. 'To the left!'
>
> I had persuaded my mother that she should follow the children and take care of them. At her age she had a right to the treatment accorded to the elderly and there would be someone to look after Arvad and Thomas.
>
> 'My mother would like to remain with the children,' I said.
>
> 'Very well,' he again acquiesced. … 'And in several weeks you'll all be reunited,' another officer added, with a smile. 'Next!'
>
> How should I have known. I had spared them from hard work, but I had condemned Arvad and my mother to death in the gas chambers.[80]

Lengyel's account of the ramp is told with a mixture of temporal effects: the irony of ignorance – 'she had a right to the treatment accorded to the elderly' – contrasts with the irony of retrospective knowledge – 'which was to mean immediate extermination'. In *Sophie's Choice*, everything is made much starker. Sophie knows full well that death by gassing awaits the unlucky; the choice she must make is between a boy and a girl;[81] and she has a significant conversation with Dr Fritz Jemand von Niemand about her Polishness, her Christian faith, and the fact that he finds her attractive (638–43). The changes Styron makes to

Lengyel's account suggest he felt that at every stage Sophie's experience must be clearly dramatized and moralized. The ambiguity, anonymity and error which characterize Lengyel's experience – and make it so striking – are absent.[82]

There are similarities here with the narrator's obvious clinging to a familiar Manichaean way of interpreting von Niemand's actions – 'he still retained a potential capacity for goodness, as well as evil'. Styron seems to have been moved in this direction by some hints given by Lengyel later in her account that Dr Klein sometimes appeared taken aback by particular excesses, although this was not inspired by anything as grand as 'religious' or suffering a 'private misery'. For instance, Lengyel witnesses Klein saving thirty-one of the 315 victims of a particularly brutal selection: 'Dr Klein was aroused to a rare gesture of humanity – for an S.S.'; and later she adds, 'I must say that [Klein] was less sadistic than his colleagues. I had the impression that whatever he did, he too, was a victim of circumstance. *Perhaps he had a conscience*. Anyway, he was the only S.S. butcher from whom I saw any humane reactions toward the deportees.'[83] However, Lengyel acknowledges on the same page that Klein may just be exhibiting the banality of evil: 'What sentiment caused such a reaction? Pity? Or was it simply indignation at the slovenly attitude of the guards?': this is after all the man who allowed her mother and son to go to the gas chambers. It seems that again Styron has either taken only those parts of Lengyel's text which fit his plot, or that the conflict between the ambiguity of her rendering of Dr Klein and his own literary conception of an evil character has not been resolved.

Styron describes Sophie's choice on the ramp as 'a metaphor for the most horrible, tyrannical despotism in history, that this was a new form of evil'; and when describing what happened to Lengyel he claims that, 'For me, this transaction, with its imposition of guilt past bearing, told more about the essential evil of Auschwitz than any of its most soulless physical cruelties.'[84] This is a very revealing comment. One might argue that Styron's emphasis on guilt betrays his Christian view of events, and Lengyel's (Christian) testimony of course also begins, '*mea culpa*'. 'Guilt' is also a term used of and by survivors, but in a rather different sense: it is not theological but material.

Styron's avoidance of anything like banal evil in von Niemand's case marks a significant divergence from one of his sources, *KL Auschwitz*, in which the diary of Johann Paul Kremer, a doctor who assisted at Auschwitz-Birkenau for three months in 1942, appears to be the epitome of incorporating atrocities into everyday life.[85] Kremer laments the death of his canary Hännschen, lists in detail the meals consumed in the Waffen-SS clubhouse, and is upset at his brother-in-law's money-grabbing habits, in between noting how many 'special actions', that is, gassings, he attended – at which he was something like a 'Chief Selector'.[86] Kremer appears hardly to have acknowledged the meaning of his own actions, and is puzzled that the American occupation forces in Münster decide to arrest him in 1945.

Styron chooses what seems like the central event of Lengyel's narrative – the effort to save her family which resulted in their destruction – yet cannot incorporate the rest of her description of the 'core' of Auschwitz into his novel. The other material he does use is at the level of individual detail, abstracted from its 'core' context. At this level Styron's borrowings include the slit in Lengyel's boot where she hid poison,[87] which in the novel becomes the place where Sophie, ironically enough, hides her father's antisemitic tract (369). Lengyel describes how the Auschwitz barbers 'were in such haste that they left irregular tufts on the skulls, as though they deliberately sought to make us look ridiculous' (31), which becomes Sophie's 'ludicrous frizzy locks, growing back in unsightly clumps after having been shorn to the roots' (307); Lengyel's comment on the toll taken on teeth and gums (39) may be the basis in the novel for Sophie's much-vaunted false teeth.[88] An incident Lengyel records links the gift of a shawl for her head from Tadek, another prisoner, with unwanted sexual advances: Tadek says to her, ' "It's a strange thing, even though you have no hair and are dressed in rags, there is something very desirable about you" ',[89] which is the source of Sophie's consciousness of her appearance in the plan to seduce Höss. The latter compliments her on her 'kerchief', and the narrator notes that 'only those prisoners fortunate enough to work at Haus Höss were ever permitted thus to secrete the degrading baldness' (306–7).

Lengyel describes how certain ranks of prisoner who did not have to eat the camp food continued to menstruate, both of which Sophie does at Höss's house. Lengyel describes in detail the sadism and sexual appetites of 'the beautiful' Irma Griese,[90] to whom Nathan cruelly likens Sophie on several occasions. While Griese only exists as an insult in *Sophie's Choice*, as she belongs to the 'core' of Auschwitz which is not represented, the ironic contrast between her beauty and her cruelty is transposed to the fictional housekeeper Wilhelmine. This is what Lengyel says of Griese:

> It may seem strange to repeat it so often, but [Griese] was exceptionally beautiful. Her beauty was so effective that even though her daily visits meant roll call and selections for the gas chambers, the internees were completely entranced.... Were a novelist to compose such a scene, his readers would accuse him of the wildest imagination. But pages from real life are often more horrible than those in novels.[91]

This is from *Sophie's Choice*:

> 'If you ever write about this, Stingo, just say that this Wilhelmine was the only beautiful woman I ever saw – no, she was not beautiful really, but good-looking with these hard good looks that some streetwalkers have – the only good-looking woman that the evil inside her had caused this absolute ugliness.'

(349)

In both passages, the already-fictive nature of the phenomenon of a beautiful yet murderous woman is emphasized. In Lengyel's account this is part of the common truth-assertion that reality is stranger than fiction; in *Sophie's Choice* it is part of a different kind of verisimilitude, appearing to prop up the impression of a factuality we do not credit at this point in the narrative. It is as if the denial of fictiveness in Lengyel's work inspired Styron to include a version of this passage in his fiction; again he has made its troubling ambiguity into something much more clear-cut, again 'Manichean', to use the narrator's own term (349). In *Sophie's Choice* the beautiful but 'mean' Wilhelmine is actually ugly; in Lengyel's *Five Chimneys* Griese, as an SS officer in charge of women's barracks, has much more power and status than the fictional housekeeper, who is also a prisoner, but her looks 'entrance' even her victims.

Lengyel describes an uncanny encounter with a certain Mr Capezius, whom she had known before the war when he was a director of the German Bayer Company in Transylvania, later 'Hauptsturmfuehrer at Birkenau and the powerful head of the pharmaceutical depots of the camps in the area'; he is clearly the basis for the much more involved coincidence of Sophie seeing her father's friend the Nazi industrialist Dürrfeld in Höss's company at Auschwitz.[92] As in the case of Lengyel's encounter with Klein at the ramp, Styron significantly sexualizes the fictional version of Sophie's meeting.[93] Finally, Lengyel describes the 'quick and cheap' method chosen by the Nazis to get rid of children interned at Birkenau in December 1944, in which she had to participate:

> In the next few minutes, with neither soap nor towels, we had to 'bathe' the children in the icy water [of the showers]. We could not dry them. We put their rags back on their poor dripping bodies and sent them into the usual columns – to wait. That was the device which the ingenious Germans employed to 'solve' the children's problem, the problem of the innocents of Birkenau. ... Few of the children of Birkenau survived that roll call. Those who did were to fall under the blows of the German cudgels. And they were mostly 'Aryans', too; but Polish, and therefore not of the 'master race'.[94]

In *Sophie's Choice*, Sophie hears of a very similar event and decides that it is most likely that her son Jan – an 'Aryan' but also Polish – died in that manner. She tells Stingo, ' "So in the freezing cold [the SS] marched the children down to the river and made them take off their clothes and soak them in the water as if they were washing them, and then made them put on these wet clothes again.... They died of exposure and pneumonia, very fast. I think Jan must have been among them ..." ' (655). Although the outline of the atrocity from Lengyel's book is preserved in Styron's fictional version, particularly the detail about the children being Polish, the most disturbing aspect of it – that Lengyel and her fellow prisoner-doctors were made to kill the children while the SS stood by – vanishes in Sophie's account. This is partly because of the way the event is narrated, but also because once more Styron has succumbed to a simplifying impulse: it is much clearer morally and narratively to attribute responsibility for Jan's horrible death directly to the SS.

In all these instances, Styron has borrowed details from Lengyel's account to construct something of the mental and physical experience of Auschwitz, and patched together a fictional female form from them. His is often a jackdaw technique: he borrows small eye-catching details from his various sources and transplants them to a new setting where they may not always fit – hence some of the jarring effects we have noted.[95] Styron has reversed some of Lengyel's attributes in constructing his fictional heroine. While Lengyel's resistance activities give her a reason to live,[96] Sophie at first refuses to get involved in the resistance on account of her children and then fails in her mission when she does join. The same kind of alteration is made to Lengyel's encounters with Dr Klein at the ramp, Capezius and Tadek in the camp. In Lengyel's account these are either not sexual encounters, or Lengyel is unwilling that they should be. In the fictional case of Sophie, as Rosenfeld and others point out, every man she meets responds sexually to her, and Dr von Niemand is no exception; neither is Höss or Dürrfeld. Styron turned Lengyel's 'choice' into a terrible but recognizable moral dilemma, rather than the kind of guilt-inducing action taken unwittingly in confusing circumstances and which produces what Lawrence Langer calls 'ruined memory' in his discussion of a similar case.[97] The same is true of Sophie's encounters with men; it is as if Styron feels he cannot afford to omit from his novel standard features such as choice, the battle between good and evil, and sexual desire, even when treating a subject like Auschwitz. The form of Styron's novel has not attempted to imitate its subject; rather, he has altered the ambiguous, inconclusive events from his source *Five Chimneys* and turned them into more traditional narrative fare.

According to Styron, the origin of Sophie's two stories – the first in which she tells Stingo that her beloved father helped shelter Jews during the war, the second in which she admits that both her husband and father were rabidly antisemitic and that she felt no affection for either of them – is rather different, although it testifies once more to Styron's urge to provide a recognizable moral narrative for his text. Its morality is not affected by the fact that it apparently underwent a reversal mid-way through. Styron claims that he realized Sophie, his fictional character, was lying about her father after his visit to Auschwitz during which he amassed his collection of SS accounts of the camp: 'when I returned home … I had an amazing revelation.… *The girl's a liar*', as he put it in an interview.[98]

Holocaust girls

As a fictional character, Sophie's discursive origins lie in a variety of texts, especially Lengyel's *Five Chimneys*. The older Stingo's representation of Sophie's voice also takes several different forms. For its most direct representation the narrator uses reported speech, which shades into various kinds of third-person narration and free indirect discourse. Sophie's voice sometimes sounds out within the third-person narration, for instance: 'Then, blinking awake with a feeling in which sorrow and cheer were curiously commingled, she would say to herself: You are not in Cracow now, Zosia, you are in America' (122). Like the particular arrangement of tenses in *Schindler's List*, which showed the buried presence of oral testimony, these traces of first-person utterance by Sophie within the narrator's discourse are reminders of where his story comes from. Occasionally an image of Sophie's voice, rather than just its formal trace, is present, as the use of her pet-name 'Zosia' in the quotation above shows; for example: 'her distress ... pushed her back toward the cauchemar, the nightmare from she was ... trying to retreat' (127); and, particularly strikingly, 'Kiss [Wilhelmine's] ass, Lotte advised Sophie, lick her ass good and you won't have no trouble' (340). Here, the narrator reports what Stingo heard Sophie tell of another person's utterance, and it is Sophie's distinctive grammatical errors which are preserved. Verisimilitude and actual control of the narrative by a narrator thus coexist.[99]

What this coexistence actually conveys, of course, is that this is a fiction in which Sophie and all her doings are invented (in contrast to *Schindler's List*). This is especially clear in the recreation – which is actually creation – of Sophie first meeting Nathan, where the dialogue appears to be the narrator's laborious reconstruction based on what Sophie told his younger self, as in the following conversation about Sophie's iron deficiency:

> 'It's one of the easiest things in the world to treat, once you've got it nailed down.'
> 'Nail down?'
> 'Once you understand what the trouble is. It's a very simple thing to cure.'
>
> (185)

This exchange ostensibly represents the transformation of Sophie's words ('And then I misunderstood a phrase ...') into the older narrator's dramatized version. The effect which Styron said he was aiming for – 'when I go into the third person and start describing what happened to Sophie the reader will believe it' – has borne fruit. Sophie's lying has the same effect; when the narrator points out that she is telling the truth this time, it seems doubly real: 'And, dear reader, at least then I knew she was not lying ...' (380).

Alvin Rosenfeld remarks on a phenomenon other critics have also noted, that the representation of Sophie in Styron's novel as a universal object of male desire suggests 'the desirability of the Mutilated Woman' and places *Sophie's Choice* under the rubric of one of three new artistic categories: the 'Erotics of Auschwitz', 'an unwitting spoof' of a Holocaust novel, or, worst of all, 'a new Southern Gothic Novel'.[100] Rosenfeld persuasively insists that 'Sophie *is* choice', as the stream of sexual invitations she receives suggests, 'but her desires bring her to choose Nathan, one of the chosen' – to Stingo's rivalrous chagrin. This is not too far from Styron's own remark that his 'Holocaust protagonist' had to be female not because of his adherence to a particular Holocaust aesthetics, but because she must be faced with a mother's choice at Auschwitz.

Gloria Steinem, in a spirited 1981 review of Styron's novel in *Ms* magazine, sees his triple role of 'author/narrator/protagonist' as one calculated to ensure domination over Sophie in these three realms. She concludes, 'The reader comes away convinced that, if she weren't beautiful and the author [*sic*] hadn't spent a whole summer trying to go to bed with her, he wouldn't have bothered to record her experience at all.'[101] There is certainly some truth in this, as Stingo's repetitively recorded desire for Sophie is integral to the way we hear her narrative: at her moments of greatest vulnerability during the telling of this story Stingo considers taking advantage of her (for instance, just after Nathan has left her for the last time (412)). He consistently likens novel-writing to the bodily: 'I was possessing the heroine of my own novel' (399); 'I'm going to make a *book* out of that slave' (561). Georgiana Colville perceptively notes that Sophie is surrounded by a rhetoric of the artificial, as if being objectified by the Nazis is an effect which lingers on. Joan Smith describes Stingo's fascination with Sophie as 'necrophilia': better even than his dead sweetheart Maria Hunt, Sophie with her 'plasticity' and looking like a death's head without her false teeth, is 'the living dead'. Several critics also note the unreal sound of Stingo's final night with Sophie.[102] Rather than seeing her as 'choosing' to die with Nathan but with Stingo's touch still upon her, it seems that Stingo can say what he likes about her final days as she is no longer there to contradict him.[103]

The episodes concerning the two other women with whom Stingo attempts romantic interaction are narratively and literally uncomfortable to read.[104] Sympathetic critics have attempted to read them, particularly the one concerning Leslie Lapidus, as light relief in a novel about a Holocaust survivor and her deranged lover; or as revelations of how terrible sexual relations were in the late 1940s.[105] Any 'resisting reader', in Judith Fetterley's phrase, will have a hard time finding funny these episodes in which Stingo thinks he will be relieved of his virginity and is disappointed.[106] The metatextual point of the Leslie Lapidus incident is the idea that in American fiction the Southern sensibility is about to be superseded by a Jewish one,[107] an idea which is brought to Stingo's attention by Nathan, who has read Saul Bellow's *Dangling Man* (1963). Stingo at once has a vision of himself as an also-ran on the literary race-track, eating 'the dust of a pounding fast-footed horde of Bellows and Schwartzes and Levys and Mandelbaums' (157), a mixture of real and imagined Jewish writers. The older narrator performs another temporal conjuring trick: he claims to be drawing on his own callow diary of the time (the narrator may have been, but Styron was not: they are invented), but the self-conscious debt of this diary to Philip Roth, unheard of in 1947, is clear. In *Portnoy's Complaint*, for instance, Alex's mother is named Sophie, née Ginsky, a desirable fellow student is called Lenore Lapidus, and he has an uncle named Nate; the entire narrative consists of Alex Portnoy's chronicle of ' "*unearned unhappiness*" ', in Sophie Zawistowska's phrase (177), spoken to his analyst;[108] as if Stingo were Alex, Styron describes Stingo being 'imprisoned in dungeons of masturbation' while Nathan, like Alex, indulges in outdoor sex in New England and Vermont; the text is peppered with the Yiddishisms that Styron coveted; Alex's cousin Heshie is prevented from continuing a relationship with a blonde Polish woman by the intervention of Heshie's father; and even Stingo's frequent comparison of Sophie's behind to a piece of fruit, whether pear or peach, appears to be indebted to Alex's observation that the Monkey's resembles a nectarine.[109] As with the Höss material, the older narrator returns to a past which is actually *constituted* by the author's superior knowledge of what is to come, this time as part of a battle of wits with another author. The most that can be said about this is that it offers the alert reader a metafictional handle on *Sophie's Choice*, although it has provoked caustic comments on Styron's apparent wish to pass for a Jewish writer.[110]

In her memories of Auschwitz Sophie inhabits a version of Primo Levi's 'gray zone' in which the usually clear-cut divisions between good and bad behaviour break down. While the reader must feel with Stingo that Sophie berates herself excessively for her past, she is apparently honest about all kinds of painful decisions she took or was forced into: not only the choice between her two children on the ramp at Birkenau, but her choice not to join the Resistance despite Wanda's insistence (' "I have already made my choice" ', as she puts it), and her final decision to kill herself. The phrase is also used of her rehabilitated life in the United States, where 'The privilege of choice', especially of food, contrasts with earlier privations. The novel's title is doubly ironic, first, morally, in that, as Irving Howe points out (see Chapter 4), acts undertaken in such circumstances are only parodies of choice; and second, narratively, in that the terrible revelation about Sophie's choice is one of many such agonizing choices. Styron speaks of Sophie in terms which combine the moral and narrative dimensions:

> I couldn't just make her a victim. That was very essential to the dynamism of the story. If she was just a pathetic victim she wouldn't be very interesting; but to put her in juxtaposition with the commandant – not really as a collaborator by any means but as a person who in desperation is acting in an unconventional way vis-à-vis the Nazis, trying to masquerade as a collaborator – this would give her a larger dimension.[111]

It might sound as if Sophie's non-Jewishness is thus integral to the 'dynamism' and 'larger dimension' of the novel, since many of the Jews were indeed simply 'pathetic victims' who were gassed at once and got nowhere near the commandant for any kind of bargaining. The irony of the date of Sophie's arrival at Auschwitz seems to have the same force: just three days later the Nazis would no longer be gassing anyone but Jews, who remain unrepresentably outside the story's frame.[112] On the other hand, this is to see Styron's own narrative choices the wrong way round. Having made the decision not to 'convert' Sophie into a Jew and to keep her away from the core of the death camp, Styron is able to represent certain scenes (such as the interior of the Höss house) but has to sacrifice others. Styron's consciousness of having to cut out such plotline potential – again for the reason that it would be 'presumptuous' of him 'to try to re-create life in a concentration camp in any way'[113] – is registered in the small details he has retained from Lengyel's account.

Sophie's Choice is interesting for the ways in which Styron has used historical and intertextual material, and it is these ways which have landed him in critical trouble. Using certain texts only for certain purposes (Lengyel's *Five Chimneys* for the construction of Sophie, Höss's *Commandant of Auschwitz* for the fictional Höss and the camp); using texts several times in differing ways (Höss's autobiography is both quoted by the narrator and used intertextually); imitating the form of autobiography; playing out a literary war; and even misreading intertexts: all these features of the novel have been seized upon as evidence of personal bad faith, historical ignorance and even antisemitism.[115] It is true that the novel has various flaws. The potential for ironizing a particular view of the world through the gap between the younger and older Stingos is not taken up; the interesting idea of how Auschwitz appears to American eyes is often dissipated into sentimentality and melodrama. But paying close attention to the discursive construction of *Sophie's Choice* rather than making instant value judgements reveals the novel to be sometimes aesthetically but not necessarily morally disappointing. The novel's construction is an instructive example of the constraints and leeways of using historical material in a Holocaust fiction.

Chapter 6

Historical polemic

Helen Darville, *The Hand that Signed the Paper*

The 'Demidenko affair' caused a furore in Australia in the mid-1990s, following the publication of Helen Demidenko's novel *The Hand that Signed the Paper* (1994). There were two main issues at stake in this critical and cultural scandal. First, Demidenko claimed that her text was 'faction'. This provoked fury among those who were dismayed by her story of Ukrainians goaded by the Jewish-Bolshevik-inspired famine of the 1930s into eager participation in Holocaust massacres. Second, in August 1995 Demidenko was unmasked as someone quite other than the Ukrainian persona she had assumed since 1992; *The Hand* was actually written by Helen Darville, of Anglo-Saxon extraction. Added to these central features of the scandal were related ones concerning the originality of Darville's work, which turned out to be reliant on historical and literary sources; the text's attempt to 'domesticate' or even 'humanize' the actions of Holocaust perpetrators; and the fact that, while she was masquerading as Demidenko, Darville had won no less than three literary prizes for her novel.

The effects of this saga in Australia were profound (the book is still not available in Britain or the US for legal reasons). An editorial by Helen Daniel in the *Australian Book Review* of March 1996 concluded: 'It seems to me that the cultural aftershocks of the whole affair will continue for some years, undermining our intellectual, moral, racial and cultural assumptions and leaving us collectively shaken.' There was a breakdown in relations between the Jewish and Ukrainian communities in Australia during this time, and the Ukrainians threatened Alan Dershowitz, the Claus von Bulow lawyer, with legal action over a statement he made on the affair while visiting Sydney.[1]

As the different stages of the Demidenko saga emerged, all kinds of scholars and celebrities were drawn into the debate, ranging from Dale Spender and Peter Singer to Thomas Keneally. The historian W.D. Rubinstein said he considered that the novel might be actionable under Australian Racial Vilification legislation. Four books on the scandal were published within six months. The literary critic Ivor Indyk observed, 'There is a whole world at work in this controversy: it is called Australia', while another critic, Peter Craven, claimed that 'Helen Demidenko is us'.[2] Antisemitic letters appeared in national newspapers, and a cartoon was published in the *Australian* depicting the blonde

Demidenko roasting over a Chanukah candelabra, so pilloried was she thought to be by 'the unacceptable face of anti-anti-Semitism'.[3]

This furore is an extreme version of the critical scandals I have examined in connection with Holocaust fiction, as it unites all of the features which occur in other texts – alleged plagiarism, antisemitism, inauthenticity, appropriation, historical revisionism – with some of its own, such as Darville's personal act of masquerade, and the particular politics of literary prize-giving in Australia.[4] Subsidiary but related infringements on the part of the novel were considered to be the representation of the everyday nature of mass murder, and the absence of an authoritative narrator. There is a sliding scale of value-judgement at work here: it begins with negative literary estimates and quickly shades into moral judgement.[5]

'A frightful dose of Demidenko'[6]

The Hand that Signed the Paper was published as the first work of a 24-year-old Australian woman, Helen Demidenko. Her own extra-textual utterances, and obviously her surname, encouraged the idea that this work was a fictionalized autobiography, and that she was telling the secrets of her own immigrant Ukrainian family. She implied that the work was a 'faction', by implication in the Author's Note to the first edition:

> What follows is a work of fiction. The Kovalenko family depicted in this novel has no counterpart in reality. Nonetheless, it would be ridiculous to pretend that this book is unhistorical: I have used historical events and people where necessary throughout the text.
>
> (vi)

This impression was backed up by statements made in public by Demidenko, for instance in a notorious televised debate broadcast in June 1995.[7]

The Hand that Signed the Paper is narrated by a young woman called Fiona Kovalenko; the similarity of her name to Demidenko's acts ambiguously both to suggest and deny a direct autobiographical link. The plot concerns Fiona's uncle Vitaly Kovalenko who is awaiting trial as a war criminal for his part in the Holocaust in the Ukraine, especially the massacre at Babi Yar, the ravine outside Kiev where 34,000 Jews were killed over two days in 1941. He is also shown serving in the Warsaw Ghetto and Treblinka, as a member of the Ukrainian SS. Flashbacks to his pre-war boyhood suggest that in Vitaly's mind the artificially induced Ukrainian Famine of 1930–33, which claimed many thousands of lives, was associated with the presence of 'Jewish Bolsheviks' sent from Moscow to tame the locals. This part of the story is not told by Fiona, but by an impersonal, or at least unidentified, narrator; and a range of other characters offer first-person reminiscences, including Vitaly's sister Kateryna, his first wife Magda, and, through their letters, a bishop and a Soviet commissar's Jewish wife. Back in the present, Vitaly dies in hospital before his trial, leaving Fiona feeling let down by her uncle and by the legal system. The novel concludes with Fiona noting she has written letters to newspapers protesting at the war crimes trials, and that on a visit to present-day Treblinka she admitted to the relation of a victim she met there that she was 'sorry' about her uncle's role in the mass murder.

Helen Demidenko was awarded three major Australian literary prizes for her novel,[8] and became a celebrity: dressed in Ukrainian peasant blouses and sporting long blonde hair, she appeared on chat shows and was widely interviewed about her family history and her writing. Her statements on her forebears ranged from relatively harmless anecdotes – her father, a taxi-driver, drove a battered Valiant 'complete with pink fluffy dice' and could barely read, and at her graduation her family poured vodka over her head – to claiming that almost all of her father's family had been killed in Vinnitsa by 'Jewish Bolsheviks'. The latter tale was supposed to back up the equation between these two groups made by Demidenko throughout her novel.[9]

In August 1995 the Australian journalist David Bentley discovered that Helen Demidenko was the pseudonym of a woman of British descent, Helen Darville, whose mother, Grace Darville, admitted, 'We are Poms'; the family was said to have emigrated from Scunthorpe rather than Vinnitsa.[10] Helen Darville's father was neither a taxi-driver nor illiterate, she had no Ukrainian relations, and her hair was not really blonde.[11] Thus the opinions of certain characters in her book – that the majority of Bolsheviks were Jews, and Jews were responsible for the terrible famine in the Ukraine in the 1930s – were figments of her own imagination, not attributable to the antisemitism of unregenerate real-life Ukrainians. Even more damagingly, it turned out that Darville's imagination was not the only moving force of the book, for she had taken material from various sources, including survivor testimonies quoted in Martin Gilbert's *The Holocaust* (1986) and in S.O. Pidhainy's collection of Ukrainian reports of Soviet atrocities in the 1930s, *The Black Deeds of the Kremlin* (1953).[12]

An uproar in the Australian literary world ensued. Some asserted that an uncritical celebration of ethnic minority (and working-class) culture was to blame, and that Darville would never have won any prizes if she had published the book under her own name.[13] Others scorned the novel as a whitewash of Ukrainian participation in the Holocaust; it returned to the old antisemitic link between Communism and Judaism, and suggested that Ukrainians were simply avenging themselves for what 'Jewish Bolsheviks' had done during the famine. Darville herself, whose mental health was called into question, went into hiding, after calls by critics that she should be stripped of her prizes and sued for breach of copyright. Ironically, as a result of the furore the book became a best-seller in Australia, where it has been reissued under Darville's proper name with credit now given to the other works 'quoted' in her novel.[14]

The connection to the events of the Holocaust which Darville invented for herself was, as her critics noted, extremely important, as it appeared to give her an 'authentic' position from which to speak about the Holocaust. The charge of inauthenticity is one which underlies all the other accusations in the scandal surrounding *The Hand*. Plagiarism is seen to be the logical outcome of inauthenticity because the writer has no other access to what he or she is trying to portray; antisemitism may be the result of clumsiness, or a secret agenda (since these writers are not survivors, anything is possible); and sensationalism has a similar root – that is, the charge that the Holocaust appears in a text merely to symbolize something else, or to gain literary cachet by easy means.

'On the Other Hand'[15]

It is instructive to examine each of the main charges laid against Darville's novel: its inauthenticity, plagiarism, antisemitism and amoral narration. First, 'authenticity' is obviously breached by Darville's assumption of the Demidenko pseudonym. Critics described their reactions to her 'unmasking', ranging from the loss of the frisson which accompanied reading about a family's secrets to increased admiration of the book as an imaginative work. Robert Manne suggested that when she took on the Demidenko persona Helen Darville also took on a discourse of antisemitism, which led her to make certain unwise public pronouncements. In her public apology, published in most Australian newspapers a week after the unmasking, Darville admitted that she had 'said foolish things' while known as Helen Demidenko.[16]

Second, plagiarism is seen as a subsidiary attack on authenticity. The very term 'plagiarism' begs various questions. As is clear even in Darville's case, other terms may be more suitable for different instances of literary borrowing, ranging from allusion to creative adaptation. As Linda Hutcheon points out in an essay on the subject,

> On the one hand, we are dealing with *authorial* intent and with the historical issue of sources and influences; on the other, it is a question of *reader* interpretation whereby invisible sources become signs of plagiarism, and influences yield to 'intertextual' echoes.[17]

In the case of *The Hand*, both *loci* of textual appropriation, in Hutcheon's phrase, are relevant. Darville's statements allow for an overdetermination of the authorial role, while the extreme reactions of critics, readers and plagiarees alike represent the pole of reader interpretation. In Darville's case, plagiarism takes various forms. It seems astonishing that the *nom de plume* Helen Darville chose should be the name of a Ukrainian accomplice in the Babi Yar massacre, which appears in Anatoli Kuznetsov's 'documentary fiction', *Babi Yar*, based on eyewitness accounts. Even more extraordinary is the fact that the passage where this name appears is the exact one D.M. Thomas was accused of plagiarizing in his novel *The White Hotel* (1981) (see Chapter 2).[18] As in Thomas's case, the sections of Darville's novel which were judged to be the most effective turned out to be the plagiarized ones.[19] It is as if the name 'Demidenko' signals both authenticity and, at a deeper level, inauthenticity too. Indeed, as Darville's sternest critic Robert Manne points out, the name Demidenko now appears in bold script in Kuznetsov's text to show that originally (in 1966) the Soviet censor excised it because it revealed Ukrainian participation in the massacre at Babi Yar. This is Kuznetsov's version of part of the story related to him by a survivor, Dina Pronicheva. The words in bold print indicate material restored in later editions of the book:

> A few minutes later she heard a voice calling from above:
>   **'Demidenko!** Come on, start shovelling!'
> There was a clatter of spades and then heavy thuds as the earth and sand landed on the bodies, coming closer and closer until it started falling on Dina herself.
>   **The Ukrainian policemen** up above **were apparently tired after a hard day's work**, too lazy to shovel the earth in properly, and once they had scattered a little in they dropped their shovels and went away.[20]

Even in Kuznetsov's text, the name 'Demidenko' is a complex sign: of a restored textual state, but also of an uncomfortable truth about Ukrainian collaboration with the Nazis. Darville's return to this overdetermined moment may be a part of her project of 'fictional revisionism', as it has been called, based on her unfortunate comment in an interview that she had sought to reassess the image that Jews are victims, everyone else in Europe victimizers.[21] On the other hand, it may be evidence of a trap set to catch the reader who does not recognize the battle for meaning within the signifier 'Demidenko'.

The real counterpart in *The Hand* to D.M. Thomas's appropriation of Kuznetsov is Darville's use of an eyewitness account about the pre-war Ukrainian Famine taken from Pidhainy's collection of eyewitness accounts, *The Black Deeds of the Kremlin*. This is a relatively standard borrowing, used to give a factual backbone to a work of fiction. It is also the method exploited by Martin Amis in *Time's Arrow*, but Darville was unable to get away with it partly because of her earlier act of stealing an identity for herself. Moreover, she also took less trouble to fashion a new aesthetic artefact out of historical material than Amis did with the material he 'borrowed' from Robert Jay Lifton's study, *The Nazi Doctors*. The material in her work looks as if it has been lazily transposed to its new context, with little novelistic amendment; this was also the charge laid against Thomas for his use of Kuznetsov's material. However, even Robert Manne does not spend much time discussing this particular act of appropriation from 'an extremely obscure Ukrainian collection of eye-witness accounts', presumably because it does not appear to have a particular axe to grind. Its status, as Manne's remark suggests, is also historically questionable; it was written for polemical purposes – to draw the world's attention to the Famine and demand justice against its perpetrators – and relies heavily on oral testimony. Susan Moore similarly dismisses Darville's reliance on 'weak (not standard) historical sources', while Fraser terms them 'folk histories'.[22] As we have seen throughout this study, such non-standard sources are more often chosen as the intertexts for Holocaust fiction than standard historical texts, precisely because of their polemical or oral aspects.

The most significant borrowing Darville makes from *The Black Deeds of the Kremlin* is an account by I. Mariupilsky of an incident in Mariupil from 1933, entitled 'The Girl who Begged for Bread', in which a zealous Communist shopkeeper turns away a starving child who, he says, should be out working:

> I saw a farm girl of about 15 years of age, in rags, and with starvation look-ing out of her eyes. She stretched her hand out to everyone who bought bread, asking for a few crumbs. At last she reached the storekeeper. This man must have been some newly arrived stranger who either could not, or would not speak Ukrainian. He began to berate her, said she was too lazy to work on the farm, and hit her outstretched hand with the blunt edge of a knife blade. The girl fell down and lost a crumb of bread she was holding in the other hand. Then the storekeeper stepped closer, kicked the girl and roared:
>
> 'Get up! Go home and get to work!' The girl groaned, stretched out and died. Some on the queue began to weep. The communist storekeeper no-ticed it and threatened: 'Some are getting too sentimental here. It's easy to spot enemies of the people!'[23]

In the version of this incident in *The Hand*, Vitaly relates what happened to the young girl, now his cousin Lara. Although Lara does not die, unlike the girl in the original, the description is not much amended, except to follow Vitaly's simple, ungrammatical diction, and to make Lara's discourse about the incident Christian:

> [Lara] begged next to the people in the bread queue. No one had anything to give, they were all starving as well. Finally she got to the storekeeper, a Russian colonist. She begged at him. He said she was too lazy to work on the farm. He yelled at her, and hit her hand with the knife. Luckily it was blunt. Lara fell down and lost the crumb she had in one hand. Then the storekeeper came out from behind the stall and kicked her, all the while yelling at her to get up, go home, and work.
>
> People in the queue started to cry, and two men pulled her away from the Russian. He said we are soft, and don't want to work for socialism. He said we are enemies of the people. Lara finally came and took my hand. She said … we must just wait and suffer, like it say in the Bible.
>
> (91)

When Darville's publisher, Allen and Unwin, enlisted legal counsel on the matter of copyright the verdict was that postmodern fiction need not document its historical sources.[24] Going as far as literal litigiousness to establish such a critical fact has serious implications for a genre of fiction which is likely to rely on anterior sources. Authors of historically based texts are likely to be caught in a double bind: if they enlist historical material, they may be open to the charge of plagiarism; if they do not, they may be accused of inaccuracy. There are two ways out of this trap: either to signal very clearly where the historical material is taken from, or to blend it with the rest of the novelistic material.

Riemer claims that *The Black Deeds* argues for Jewish complicity in the Famine.[25] However, the opposite seems to be the case: while Pidhainy's anthology lays the blame squarely at the door of the Bolsheviks, Darville has taken details from the text and transformed them into atrocities committed by Jews (although not in the instance cited above). *The Black Deeds* only refers to the perpetrators of the murder and cultural destruction carried out in the Ukraine during the 1930s as 'Bolsheviks', 'the Soviet Russian Government', Muscovites, NKVD chiefs, 'Russian red fascis[ts]' or Russians.[26] Jews are mentioned only extremely infrequently. The one description apparently linking the two groups – 'The personnel of [Horliwka NKVD prison] consisted of ... other agents exclusively of Russian or Jewish origin' – makes nothing of this link, and adds, 'Among the prison guards there may be Ukrainians': that is, Ukrainians were oppressing their own people. Even when a commissar has the kind of surname – Rosenberg, Katsnelson – one imagines Demidenko might have seized upon as evidence for her 'ratio' (see n. 39), no comment is made on this. Kaganovich is never mentioned and all blame is ascribed to Stalin.[27] The 'tragedy of Vynnytsa', at which Demidenko claimed Jewish Bolsheviks had killed her father's family, is described without reference to Jews; the murders were committed by 'Russian police'.[28] Furthermore, Ivan Bahryany, in a chapter called 'I Accuse', notes that many Ukrainians were themselves imprisoned in 'the concentration camps of the Gestapo ... Dachau, Belsen, Buchenwald, Auschwitz':[29] far from seeing the Nazis as liberators, Ukrainians were victimized by the Nazis just as by the Bolsheviks.

It is important to note, though, that reading this book does give a horrifying insight into the Bolshevik treatment of Ukrainians: a mother is nearly shot for allowing her son to call his dog 'Bolshevik' in fun; a locksmith is sent to Siberia for using a method not recommended by the Bolsheviks; poets are exiled for writing in Ukrainian. The book demands publicity and revenge, but the latter is against Russian Communists, not anyone else. As the witness F.D. puts it, 'My wretched childhood and adolescence had planted in me an intense abhorrence of the despicable Soviet-Muscovite imperialism and the infernal NKVD persecutions':[30] the emotion is the one described in *The Hand*, but directed at a different target. *The Black Deeds* uses vocabulary more usually associated with the Nazi era. NKVD prisons are called 'concentration camps', exiles are 'deportees', Ukrainians suffered 'extermination' and 'genocide'. This may explain the impetus behind Darville's shift of the park sign back into the pre-Nazi era, to signal their similarity (see n. 28). The role of *The Black Deeds* – published post-war about the 1930s – in inspiring historical shifts in the novel is borne out by the use of the phrase 'Russian colonists' by one witness, Y.P.; in *The Hand* this phrase becomes 'Russian and Jewish colonists' (13), a rhetorical shift that inspired Manne to explain the meaninglessness of the phrase.[31] In another incident, the witness F.D. describes how a (Bolshevik) policeman took pity on him as the homeless child of an exile: the policeman 'handed me a piece of bread and said in Ukrainian, "Here, take this, you poor wretch." '[32] In *The Hand* this incident has been transmogrified into one where the starving young Evheny is given bread and cheese by an old Jew.

Although there is no evidence to suggest that Darville also read the second volume of *The Black Deeds*,[33] it does include an especially striking example of an event which has an antisemitic variant in *The Hand*. In volume II Natalka Zolotarevich records two incidents, the first told to her by Varka, a starving girl placed on a pile of corpses: the girl was rescued by 'Olga Volkova, the wife of the local Jewish doctor' who 'took care of the child and consequently saved her life'.[34] The other incident concerns the Jewish doctor himself, Moisei Davidovich Fishman, who 'never lost the milk of human kindness during those difficult years, and, instead of carrying out the orders of the authorities … helped the starving populace'.[35] Zolotarevich's testimony is in marked contrast to the incident in *The Hand* where a Jewish doctor, wife of the local commissar, refuses on principle to treat Ukrainian children (15). In conclusion, we can say that Darville has used particular details from *The Black Deeds* but reversed their meaning by the addition of an antisemitic discourse taken from elsewhere in an effort to link two atrocities – the Famine and the Holocaust – and to provide for her Ukrainian characters a motive for mass murder.

However, not all the fictional features of Darville's Demidenko persona were to do with her supposed Ukrainian ancestry – she also claimed to be working class, to have practised law, to be a graphics artist and an expert mathematician: none of these claims was true. Equally, not all the instances of plagiarism in *The Hand that Signed the Paper* were to do with the construction of a factual backbone. In some instances, Darville apparently just coveted a particular image or phrase; debts were traced back by hawk-eyed critics to writers as diverse as Toni Morrison, Robin Morgan, Graham Greene, Thomas Keneally, James Lowell and Patrick White.[36] (Robin Morgan objected to having her book *The Demon Lover: On the Sexuality of Terrorism* used by Darville in this way, although Keneally did not mind the use made of material from his *Gossip from the Forest*. Morgan said it made her feel as if her 'brain had been burgled', and that she would not press charges only because she felt Darville was 'severely ill'.)[37] Again, the brush of inauthenticity tarred Darville's use of these intertexts, a method used by many other modern authors, ranging from to T.S. Eliot to Malcolm Lowry. Also, and more significantly, they deployed their intertexts in an obviously aesthetic, modernist manner, and their subject was not the Holocaust.

Perhaps the most interesting category of this particular act of plagiarism, if that is still the appropriate word, is Darville's *misquotation* of her sources. For instance, at the beginning of *The Hand that Signed the Paper*, which is set in pre-war Soviet Ukraine, a character sees a sign in a city park that reads, 'No Ukrainians and no dogs allowed' (20); this is borrowed from Kuznetsov's account of Kiev ten years on, under Nazi occupation.[38] The shift backwards in time which Darville has effected is primarily rhetorical, to back up the idea that maltreatment of Ukrainians by Jewish Bolsheviks in the 1920s and 1930s was repaid by the enthusiasm of Ukrainians for joining the SS. It could also imply that the Jewish Bolsheviks' treatment of Ukrainians was analogous to, and as racially based as, the Nazis' treatment of Jews. It contributes to the more general telescoping of history in the novel: for instance, the bloody tradition of Ukrainian antisemitism, dating from centuries before the Russian revolution, is barely mentioned. The transposition of the Nazis' racist sign to an earlier era governed by a different ideology gives away such historical telescoping within the text, once we know the origin of the notice, but it was Darville's extra-textual utterances which sealed the impression of questionable motives. She claimed in an interview that there was a clear 'ratio' between the numbers of Jewish commissars present in a certain areas of the Ukraine during the Famine, and numbers of Ukrainian volunteers for death-squads during the war.[39] Within the text itself, however, it is important to notice that the sign banning Ukrainians from the park is part of Evheny Kovalenko's recollections of travelling cross-country after fleeing a Komsomol school, and that it is narrated in free indirect discourse. This is an instance of a voice at least twice removed from what it is describing.

Darville's public pronouncements were clearly misjudged, and obviously at least as fictive as her own novel. The fact that she was speaking in the Demidenko persona is hardly a mitigation. It is more helpful to accept the novel's ambiguous version of events, despite its occasional lapses of consistency and other breaches of textual decorum, and to see Darville's unambiguously biased comments as irrelevant curiosities. If we do not insist upon this separation, then all the historical myths which feature in Darville's novel – that Bolsheviks and Jews were the same people, that they caused the Ukrainian famine, and that the Ukrainians therefore had an 'experiential' reason to murder Jews during the Nazi occupation – must be ascribed to the novel as a whole, or to its author, rather than to its characters. The counter-argument I would use is one also uttered by the copy-editor of the book: ' "How do you depict antisemites if they don't act and speak in an antisemitic way?" '[40]

Another instance of a misquoted source where the locus of sympathy is shifted even more subtly is Darville's use of a horrifying event from Alexander Donat's eyewitness account of the Warsaw Ghetto, quoted in Martin Gilbert's *The Holocaust*. Donat describes how a father waiting to board a death-train at the Umschlagplatz hid his baby in his knapsack. The baby cried, a Ukrainian guard bayoneted it and then shot the father; Donat reports, 'Mercifully, the Ukrainian's bullet put an end to the father's ordeal then and there.' In the version in *The Hand that Signed the Paper*, the incident is seen through the eyes of Vitaly

Kovalenko, who is the 'Ukrainian guard' of Donat's account. The idea of 'mercy' is transposed from Donat, the watching fellow Jew, to the guard: the narrator reports that Vitaly, 'in what he will always regard as an act of mercy', shot the baby's father. Astonishingly, while she was still making appearances as Demidenko, Helen Darville would include this particular passage in public readings. After all was revealed, the meaning of this change – the movement of subjectivity from eyewitness Donat to fictional Vitaly – was widely debated. Robert Manne claims that Darville has 'disfigured the moral meaning of this passage by her apparently minor change'. On the other hand, Andrew Riemer, who takes a more sympathetic view of Darville's novel – in particular by recognizing its status as a *representation* of the Holocaust rather than a historical commentary on it – observes that the adverb 'mercifully' in Donat's account (where it refers to the action of shooting) has been used, or misread, as an adjective in Darville's novel (where it refers to the guard). In Riemer's view, this is a matter of textual analysis rather than morality, and he argues that the two realms should be keep separate.[41] What also seems true is that, like the instances from *The Black Deeds* which Darville altered to appear to blame the Jews, this misquotation attempts to supply some interiority for a perpetrator. In the case of *The Black Deeds* it was motive rather than subjectivity that was at stake; in the case of Donat's eyewitness account, Darville has taken the horrible irony of death as 'merciful' and in attributing it to Vitaly has given that irony a different and uncomfortable resonance.

Hearing voices

The Hand is constructed idiosyncratically to give the effect of ventriloquizing antisemitism and does not promulgate it through a single voice. It begins with a first-person narrator in the Australian present, Fiona Kovalenko, who has had conversations with her uncle Vitaly and listened to the taped reminiscences of her aunt Kateryna, the widow of a member of the German SS. Fiona has transcribed both voices along with the first-person utterances of some other related characters. Thus about half the novel is in the form of first-person accounts by these people. However, interspersed with this material, and within the frame of Fiona's narration, is a third-person narrator, sometimes giving a different perspective on action we have already seen from a first-person view.

The most common judgement of this third-person narrative voice is that it is a technical error on Darville's part. Manne, again putting forward a worst-case scenario, identifies it clearly as Darville's own voice.[42] He says that as a matter of simple fact the third-person narrator cannot be Fiona Kovalenko, the present-day first-person narrator, since it knows things she could not (such as details of the relationship between Stalin and Kaganovich, and the psychology of various SS men) – therefore it must be Darville's.[43] Yet there are of course other ways of accounting for the third-person narrator in this text. Most narrative theories would have little problem with accommodating the unusual but not impossible form used by Darville: a named first-person narrator in the present orchestrates and overhears the first-person testimonies of three other characters, who are also intermittently narrated by a third-person voice. In fact, it is an almost literal example of Mikhail Bakhtin's concept of polyphony, which he discusses at length in *Problems of Dostoevsky's Poetics*. According to this theory, in contrast to the conventional third-person narrator of, say, George Eliot's novels, where moral and physical facts are told to us over the heads of the characters, in a polyphonic novel the narrator has no such privileged information. Its voice operates on the same level as the characters and their voices, and is constructed in the same way; if we learn anything of the moral nature and appearance of the characters, it is through the utterances of the characters themselves, not straightforwardly through the narrator. In the polyphonic novel, Bakhtin says, the author (or narrator) acts as a 'participant in the dialogue without retaining for himself the final word'.[44]

If we view Darville's novel as polyphonic, albeit rather unevenly put together, accusations of antisemitism can be countered. Antisemitism is to be seen as a component of the stylized voices we hear, including the voice of the narrator, which is on the same level as those of the characters. This can explain the 'errors' that critics have exposed in Darville's text. For instance, the narration concerning Stalin's relationship with Kaganovich is taken by Manne as proof of the presence of an omniscient third-person narrator who must be taken as the moral centre of the text, that is, as the author's voice. The narrator of *The Hand* says this of Vitaly and his wish for vengeance:

> He does not know the truth: Kaganovich only kept his power because he was shorter than Stalin, a good two inches shorter. Vitaly thinks that he kept his power through Jewish cunning. … Kaganovich's reward for his extraordinary loyalty was to be posted to the Ukraine, land of giants. Oh, how it irked him that these people were taller than he! So he wanted power. Power over this sullen race that refused to part with its fields.
>
> (96)

Manne points out that the only biography of Kaganovich in English claims he was actually considerably taller than Stalin, and that by the time of collectivization his Ukrainian posting was over, so he can have played no direct role in the Famine. Manne takes these inaccuracies to be evidence of a monologic antisemitic voice in *The Hand*, which explains 'Kaganovich's power-lust and anti-Ukrainianism as the consequence of the malicious envy of a Jewish dwarf'.[45]

Nevertheless, an alternative way to evaluate the matter is, again, in Bakhtinian terms. The narrator's voice in the extract above is an example of what Bakhtin, following the Russian formalists, calls *skaz*: a narratorial imitation of an oral utterance. We can see that this is the case in such phrases as, 'Oh, how it irked him'. Bakhtin argues that there are automatically two voices present in any example of *skaz*: the represented voice, which looks like an oral utterance, and the representing voice, which is responsible for its presence – that of the implied author or narrator.[46] Manne's criticism makes the assumption that these two voices – represented and representing – are one and the same. Throughout *The Hand* the anonymous narrator is given just such a stylized voice. This narrator is someone more sophisticated than Vitaly, is capable of seeing through the myth of Kaganovich's Jewish cunning, but is fallible or at least selective in other ways. Manne insists that this narrator has access to the psychology of the SS; but this often takes the form of a mixture of arcane facts and opinions, not an authoritative commentary (see, for instance, the remarks on 'Eberl and his Liszt records' (101), and the post-war fate of Erich Kretschmann after attending a Beatles concert (68)). It is true that the polyphonic nature of such a narrator is not consistent, as the quotation above shows; it is a typical 'monologic' move to observe that a character does not know a fact which is available to narrator and reader. However, elsewhere, in polyphonic patches, the narrator of *The Hand* simply *shows* ignorance on the part of the characters, without commenting on it, and it is these ambiguous moments which have unnecessarily outraged Robert Manne.

Enlisting Bakhtin's notion of polyphony can also help us deal with the apparent argument of Darville's novel, that Jewish Bolsheviks were responsible for the Ukrainian Famine and that they therefore got what they deserved later on. Critics have pointed out that this is the very argument used by the Nazis.[47] However, to argue in such a way is to assume a mono-vocal source for these myths within the novel. On the contrary, it is important to investigate precisely whose opinions these are. As Bakhtin says, in a polyphonic text: 'Fewer and fewer neutral, hard elements ("rock bottom truths") remain that are not drawn into dialogue.' Bakhtin suggests that, in a novel, the presence of a 'direct and unmediated' word is so 'impermissibly naive' that it is at once dialogized by taking on the nature of 'an internal polemic'. That is, an apparently univocal word exists as the *representation* of such a word, and must interact dialogically with the other words around it, which may contradict it. The same is true even if the contradictory heteroglossia remains outside the novel and the 'novelist comes forward with his own unitary and fully affirming language'.[48] One could argue that such heteroglossia, in the case of Darville's novel, includes historical and logical correctives to the prejudiced voices we hear in it, correctives which are often helpfully – if unwittingly – unearthed by Manne. Such correctives are not present within the text, but the voices we do hear require, or even demand, the reader's dialogic response.

For instance, Simon Petlyura, Ukrainian patriot and leader of terrible pogroms just after the First World War, is described in *The Hand* – by Kateryna – as a champion of 'ethnic peace'. He was assassinated by Shalom Schwarzbard in Paris in 1926, and Schwarzbard used his trial to reveal the extent of the pogroms in the Ukraine. Schwarzbard appears in *The Hand* as a hired assassin ' "under instructions from Moscow" ' (33) – but these are the words of a character, Ivan, from Lvov. This seems to constitute the novelistic 'testing of an idea', as Bakhtin puts it, rather than a monologic truth. Petlyura's reputation has been the subject of disagreement among historians, with Ukrainian-identified historians insisting that he was a patriot and denying his antisemitic record:[49] an inflammatory controversy which, like the Bolshevist slur against Jewry, reappears in Darville's novel. For this kind of reason Manne demands a 'clearly identified and morally unambiguous authorial voice' – that is, a non-polyphonic voice – where a subject like the Holocaust and its antecedents is concerned. He argues that if Darville's novel is read 'without knowledge or curiosity' then it may be a very dangerous text; there is 'nothing to suggest that any detail is imagined or false'.[50] This is true, but only *within the text*. We can argue that the Bakhtinian notion of heteroglossia, which may well exist only *outside* the text, performs the function of knowledge and curiosity, by providing a context for novels like Darville's and filling the loopholes in them. Furthermore, it is not necessary to be an expert on Jewish–Ukrainian history to notice the partial cast of Ivan's words on Petlyura – they are accompanied by an imitation of a 'Jewish' voice (32) – and to doubt them for that, contextual, reason.

Bakhtin's concept of polyphony, in which characters reveal their own and each other's traits without a narrator spelling them out, is a way of accounting for an incident which has troubled several critics. In the part of the novel set in the Ukraine in the 1930s, village life under collectivization is described; the commissar of the village where Vitaly lives is married to a Jewish doctor. The latter is presented as an ideologically committed Communist, who cannot understand why Soviet policy is leaving the Ukrainian peasants starving. However, the doctor's devotion to Stalinism also means that she despises the peasants: she accuses them of cattle-like passivity and breeding like animals. Anatoly Kovalenko's mother begs her to treat her baby son:

> Mrs Kommissar refused. 'I am a physician, not a veterinarian', she said softly, enunciating the words with a kind of feral sharpness. 'Get away.'
>
> (15)

This incident is transcribed by Fiona Kovalenko from her aunt Kateryna's testimony, so it is twice-reported speech. Rather than viewing the portrayal of this Jewish doctor as an antisemitic and Holocaust-denying act, it is more helpful to see the representation of Kateryna as that of a character with antisemitic prejudices. In other words, Kateryna's narration reflects back upon herself as well as giving a perspective on the physician. This is not information so much as another partial view.

The same defence, that this is a polyphonic text, can be made against the charges of plagiarism. It is hard to see what the future of Holocaust fiction could be if intertextual methodologies were outlawed. Indeed, the second edition of *The Hand*, which credits on its title page full details of the works by Gilbert and Pidhainy from which material is quoted, only does what other novels on this subject do, ranging from Lucy Ellmann's *Man or Mango?* (1998) to Anne Michaels's *Fugitive Pieces* (1996).

The third-person narrator may present problems to the reader in appearing to endorse the characters' voices; Fiona herself, as a character-narrator, is just as problematic. As Morag Fraser puts it, Fiona's simple-sounding remark, 'I did not tell Cathe about the hate, or how the Ukrainian famine bled into the Holocaust and one fed the other' (3), summarizes 'a profoundly controversial political and ethnic history' as if it were none of these things.[51] But the same argument could be made of Fiona as of the third-person narrator. Hers may be a scene-setting voice, but it is as fallible and unreliable as any of the others we read. Fiona's question to Vitaly, for instance, is both oriented towards the reader yet naive: ' "But you didn't have to volunteer! You could have run away! If you could go back, would you join the SS or go to Finland?" ' (41). Alan Dershowitz, on the other hand, reacts to the characters, let alone the narrators, as simple mouth-pieces: 'The author, afraid to write a non-fiction apologia for the Ukrainian genocide, lest she be rightly ostracized, smuggles her views into the mouths of her characters.'[52] Manne is similarly of the severe opinion that it is a 'simple fact' that the novel's omniscient narrator, who never cares to correct the characters' antisemitic opinions, can be identified with the author herself. He adds that 'Demidenko's purposes are thoroughly didactic'.[53] These remarks do not take account of the novel's implied reader and that reader's ability to resist and respond to such opinions; as Fraser puts it, '[Demidenko's] effect is to leave her reader appalled, not partisan.'[54]

However, as the philosopher Peter Singer insists, this is a novel in which 'the horrors of Nazism are displayed' for all to see, in 'an attempt to explain – not to justify – how it could happen that people who grew up as simple village boys could end up committing the vilest atrocities'.[55] The historical omissions and foreshortenings are sites of irony; the reader should know better than Vitaly Kovalenko, can supply missing contexts, and does not believe the reasons he gives for his own actions, and (in a passage Manne especially dislikes) Ivan the Terrible's actions during the war. Vitaly says Ivan saw his family burn to death in their home at the hands of Jewish Bolsheviks, hence his murderous behaviour towards Jews during the war. However, even Vitaly's wife does not accept this account and says, ' "He doesn't look mad" ' (115). This is a quarrel between the text's characters, rather than one between the author and her critics.[56] Of course, saying so puts a heavy burden of responsibility on the reader, who is required to recognize self-delusion and historical ignorance for what they are.[57]

A particularly revealing anecdote about the Demidenko affair is that a troupe of Demidenko lookalikes, men sporting long blonde wigs and sequinned cocktail dresses, appeared at the 1995 Sydney Gay and Lesbian Mardi Gras, in homage to Helen Darville's literary dressing-up. The critic Sneja Gunew argues that, as Demidenko, Darville was enacting a *representation* of ethnicity – a category from which, in contemporary Australia, Anglo-Saxon ancestry is exempt – in just the terms we have been schooled to read it, through the superficial cultural details of drink, food and appearance. This explains Darville's success as a novelist of Ukrainian descent, and her abject failure as a Pom (and envy of the exotic is certainly one way of explaining Darville's personal and literary façade).[58] To criticize Darville for writing a tendentious novel is to allow oneself to be addressed by only one of the several voices which go to make it up. The literal-minded and litigious response to the Demidenko scandal represents a misunderstanding about what a literature of the Holocaust might look like now and in the future as we reach the third millennium.

The begetters of violence

Darville's novel is outstanding in its efforts to show how 'ordinary men' became agents of genocide; it is this quality which led to its initially very positive reception. Such ordinariness is represented in a double way in *The Hand*, most clearly at the level of the content, but also at the level of style, which has an everyday, affectless tone. It is often on the grounds of just this innovation that Darville's novel was highly praised; and on the same grounds that it caused outrage. Andrew Riemer notes approvingly that Darville attempts to 'endow unspeakable acts of barbarism with an air of the commonplace and ordinary'.[59] The ever-critical Manne, however, describes the novel's representation of violence as, 'at best kindergarten Hemingway, at worst the product of an imagination shrivelled on splatter movies'.[60] The comparison with Hemingway is an implicit slur on Darville's style too, and Manne goes on to make what he sees as the disparity between content and form into a moral issue: 'how little pity or terror or astonishment or humility she feels in the presence of what is, after all, the subject matter of her book – radical evil. Hers is one of the coldest books I have ever read.'[61]

Susan Moore, another fierce critic of *The Hand*, arraigns 'the eerily impersonal matter-of-factness which goes hand in hand with the desire to shock, so characteristic of the tone of Demidenko and of many other young people of her generation'.[62] Raymond Gaita, in a long, anti-Darville essay on Holocaust representation, finds the structure and style of *The Hand* to be intimately related; he avers that 'It is a terrible mistake, made by some of Darville's defenders, to believe that numbness could be an appropriate (as distinct from understandable) response to evil.'[63] He argues that the novel includes numerous speakers but not voices. But even the far less censorious Fraser sees the narratorial voice as often indistinguishable from the characters', while Moore insists that all of the major characters in a superior novel 'can be identified by their uniquely individual voices; and both authors, for the same reason, can be identified straight away'.[64] It is interesting that such sharp distinguishability is seen by these critics as an index of novelistic multi-voicedness, when for Bakhtin it signals quite the opposite. His claim is that

> language differentiation and the clear-cut 'speech characterizations' of characters have the greatest artistic significance precisely in the creation of

objectified and finalized images of people. The more objectified a character, the more sharply his speech physiognomy stands out.[65]

It may be true that the lack of such differentiation in Darville's novel is the product of clumsiness rather than a polyphonic project, but it is also true that the absence of differentiation is *not* the sign of a hidden and sinister agenda on the author's part. Darville revealingly claims that Akira Kurosawa's 1950 film *Rashomon* was the inspiration for her novel's form: 'I saw a Japanese film where eight people describe the same incident (in this case, a rape) and tell wildly divergent stories about what had actually occurred. I was impressed and sought to capture that moral ambiguity in my own writing.' In Kurosawa's film, mutually exclusive accounts of a robbery, rape and murder are given by each of those involved and no final, 'true' version is offered at the film's end. Darville's indebtedness to *Rashomon* for the form of her novel could account for its awkward combination of first- and third-person narration. In the film, some of the accounts of the events are second-hand – as if told through reported speech – though in all cases we actually see enacted what might have happened. Critics of the film have suggested that the camera is not neutral but constitutes a 'fifth witness', just as Fiona Kovalenko and the third-person narrator in *The Hand* are partial witnesses.[66]

Criticizing *The Hand* for its numbed style is another way of saying that the text needs a morally upright, omniscient narrator, or, as Moore asserts, author: 'A clear authorial presence, however it makes itself felt, deeply matters, and it is nonsensical to pretend that it doesn't.' The critic William Schaffer speaks of the 'cold, cathode light' which accompanies the novel's 'penchant for graphic description of violent acts and scenes of humiliation'.[67] He calls this a 'pornography of representation' in which the rhetorical point has somehow been forgotten: that is, the specific fate of the Jews in the Holocaust has been overlooked. However, the representation of 'ordinary men' in *The Hand* exists within a structure of oblique, non-narrational methods of registering attitudes to horror. Physical reactions on the part of the characters, or descriptions of atrocities without a piling-up of adjectives, replace overt narratorial commentary. In Bakhtin's phrase, 'All direct meaning and direct expressions are false, and this is especially true of emotional meanings and expressions.'[68] Instances of such oblique narration include the incident in which Vitaly's lawyer does not respond to his client's observation that ' "now [the hate] starts again" ' except by shattering a biro and injuring himself (83); and the young boy who beats his head against the bannister of Madga's house, leaving behind 'a fat, brown blotch on the slat flooring' (114). On several occasions in the novel vomiting takes the place of a moral or emotional reaction, also relieving the narrator of the need to provide any commentary: Fiona refuses to play the part of Anne Frank in a school play and goes home to throw up (39); Madga feels 'bile' rise in her throat at the sight of a roundup in Warsaw (125); the mobile infirmary of Einsatzgruppe C at Babi Yar is awash (66–7). Such extreme bodily reactions are appropriate in a novel where characters are often said to *feel* nothing (44, 53, 58). Although critics have taken Darville to task for not supplying her characters with feelings of remorse or shame, such an expressively void response again avoids the accumulation of adjectives in an effort to represent something 'unspeakable'.

The critic Serge Liberman sees the matter of *The Hand's* affectless style more positively: the scenes set in Babi Yar are 'certainly effectively rendered in an uncluttered prose that carries the narrative element in an absorbing way'.[69] He cites some of the conversations that take place in the novel between Fiona and her uncle Vitaly, which are indeed remarkable for their banality. The 'shame' of imprisonment ranks higher in both minds than remorse for murders committed (40), and Vitaly's explanations to his niece are at the level of, ' "It was a crazy time" ', and, ' "If you leave people alone, they don't do bad things" ' (3, 154). Liberman notes the 'peculiar' fact that Fiona juxtaposes these bathetic conversations with an apparently contradictory urge to record 'with the fullest clarity' the atrocities in which her father and uncle have been involved, and which 'cut across virtually every one of these glib and wimpish hand-me-downs'.[70] This is surely just the point of such an uncomfortable juxtaposition of discourses: inappropriate platitudes and terrible crimes coexist, in this case within the same lifetime. Liberman calls this 'a near-schizoid dissociation, a *belle indifference*' on Fiona's part;[71] yet on the *novel's* part it is an especially striking instance of dialogized heteroglossia. (This phrase of Bakhtin's refers to the combative relations that different discourses enter into when they come into contact with each other in a novel.)[72]

However, Liberman does seem to recognize that an idea is being subjected to a dialogic, novelistic testing in *The Hand*, without being able either to see the positive aspects of such a process or to name it.[73] As well as the comment quoted above about everyday discourse which 'cuts across' the out-of-the-ordinary – a remarkably dialogic notion – Liberman cites the frequent insistence made in the novel by the brothers Kovalenko that they had no choice about enlisting with the SS. Liberman realizes that such an alibi is not represented monologically: 'But undercutting this very same plea of choicelessness is the episode of a certain Barsek Ohlobla, a Ukrainian who guides Jews away from Babi Yar, even plucking them out of the slow-marching columns.'[74] Even the term 'undercutting' suggests that Liberman is aware of the clash of evaluations present in the novel, but attributes them to the narrator's faulty logic rather than the novel's dialogized heteroglossia.

Liberman makes a similar point about what it was that 'really ... underlay the Ukrainian assault upon the Jews', claiming that, 'Oddly, Demidenko's book actually contains the material for an answer, although Fiona Kovalenko fails to see its implications.' He cites as an answer the scene in which 400 locally recruited SS members greet their officer's antisemitism with rapturous applause: 'Clearly the Nazis knew their clients well. Ukrainian (and, here, Latvian) antisemitism was already legendary – but not for the reason Demidenko is content to give.'[75] Liberman confuses Kovalenko and Demidenko, paradoxically claiming that what Kovalenko cannot see is something her author has failed to put into the text: yet he can quote it. This suggests that the second voice which takes issue with and contradicts the monologism of, for instance, the antisemitic stereotype does not always have to be sought outside the text. At times it is even present within the novel, though there is some truth in Liberman's final accusation that 'Ms Demidenko ... has displayed little interest in finding out even the least of [the Ukrainian–Jewish symbiosis and strife's] numerous interwoven complexities'.[76] Bernard Cohen echoes Liberman's regret that there is not more evidence in the text of thorough research, or, in other words, of heteroglot variety: 'The book *forgets* to note that most Jews – including most Ukrainian Jews – were not Communists; most Communists were not Jews; Stalin conducted virulent anti-Semitic purges; a large proportion of Jews murdered by Ukrainian fascists lived in what was Poland in 1933.'[77] However, this is to miss the point; although some varieties of discourse are present in the text, others are only known by their absence, as Cohen's list reveals.

Furthermore, Schaffer also comes close to recognizing that conflicting voices and scenarios exist within *The Hand*, but, like Liberman, he criticizes the novel for not making explicit such dialogism. He notes the 'odious comparison' of the fate of Ukrainian children at Jewish, or at least Bolshevik, hands with the fate of Jewish children at Ukrainian SS hands; and that the differences between these children's fates summarizes the 'false' and 'noxious' nature of the implied equivalence between Ukrainians and Jews. While the Ukrainian children were destined for a future of re-indoctrination, the Jewish ones were destined for extermination.[78] Like Liberman, Schaffer is pointing to scenes *within the text itself* for his evidence of its omissions. It would be much more interesting to acknowledge the effect of those voices which run counter to the narratorial, or specifically Kovalenkan, drift of the novel.[79]

Throughout *The Hand* there are signs of incipient narratorial double-voicedness which, if fully developed, would have sharpened its ironizing of 'ordinary' perceptions of atrocity. Several of these instances are attached to the representation of Evheny, brother of the more central Vitaly and father of Fiona. Evheny is a suitable subject for double-voiced narration because he is shown to be 'stupid'. When an old Jew gives some food to the young Evheny during the time of the Famine, the narrator observes, 'His mother said that Jews polluted everything they touched, but he was hungry' (21). This is an instance of free indirect discourse which is also dialogized heteroglossia: Evheny's consciousness is constructed out of his mother's ironized words which conflict with his experience. Evheny's partial view of his inability to learn to read is conveyed in a similar way: 'He is just stupid – that is what the teachers said. Just plain stupid' (64). Although these utterances may look authoritative and monologic, particularly the latter one – 'Just plain stupid' – they actually contain the conflicting evaluations of several voices. The phrase expressing Evheny's stupidity is not a narratorial judgement but the repetition of others' words. Finally, here is an example which takes exactly the same form of showing the development of apparently unified narration out of what is clearly double-voiced discourse: '[Magda] does not know who Jewish Bolsheviks are, only who the Jews are. Her father says they are bad people, who steal. Kazimier made a great mistake letting them come to Poland' (108). Free indirect discourse is succeeded in the second sentence by an instance of heteroglossia (the antisemitic discourse of her father), and in the third by dialogized heteroglossia (an apparently monologic statement is washed over by an unheard conflicting voice: perhaps best thought of as having absent quotation marks). These are small but rewarding instances of the alternation between authoritative and qualified discourse which characterizes *The Hand* as a whole. What makes Darville's text novelistic is just this battle among discourses and perspectives. One might not feel that the Holocaust is a subject suitable for such a battle; the columnist Pamela Bone notes: 'This [*The Hand*] is the other side of the Holocaust. Except, as John Pilger has said, there is no other side to the Holocaust.'[80] However, it is more dramatically effective to present even something to which there is 'no other side' in a dialogic, polyphonic manner, than to insist monologically on a truth already known.

It may seem to be unnecessary repetition to insist that *The Hand that Signed the Paper* is a novel;[81] but it is important to remember that its novelistic features, particularly the utterances of characters and its partial narrator, mean that its 'opinion' cannot be pinned down in the way its detractors claim. Even Andrew Riemer thinks he can detect an 'authorial' voice within the novel, one which does speak with an antisemitic tongue.[82] Yet the novel's morally inflamed critics overlook the fact that what we read in the novel are viewpoints, not verities, which clash with one another and with the reader's viewpoint. The case is only slightly less clear for the narrator, whose view is equally partial. This partiality is especially striking when the narrator uses such phrases as, 'It was true' (25), which sounds authoritative but has the ring of reported speech. However, it is not a question of a narratorial withholding of the correct moral judgements, as the criticisms of Manne and others allege; there is no omniscient narrator in this text, but an unreliable one, who is incapable of such judgement. Even if straightforward condemnations were uttered by the narrator, they too would have the status only of opinion.

None the less, *The Hand* makes for provoking rather than pleasant, or even familiar, reading. Unlike *Schindler's List* and *Sophie's Choice*, the novel's battles are not clearly Manichaean. We are unsure which moral labels to apply, as some of the perpetrators are also victims. Of course the novel can only accomplish such an impression by failing fully to represent the Jewish victims of the events it narrates; its only significant characters are the SS, whether German or Ukrainian.[83] For this reason one might ask whether it is best described as a 'Holocaust novel'. Its effects are sometimes unsubtle or uneven, which can upset its polyphonic discourse – at times, for instance, the narrator does seem to be endowed with objective historical knowledge: 'The invasion of the Soviet Union had a grim structure to it' (43). Readers may simply prefer not to read a novel in which the old 'Jewish-Bolshevik' slur is so energetically dramatized,[84] particularly when it becomes clear that authentic witnesses to the Ukrainian famine harboured no illusions about who was really responsible for their suffering: it was the Bolsheviks, plain and simple. However, the intensity of the debate surrounding *The Hand*, both before and after the watershed of mid-August 1995 when Demidenko was unmasked, testifies to the great power and potential of the polyphonic novel and dialogized heteroglossia, particularly in a novel about the Holocaust.

Conclusion

I have argued throughout this book that, despite much received wisdom, Holocaust fiction which is unaccommodating to the reader may be more successful in conveying the disruption and unease that the subject demands than more seamless, aesthetically pleasing work. The examples I have discussed show that although there are no norms where fiction about the Holocaust is concerned, critical estimates tend towards establishing them. Fine imaginative prose, particularly when written by an author with good credentials, is valued more highly than generically unstable, intertextual, ironic or experimental texts. The fact that Martin Amis's *Time's Arrow* has received as polarized a reception as the manifestly less subtle *Sophie's Choice* bears this out. Amis's sure and inventive handling of novelistic form leads to accusations of bad faith, as poor artistry is harder to prove; indeed, whereas William Styron's novel at times sinks under the weight of its imperfectly digested sources, Amis's is in perfect control of them.

As I have argued, intertextuality is very likely be the central element in Holocaust fiction; even Anne Michaels's mostly imaginative *Fugitive Pieces* concludes with a section acknowledging anterior sources. Thomas Keneally's *Schindler's List* registers in unexpected ways its reliance on witness testimony; its status as the biography of a hero is in constant tension with its author's necessary reliance on the words of victims. D.M. Thomas's *The White Hotel* revolves self-consciously around its main borrowing; indeed, the horrible revelation of its character's destiny and the revelation that to describe certain events the author must resort to the historical record are simultaneous. The case of Helen Darville's *The Hand that Signed the Paper* shows the eagerness with which extra-textual material is seized upon where Holocaust representation is at stake, and the literary liability this can become if the author is not vigilant. *The Painted Bird* suffered from the same syndrome, as its author allowed himself to be tempted to exaggerate his experiences during the war in order to establish his legitimacy as a Holocaust novelist and his book's 'authenticity'. However, *The Painted Bird* does work much better as a novel than as any kind of testimony.

The two issues which are most central to the negative reception of much Holocaust fiction – even more so than the literary matter of intertextuality – are the philosophical issues of authenticity and accuracy. First, lack of perceived authenticity, and consequent suspicion of authorial motives, underlies the negative estimates of *Time's Arrow*, *The Hand that Signed the Paper*, *The White Hotel*, *Sophie's Choice* and *Schindler's List* – even though of these five novels only Thomas's deals centrally with a Holocaust victim who is targeted on account of her Jewishness. The other four novels concern instead perpetrators, a non-Jewish victim, and a rescuer respectively. Unable to accuse Kosinski of lacking a personal connection with the Holocaust, critics instead subjected the precise details of his connection to unforgiving scrutiny.

Second, charges of inaccuracy have been levelled at all six of these authors, despite the unusual nature of such a charge where fiction is concerned. Critics in effect accused *Time's Arrow* of inaccuracy in its backwards representation of the Holocaust: it seems that the only accurate way to represent it is forwards, as part of a predetermined teleology. Experimenting with form is treated as if it were inaccuracy; in other words, accusing the novel in this way is tantamount to accusing it of fictionality, and is a contradiction in terms. Thomas, Keneally, Styron and Darville have each been accused of dishonestly distorting historical sources. As I have argued in relation to *The White Hotel*, this is also a contradictory position. Novelists are expected to keep to the facts, yet doing so too slavishly can be viewed as plagiarism; as novelists they are expected to invent material, yet doing so amounts to inaccuracy. Once more the establishment of this double bind indicates that critical opinion has a narrow view of what a Holocaust novel should be like, and who should write it. Even Kosinski, whose technical legitimacy is impeccable, has been taken to task for inaccuracy, in painting too black a picture of how local populations reacted to Jews during the Holocaust years. It is as if such responses to Holocaust fiction demand both too much and too little from the novel. On the one hand, Holocaust novels are supposed to convey accurately facts which are not even agreed upon by historians; on the other hand, the novelistic staples of altering viewpoint, playing narrator off against character, testing the reader, are to be eschewed in favour of a limited variety of realism.

In concluding here, I will discuss two further literary scandals concerning the issues of authenticity and accuracy. The controversies also demonstrate that, despite publishers' expectations,[1] there is no reason to believe the Holocaust will cease being the – unstable – subject of fiction in the new millennium. In the first case, Binjamin Wilkomirski's *Fragments: Memories of a Childhood, 1939–1948* was received with great acclaim as a memoir, and then slated as a work of fiction: a turnaround due to critical reaction to its author's deception rather than to its literary merits. In the second case, concerning Jim Allen's play *Perdition*, issues of historical accuracy were enlisted by those who took exception to Allen using the Holocaust as an analogy for another historical moment. In this case, however, problems with the work's form are inextricable from those concerning its content: I will argue that the manipulation of historical facts is necessary to such a polemic, which is not really about the Holocaust at all.

When fact turns into fiction: Binjamin Wilkomirski's *Fragments*

As several of the cases discussed in this study have shown, critical estimates vary according to what is known of a writer's biography, and what relation a narrator has to the text's author. *Fragments* was published in 1995 as the autobiography of Binjamin Wilkomirski. According to interviews with Wilkomirski, this text is a representation of the recovered memory of the classical musician, known after the war as Bruno Doessekker.[2] Recent work has shown, however, that 'Binjamin Wilkomirski' does not exist; although the author of *Fragments* appears to believe that he was once an inmate of the death camps, Elena Lappin and Philip Gourevitch have argued that this cannot be the case.[3] Wilkomirski (as I shall continue to call him) claims to have been born in Latvia around 1939 and, after the murder of his family, was imprisoned in Majdanek and Auschwitz between the ages of three and nine. He was adopted by a Swiss family after liberation, and encouraged not to dwell on his childhood experiences in the death camps. As an autobiography, albeit one constructed according to the logic of blurred and distant memory, *Fragments* was received with acclaim.[4] Then, in September 1998, an article by the Swiss journalist Daniel Ganzfried was published in the Zurich *Weltwoche* claiming that 'Wilkomirski' was born in Switzerland, not Latvia, in 1941; he was not Jewish, and had spent no time in Majdanek or Auschwitz. On the contrary, he was the illegitimate son of a woman named Yvonne Grosjean, later adopted by the Doessekker family.[5] The implication of Ganzfried's article is that the man who calls himself Wilkomirski is at best the deluded victim of 'false memory syndrome', and his text the expression of over-identification with the trauma of the Holocaust.

It is undeniably the case that readers want to know details of an author's biography, particularly in a case like this where the text purports to be a Holocaust testimony – its subtitle is *Memories of a Childhood, 1939–1948*. One worry is the usual one that the historical record may be muddied by the appearance of works which are known to be imaginative, let alone works which claim to be factual but are not. Writing in *The Times*, Roger Boyes observed that 'witness accounts are essential' to deflect the efforts of Holocaust deniers, and that 'fake Holocaust testimony distorts the debate'.[6] Yet it seems that such a pragmatic consideration, however important it may be, is not the only one at issue here. Other reasons for feeling disquiet or even outrage at the kind of deception practised by Wilkomirski are less quantifiable, and are once more to do with moral issues masquerading as critical ones. Impersonation is in itself seen to be reprehensible; readers do not like to expend energy and emotion on a book they believe is true, only to discover that they have been reading a work of fiction. As the critic Andrew Riemer puts it, dishonest literary practices, such as plagiarism or use of a pseudonym, are often taken as evidence of 'slanderous and partisan attitudes' in general[7] – that is, of the author's thoroughly bad character and even of an inability to write well.

Boyes quotes Ganzfried saying that there would have been no objection to Wilkomirski's book had it been presented as fiction from the outset,[8] and it is true that the author-related aspects of the scandal would not have taken place in the same way had it been differently categorized. But it is hard to believe that *Fragments* would have been uniformly well received even if it were marketed as a novel, for exactly the reasons I have been discussing throughout this study. Novels about the 'core' of the Holocaust, in William Styron's phrase, that is, the machinery of mechanized death in the extermination camps, are not common.

Wilkomirski's text is full of the kinds of uncertainty principle which critics claim distinguish testimony from fiction;[9] but in this case such uncertainty gives *Fragments* a fictive feel, rather than increasing its resemblance to testimony. In the first place, it should be remembered that even *Night*, Elie Wiesel's survivor testimony,[10] necessarily uses novelistic methods: it is retrospective, it is clearly the result of narrative choices and omissions, and its first-person narrator is at a distance from its character, whose name, Eliezer, is different from that of the author. The blurb for *Fragments*, which notes that it is 'Beautifully written, unselfconscious and powerful', is unwittingly aware of the text's confected nature, as the contradictoriness of the first two epithets shows. Testimonial uncertainty is often different from the kind of fictive instability I have been concerned with in this book, although – as the case of Wiesel suggests – the two categories are not always neatly separable.

Fragments is more *about* memory than mimetic of its logic, even when it gives the impression of immediacy: 'I'm just an eye, taking in what it sees, giving nothing back.'[11] Like Wiesel's *Night*, *Fragments* is retrospective, and the narrator is not the same person as the text's character Binjamin. (This is the case regardless of what relation the real-life author has to the textual character.) The present-tense sentence 'I'm just an eye' elides the distinction between character and narrator: the child may have been such a recording device, but it is the adult narrator who is telling the story. This utterance is an example not of reported speech or authentic testimony, but of the much more literary free indirect discourse. The narrator's voice is present along with the character's.

The relevance of *Fragments* to my argument here is that it shows once more the problems Holocaust texts and their authors encounter when there is any generic uncertainty about them. Now that it seems clear that Doessekker invented Wilkomirski as a historically embodied figure for childhood trauma, the work of textual analysis can begin on what remains a striking and unusual *novel* about a childhood in the death camps.

Historical inaccuracy: Jim Allen's *Perdition*

There was great controversy over *Perdition* in Britain in 1987, when it became the first play to be banned by the Royal Court Theatre. Rather like Helen Darville's novel *The Hand that Signed the Paper*, Allen's play was judged according to its historical claims and implications;[12] and its literary merits were presented as if inextricable from its historical ones. This is clear even from a letter written by Arnold Wesker to the *Guardian* declaring his new-found support for the play to be performed in June 1999: 'I was one of the signatories 12 years ago calling for a ban on Jim Allen's play *Perdition*. It seemed to me a *bad play*.'[13] Wesker's phrase neatly unites the moral and aesthetic dimensions of the debate. However, in this case, unlike Darville's, this link is appropriate.

Perdition is a fictionalized version of the Kastner trial, held in Israel in 1954. Rudolf Kastner had been a member of the Budapest Rescue Committee during the Nazi occupation of Hungary; when a fellow civil servant, Malchiel Gruenwald, accused Kastner of collaboration with the Nazis, the Israeli government brought a criminal libel case against Gruenwald on Kastner's behalf. The judge awarded Kastner one Israeli pound in damages, which was tantamount to upholding Gruenwald's charge. The verdict was overturned in 1957, but Kastner was assassinated before the issue could be resolved.

The relation of *Perdition* to this material is presented in a contradictory fashion, presumably to avoid charges of libel.[14] It is clear that its characters, Miklos Yaron and Ruth Kaplan, are the fictional counterparts of Kastner and Gruenwald. Kastner – 'an ice-cold lawyer and a fanatical Zionist' – and his trial are also mentioned several times in the play. Although the Author's Note observes that 'the characters on the stage of this play are all fictions and no resemblance to any person living or dead is intended', it also notes that '*Perdition* is a play which shows how some Zionist leaders collaborated with the Nazis before and during the Second World War', and refers the reader to a lengthy Bibliography – titles from which the characters have a habit of citing.[15] The blurb on the cover of the published script has no hesitation in claiming that the play is 'largely based on evidence produced at a libel action which took place in Israel in 1953 [*sic*] involving Dr Rudolf Kastner'. The appendix to the text, '*Perdition* and the Press', is a collection of historical and critical pieces which Allen drew upon or which were published in response to his play; all of the critical texts take for granted the play's close relation to the Kastner trial.

It is obvious that *Perdition* is a factional play. Its divergences from the historical record are more revealing than its fidelities. According to David Cesarani, the play is 'a distortion of history based on a selective interpretation of the facts and the citation of actions and documents taken out of context'.[16] It is also obvious that *Perdition* is a polemical play. The published version[17] includes in its cast-list the part, 'MEMBERS OF THE JURY: The Audience'.[18] This suggests that the audience has a free role in deciding the outcome of the play's trial, but it is clear at the end what the verdict is – although it is not heard – and that it will exonerate Kaplan and condemn Yaron. Yaron already had such a keen sense of his own guilt that, it emerges, he allowed the trial to proceed in order to reach a historical and personal truth:

> I needed a judgement, Mr Scott [the counsel for the defence]. The question remained: was it right to co-operate with the Nazis? With good faith we believed we were contributing to a great mission.[19]

The 'great mission' to which Yaron refers is the establishment of a Jewish homeland, and *this* is the subject on which a verdict is sought from the audience-jury, rather than Yaron's personal guilt.

The construction of *Perdition* is such that it would take a very resistant – or 'Zionist' – audience, relying on information quite outside the play itself, to dissent from the overpoweringly implied conclusion: that 'Zionist' leaders made all kinds of deals with the Nazis before and during the Second World War, including bartering the lives of other Jews, to press ahead with their dream of a Jewish state – which turned out to be as racist as the Jews' oppressors. In his summing up, Alec Scott refers to the 'calculated treachery' of the Hungarian Jews' own leaders, 'the only "chosen people" left in Budapest', which contributed to the murder of half a million people; and implies that the next holocaust will be perpetrated by the Israelis against the Arabs.[20] In formal terms, the weakness of the defence, Yaron's dubious motives for bringing a libel action, and the successive defeat of two witnesses for the defence, all point inexorably to a guilty verdict on 'Zionism' – a word which is used with all the frequency and over-determination of the phrase 'Jewish Bolshevik' in *The Hand that Signed the Paper*.[21] Voices in the play which hint at the possibility of a polyphonic structure by offering counter-evidence to its theme are quickly defeated, often by the Judge – whose role seems to be one not of impartial orchestration, but of authoritative monologism and the poser of leading questions.[22]

Several of the objections I have just made to *Perdition* are the very ones that I dismissed in relation to Helen Darville's novel *The Hand that Signed the Paper*. Critics declared that her novel excluded germane historical evidence, and that its narration was biased towards a particular thesis: that there is an impersonal cycle of violence in human history, where the victims in one phase (for instance, the Ukrainians during the Famine years) will be the perpetrators next time around (during the Holocaust), and their victims will in turn exact further revenge (in the form of war crimes trials in the present). I suggested that the dialogized heteroglossia and polyphonic narration of Darville's novel militated against such a clear reading of its supposed thesis. At the risk of subscribing to a Bakhtinian orthodoxy,[23] I suggest that the *absence* of these elements from Jim Allen's play makes its thesis stand out only too clearly. Allen's own comment in an interview sums up this thesis as well as any critical paraphrase could do:

> Without any undue humility I'm saying that this is the most lethal attack on Zionism ever written, because it touches at the heart of the most abiding myth of modern history, the Holocaust. Because it says quite plainly that privileged Jewish leaders collaborated in the extermination of their own kind

in order to help bring about a Zionist state, Israel, a state which is itself racist.[24]

It is true that the role of the *Judenräte* and Jewish police during the Holocaust is a subject which has not yet been fully investigated; that Rudolf Kastner and the Rescue Committee in Budapest in 1944 did not succeed in their mission; and that a play about these issues should not be banned.[25] However, *Perdition* is not a modulated investigation into painful facts, but the acting out of a predetermined view of the term 'Zionist' and of Jewish leadership in Europe under the Nazis. More than this, *Perdition* is using the Holocaust as a cover for its real target: recent Israeli domestic and foreign policy.[26] While *The Hand that Signed the Paper* used factual sources to construct a novel, *Perdition* cloaks its ideological reading of historical facts in the semblance of a play.

A comparison of Allen's play and Darville's novel risks subscribing to another Bakhtinian truism by likening what Bakhtin considers the least dialogic of genres – drama – to the most dialogic – the novel. Naturally this assertion has been challenged either explicitly or in practice by critics who consider Bakhtin's categories can be applied to any genre, including drama and poetry.[27] Indeed, as I argued in the Introduction, Bakhtin's categories can be applied trans-generically, and there are many instances of monologic novels. However, I think that Allen's play is on its own merits a monologic work masquerading, through its representation of different viewpoints, as a dialogic one.

The case of *Perdition* shows that isolating features such as historical inaccuracy as reasons to condemn a Holocaust fiction is not enough; historical inaccuracy, of itself, tells us very little about a text or how effective its representation is of the Holocaust. In *Perdition*, inaccuracy is deployed in particular ways for a particular reason, and it is this polemic which makes it only ostensibly about the Holocaust. Equally, the case of *Fragments* shows that while it is necessary to know on what basis the narrator of a Holocaust fiction is related to its author, such information is only the bare minimum needed to allow for the literary evaluation of such a text. This is true of the six novels I have analysed in this study as well as the less easily categorizable works by Wilkomirski and Allen.

Notes

Introduction

1 Rolf Hochhuth, *The Deputy* (New York: Grove Press, 1964) (and see Eric Bentley, ed., *The Storm Over the Deputy: Essays and Articles about Hochhuth's Explosive Drama*, New York: Grove Press, 1964). Peter Weiss, *The Investigation*, trans. Jan Swan and Ulu Grosbard (Chicago: Dramatic Publishing Co., 1966). Gerald Green, *The Holocaust* (London: Corgi, 1978). Jim Allen, *Perdition: A Play in Two Acts* (London and Atlantic Highlands: Ithaca Press, 1987). Binjamin Wilkomirski, *Fragments: Memories of a Childhood, 1939–1948*, trans. Carol Brown Janeway (London: Picador, 1996). On issues of Holocaust representation and the problems of authenticity see, for instance, Jean-François Lyotard's *Heidegger and 'the jews'* (Minneapolis: University of Minnesota Press, 1990); Dominick LaCapra, *Representing the Holocaust: History, Theory, Trauma* (Ithaca and London: Cornell University Press, 1994), and his *History and Memory after Auschwitz* (Ithaca and London: Cornell University Press, 1998); Philippe Lacoue-Labarthe, *Heidegger, Art and Politics* (Cambridge: Polity Press, 1991); and Ann Parry's application of these ideas to popular fiction, 'Idioms for the Unrepresentable: Postwar Fiction and the Shoah', *Journal of European Studies* 27 (4), 108, 1997, pp. 417–32.

2 There are obviously exceptions to this rule, in particular Louis Begley's survivor novel *Wartime Lies* (London: Picador, 1991) and writings by second-generation survivors, for instance Helen Epstein, *Where She Came From* (New York: Plume [Penguin], 1998); and Elizabeth Ehrlich, *Miriam's Kitchen* (New York: Penguin, 1998).

3 In a review of Roberto Benigni's 1998 film *Life is Beautiful*, the critic David Denby observed that 'the enormous worldwide success of the film suggests that the audience is exhausted by the Holocaust, that it is sick to death of the subject's unending ability to disturb' ('In the Eye of the Beholder: Another Look at Roberto Benigni's Holocaust Fantasy', *New Yorker*, 15 March 1999, p. 99).

4 Michael André Bernstein, *Foregone Conclusions: Against Apocalyptic History* (Berkeley and London: University of California Press, 1994), p. 23.

5 See Richard Menkes, 'Narrative Reversals and the Thermodynamics of History', *Modern Fiction Studies* 44 (4), 1998, pp. 959–80. Thanks to Sue Owen for discussing this with me.

6 Martin Amis, in Martin Amis, Bryan Cheyette, Lucy Ellmann, Joseph Skibell, 'Writing the Unwritable: A Debate on Holocaust Fiction', *Jewish Quarterly* 170 (Summer 1998), pp. 12–15: p. 12; William Styron, 'The Message of Auschwitz', in A.D. Casciato and J.L.W. West III (eds), *Critical Essays on William Styron* (Boston: G.K. Hall, 1982), p. 285. Emily Budick Miller contrasts the differing receptions of William Styron's *Sophie's Choice* and its 'Judaic' version, Cynthia Ozick's *The Shawl*

('Acknowledging the Holocaust in Contemporary American Fiction and Criticism', in Efraim Sicher (ed.), *Breaking the Crystal: Writing and Memory after Auschwitz*, Urbana and Chicago: University of Illinois Press, 1998, pp. 332–3).

7 Roland Barthes, 'The Death of the Author', *Image, Music, Text*, ed. and trans. Stephen Heath (London: Fontana, 1977).

8 Sara Horowitz, in an otherwise interesting discussion of generic hybridity in Holocaust novels by survivors, notes that this is the case without adding that it is a curiously unliterary way to approach a text ('Auto/Biography and Fiction after Auschwitz: Probing the Boundaries of Second-Generation Aesthetics', in Efraim Sicher, *Breaking the Crystal*, p. 278).

9 Quoted by Charles Spencer, 'Poor testament to great tragedy', *Daily Telegraph*, 9 November 1996, p. 8.

10 David Denby notes that the press kit for Benigni's *Life is Beautiful* insisted on the historical research and accuracy of the film, which Denby holds to be at odds with the director's claim that his film was not realist ('In the Eye of the Beholder', *New Yorker*, 15 March 1999, p. 99).

11 George Steiner, 'Dying is an Art', *Language and Silence* (Harmondsworth: Penguin, 1979); for more positive views of Plath's Holocaust imagery, see Stan Smith, 'Waist-deep in History', *Inviolable Voice* (Dublin: McGill, 1982); James E. Young, 'The Holocaust Confessions of Sylvia Plath', *Writing and Rewriting the Holocaust: Narrative and the Consequences of Interpretation* (Bloomington and Indianapolis: Indiana University Press, 1990); Jacqueline Rose, *The Haunting of Sylvia Plath* (London: Virago, 1991).

12 Cynthia Ozick, *The Shawl* (London: Jonathan Cape, 1991 [1980]); Susan Fromberg Schaeffer, *Anya* (Harmondsworth: Penguin, 1974); Diane Samuels, *Kindertransport* (London: Nick Hern Books, 1995); David Hartnett, *Black Milk* (London: Jonathan Cape, 1994); John Hersey, *The Wall* (New York: Alfred A. Knopf, 1950). Sicher ('Introduction', *Breaking the Crystal*, p. 5) asserts that he is concerned with the 'depiction of the Holocaust by those who were not there', but by this he means specifically 'children of survivors … [and] also members of their generation': all the writers he cites are Jewish. See also Alan L. Berger's study, *Children of Job: American Second-Generation Witnesses to the Holocaust* (Albany, N.Y.: State University of New York Press, 1997), which is clearly concerned with Jewish responses to the Holocaust.

13 For instance, Joel Shatzky refers to the imagined reincarnation of Anne Frank in Roth's novel as 'a sick Jewish joke' ('Creating an Aesthetic for Holocaust Literature', *Studies in Jewish American Literature* 10 (1), 1994, pp. 104–14: p. 110; Philip Roth, *The Ghost Writer* (London: Jonathan Cape, 1979); Melvin Jules Bukiet, *After* (New York: St Martin's Press, 1996).

14 By contrast, Sara Horowitz declares that the way in which 'literature foregrounds its own rhetoric' makes fiction a poor witness for the Holocaust ('Auto/Biography and Fiction after Auschwitz', p. 292). Her argument is structured the wrong way round: rather than assessing the available options and deciding that fiction is the least appropriate, it seems more sensible to address each genre separately.

15 Elie Wiesel, 'The Holocaust as Literary Inspiration', *Dimensions of the Holocaust: Lectures at Northwestern University by Elie Wiesel, Lucy S. Dawidowicz, Dorothy Rabinowitz, Robert McAfee Brown* (Evanston, Ill.: Northwestern University Press, 1977).

16 Quoted in Irving Howe, 'Writing and the Holocaust', in Berel Lang (ed.), *Writing and the Holocaust* (New York: Holmes and Meier, 1988), p. 179.

17 Irving Howe uses the same argument to support the priority of memoir, 'a kind of writing in which the author has no obligation to do anything but, in accurate and sober terms, tell what he experience and witnessed' ('Writing and the Holocaust', p. 182); according to this view, the memoirist uses a kind of transparent, non-figurative prose.

18 Quoted in Miriam Bratu Hansen, '*Schindler's List* is not *Shoah*: Second Commandment, Popular Modernism, and Public Memory', in Yosefa Loshitzky (ed.), *Spielberg's Holocaust: Critical Perspectives on 'Schindler's List'* (Bloomington and Indianapolis:
Indiana University Press, 1997), p. 200.

19 Lanzmann announces: 'If I had stumbled on a real SS film – a secret film, because
filming was strictly forbidden – that showed how 3,000 Jewish men, women and
children were gassed in Auschwitz's crematorium 2, not only would I not have
shown it, I would have destroyed it' ('Why Spielberg has distorted the truth', *Guardian Weekly*, 3 April 1994, p. 14).

20 Ibid.

21 Instead, *Shoah* is 'a presentation of representation. It is a documentation of the
process of producing events in front of the camera' (Hansen, '*Schindler's List* is not
Shoah', p. 108).

22 Wiesel, 'The Holocaust as Literary Inspiration', p. 7.

23 Saul Friedlander refines this argument further by quoting Perry Anderson's
comments on the 'limits' of representation: 'the Final Solution cannot *historically* be
written as romance or as comedy', or as 'pastoral' ('Introduction', Saul Friedlander
(ed.), *Probing the Limits of Representation: Nazism and the 'Final Solution'*, Cambridge,
Mass.: Harvard University Press, 1992, pp. 8, 10). This is a revealing use of the
vocabulary of prohibition – 'cannot' really means 'must not', as such writing not
only can but does occur. Benigni's film *Life is Beautiful* is an instance of a Holocaust
romance; Melvin Bukiet's *After* a Holocaust comedy; Ida Fink's stories *A Scrap of
Time* (Harmondsworth: Penguin, 1989) are pastorally set in the gardens and fields of
wartime Cracow. The attempt to rule out certain representational genres rests on
the assumption that these genres only appear monologically, as themselves. What
Anderson means by a Holocaust comedy is presumably one which straightforwardly
views the event as a source of humour, of the kind which, as Friedlander says, would
have been *de rigueur* had the Nazis won the war (p. 10), rather than the stylized,
double-voiced black comedy of, for instance, Tadeusz Borowski's *This Way for the
Gas, Ladies and Gentlemen* (New York: Penguin Books, 1976) or Art Spiegelman's
cartoon narratives, *Maus I* and *Maus II* (New York: Pantheon Books, 1986, 1991).
Such prescriptions may appear to be clear and sensible, but they do not take into
account the dialogic construction of literary genres and their ironized relation to
Holocaust fiction.

24 See, for instance, Horowitz's account of three genres: the pale imitation of
'invention' (fiction); 'chronology' (historical records); and 'Holocaust fiction' (fiction
written by survivors) ('Auto/Biography and Fiction after Auschwitz', p. 287); and
Howe, who allows for invention only in the writing of such survivors as Tadeusz
Borowski and Piotr Rawicz which is founded in 'mimesis' ('Writing the Holocaust',
pp. 192–3).

25 Erich Auerbach, *Mimesis: The Representation of Reality in Western Literature* (New York:
Doubleday, 1957), p. 20.

26 Ibid., pp. 19, 20.

27 It is not only fictional representations of the Holocaust which give rise to critical
scandals. Other histories, particularly those to do with self-determination or oppression, are also the sites of critical unease based on uncertainty about who is to nar-
rate such stories, and how they will do it. Such histories include plantation slavery;
Vietnam; and the fate of aboriginal peoples in Australasia.

28 Bryan Cheyette, in 'Writing the Unwritable', p. 14.

29 However, even this truism is open to debate. Irving Howe describes the effect of
reading Filip Müller's memoir *Eyewitness Auschwitz* (1979): 'Somehow Müller survived. His narrative is free of verbal embellishment or thematic reflection; he indulges neither in self-apology nor self-attack.... His book is simply the story of a

simple man who processed many corpses' ('Writing the Holocaust', p. 184). It is true that Müller's testimony, instantly recognizable to anyone who has seen *Shoah* as that of the man who recounts his experience in an Auschwitz Sonderkommando, is remarkable. But for Inga Clendinnen, *Eyewitness Auschwitz* reads as a highly structured text, so plotted for dramatic effect that at times it is implausible: 'Time and again, after gruelling descriptions of gas-chamber killings – descriptions which can be broadly authenticated from other sources – the reader is comforted by notably less well-authenticated scenes of defiance and/or faith' (*Reading the Holocaust*, Melbourne, Victoria: Text Publishing, 1998, p. 28).

30 See, for instance, the several accounts of the Warsaw Ghetto uprising, including Tuvia Borzykowski, *Between Tumbling Walls* (Israel: Ghetto Fighters' House, 1972); Mark Ber, *Uprising in the Warsaw Ghetto* (New York: Schocken Books, 1975); Yitzhak Zuckerman, *A Surplus of Memory: Chronicle of the Warsaw Ghetto Uprising* (Berkeley: University of California Press, 1993).

31 Hannah Arendt, *Eichmann in Jerusalem: A Report on the Banality of Evil* (Harmondsworth: Penguin, 1965); A. Anatoli (Anatoly Kuznetsov), *Babi Yar* (London: Sphere Books, 1970); Martin Gilbert, *The Holocaust: The Jewish Tragedy*, (London: HarperCollins, 1986); *KL Auschwitz Seen by the SS: Rudolf Höss, Pery Broad, Johann Paul Kremer*, footnotes and biographical notes ed. by Jadwiga Bezwinska and Danuta Czech (Oswiecim: The Auschwitz-Birkenau State Museum, 1994 [1970]); Robert Jay Lifton, *The Nazi Doctors: Medical Killing and the Psychology of Genocide* (New York: Basic Books, 1986).

32 Quoted by Lacey Baldwin Smith, 'Foreword', *Dimensions of the Holocaust*, p. 2.

33 Joseph Skibell, 'Writing the Unthinkable', p. 13; *A Blessing on the Moon* (London: Little, Brown and Company, 1997).

34 Lucy Ellmann, 'Writing the Unthinkable', p. 13; *Man or Mango?* (London: Headline Books, 1998).

35 Michael André Bernstein, 'Homage to the Extreme: The Shoah and the Rhetoric of Catastrophe', *Times Literary Supplement*, 6 March 1998, pp. 6–8: p. 8. Wiesel, 'The Holocaust as Literary Inspiration', p. 9.

36 Pat Barker, *Regeneration* (Harmondsworth: Penguin, 1991); *The Eye in the Door* (Harmondsworth: Penguin, 1993); *The Ghost Road* (Harmondsworth: Penguin, 1996).

37 Howe expresses this fear, 'Writing the Holocaust', p. 187.

38 Shatzky takes a prescriptive line and insists that the three important factors to be borne in mind when assessing the merit of a work about the Holocaust are 'historical accuracy, literary quality, and what I would call "intellectual integrity" '. He explains the latter phrase: 'Thus the intellectual integrity of a work about the Holocaust *must* be measured by the extent to which it centers its meaning upon the Holocaust itself rather than "borrowing" the Holocaust to mean something else' ('Creating an Aesthetic for Holocaust Literature', pp. 105, 107, my italics).

39 Anne Michaels, *Fugitive Pieces* (London: Bloomsbury, 1997). All the extracts from reviews quoted on the novel's cover emphasize its fine writing and do not mention its subject matter at all.

40 Ibid., p. 216.

41 Ibid., p. 53.

42 Ibid., p. 168.

43 Mikhail Bakhtin, 'Discourse in the Novel', *The Dialogic Imagination: Four Essays*, trans. Caryl Emerson and Michael Holquist, ed. Michael Holquist (Austin, Tex.: University of Texas Press, 1981), p. 272.

44 Why, for instance, does Jakob's lost sister Bella have to be a talented piano player,

and beautiful? Why does Athos have to be a saint in human form, *and* a palaeobotanist?

45 Natasha Walter, 'Memorable miniatures', *Guardian* section 2, 20 February 1997, p. 12.
46 Ozick, *The Shawl*, p. 18. Of course there are counter views to the one I have expressed: Elaine M. Kauvar discusses the metaphor of flight in Ozick's novel and the literary traditions she is drawing on (*Cynthia Ozick's Fiction*, Bloomington and Indianapolis: Indiana University Press, 1993, p. 180). Lawrence L. Langer comments on the very same lines, noting that they convey a 'view both poetic and remote, since Rosa is not very close to the scene of the murder'; however, he judges that if there is 'a branch of art called the poetry of atrocity' then Ozick is its 'master' [*sic*] (*Pre-empting the Holocaust*, New Haven and London: Yale University Press, 1998, p. 123).

1 Formal matters: Martin Amis, *Time's Arrow*

1 Mark Lawson, 'The Amis Babies', *Independent Magazine*, 7 September 1991, p. 43.
2 Simon Louvish, 'No Business Like Shoah Business', *New Moon*, November 1991, p. 10.
3 Zsuzsanna Ozsvath and Martha Satz, 'The Audacity of Expressing the Inexpressible: The Relation Between Moral and Aesthetic Considerations in Holocaust Literature', *Judaism* 34 (2), 1985, pp. 197–210: p. 200.
4 Quoted in Lawson, 'The Amis Babies', p. 43.
5 Amis did not win the Booker Prize, although he was the favourite (Ben Okri won it for *The Famished Road*), but he was the recipient that year of the Hooker Prize for his novel *London Fields*, 'bestowed by a group of female writers for male chauvinist writing' (Tim Cooper, 'Beating St Paul to Hooker Prize', *London Evening Standard*, 1991, n.d.).
6 Allan Massie, *The Sins of the Fathers* (London: Hutchinson, 1991).
7 Anonymous review, *Sunday Times*, 11 October 1992. Karl Miller, *Doubles: Studies in Literary History* (Oxford: Oxford University Press, 1985), pp. 410, 412.
8 Lawson, 'The Amis Babies', p. 43.
9 Lawrence L. Langer, *Admitting the Holocaust: Collected Essays* (Oxford and New York: Oxford University Press, 1995), p. 6.
10 Martin Amis, *Time's Arrow* (Harmondsworth: Penguin, 1992 [1991]), p. 139; all further page references are cited in brackets in the text. James Buchan, a sceptical reviewer, puts the reverse of cause and effect rather differently: 'things happen because they have happened, not from cause or motive' ('The Return of Dr Death', *Spectator*, 28 September 1991, p. 37).
11 Louvish, 'No Business', p. 10; and the anonymous reviewer 'A.B.' in the *Glasgow Herald*, 19 October 1992: 'maverick voices raised the objection that Amis was using the Holocaust as the latest notch on the headboard of his own self-importance.' Buchan is not impressed by the weight placed on the formal aspect of the novel: 'Listen: Auschwitz is not just about style. It is about aberrant behaviour by people en masse which is hard to understand even with great thought and study. Martin Amis is just about style' ('The Return of Dr Death', p. 37). And see Amis's reply, 'Creepier Than Thou', *Spectator*, 5 October 1991, p. 25. On the British television review *The Late Show*, the poet Tom Paulin accused Amis's novel of constituting a 'designer Auschwitz' (BBC2, November 1991).
12 David Roskies, *Against the Apocalypse: Responses to Catastrophe in Modern Jewish Culture* (Cambridge, Mass.: Harvard University Press, 1984), p. 198.

13 However, in Wiesel's memoirs there is no trace of any bad feeling on his part. He ascribes the change of title simply to the publisher's preference for a biblical phrase (*All Rivers Run to the Sea: Memoirs Volume One, 1928–1969*, London: HarperCollins, 1996, pp. 319–20).

14 There is, it is true, nothing as polemical as a reproach in either Begley's novel, which won the *Irish Times/*Aer Lingus International Fiction Prize, or Fink's stories *A Scrap of Time*, which won the Anne Frank Prize for Literature.

15 Maya Slater, 'Problems When Time Moves Backwards: Martin Amis's *Time's Arrow*', *English* 42 (173), Summer 1993, pp. 141–52; V.N. Volosinov, *Marxism and the Philosophy of Language*, trans. Ladislav Matejka and I.R. Titunik (New York: Seminar Press, 1973 [1929]), p. 23.

16 Robert Jay Lifton, *The Nazi Doctors: Medical Killing and the Psychology of Genocide* (New York: Basic Books, 1986), p. 373.

17 Frank Kermode, 'In Reverse', *London Review of Books*, 12 September 1991, p. 11.

18 Langer, *Admitting the Holocaust*, p. 77; Langer is discussing an observation made by Norma Rosen, which Michael André Bernstein calls a 'sadomasochistic identification' (*Foregone Conclusions: Against Apocalyptic History*, Berkeley and London: University of California Press, 1994, p. 58). Writing from the viewpoint of a survivor, Wiesel observes, 'I cannot write the words "concentration", "night and fog", "selection" or "transport" without a feeling of sacrilege' (*All Rivers Run*, p. 321).

19 Slater, 'Problems When Time Runs Backwards', p. 146.

20 Ibid., pp. 145, 149. John Updike, and others, have unearthed more genuine inconsistencies, the result of an apparently irresistible impulse to show up Amis's 'slips' – Updike ascribes their inevitability to the fact that 'the forward arrow of time is so deeply embedded in the syntax of the language and our habits of narration' ('Nobody Gets Away with Everything', *New Yorker*, 25 May 1992, p. 86).

21 Neil Easterbrook, ' "I know that it is to do with trash and shit": Narrative Reversal in Martin Amis's *Time's Arrow*', *Conference of College Teachers in English Studies* 55, 1995, pp. 52–61.

22 James Wood, 'The literary lip of Ladbroke Grove', *Guardian* 7/8 September 1991, p. 14; Kermode, 'In Reverse', p. 11; and neither the 'Commentary' nor the 'Summary' in the *Time's Arrow* section of the Martin Amis Homepage makes the Holocaust a central part of the novel.

23 Lifton, *The Nazi Doctors*, p. 149.

24 Quoted in Gary Saul Morson, *Narrative and Freedom: The Shadows of Time* (New Haven: Yale University Press, 1994), p. 155.

25 Bernstein, *Foregone Conclusions*, p. 1. One of the examples Bernstein gives of an oppressive backshadowing is the New Testament view of the Hebrew Bible as the precursor and predictor of the coming of Christ.

26 Morson, *Narrative and Freedom*, p. 6.

27 Ibid., pp. 2, 118.

28 Ibid., pp. 3, 45. Morson claims there is no foreshadowing in life.

29 Ibid., pp. 7, 117.

30 Bernstein, *Foregone Conclusions*, pp. 9, 13.

31 Ibid., p. 16. As Bernstein points out, backshadowing is crucially different from the classical tragic inevitability of anticipation, which we see in *King Lear*, where 'the end is not used retroactively to judge the characters' (*Foregone Conclusions*, p. 67).

32 Ibid., p. 23.

33 See also the controversy which erupted in 1997 about British knowledge of extermination as early as 1941, and the British government's disinclination, for a variety of reasons, to do anything about it; for example, Dan Stone, 'We know we knew', *Guardian*, 21 May 1997, p. 17.

34 Bernstein, *Foregone Conclusions*, p. 16.

35 Morson, *Narrative and Freedom*, p. 13.
36 Bernstein, *Foregone Conclusions*, p. 101.
37 Ibid., p. 42.
38 Easterbrook, ' "I know that it is to do with trash and shit" ', p. 52.
39 Lifton, *The Nazi Doctors*, p. 458; he suggests that doctors have a greater propensity for doubling than other professionals.
40 Peter Faulkner, *New Humanist* 1, 1991, p. 20.
41 Lifton in *The Nazi Doctors* quotes a strikingly similar phrase from the interview he conducted with former Nazi doctor Wolfgang R., who managed to leave a killing centre for the disabled after a month, but who continued to be plagued with questions about what might have happened ' "if I had been the right man on the right spot" ', p. 110).
42 Bernstein, *Foregone Conclusions*, p. 161, n. 7.
43 Ibid., p. 98.
44 Catherine Belsey, 'Constructing the Subject: Deconstructing the Text', in Judith Newton and Deborah Rosenfelt (eds), *Feminist Criticism and Social Change: Sex, Class and Race in Literature and Culture* (New York and London: Methuen, 1985), p. 53.
45 Mikhail Bakhtin, *Problems of Dostoevsky's Poetics*, trans. and ed. Caryl Emerson (Minneapolis: University of Minnesota Press, 1984), p. 75.
46 Bernstein, *Foregone Conclusions*, pp. 16, 37; see Ken Hirschkop on the difficulty of recognizing Bakhtin's notion of voices with 'equal rights' in a text: 'Is Dialogism for Real?', *Social Text* 30, 1987, p. 105.
47 Bernstein, *Foregone Conclusions*, p. 65.
48 Morson, *Narrative and Freedom*, p. 103.
49 Bernstein, *Foregone Conclusions*, p. 65.
50 Ida Fink, 'A Scrap of Time', in *A Scrap of Time: Stories* (Harmondsworth: Penguin, 1989 [1987]).
51 Kermode, 'In Reverse', p. 11.
52 Bernstein, *Foregone Conclusions*, p. 52, and p. 18 on George Berkeley's *Vienna and its Jews*.
53 Ibid., p. 18; he calls this 'Hitler-kitsch' and considers it an example of an 'alarming … fascination with Hitler'. In a review of *Foregone Conclusions*, Sander L. Gilman disagrees that Pawel is trying to elicit a 'tawdry frisson' by drawing a parallel between the birth of Hitler and the birth of Kafka's sister Elli, and argues that instead Pawel shows that 'the culture that both nurtures and deforms Kafka and Hitler provides the origins of the Shoah' (*Modern Philology* 94 (2), November 1996, p. 278).
54 Quoted in Morson, *Narrative and Freedom*, p. 186.
55 See Jonathan Webber, *The Future of Auschwitz* (Yarnton, Oxon: Oxford Centre for Postgraduate Hebrew Studies, 1992), on the different literal and figurative meanings of the word 'Auschwitz'.
56 Easterbrook, ' "I know that it is to do with trash and shit" ', p. 55.
57 Quoted in ibid.
58 Ibid., p. 58. John Updike gives an interesting reading of the narrator's comment on Irene's *aperçu*: telling him he has no soul 'sounds like a hectoring author scolding one of his characters for being subhuman' ('Nobody Gets Away with Everything', p. 87). Updike ironically transfers the Nazis' vocabulary of human hierarchy to that of the novelist, as Amis 'permits [Unverdorben] hardly a thought or deed that would encourage sympathy to work its way in': this is the point of the narrator, and the representation he facilitates of the plausible but damned 'doubled' self.
59 Updike, 'Nobody Gets Away with Everything', p. 87.
60 Easterbrook, ' "I know that it is to do with trash and shit" ', p. 57.

61 Philip K. Dick, 'Your Appointment will be Yesterday', *We Can Remember it for You Wholesale: Volume 5: The Collected Stories of Philip K. Dick* (London: HarperCollins, 1994 [1966]), p. 155. Thanks to Isabelle Doyle for this reference.

62 Ibid., pp. 156–7.

63 Ibid., pp. 173, 160.

64 Easterbrook, ' "I know that it is to do with trash and shit" ', p. 58.

65 The intertext for this *aperçu* on suicide could come from Dick, 'Your Appointment will be Yesterday' (p. 173), or Lifton, *The Nazi Doctors* (p. 150), where he observes: 'But prisoners could not be permitted to kill themselves; suicide violated the logic of the healing–killing paradox' – again, reverse narration makes the death camp logic seem 'right'.

66 Claude Lanzmann, *Shoah: An Oral History of the Holocaust* (New York: Pantheon Books, 1985), p. 20. In fact, Germans before the war did ask where the insane were taken to, in a rare act of popular opposition to state-sponsored murder; see Lifton, *The Nazi Doctors* (pp. 90–6).

67 Dick, 'Your Appointment will be Yesterday', p. 174.

68 Martin Amis, 'Kurt Vonnegut: After the Slaughterhouse', in *The Moronic Inferno and Other Visits to America* (London: Jonathan Cape, 1986), p. 135.

69 Kurt Vonnegut, *Slaughterhouse 5* (London: Triad/Granada, 1979 [1969]), p. 77.

70 Ibid., p.77.

71 Ibid., p. 54.

72 Ibid., pp. 36, 45.

73 Morson, *Narrative and Freedom*, p 17.

74 Ibid., p.134.

75 Vonnegut, *Slaughterhouse 5*, p. 61.

76 Ibid., p.77.

77 Morson, *Narrative and Freedom*, p. 118. Strictly speaking, as Morson says (p. 236), this is a trope of backshadowing, as the narrator is describing past events from the standpoint of the present.

78 Vonnegut, *Slaughterhouse 5*, p. 100.

79 Ibid., p. 102.

80 Ibid., p. 98. References made in the text to Ronald Reagan and David Irving cannot have had the effect of striking backshadowing which they do thirty years later: ' "Reagan for President!" a bumper sticker said' (p. 122) of the then Governor of California; and a character reads *The Destruction of Dresden*, a book proclaiming it a tragedy equal to the war's other massacres, by 'an Englishman called David Irving' (p. 124) – an early step on his route to Holocaust denial.

81 See Amis's essay 'Kurt Vonnegut: After the Slaughterhouse', p. 135.

82 Lifton, *The Nazi Doctors*, pp. 4, 147.

83 Ibid., pp. 14–15, 150.

84 Ibid., p. 70.

85 Wood observes, 'sometimes, like his friend and former Oxford tutor, the poet Craig Raine, Amis goes Martian' ('The literary lip', p. 13).

86 One might ask what is the point of the irony; do we not already know this? Wood comments, 'even Amis realises that he does not need to tell us how evil the Holocaust was', though follows it with a slide into commentary on the novel's form: 'Indeed, he doesn't: in this book, by way of compensation, he tells us how *good* the Holocaust was' (p. 12). Updike, on the other hand, laments the fact that *Time's Arrow* 'seems, flashily, to propose a fresh investigation, but comes up with no new evidence' ('Nobody Gets Away with Everything', p. 87).

87 Lifton, *The Nazi Doctors*, p. 355.

88 Ibid., p. 350.

89 Ibid., pp. 361–2.
90 See also Mario Biagioli's 'Science, Modernity, and the "Final Solution" ', in Saul Friedlander (ed.), *Probing the Limits of Representation: Nazism and the 'Final Solution'*, Cambridge, Mass.: Harvard University Press, 1992).
91 The details of sterilization experimentation seem to have been transferred by Amis from Lifton's account of Wladislaw Dering, the infamous subject of Leon Uris's novel *QB VII* (*The Nazi Doctors*, pp. 246–9). Lifton points out that Mengele was 'not a major Auschwitz experimenter in this area', and that prisoners, who undoubtedly did witness these kinds of experiment, were sometimes unclear about which Nazi doctor was conducting them (p. 363).
92 Lifton, *The Nazi Doctors*, p. 8.
93 Ibid., p. 430.
94 Ibid., p. 150, my italics
95 Anonymous review, *Scotland on Sunday*, 11 October 1992.
96 Lifton, *The Nazi Doctors*, pp. 195 ff., 151.
97 Ibid., p. 419.
98 Ibid., p. 422.
99 Wood, 'The literary lip', p. 14.
100 Bryan Cheyette, 'Fathers and Sons and Sins', *Jewish Chronicle*, 18 October 1991.
101 Anonymous review, *Glasgow Herald*; cf. Wood on Amis's Afterword, 'which reads like a massing of Jewish friends on his behalf' ('The literary lip', p. 14), and Aviva Kipen, 'Hitting and Missing the Mark', *Jewish Quarterly*, Summer 1992, p. 71: 'some of his best friends might even be Jewish'. See D.M. Thomas's defensive comment in his letter to the *Times Literary Supplement* (30 April 1982) during the debate over plagiarism in *The White Hotel* that he feels no 'unease' about his appropriation of a real-life testimony 'because the response of Jewish readers has been overwhelmingly positive'.
102 Kipen, 'Hitting and Missing the Mark', p. 70.
103 Easterbrook argues interestingly that the text 'allegorizes a Jewish double: the narrator literally reads backward', referring to the moment in which the narrator notes that observant Jews read the same way round he does (p. 51) (' "I know that it is to do with trash and shit" ', p. 58).
104 Kermode, 'In Reverse', p. 11.
105 Lawson, 'The Amis Babies', p. 44.
106 Anonymous review, *Sunday Times*, 11 October 1992.

2 Documentary fiction: D.M. Thomas, *The White Hotel*

1 In his autobiographical *Memories and Hallucinations* (London: Abacus, 1989), Thomas claims to have taken the idea of a woman fantasizing a sexual relation with Freud's son from Ernest Jones's biography (p. 24); details of hysteria from the 'Elizabeth von. R.' case history in Freud and Josef Breuer's *Studies in Hysteria* (Harmondsworth: Penguin, 1974); and acknowledges *passim* quotation from Freud's letters and works (Author's Note, *The White Hotel*, Harmondsworth: Penguin, 1981, p. iv; all further page references are cited in brackets in the text). See also Robert E. Lougy, 'The Wolf-Man, Freud, and D.M. Thomas: Intertextuality, Interpretation, and Narration in *The White Hotel*', *Modern Language Studies* 23 (3), 1991, pp. 91–106: pp. 91–2.
2 Hana Wirth-Nesher points out that in 'The Gastein Journal' 'Freud's paradigm seems to have replaced the laws of physics' ('The Ethics of Narration in D.M. Thomas's *The White Hotel*', *The Journal of Narrative Technique* 15, 1985, p. 19). Wombs may fly, in a literalization of the etymology of 'hysteria', and petrified foetuses float above the lake, but there is a very good explanation for this: we are in the realm of

the unconscious. Thomas says the novel turns 'poetic metaphors into literal fact – so that hair actually caught fire' (*Memories and Hallucinations*, p. 44).

3 Thomas, *Memories and Hallucinations*, p. 130.

4 Letter from Susan Fromberg Schaeffer to Peter Redgrove, 17 May 1981, in which she says, 'I seem to have been the only person in this country [the US] not to have loved *TWH* and to have said so in print. I loved the beginning and the rest of the novel struck me as pretentious nonsense in which Freud was made a mockery of and the plot and characters fail in every possible novelistic way' (Peter Redgrove Archive, 24.16). Thomas, *Memories and Hallucinations*, p. 73; letter from Sylvia Kantaris to Peter Redgrove, 4 May 1982. Zsuzsanna Ozsvath and Martha Satz document some of the 'superlative reviews' *The White Hotel* received in the American press ('The Audacity of Expressing the Inexpressible: The Relation Between Moral and Aesthetic Considerations in Holocaust Literature', *Judaism* 34 (2), 1985, p. 209, n. 23). In Martin Amis's words, 'a little offering, *The White Hotel*, had tiptoed through the review pages of the London press and had sold the usual 500 copies' until the rave American reviews, whereupon back in Britain 'red-faced reviewers began to take a second look' ('The D.M. Thomas Phenomenon', *Atlantic Monthly*, April 1983, p. 124). He ascribes the novel's success in the US to its combination of sex, the Final Solution and psychoanalysis: 'the full triumvirate of national fixations'. A second attempt is being made to film the novel in 2000, directed by Emir Kusturica.

5 D.A. Kenrick, letter to the *Times Literary Supplement*, 26 March 1982: 'should the author of a fiction choose as his proper subject events which are not only outside his own experience but also, evidently, beyond his own resources of imaginative recreation?' Linda Hutcheon, in a sensitive and sympathetic discussion, gives *The White Hotel* the label of 'historiographic metafiction', that is, 'a novel about how we produce meaning in history and fiction' ('Subject In/Of/To History and His Story', *Diacritics* 16 (1), Spring 1986, pp. 78–91: pp. 78, 83).

6 Thomas, *Memories and Hallucinations*, p. 47. See also his letters to the *Times Literary Supplement* (*TLS*), 30 March 1982 and 2 April 1982.

7 Susanne Kappeler, *The Pornography of Representation* (Cambridge: Polity Press, 1986), pp. 85, 87.

8 Ibid., pp. 88, 89–90. Hutcheon gives a different reading, likening the 'impossibility of a "fixed subject-vision" ' in *The White Hotel* to that in Oshima's film *In the Realm of the Senses*: another site of contested sexual meaning ('Subject In/Of/To History', p. 79). She ascribes the novel's ability to disturb to its 'antihumanistic' qualities, which simultaneously install and subvert the female subject (ibid., p. 90).

9 Wirth-Nesher, 'The Ethics of Narration', p. 456; Hutcheon, 'Subject In/Of/To History', p. 80. Margaret Soltan compares the 'dumbly registered' fact of Lisa's death with the 'meaningful' death of Malcolm Lowry's Consul in *Under the Volcano* as typifying a postmodern approach to fate: she argues that Lisa Erdman's name itself betokens a 'physical' nature as opposed to the Consul's 'metaphysical' name, Geoffrey Firmin; see her 'From Black Magic to White Noise: Malcolm Lowry and Don DeLillo', in Frederick Asals and Paul Tiessen (eds), *A Darkness that Murmured: Essays on Malcolm Lowry* (Toronto: University of Toronto Press, 2000).

10 Kappeler, *The Pornography of Representation*, pp. 94, 90. Hutcheon has a different view of the same phenomenon: all the differing narratorial practices are part of the presentation of 'the process of the constitution of [*The White Hotel's*] protagonist, Lisa' ('Subject In/Of/To History', p. 86).

11 Thomas, *Memories and Hallucinations*, p. 84; letter to the *TLS*, 2 April 1982. The case of *The White Hotel* was not the first time Thomas had been accused of plagiarism, as Lynn Felder charts in 'D.M. Thomas: The Plagiarism Controversy', in Richard Ziegfeld (ed.), *Dictionary of Literary Biography Yearbook 1982* (Detroit: Gale Research,

1983, pp. 79–82: pp. 80–1). His translations of Pushkin and Akhmatova were seen as over-reliant on earlier translations. Felder notes (ibid., p. 80) that Thomas acknowledged the inspiration of science fiction writers Isaac Asimov and Ray Bradbury in an early collection of poems, which Geoffrey Grigson described, during the *White Hotel* controversy, as 'admission of plagiarism in poetry': a case of neither having your cake nor eating it. On the hierarchy of intertexts which Thomas denies, James Fenton oddly observes in a letter to the *Times Literary Supplement* (2 April 1982) that there is justice in the greater prominence of the acknowledgement to Freud in *The White Hotel*, as without Freud '*The White Hotel* could not have been written. On the other hand, there were other massacres beside Babi Yar. The debt to Freud is fundamental. The debt to Kuznetsov's unique witness is contingent.' This seems incorrect even if Fenton means there were other *Holocaust* massacres that Thomas could have included; as we have seen, there are several reasons why this ravine and Kuznetsov's text were chosen.

12 Anatoly Kuznetsov [A. Anatoli], *Babi Yar*, trans. David Floyd (London: Sphere Books, 1970), pp. 38, 34, 446, 112 (some censoring of religious metaphors here too), 186, 378, 399, 225. In all quotations, bold type indicates material deleted by the Soviet censor for the book's 1966 Russian edition and restored in the English edition; square brackets indicate material added by Kuznetsov in 1970. Hutcheon points out that for all Kuznetsov's insistence that what he writes is only factual, 'he does not consider the discursive context of [Dina's] account (the 1946 Ukraine war crimes trial) or the fact that he (a male) has reinscribed her (female) experience' ('Subject In/Of/To History', p. 86). In his final letter to the *Times Literary Supplement* (30 April 1982), Thomas describes the 'tone' of Pronicheva's account as that of 'public testimony not of a private memoir'.

13 Thomas, *Memories and Hallucinations*, p. 47.

14 Kuznetsov, *Babi Yar*, p. 209; and Thomas, *The White Hotel*, p. 104. Kuznetsov, *Babi Yar*, p. 211; and Thomas, *The White Hotel*, p. 105. Patrick Swinden praises Thomas's changes to the description of the coat as 'delicately humanising' ('D.M. Thomas and *The White Hotel*', *Critical Quarterly* 24 (4), 1986, p. 80).

15 Thomas describes coming upon *Babi Yar* in *Memories and Hallucinations*: 'There were extraordinary connections [with the monologue, 'The Woman to Sigmund Freud']. My anonymous heroine had also made a terrified escape from an unspecified danger. I had based her fantasy on the elements: water, fire, earth and air. The lake had flooded, the hotel burned, mourners had been buried in an avalanche, skiers had fallen through the air to their deaths. All these events were echoed at Babi Yar: the victims had fallen into the ravine; Dina Pronicheva, the survivor, had been terrified of being buried alive as earth was flung down on the sea of bodies; later the Nazis had burned the dug-up corpses, trying to hide their crime; then, under the Soviets, a dam had burst, flooding the ravine and most of Kiev' (p. 39).

Hutcheon points out that Lisa's fate in the Yar is like a horrible materialization of the Freudian definition of femininity as (quoting Kaja Silverman) 'ideally passive, masochistic and exhibitionisitic to fit male aggression, sadism and voyeurism', although it is going too far to add that the SS's (Hutcheon calls them 'soldiers') method of asserting masculinity is 'perhaps a more immediately effective way than "Freud's" equally patriarchal inscription of [Lisa] as subject' ('Subject In/Of/To History', p. 89). Patrick Swinden makes the similarly glib remark that although one would of course prefer analysis to the Nazi boot, 'their *effect* is identical: the reduction of personality to manageable and unself-contradictory proportions' ('D.M. Thomas and *The White Hotel*', p. 79).

16 Kuznetsov, *Babi Yar*, p. 110. See Hutcheon, 'Subject In/Of/To History', p. 83: Dina's voice is ' "borrowed" *by the narrator* of the novel, so women are no longer to be "absented" from history and cultural process' (my italics). It is very significant

that Hutcheon ascribes the act of borrowing to the narrator rather than the author, thus defusing the plagiarism controversy in one word. She adds that 'man' is not the centre of action in *The White Hotel*: '*woman* is, on one level, and collective history is, on another' (p. 84).

17 Hutcheon, 'Subject In/Of/To History', p. 112.

18 Ibid., p. 117ff.; Kuznetsov, *Babi Yar*, p. 222; and Thomas, *The White Hotel*, p. 379.

19 Wirth-Nesher, 'The Ethics of Narration', p. 25. See also David Frost's letter to the *Times Literary Supplement* (9 April 1982), in which he argues that Thomas's use of the *Babi Yar* material commits him to ' "back-projection" ': 'he must create a character and a past for that character which may plausibly emerge in Dina Pronicheva's real experiences', but Frost finds the link between the two women unconvincing (in fact, they are two separate people in the novel; Lisa knows Dina from the opera).

20 Letter to the *Times Literary Supplement*, 2 April 1982. Linda Hutcheon comments that the tracing of influences through 'textual or biographical evidence' is now a largely outmoded genre of literary criticism which has been replaced by interest 'in the functional reverberations caused by textual strategies in the mind of the reader': this is the relevance of Thomas's comment about the 'transition' between discourses ('Literary Borrowing … and Stealing: Plagiarism, Sources, Influences, and Intertexts', *English Studies in Canada* XII (2), June 1986, p. 234).

21 Kappeler, *The Pornography of Representation*, pp. 93, 99.

22 Quoted in Barbara Foley, 'Fact, Fiction, Fascism: Testimony and Mimesis in Holocaust Narratives', *Comparative Literature* 34 (4), Fall 1982, pp. 330–60.

23 Wirth-Nesher says of the dilemma she constructs for Thomas: 'while pain can be imagined artistically, fictions about factual accounts of human suffering betray those who suffer, either by creating an object of beauty and enjoyment out of another's pain or through fictionalizing, calling into question the "reality" of the pain having ever occurred' ('The Ethics of Narration', p. 24).

24 'The Woman to Sigmund Freud', originally published in *New Worlds*, 1979.

25 Quoted in Kappeler, *The Pornography of Representation*, p. 87; elisions are Kappeler's.

26 Ibid., p. 87.

27 Thomas, *Memories and Hallucinations*, pp. 39, 40.

28 Laura E. Tanner, 'Sweet Pain and Charred Bodies: Figuring Violence in *The White Hotel*', *Intimate Violence* (Bloomington and Indianapolis: Indiana University Press, 1994), p. 58.

29 James Strachey, 'Sigmund Freud: A Sketch of His Life and Ideas', in Freud and Breuer, *Studies in Hysteria*, p. 14.

30 Tanner, 'Sweet Pain', p. 64.

31 Ibid., pp. 88, 65.

32 Mary F. Robertson, 'Hystery, Herstory, History: "Imagining the Real" in Thomas's *The White Hotel*', *Contemporary Literature* 25, 1984, p. 457.

33 Tanner, 'Sweet Pain', pp. 65, 64, 69.

34 Thomas's Freud says, 'it may be that we have studied the sexual impulses too exclusively, and that we are in the position of a mariner whose gaze is so concentrated on the lighthouse that he runs on to the rocks in the engulfing darkness' (*The White Hotel*, p. 13). Ozsvath and Satz agree with Tanner's argument that 'psychological investigation is incommensurate with the Holocaust', but add that the novel's 'structure belies its statement' ('The Audacity of Expressing the Inexpressible', p. 210).

35 Tanner points out that sexual images acquire an awful reality at Babi Yar. Instead of the beautiful arctic sea of her imaginings, at the Yar Lisa is immersed in a 'sea of bodies covered in blood'; 'The "whale who moaned/a lullaby to my corset" disappears, replaced by a brutal soldier who "started hitting her with his club, on her back and shoulders" because "she couldn't unhook her corset fast enough" ' ('Sweet

Pain', p. 69); and perhaps most strikingly, the image Lisa uses for her empathy with other people's suffering ' "just the other side of the hill" ' (p. 170) comes true when she is made to sit on a 'hillock' at Babi Yar watching the agony of others before being shot herself (p. 213).

36 Robertson, 'Hystery, Herstory, History', pp. 460, 461.

37 Tanner, 'Sweet Pain', p. 72.

38 David Wingrove/D.M.Thomas, 'Different Voices', *London Magazine*, February 1982, pp. 27–43: p. 42.

39 Tanner, 'Sweet Pain', p. 72. See also Hutcheon, who describes how the novel disrupts any 'reader position from which the text is easily understandable', despite the 'lure' of historical figures and traditional novelistic discourses such as 'biographical and epistolary form' ('Subject In/Of/To History', pp. 85, 87); Jerzy Kosinski calls the easily understandable 'the Fiddler-on-the-Roof' readerly approach (quoted in Daniel J. Cahill, 'Kosinski and His Critics', *North American Review*, Spring 1980, p. 68).

40 Michael André Bernstein, *Foregone Conclusions: Against Apocalyptic History* (Berkeley and London: University of California Press, 1994), p. 161, n. 7. Some critics think it necessary to defend Lisa against the charge of 'wanting' her fate because she predicts it (K.J. Phillips, 'The Phalaris Syndrome: Alain Robbe-Grillet vs. D.M. Thomas', in Katherine Anne Ackley (ed.), *Women and Violence in Literature: An Essay Collection*, New York and London: Garland Publishing, 1990, p. 195; David Cowart, 'Being and Seeming: *The White Hotel*', *Novel* 19, Spring 1986, pp. 216–31: p. 220). Even in cases where such a defence might be appropriate, such as Lise in Muriel Spark's *The Driver's Seat* (Harmondsworth: Penguin, 1970) or Nicola in Martin Amis's *London Fields* (Harmondsworth: Penguin, 1988), the texts self-consciously draw attention to the necessary novelistic confusion between contingency and necessity, just as Thomas does.

41 Lougy discusses the Wolf Man's case history as intertext, 'The Wolf-Man, Freud, and D.M. Thomas', pp. 93, 104, n. 6.

42 Sigmund Freud, *The Standard Edition of the Complete Psychological Works of Sigmund Freud*, vol. XVII (London: Hogarth, 1953), p. 109.

43 J. Laplanche and J.B. Pontalis, *The Language of Psychoanalysis*, trans. D. Nicholson-Smith (London: Karnac Books, 1988), p. 112.

44 Lougy, 'The Wolf-Man, Freud, and D.M. Thomas', p. 96; Freud, *Standard Edition*, vol. XVII, p. 103.

45 Neil Easterbrook, ' "I know that it is to do with trash and shit": Narrative reversal in Martin Amis's *Time's Arrow*', *Conference of College Teachers in English Studies* 55, 1995, pp. 52–61: p. 58.

46 Laplanche and Pontalis, *The Language of Psychoanalysis*, p. 111.

47 Wingrove/Thomas, 'Different Voices', pp. 34, 42.

48 Ibid., p. 33.

49 Lougy sees the effect of the epistolary calm being 'shattered' by the eroticism and violence of the next two sections as a fruitful stumbling block in the way of simple quests for 'that elusive culprit called meaning' ('The Wolf-Man, Freud, and D.M. Thomas', p. 91).

50 Wingrove/Thomas, 'Different Voices', p. 33.

51 Ibid., p. 35.

52 Tanner, 'Sweet Pain', p. 72.

53 Linda Hutcheon asks if controversy arises as a consequence 'less of the *manner* in which one uses another text than of the *kind* of text from which one borrows – or steals?' ('Literary Borrowing ... and Stealing', p. 230), suggesting that to borrow from Freud is seen as less heinous than borrowing from the historical record, that is, Kuznetsov.

54 James E. Young, 'Holocaust Documentary Fiction: The Novelist as Eyewitness', in Berel Lang (ed.), *Writing and the Holocaust* (New York: Holmes and Meier, 1988), pp. 200–15: p. 212 (my italics), pp. 204, 206. Young adds that the fact of the text's originally censored, translated nature also makes it less than historically perfect. Barbara Foley, in her discussion of the documentary novel, also argues that 'it is a species of fiction distinctly characterized by its adherence to referential strategies associated with nonfictional modes of discourse but also demanding to be read within a fictional Gestalt familiar to contemporaneous readers' ('The Documentary Novel', in Michael J. Hoffman and Patrick D. Murphy (eds), *Essentials of the Theory of Fiction*, London: Leicester University Press, 1996, p. 405). Wirth-Nesher, however, gets the wrong end of the stick on this issue: 'One could accuse Thomas of naivete in his definition of history, given Kuznetsov's method of recording and reconstructing narratives after conversations with eyewitnesses' ('The Ethics of Narration', p. 23): the importance of *Babi Yar* for *The White Hotel* is exactly the kind of unofficial history Kuznetsov presents.

55 Young, 'Holocaust Documentary Fiction', p. 201. Linda Hutcheon describes the material borrowed from Kuznetsov as '*re*-fictionalized', as it is 'already twice removed from any historical reality: it is his version of [Dina's] narrativization of her experience' ('Subject In/Of/To History', p. 84).

56 Kuznetov, *Babi Yar*, p. 110.

57 This is *pace* Lougy, who says Lisa 'irrevocably choose[s] her Jewish heritage' ('The Wolf-Man, Freud, and D.M. Thomas', p. 94); in the scene at Babi Yar, it is rather that it is chosen *for* her.

58 Tanner, 'Sweet Pain', p. 59.

59 Ibid., p. 61.

60 Frank Kermode, 'In Reverse', *London Review of Books*, 12 September 1991, p. 11.

61 Cf. Kuznetsov, *Babi Yar*, p. 102.

62 Tanner, 'Sweet Pain', p. 102.

63 William G. Niederland, *The Schreber Case: Psychoanalytic Profile of a Paranoid Personality* (New York: Quadrangle/The New York Times Book Co., 1974); and Morton Schatzman, *Soul Murder: Persecution in the Family* (Harmondsworth: Penguin, 1976).

64 Eric Santner, *My Own Private Germany: Daniel Paul Schreber's Secret History of Modernity* (Princeton, N.J.: Princeton University Press, 1992). On Schreber's gender identification, see Marjorie Garber, *Vested Interests: Cross-Dressing and Cultural Anxiety* (Harmondsworth: Penguin, 1993), pp. 206–8.

65 Ann Pellegrini argues that Freud sought to avoid the issue of the Jewish man's 'pathological femininity' by shifting 'the burden of signifying castration and lack wholly onto women's bodies' ('Jewishness as Gender', *Performance Anxieties: Staging Psychoanalysis, Staging Race*, London: Routledge, 1997, pp. 18–37: p. 25); on race and gender, p. 28; he 'maximizes one relatively minor difference ("sex"), so as to minimize another ("race")' (p. 34).

66 Peter Gay points out that Freud observed, ' "if my name were Oberhuber, my innovations would have encountered far less resistance" ', and that he 'persisted, in doing psychoanalytic work and calling himself a Jew' (*Freud, Jews and Other Germans: Masters and Victims in Modernist Culture*, Oxford: Oxford University Press, 1978, pp. 76–7). This is *pace* Wirth-Nesher, who quotes from Carl E. Schorske's book *Fin-de-Siècle Vienna* on the ' "a-historical theory of man and society" ' that Freud adopted to ' "make bearable a political world spun out of orbit" ' ('The Ethics of Narration', p. 28, n. 11).

67 Phillips points out that the 'jew/jaw' slip reveals that Freud 'understands unconsciously that it hurts to *be a Jew*', but diverts this realization on to his own jaw ('The Phalaris Syndrome', p. 196).

68 Wingrove/Thomas, 'Different Voices', p. 33.

69 See Thomas's response, 'Altering my ego' (*Guardian*, 3 March 1993, p. 4), in which he claimed that the Pass Notes was about a non-existent Hyde to his inoffensive Jekyll, someone whose new novel 'is coldly calculated to become a bestseller, cashing in again on the Holocaust and Freudianism', author perhaps of *The Blue Motel* mentioned in *Memories and Hallucinations*, p. 113, or John Bayley's 'Off-White Motel' named in a postcard to Peter Redgrove, 7 March 1988 (Peter Redgrove Archive). It is true that the Minnesotan and 'big-thighed' student escapades in *Memories and Hallucinations* are related self-parodically, as are references to plagiarism (p. 2) and even prolepsis. Of an unwanted foreign tour, Thomas says, 'I told them I was resigning on the grounds of future ill-health' (p. 79). In 'Altering my ego', Thomas repeats the credo of *Memories and Hallucinations*: the impostor-double 'hates it that I prefer women to men, finding them more open to emotions and feelings. ... For me sex is a creative, no the creative force; which gives my novels the obsessional feel disturbing to many.' In an interview with Sabine Durrant ('The sins of the father', *Observer*, 8 September 1996, p. 14), Thomas argues that for the novelist to censor him- or herself in order not to offend would result in a Soviet realist kind of writing, of the kind described by Kuznetsov: ' "Socialist realism" requires an author to describe, not so much what really happened, but what ought to have happened, or at any rate what might have happened' (*Babi Yar*, p. 14).

70 Thomas, 'Altering my ego'; Thomas, *Memories and Hallucinations*, p. 131; Wingrove/Thomas, 'Different Voices', p. 30.

71 Kappeler, *The Pornography of Representation*, p. 104.

72 Robertson quaintly calls this 'the question of Woman' ('Hystery, Herstory, History', p. 463); Ronald Granofsky says that 'The violation of human dignity which holocaust entails encompasses the sources of nourishment and generation – the breast and pelvic region – which Lisa's body represents' ('Holocaust as Symbol in *Riddley Walker* and *The White Hotel*', *Modern Language Studies* 16 (3), 1986, pp. 172–82: p. 178).

73 Letter to the *Times Literary Supplement*, 23 April 1982; Kantaris sees Lisa's erotic fantasies not as an expression of the unconscious which is lost at Babi Yar, but 'symptomatic' of a sick society and prophetic of the consequences of sickness. In her letter to Peter Redgrove, 4 May 1982 (Peter Redgrove Archive, 70.01), Kantaris says she finds the scene where Lisa lactates at the hotel hard to take and adds: 'Interesting that Don finds milk so repulsive and told me he can't stand the milky scenes either – though he likes corsets of course.'

74 Kappeler, *The Pornography of Representation*, p. 86.

75 This is also Catherine Bernard's argument in her essay 'A Certain Hermeneutic Slant: Allegories in Contemporary English Fiction', where she briefly discusses *The White Hotel*'s subject as 'an absurd dance of death on the ash urn of the world', described in a 'stylization [which] exhausts meaning' (*Contemporary Literature* 38 (1), Spring 1997, p. 168).

76 Kantaris, letter of 4 May 1982.

77 In a letter to Peter Redgrove, 15 January 1984 (Peter Redgrove Archive, 69.06), Thomas says, 'Your observations on sex-magic in TWH strike me as absolutely true', and cites a review in the *North West Review*, by Thompson, who also hit on what is presumably the idea that Nazism annihilated the 'sex-magic' of femininity. Phillips argues that Lisa's writings are 'disappointing' because 'Thomas fails to make them entirely convincing as female fantasies of sexuality, since he has her emphasize penetration rather than orgasm in the erotic scenes' ('The Phalaris Syndrome', p. 192).

78 Sidra DeKoven Ezrahi, ' "The Grave in the Air": Unbound Metaphors in Post-Holocaust Poetry', in Saul Friedlander (ed.), *Probing the Limits of Representation* (Cambridge, Mass.: Harvard University Press, 1992), pp. 259–76: pp. 260–1. Interestingly, Kuznetsov himself uses the concept of Babi Yar figuratively: '**The world**

was just one big Babi Yar' (*Babi Yar*, p. 204); ['Babi Yar: that is the real symbol of your cultures and of your humanisms]' (p. 226); 'What new Babi Yars, Mai-daneks, Hiroshimas, [Kolymas and Potmas] ... lie hidden in the future?' (p. 477, square brackets Kuznetsov's own). Jay Bergman points out that Kuznetsov uses Babi Yar as 'a metaphor for the preservation of history', and quotes his words: ' "History cannot be deceived, and it is impossible to conceal something from it forever" ' ('Soviet Dissidents on the Holocaust, Hitler and Nazism: A Study of the Preservation of Historical Memory', *Slavic and East European Review* 70 (3), July 1992, pp. 477–504: p. 496).

79 Lougy, on the other hand, sees this as part of the novel's humanist, rather than psychoanalytic, agenda, 'Eloquently affirming the mysterious and irreducible individuality of each human being' ('The Wolf-Man, Freud, and D.M. Thomas', p. 102).

80 Quoted in Clair Wills, 'Upsetting the Public: Carnival, Hysteria and Women's Texts', in Ken Hirschkop and David Shepherd (eds), *Bakhtin and Cultural Theory* (Manchester: Manchester University Press, 1989), p. 138; among the many other instances of such sentiments is Peter Redgrove's observation that 'those peoples who hate and avoid the feminine in life become the most bellicose' (*The Wise Wound*, London: Paladin, 1986, p. 66); Kantaris links political and sexual malaise by describing *The White Hotel* as an exploration of 'the relationship between *repression* and brutality' (letter to the *Times Literary Supplement*, 23 April 1982, my italics).

81 Robertson says 'this novel could not have had a male hero' because of Lisa's special knowingness 'as woman, as analysand, and as Nazi victim' ('Hystery, Herstory, History', pp. 465, 477), a knowingness which can predict the historical disasters that remain opaque for instance to Freud; but she undermines her argument somewhat with a recourse to biology (p. 466).

82 Wirth-Nesher, 'The Ethics of Narration', p. 22.

83 Thomas himself contrasts the parts of the novel dealing with 1919 with those dealing with 1941: 'The style [is] realistic and impersonal, but also lyrical in parts: so leading to, yet contrasting with, the grim slow-moving realism of Babi Yar' (*Memories and Hallucinations*, p. 41).

84 Wirth-Nesher, 'Hystery, Herstory, History', p. 22 (my italics); she also says, 'History supplants psychology' (ibid., p. 25), though Lougy argues that 'Lisa's fantasies ... become *translated* into history' ('The Wolf-Man, Freud, and D.M. Thomas', p. 100, my italics); John Burt Foster, 'Magic Realism in *The White Hotel*: Compensatory Vision and the Transformation of Classic Realism', *Southern Humanities Review* 20, 1986, pp. 205–19.

85 Sander L. Gilman, *Jewish Self-Hatred: Anti-Semitism and the Hidden Language of the Jews* (Baltimore and London: Johns Hopkins University Press), p. 86; see also Pellegrini, who says Gilman 'has framed his arguments through and around the Jewish male' ('Jewishness as Gender', p. 19), and '*All Jews are womanly, but no women are Jews*' (p. 28). She concludes that 'The leading sign and originating occasion for Jewish male effeminacy was the circumcised penis' (p. 22), which was linked to the myth of Jewish male menstruation. Pellegrini goes on to comment on Gilman's finding that in early twentieth-century Viennese slang the clitoris was called the *Jud*, or 'Jew', that this effects a pejorative synthesis of female and Jewish male inferiority; both women and Jews possessed organs which were 'lesser', 'truncated versions of the "real" thing' (p. 29). Robertson argues, less convincingly, that there is a natural homology between representations of women and Holocaust victims ('Hystery, Herstory, History', p. 464).

86 Quoted in Gilman, *Jewish Self-Hatred*, p. 223.

87 Ibid., pp. 243–6.

88 Ibid., p. 245.

89 Sander L. Gilman, *The Case of Sigmund Freud* (Baltimore: Johns Hopkins University Press, 1993), p. 3; see also discussion of the Jewish dialect '*mauscheln*', pp. 140–5.

90 Ibid., p. 88.

91 Ibid., p. 104; for women, there were Charcot's photographs of hysterics, for Jews, physiognomy charts. Jews could be seen as members of the group identified by Julia Kristeva as the marginal 'feminine' (see Toril Moi, *Sexual/Textual Politics*, London: Methuen, 1985, pp. 163–7).

92 Gilman, *The Case of Sigmund Freud*, p. 127; see also Peggy Phelan, 'Dance and the History of Hysteria', in Susan Leigh Foster (ed.), *Corporealities: Dancing Knowledge, Culture and Power* (London: Routledge, 1996), pp. 90–103; Luce Irigaray, 'Gesture in Psychoanalysis', *Sexes and Genealogies*, trans. Gillian C. Gill (New York: Columbia University Press, 1993).

93 Pellegrini, 'Jewishness as Gender', p. 20.

94 Kuznetsov, *Babi Yar*, p. 99.

95 Robertson, 'Hystery, Herstory, History', p. 462; Phillips, 'The Phalaris Syndrome', p. 189: it goes quite against the temporal structure of the novel and its satiric purpose to argue, as Phillips does, that 'Thomas makes the events [Lisa] foresees seem preventable' (ibid., p. 194). The relationship of psychoanalysis and history or politics has been widely discussed, from Louis Althusser's *Essays on Ideology* (London: Verso, 1984) onwards; to mention just an eclectic few: Studs Turkle, *Psychoanalytic Politics: Jacques Lacan and Freud's French Revolution* (London: Free Association Books, 1992); Slavoj Zizek, *The Sublime Object of Ideology* (London: Verso, 1989); R. Saclel, 'Nationalism, Anti-Semitism and Anti-Feminism in Eastern Europe', *New German Critique* 57, Fall 1992, pp. 51–65 (thanks to Sean Homer for these references).

96 Quoted in Robertson, 'Hystery, Herstory, History', p. 462; Lougy, 'The Wolf-Man, Freud, and D.M. Thomas', sees them as a questioned image of cyclical time (p. 101).

97 The analogy comes from Kuznetsov, who specifically likens the posture of those killed by the bursting of the Babi Yar dam in 1961 to that of people frozen in time at Pompeii: 'One person had been making a call in a telephone booth, and perished there, with the receiver in his hand' (*Babi Yar*, p. 473). Freud appositely notes, 'the archaeological object occurs only in such rare circumstances as those of Pompeii or the tomb of Tutankhamun. All of the essentials are preserved; even things that seem completely forgotten – are present somehow and somewhere, and have merely been buried and made inaccessible to the subject. Indeed, it may, as we know, be doubted whether any psychical structure can really be the victim of total destruction' (*Standard Edition* vol. XXXII, p. 260). A different intertext may be Seamus Heaney's collection of poems, *North* (London: Faber, 1975).

98 Wirth-Nesher, 'The Ethics of Narration', p. 17. There was a debate about inorganic versus polyphonic structure in the letters pages of the *Times Literary Supplement*, David Frost advocating the former (9 April 1982), Sylvia Kantaris the latter (23 April 1982).

99 Aviva Kipen, 'Hitting and Missing the Mark', *Jewish Quarterly*, Summer 1992, p. 70.

100 Tanner, 'Sweet Pain', p. 65. Phillips sees the novel's move to 'historical' discourse as a way out of the problem of aestheticizing violence: 'Thomas may divert us and please us with his layered pattern in which to wrap falling bodies. Yet he withdraws the veils from Babi Yar at the necessary moment, to present a violent historical fact starkly, not evaded' ('The Phalaris Syndrome', p. 200).

101 Freud, *Standard Edition* vol. XVII, p. 13.

102 Peter Brooks, *Reading for the Plot* (New York: Columbia University Press, 1984), p. 273.

103 James Young interestingly points out that Thomas seems also to have based his account of Babi Yar on photographs of massacres in Lijepaja, Latvia, and Sniadowa,

Poland, reproduced in Gerhard Schoenberner, *The Yellow Star* (New York and London: Bantam, 1969), pp. 92–7. These photographs, taken by the perpetrators, are the equivalent of those moments in *The White Hotel* where Lisa is transformed into an object under the gaze of the SS.

104 Thomas says the white hotel is 'life': *Memories and Hallucinations* pp. 40, 73; David Cowart says that the hotel is 'corporeal existence', in contrast to the incorporeal existence of the camp (*Being and Seeming: 'The White Hotel'*, *Novel* 19, 1986, pp. 216–31).

105 Kuznetsov, *Babi Yar*, p. 91; he credits the Central State Archives of the October Revolution, Moscow. Fund 7021, index 65, item 5, fn.

106 Wingrove/Thomas, 'Different Voices', p. 42.

107 Lougy describes a first-time reader and how s/he is on the same footing as the characters ('The Wolf-Man, Freud, and D.M. Thomas, p. 91); see also Thomas, *Memories and Hallucinations*, p. 49; and Hutcheon, 'Subject In/Of/To History', p. 89: our 'hindsight that corresponds in part to Lisa's foresight' on a second reading.

108 Thomas, *Memories and Hallucinations*, p. 49.

109 Robertson says, 'we now must ask whether Thomas means us to have read the realistic chapter as "just one more possible discourse", no more compelling than the others' ('Hystery, Herstory, History', p. 462).

110 John Updike, 'Nobody Gets Away with Everything', *New Yorker*, 25 May 1992, p. 87.

111 *Pace* Wirth-Nesher, 'The Ethics of Narration', p. 25, but, as we have seen, taken from Kuznetsov, *Babi Yar*, p. 391.

112 Kuznetsov, *Babi Yar*, pp. 102, 391.

113 Robertson, 'Hystery, Herstory, History', pp. 462, 472.

114 Robertson sees it as the response to *The White Hotel*'s epigraph from Yeats, discussed ibid., p. 476.

115 Thomas, *Memories and Hallucinations*, pp. 49, 73.

116 Ibid., p. 49. Other reasons for Lisa not being Jewish are more structural: she must be an observer and one of the last to die (p. 48). Ozsvath and Satz argue that the novel itself 'prominently displaying the terrible monument of Babi Yar belies [Thomas's] statement' that ' "People have talked a lot about *The White Hotel* as a Holocaust book but it's almost accidental that [Lisa's] half-Jewish … all of us end up in holocausts as individuals" ' ('The Audacity of Expressing the Inexpressible', p. 207, n. 20).

117 Wirth-Nesher, 'The Ethics of Narration', p. 23 (my italics).

118 Letter to the *TLS*, 30 March 1982.

119 Emma Tennant, letter to the *TLS*, 9 April 1982. She adds that 'no writer has the *moral right* to take the experience of a real human being and attach it … to a made-up character' (my italics).

120 Wirth-Nesher, 'The Ethics of Narration', p. 17, and Thomas, in similar vein, says, 'the Holocaust raises profound questions of good and evil, and psychoanalysis deals with individual moral ambiguities' (quoted in Durrant, 'The sins of the father'). Barbara Foley quotes Victor Lange on the contextual definition of what is fact and what fiction at any given historical time: ' "The invented speeches in Tacitus are clearly part of a non-fictional intention; the actual letter which Rilke incorporated in *Malte Laurids Brigge* assumes, within the purposes of the novel, a distinctly fictional character" ' (quoted in Foley, 'Fact, Fiction, Fascism', p. 404). Lange gives an intentionalist cast to his observation, but what he describes here is a version of Bakhtin's dialogized heteroglossia: discourses from all walks of life and levels of meaning rub shoulders in the novel, and battle for supremacy. This battle is what we call novelistic meaning.

3 Autobiographical fiction: Jerzy Kosinski, *The Painted Bird*

1 Marty Bloomberg and Buckley Barry Barrett, *The Jewish Holocaust: An Annotated Guide to Books in English* (San Bernardino, Calif.: The Borgo Press, 1995), p. 266. On the different early editions of the novel, see Philip R. Rider, 'The Three States of the Text of Kosinski's *The Painted Bird*', *Papers of the Bibliographical Society of America*, 72 (3), 1978, pp. 361–84. Jerzy Kosinski, *The Painted Bird* (New York: Bantam, 1978 [1965]); all references to *The Painted Bird* are cited in brackets in the text.

2 See the epilogue, or 'Postlude', which appeared only in the novel's first Houghton Mifflin hardback edition of 1965; it described how the boy grew up, rejected collective society and fled to the West.

3 Lawrence Langer, *The Holocaust and the Literary Imagination* (New Haven: Yale University Press, 1975), pp. 166, 167.

4 David H. Richter details changes which 'generalize the locale' of the novel and avoid 'facile identification' of the boy with the author by altering or removing references to Poland and Polish, and the elimination of a specific time reference ('The Three Denouements of Jerzy Kosinski's *The Painted Bird*', *Contemporary Literature* 15, Summer 1974, pp. 370–85; p. 378); Alvin Rosenfeld says such evil transcends its historical setting (*A Double Dying: Reflections on Holocaust Literature*, Bloomington: Indiana University Press, 1980, p. 76).

5 Sidra DeKoven Ezrahi, *By Words Alone: The Holocaust in Literature* (Chicago: University of Chicago Press, 1980), p. 51.

6 This is Ivan Sanders's phrase, quoted in Langer, *The Holocaust and the Literary Imagination*, p. 173.

7 Ibid., p. 174.

8 These are also among the scenes the lawyer of Houghton Mifflin, the original publishers, wanted removed on the grounds of obscenity: the blinding of the ploughboy, the murder of Ludmila, 'the boy's relations with Ewka and her sexual relations with the goat', and the 'raping and pillaging by the Kalmuk cavalry' (see James Park Sloan, *Jerzy Kosinski: A Biography*, London/New York: Plume/Penguin, 1997, p. 212). Other problems which Sloan discusses include the possibility of libel, if the characters were based on real people (ibid., p. 215); and the representation of sadomasochistic acts (ibid., p. 333).

9 Stanley Corngold says, rightly, that it also has a 'necessary' metafictional sense, as it shows how 'Memory enters the service of a self bent on vision' ('Jerzy Kosinski's *The Painted Bird*: Language Lost and Regained', *Mosaic* 4, Summer 1973, pp. 153–68: p. 166).

10 Ivan Sanders points to a different pattern: the boy's search for explanatory 'panaceas' – 'witchcraft, Christianity, Nazism, Communism (paralleling the grim road travelled by Western man)' – ends in disappointment each time ('The Gifts of Strangeness: Alienation and Creation in Kosinski's Fiction', *Polish Review* 19, 1974, pp. 171–89: p. 174).

11 Sloan, *Jerzy Kosinski*, p. 133; and on the picaresque, Geoffrey Green, 'The Nightmarish Quest of Jerzy Kosinski', in Moshe Lazar (ed.), *The Anxious Subject: Nightmares and Daymares in Literature and Film* (Malibu: Undena, 1983), pp. 51–67.

12 Sloan, *Jerzy Kosinski*, p. 192.

13 See Paul Lilly on contemporary reviews of the novel, *Words in Search of Victims: The Achievement of Jerzy Kosinski* (Kent, Ohio and London: Kent State University Press, 1988), p. 176, n. 1.

14 Daniel J. Cahill, 'Kosinski and His Critics', *North American Review* 265 (1), 1980, pp. 66–8: p. 68; Eric Larsen finds this logic specious: 'Few people argue that what happens in television soap opera couldn't possibly happen in life; of course it can. And yet few people concomitantly argue that television soap opera is "true" '

('Kosinski Again: A Letter of Dissent', *North American Review* 265 (2), 1980, pp. 61–2: p. 62). Sara Horowitz agrees in principle with Cahill, observing that 'even a casual reading of accounts of the Nazi era reveals that actual events surpassed Kosinski's fiction in cruelty and ferocity' (*Voicing the Void: Muteness and Memory in Holocaust Fiction*, Albany: State University of New York Press, 1997, p. 79). She argues that *The Painted Bird* 'moves back and forth between vagueness and specificity' and 'hints of the historical reality seep through' (ibid., p. 80), yet interprets events according to a model of a very fixed correspondence: the indifference of the healthy horses to the maimed one 'echoes the peasants' lack of remorse', while the owner's plans for the horse's carcass are 'a reminder' of the Nazis' habit of profiting even from their victims' bodies (p. 81).

15 Quoted in Larsen, 'Kosinski Again', p. 61.

16 Horowitz observes that 'he pays with the death of animal surrogates, closely identified with him'; and he undergoes at least two 'symbolic' deaths of his own, at the hands of the German soldier who does not shoot him and the carpenter who wants his death by lightning to appease a deity; they 'allow him to represent those who did not survive' (*Voicing the Void*, p. 91).

17 Quoted in Larsen, 'Kosinski Again', p. 61.

18 Interview by Lawrence L. Langer, cited in his *The Holocaust and the Literary Imagination* (New Haven and London: Yale University Press, p. 175); also cited in interview by Szonyi in Tom Teicholz (ed.), *Conversations with Jerzy Kosinski* (Jackson, Miss.: University Press of Mississippi, 1993), p. 194.

19 Kosinski observed in an interview with Jerome Klinkowitz that the difference between his fiction and non-fiction is that the latter 'grounds [particular incidents] in a specific place – the U.S.S.R. – and by doing it torpedoes its immediacy, its proximity to the reader. On the other hand, the fiction invokes the reader directly. He cannot discard it by saying, "It already happened to someone else, hence it won't happen to me. I'm excluded; I'm a bystander" ' (quoted in Klinkowitz, 'Jerzy Kosinski: An Interview', in Teicholz, *Conversations with Jerzy Kosinski*, p. 100). Incidentally, it is interesting that when Kosinski distinguishes his fiction from his non-fiction in this way, we are in no doubt about what he means: the two early books about Communist society, *The Future is Ours, Comrade* and *No Third Path*, are non-fiction, while *The Painted Bird* and the rest of his writings are fiction. The point is rather that critics have been keen to know exactly how fictional *The Painted Bird* is.

20 See Ezrahi, *By Words Alone*, p. 158; though Corngold calls this the time when 'the burden of the hostile Other is most oppressive' as the boy has to 'put on a show' for other children ('Jerzy Kosinski's *The Painted Bird*', p. 159).

21 As Sloan puts it, 'if the peasants had been as unrelentingly brutal as Kosinski described, how had he managed to survive?' (*Jerzy Kosinski*, p. 113).

22 Leslie Epstein, 'Writing About the Holocaust', in Berel Lang (ed.), *Writing and the Holocaust* (New York: Holmes and Meier, 1988), pp. 261–70: p. 266. See also Neil Compton, who compares *The Painted Bird* with Günter Grass's *The Tin Drum*, but because he judges both to be 'semi-autobiographical fictions by writers who were children during the war' ('Dream of Violence', *Commentary*, June 1966, pp. 92–5: p. 93).

23 Epstein, 'Writing About the Holocaust', p. 266. David Richter argues that the novel constructs the reader as a kind of perpetrator: realizing by the end that we are no longer so affected by scenes of violence in the novel, we experience the return of horror and 'bitter shame' ('The Three Denouements of Jerzy Kosinski's *The Painted Bird*', p. 373).

24 Compton, 'Dream of Violence', p. 95.

25 Samuel Coale, 'The Cinematic Self of Jerzy Kosinski', *Modern Fiction Studies* 20, Autumn 1974, pp. 359–70: p. 361.

26 Typically, Kosinski contradicts his comment to the woman who objected to the eye-gouging scene (n. 18). Corngold argues that through its concern with the tendency of 'collective behaviour' to hatred and revenge, the work attempts to 'get beyond the imitation of a particular historical epoch' ('Jerzy Kosinski's *The Painted Bird*', p. 163); Meta Lale and John Williams claim that the novel is 'not simply about the insanity that pervaded Eastern Europe and permitted [*sic*] the Nazi takeover' but about Laingian notions of madness and sanity ('The Narrator of *The Painted Bird*: A Case Study', *Renascence* 24, Summer 1972, pp. 198–206: p. 198).

27 Jerzy Kosinski, 'Afterward: *The Painted Bird* Tenth Anniversary Edition (1976)', *Passing By: Selected Essays, 1962–1991* (New York: Random House, 1992), pp. 183–200: p. 186.

28 Joseph Alkana, ' "Do We Not Know the Meaning of Aesthetic Gratification?": Cynthia Ozick's *The Shawl*, the Akedah, and the Ethics of Holocaust Literary Aesthetics', *Modern Fiction Studies* 43 (4), Winter 1997, pp. 963–90: pp. 977–8; Erich Auerbach, *Mimesis: The Representation of Reality in Western Literture*, trans. Willard R. Trask (Princeton, N.J.: Princeton University Press, 1953), pp. 3–5.

29 Mikhail Bakhtin, 'Epic and Novel', in *The Dialogic Imagination: Four Essays*, trans. Caryl Emerson and Michael Holquist (Austin, Tex.: University of Texas Press, 1981), p. 13; other shared features include externalization of emotion and thought (Auerbach, *Mimesis*, pp. 3, 6; Bakhtin, ibid., p. 10); fixed 'spatial and temporal relations' (Auerbach, ibid., p. 6; Bakhtin, ibid., p. 15).

30 Bakhtin, 'Epic and Novel', p. 15. For a view which questions Bakhtin's clear division between epic and novel, see Rachel Falconer, 'Bakhtin and the Epic Chronotope', in Carol Adlam *et al.* (eds), *Face to Face: Bakhtin in Russia and the West* (Sheffield: Sheffield Academic Press, 1997).

31 Alkana, ' "Do We Not Know?" ', pp. 980, 981.

32 This juxtaposition fits with Alkana's analysis of Auerbach's project, written while he was in exile from Nazi Germany, to show that Jewish and Christian hermeneutics are so similar that Nazism is the odd one out (' "Do We Not Know?" ', p. 978).

33 Ibid., p. 980.

34 The subheading quotation is taken from Geoffrey Stokes and Eliot Fremont-Smith, 'Jerzy Kosinski's Tainted Words', *Village Voice*, 22 June 1982 (1), pp. 41–3; these are the words of an ornithologist cited to cast doubt on the 'central metaphor' of Kosinski's novel (p. 43).

35 Zbigniew Brzezinski is quoted as saying ' "I think it contributed to his death" ' (in John Taylor, 'The Haunted Bird: The Life and Death of Jerzy Kosinski', *New Yorker*, 15 July 1991, pp. 24–37: p. 26).

36 See the detailed discussion of the scandal in Sloan, *Jerzy Kosinski*, pp. 388–93. Sloan points out the irony that the *New York Times* published a list of fourteen best books of the year in late 1965, of which one was *The Painted Bird*; the list's author was Eliot Fremont-Smith, 'who seventeen years later would be coauthor of the article in the *Village Voice* that brought Kosinski down' (p. 226).

37 Kosinski's two Polish-language publications are *Documents Concerning the Struggle of Man: Reminiscences of the Members of the Proletariat* (Lodz, Poland: Scientific Society of Lodz, 1955) and *The Program of the People's Revolution of Jakob Jaworski* (Lodz, Poland: Scientific Society of Lodz, 1955).

38 Stokes and Fremont-Smith, 'Jerzy Kosinski's Tainted Words', p. 41.

39 Lilly says Kosinski used a pseudonym partly to protect his parents, who remained in Poland, and also to provide himself with 'an attitude of detachment', a fictive character (*Words in Search of Victims*, p. 174, n. 16).

40 Sloan discusses John Corry's *New York Times* 6,400-word piece rebutting the accusations against Koskinski – 'A Case History: 17 Years of Ideological Attack on a Cultural Target', 7 November 1982 – as 'a serious mistake' because it confirmed

that 'Kosinski was indeed a personal and ideological favorite of the top floor at the *Times*' and simply widened the readership of the accusations (*Jerzy Kosinski*, p. 393).

41 Sally Johns, 'Jerzy Kosinski', in Richard Ziegfeld (ed.), *Dictionary of Literary Biography Yearbook 1982* (Detroit: Gale Research, 1983), pp. 169–74; p. 172.

42 Although Kosinski was capable of denials 'in stunning neglect of the facts' (in this case about his use of literary agents: Sloan, *Jerzy Kosinski*, p. 363), only one of the three editors quoted in Stokes and Fremont-Smith's article agreed with the charges (see Sloan on other editors, ibid., pp. 198–9, 254, 280, 300, 332). See also the introduction to Teicholz, *Conversations with Jerzy Kosinski*, p. xii: 'The irony was that on the one hand Kosinski had been "telling tales" for many years challenging people to determine whether they were true or not (it was clear he cared little); on the other, Kosinski's desire for control was so great, that it was impossible to believe that any book of his in print contained a word that he had not worried over himself.'

43 Although plagiarism was not an accusation levelled against Kosinski, there were hints at it in various places. Klinkowitz cites an article in Polish by Hanna Wydzga and Jan Zaborowski, who claim that 'Kosinski plagiarized his accounts of peasant superstition and behavior from "a 400-page work of Professor Biegleisen, published in Cracow in 1929 under the title *The Healing Practices of the Polish Peasantry*" ' (*Literary Disruptions: The Making of a Post-Contemporary American Fiction*, Urbana: University of Illinois Press, 1975, p. 101). It sounds from the subject of this book and the use Kosinski would have made of it that plagiarism is not the right term here, but that it was used for authenticating background detail. This is also Barbara Tepa Lupak's opinion in *Plays of Passion, Games of Chance* (Bristol, Ind.: Wyndham Hall, 1988), p. 101; she says that Kosinski used Biegleisen's work 'to give more validity to the peasant superstitions' in *The Painted Bird*; she points out that Kosinski acknowledged his familiarity with Biegleisen in an interview in *Der Spiegel*, in which he attempted to refute readers' objections to the 'far-fetched' nature of what he describes in his novel – another instance of neither having your cake nor eating it, as, like D.M. Thomas, Kosinski is damned if he does admits borrowings, and damned if he does not. In *Jerzy Kosinski*, Sloan cites Gerald Reitlinger's *The House Built on Sand* as a source for the Kalmuk episode, Henryk Sienkiewicz's *Pan Wolodyjowski*, and Wladyslaw Reymont's *The Peasants*, a source for the killing of Stupid Ludmila. Sloan argues that *The Painted Bird* is 'not only an enhanced personal account but a researched "historical" novel, comparable perhaps to [E.L.] Doctorow's *Ragtime*' (p. 191).

44 Sloan, 'Kosinski's War', *New Yorker*, 10 October 1994, p. 50. The details are from Maria Hochberg-Marianska and Noe Gruss (eds), *The Children Accuse*, trans. Bill Johnston (London: Vallentine Mitchell, 1996 [1946]), pp. 133; 132; 119 and 139–40; 121 and 129; 129 and 176; 128 and 129; 123; 136 and several other instances; 124; 124 again; 141 and 146; 136, 190 and 138.

45 Lupak, *Plays of Passion*, p. 47.

46 Lilly, *Words as Victims*, pp. 158–71; see also Lupak's discussion, *Plays of Passion*, pp. 36–40. Sloan, *Jerzy Kosinski*, p. 170. Of the controversy over the details of Kosinski's move to the West, for instance, Lilly concludes, 'In short, the issue is unverifiable' (*Words as Victims*, p. 173, n. 5), and this may be true of other episodes too. It should be added that many critics, and Kosinski himself, note that Kosinski's particular lifestyle appeared to rub people up the wrong way and lent an extra frisson to the proceedings; this may be the reason why even the question of whether he 'docked' or 'landed' in New York in 1957, or whether his parents were born or just educated in Russia is of concern (ibid., p. 174, n. 15).

47 Klinkowitz, quoted in Lupak, *Plays of Passion*, p. 41.

48 For instance, Sloan says Kosinski's tale of rescue by the Red Army is a 'moving and revealing' adoption fantasy (*Jerzy Kosinski*, p. 51).

49 Kosinski, *Passing By*, p. 191.

50 Sloan, 'Kosinski's War', p. 50; Sloan also discusses the campaign waged against the 'German-lover' Kosinski and his novel by Wieslaw Gornicki, a correspondent at the United Nations for the official Polish Press Agency in the mid-1960s (*Jerzy Kosinski*, pp. 236, 224).

51 Sloan, 'Kosinski's War', p. 50; Kosinski notes in *Passing By* that he considers the criticisms he and his book suffered were part of 'a plot intended to force the remaining Jewish population to leave the state' (p. 189), which they increasingly did in the late 1960s.

52 Joanna Siedlecka, 'Czarny ptasior' (translated as 'Black Bird') (Gdansk: Marabut/CIS, 1994). For examples of critics who took for granted the lone-survival story, see several interviews, especially those with Klinkowitz (1973), pp. 37–59, and Warga (1973), pp. 60–5, in Teicholz, *Conversations with Jerzy Kosinski*; the entry 'Jerzy Kosinski' in *Research Guide to Biography and Criticism* vol. VI (Washington, D.C.: Beacham Publishing, 1992), pp. 456–63; articles by Barbara Geld, 'Being Jerzy Kosinski', *New York Times Magazine*, 21 February 1982, pp. 42–58, and Stephen Schiff, 'The Kosinski Conundrum', *Vanity Fair* 51 (6), June 1988, pp. 115–70.

53 Horowitz, *Voicing the Void*, p. 72.

54 Dorrit Cohn discusses 'these newest crossbreeds', which he calls 'True Life Novel, Novel Biography, Non-Fiction Novel', in 'Fictional *versus* Historical Lives: Borderlines and Borderline Cases', *Journal of Narrative Technique* 19 (1), Winter 1989, p. 11.

55 Horowitz, *Voicing the Void*, p. 74, argues that he is neither; Wiesel that he is Christian (noted in Lilly, *Words in Search of Victims*, p. 176).

56 See Lilly, *Words in Search of Victims*, p. 177.

57 Binjamin Wilkomirski, *Fragments: Memories of a Childhood 1939–1948*, trans. Carol Brown Janeway (London: Picador, 1996).

58 See, for example, Jan Blonski's essay giving the template of a debate between a Jewish and a non-Jewish Pole, rehearsing all the well-known arguments and reaching no resolution, 'The Poor Poles Look at the Ghetto', in Antony Polonsky (ed.), *My Brother's Keeper: Recent Polish Debates on the Holocaust* (London: Routledge, 1990), pp. 34–52. Corngold says the problem was *The Painted Bird* inverted 'Poland's role of war *victim*' ('Jerzy Kosinski's *The Painted Bird*', p. 154); and Sloan describes how Kosinski himself in the 1980s took to emphasizing the Poles' historical philosemitism and their own fate under the Nazis (*Jerzy Kosinski*, p. 409).

59 Cahill, 'Kosinski and His Critics', says it was the result of 'confusion' and a publisher's error, although this is not David Richter's estimate of the excised epilogue. Richter writes that Kosinski's explanation is his 'memorial reconstruction, more than six years after the event, of an apparently confused correspondence with his publishers. That Kosinski *no longer* intends the epilogue to conclude his first novel has been evident since the 1966 Pocket Books publication ... one would like to examine the correspondence out of which the epilogue sprung before being firmly convinced that such had never been his intention' ('The Three Denouements', p. 128).

60 Kosinski, 'Afterward', p. 184.

61 Sloan, *Jerzy Kosinski*, p. 53.

62 Sloan, 'Kosinski's War', p. 50.

63 Ibid., pp. 51–2; in *Jerzy Kosinski*, Sloan gives the originals for characters in Kosinski's novel (pp. 25, 28–9, 32).

64 Kosinski comments on a Polish TV programme, 'In the Footsteps of *The Painted Bird*', in which people 'who had supposedly c[o]me into contact with me and my family during the war' were interviewed: 'As these disoriented, often uneducated witnesses were brought forward, horrified at what they were supposed to have done, they angrily denounced the book and its author' (*Passing By*, p. 190).

65   Sloan, *Jerzy Kosinski*, pp. 171, 225, 90.

66   Ibid., pp. 21, 65; there are constant references in the biography to Kosinski's hatred of water and dogs, which appear to be authenticating but it is not clear which came first, the hatred or the childhood stories. Sloan gives other instances of Kosinski reversing chronology, such as putting false dates in inscribed books impishly to mislead biographers; the myth of the painted bird first appears in Kosinski's non-fiction study of the Soviet Union, *No Third Path*, as an image of Communist confor-mity, and is then transposed into the Nazi past (p. 159); while episodes in other novels were transplanted from their Eastern European origins to the West, for example, p. 256.

67   Some of the things that happen to the boy in the novel apparently happened to Kosinski's younger brother Henryk, such as becoming a mascot for the Red Army (Sloan, *Jerzy Kosinksi*, p. 49).

68   Sloan, 'Kosinski's War', p. 53; in *Jerzy Kosinski*, Sloan notes that, of sixty members of Kosinski's parents' family who attended a reunion before the war, fifty-nine per-ished (p. 50).

69   Horowitz, *Voicing the Void*, pp. 8–11; Louis Begley, *Wartime Lies* (London: Picador, 1991).

70   Sloan, 'Kosinski's War', p. 47; he adds, ' "Account", "confession", "testament", "document", "testimony" … were the key words in the book's critical reception'; and 'it has been for a generation the source of what they "know" about Poland under German occupation'.

71   Ibid., p. 46.

72   Sloan, *Jerzy Kosinski*, p. 221; interview by Tartikoff in Teicholz, *Conversations with Jerzy Kosinski* (p. 11): ' "I never claimed [my novels] to be anything but novels." '

73   Sloan, *Jerzy Kosinski*, p. 407; and, perversely, in an interview, Kosinski claimed: 'If anything, *Being There* and *Devil Tree* are more autobiographical than my other books' (interview by Warga, in Teicholz, *Conversations with Jerzy Kosinski*, p. 64).

74   Lale and Williams chart the novel's 'authenticity' in relation to studies of trauma victims ('The Narrator of *The Painted Bird*', p. 199), while Kosinski says, 'Facts about my life and my origins, I felt, should not be used to test the book's authenticity, any more than they should be used to encourage readers to read *The Painted Bird*' (*Passing By*, p. 188), whereas a 'fictional life', rather than autobiography, 'forces the reader to contribute'.

75   Rosenfeld quotes Wiesel on the difficulty of maintaining truth categories in Holocaust writing, particularly in works by survivors Charlotte Delbo and Piotr Rawicz which show an awareness of the difference between accuracy and truth (*A Double Dying*, pp. 78–9); even if *The Painted Bird* is not accurate as Kosinski's biogra-phy, it does not mean it is not a 'true' representation of the Holocaust.

76   Piotr Rawicz's highly hybrid *Blood from the Sky*, trans. Peter Wiley (London: Secker and Warburg, 1964), has not been criticized in the same way as *The Painted Bird*. In her study of muteness and Holocaust writing, Horowitz compares an incident of enforced muteness in Rawicz's novel, where a little boy's act of defiance in the ghetto, sticking out his tongue at the SS, results in his tongue being cut out: 'In both Kosinski's and Rawicz's accounts, the mutilations serve to represent atrocities far more brutal than those depicted' (*Voicing the Void*, p. 78).

77   The *Notes* were 'to clarify the novels' themes for countries which had had fascist histories' (Klinkowitz, *Literary Disruptions*, p. 84, n. 6); Kosinski claims they were 'to soften' that impact ('Afterward', p. 188); the *Notes* were also published in English separately under the imprint Scientia-Factum – a publishing company consisting of Kosinski and his wife Kiki (Sloan, *Jerzy Kosinski*, p. 217).

78   Kosinski, *Notes of the Author on 'The Painted Bird'*, in *Passing By*, p. 14. See, however, Andrew Field's review, 'The Butcher's Helpers', *Book Week*, 17 October 1965, of the

1965 Houghton Mifflin edition complete with identification of place, which took *The Painted Bird* to be a portrait of Polish antisemitism and the Poles' role in wartime genocide, *at which point* Kosinski disavowed the epilogue and the novel's specificity in a letter to the same journal; see Richter's discussion, n. 63.

79 Kosinski, *Notes*, p. 11.

80 Ibid., p. 14; Sloan calls this particular comment 'hedging' ('Kosinski's War', p. 47). We can see that Kosinski is in the difficult position of having to assert simultaneously both the positions he otherwise deployed separately: he has to imply the book both is and is not autobiographical.

81 Kosinski, *Notes*, p. 12.

82 Ibid., p. 13; first italics mine, second his.

83 Kosinski, 'Afterward', p. 185.

84 Kosinski, *Notes*, p. 11. In an interview with George Plimpton he says, 'in this country [the USA] … as a novelist you are assumed to have lived your novels' (interview with Kosinski, in George Plimpton (ed.), *Writers at Work: The 'Paris Review' Interviews*, London: Secker and Warburg, 1981, pp. 315–38: p. 331).

85 Kosinski, 'Afterward', p. xiv.

86 Sloan, 'Kosinski's War', p. 47.

87 Sloan claims that the odds of a family surviving together were 10,000 to one, whereas the odds of surviving at all were one in 100 (ibid., p. 52).

88 Ibid., p. 52.

89 Kosinski, *Notes*, p. 15. Sanders says, 'The worst fears of the boy are *always* realized in *The Painted Bird*', which gives the novel a sense of 'nightmarish unreality' ('The Gifts of Strangeness', p. 182); see studies of other child's-eye views of the Holocaust, for example Naomi Sokoloff, *Imagining the Child in Modern Jewish Fiction* (Baltimore: Johns Hopkins University Press, 1992).

90 Barbara Foley, 'The Documentary Novel and the Problem of Borders', in Michael J. Hoffman and Patrick D. Murphy (eds), *Essentials of the Theory of Fiction* (London: Leicester University Press, 1996), p. 404.

91 Ibid., p. 393.

92 For instance, Lilly suggests that 'The boy's movement away from silent victimization toward the power of eloquence, which is the structure of his narration, is also a tale of a writer's slow progress from silence to spoken to written words' (*Words in Search of Victims*, p. 37); Kosinski likens the revenge with which the novel culminates to creativity (*Notes*, p. 27): 'Like Prospero [the wielder of power] rules his kingdom, and justice is meted out according to his will'; and in *Passing By* explicitly compares the bird with artistry: 'having caught the bird, painted its feathers and released it, I simply stood by and watched as it wreaked its havoc. … Can the imagination, any more than the boy, be held prisoner?' (p. 200).

93 Marian Scholtmeijer, *Animal Victims in Modern Fiction: From Sanctity to Sacrifice* (Toronto: Toronto University Press, 1993), p. 379. Thanks to Robert McKay for this reference.

94 Foley, 'The Documentary Novel', p. 394, my italics; she argues for what she calls 'a qualitative view of mimesis', which differs from fact 'in kind rather than in degree' (p. 395). She discusses poststructuralist criticism of 'The common valorization of "creative" or "imaginative" writing [which implies] a positivist reduction of nonfictional discourse to the unmediated reportage of "what is" ' (pp. 395–400); as we keep seeing, critics of Holocaust fiction often automatically reverse this binary.

95 Kosinski, *Notes*, claims that 'the boy survives because he cannot do otherwise, because he is a total incarnation of the urge for self-realization and self-preservation' (p. 16).

96 Sloan, 'Kosinski's War', p. 52; in *Jerzy Kosinski*, Sloan argues that in his inner life, dropping the missal must have been 'momentous' for Kosinski, even if it was not the prelude for being beaten or thrown into a cess-pit.

97 Cohn's definition in 'Fictional *versus* Historical Lives' (p. 21, n. 14) begs the question: 'I would maintain that autobiographically inspired works are more appropriately labelled by the ... term "autobiographical fiction".'

98 Welch D. Everman, *Jerzy Kosinski: The Literature of Violation* (San Bernardino, Calif.: Borgo Press, 1991), p. 27; or as Shlomith Rimmon-Kenan says of Charles Dickens's *Great Expectations* in Gerard Genette's terminology, 'The narrator is Pip, the adult, while the focalizer is Pip, the child' (*Narrative Fiction: Contemporary Poetics*, London: Methuen, 1983, p. 73).

99 Sanders, 'The Gifts of Strangeness', p. 185; Plimpton, *Writers at Work*, p. 329.

100 Kosinski, *The Painted Bird*, p. 126.

101 As Sloan says, Kosinski's personal and fictive 'improvisation' of muteness is 'a powerful metaphor for his inability, at first, to give coherent articulation to the horror of his childhood experience' (*Jerzy Kosinski*, p. 193).

102 Corngold discusses the scene in which Olga buries the boy in earth up to his neck to cure him of fever as a drama of 'the very survival of consciousness in the world', and sees in it the same covert representation of time present and time past: the boy's control over language *in the present* – my italics – means that he survives through surrender *in the past*, although even Corngold admits that 'Of course the passage does not suggest that the act has contributed in even the slightest way to real survival' ('Jerzy Kosinski's *The Painted Bird*', pp. 157–8).

103 Corngold sees the structure of the whole novel representing the 'artist-hero': when the boy regains the ability to speak, the novel shows its concern has been with 'language brutalized, lost and then regained with a generality capable of interpreting each of the stages of its destiny' (ibid., p. 156).

104 Lale and Williams discuss the same phenomenon in the psychoanalytic terms of introjection ('The Narrator of *The Painted Bird*', p. 201).

105 Corngold, 'Jerzy Kosinski's *The Painted Bird*', p. 157.

106 Rimmon-Kenan says an 'implied author' (*Narrative Fiction*, p. 114).

107 The pervasive use of free indirect discourse is apt in view of the ghost-writing controversy; rather like Kosinski, the boy takes words and phrases from a variety of sources and makes them his own.

108 Gavrila is a (possibly fictional) interlocutor in both Kosinski's non-fiction books, *The Future is Ours, Comrade* and *No Third Path*, as well as a Red Army officer in *The Painted Bird*.

109 Richter, 'The Three Denouements', p. 376.

110 Bakhtin, *The Dialogic Imagination*, p. 293.

111 Corngold, 'Jerzy Kosinski's *The Painted Bird*', p. 162.

112 Lilly, *Words in Search of Victims*, p. 38.

113 Lale and Williams discuss the boy's 'classic psychophysiological gastro-intestinal reaction to "terror that shakes one until it squeezes the stomach empty of vomit" ' ('The Narrator of *The Painted Bird*', p. 199).

114 Julia Kristeva, *Powers of Horror*, trans. Léon S. Roudiez (New York: Columbia University Press, 1984), p. 8.

115 Kristeva describes the 'deject', the 'one by whom the abject exists', as a 'stray' whose universe has 'fluid confines' and whose journey is 'endless' (ibid., p. 8).

116 Ibid., pp. 3–4.

117 Ibid., p. 16.

118 Ibid., p. 120.

119 Kristeva quotes Mary Douglas saying that 'filth is not a quality in itself, but it applies only to what relates to a *boundary*' (ibid., p. 69).

120 Ibid., p. 53.
121 Ibid., p. 3.
122 The boy describes Labina's 'jerkin of rabbit pelts with many holes' (Kosinski, *The Painted Bird*, p. 171).
123 The fact that the rabbit is female is significant, linked to Kristeva's extensive discussion of the 'fascinating and abject inside of the maternal body'. In a discussion of the reasons why the Hebrew Bible's laws about the maternal body are closely juxtaposed to those concerning the diseased body, Kristeva describes birth as 'a violent act of expulsion through which the nascent body tears itself away from the matter of maternal insides'; the rabbit scene is an awful birth, as the rabbit is tearing herself away from herself, which results in death. The maternal 'skin apparently never ceases to bear the traces' of violent birth and can easily become diseased in the subject's mind, as it conceives of 'a placenta that is no longer nourishing but devastating' (*Powers of Horror*, p. 101). The subject has two choices: rejecting the mother, with the psychic 'mutilation' that entails, or continuing to desire the mother and threatening its own identity with a 'harebrained staging of an abortion' (ibid., p. 54).
124 Kristeva discusses the 'defilement' of blinding in reference to Oedipus: 'Blinding is thus an image of splitting; it marks, on the very body, the alteration of the self … into the defiled' (ibid., p. 84).
125 Kristeva emphasizes that the proper place of the abject is in literature, specifically in relation to blinding; it is better that 'we hear in language – and not in the other, nor in the other sex – the gouged-out eye, the wound' (ibid., p. 88).
126 Ibid., p. 156.
127 See, for instance, the boy's 'abject' forays under Labina's bed (Kosinski, *The Painted Bird*, p. 173): 'Touching this dark world with my flesh always filled me with revulsion and fear.'
128 For a discussion of this practice in the work of Virginia Woolf and James Kelman, see, respectively, Makiko Minow-Pinkney, *Virginia Woolf and the Problem of the Subject* (Brighton: Harvester, 1984); Sue Vice, *Introducing Bakhtin* (Manchester: Manchester University Press, 1997).
129 'Socio-historical considerations … allow us to understand why that demarcating imperative, which is subjectively experienced as abjection, varies according to time and space, even though it is universal' (Kristeva, *Powers of Horror*, p. 68). But see Judith Flower MacCannell, 'Kristeva's Horror', *Semiotica* 62 (3/4), 1986, pp. 325–55: p. 340: 'Kristeva's thesis depends on seeing the set of drives as universal, not subject *per se* to cultural modification.' MacCannell also makes a much more serious observation that in her view Kristeva implies that 'monotheism, the Jews themselves are responsible for the holocaust.… Persecution and the murder of Jews is only a return of the repressed, the repression of the "constant" forces of mother and murder' in the Hebrew Bible (pp. 341–2).
130 For instance, Ruth Rendell is quoted on the jacket of Bernhard Schlink's *The Reader* describing it 'as far above a Holocaust genre as *Crime and Punishment* is above the average thriller, a sensitive and daring, deeply moving book about the tragic results of fear and the redemption [*sic*] power of understanding'.

4 Faction: Thomas Keneally, *Schindler's List*

1 Quoted in Yosefa Loshitzky (ed.), *Spielberg's Holocaust: Critical Perspectives on 'Schindler's List'* (Bloomington and Indianapolis: Indiana University Press, 1997), 'Introduction', p. 14, n. 13.
   In his native Australia Keneally has had a mixed reception, for reasons different from the ones I will discuss in this chapter. In a 1993 article in the *Australian*,

Keneally bemoaned what he saw as his victimization at critics' hands: 'The hardest thing is that my professional competence and care is attacked so commonly here in Australia' (quoted in Imre Salusinzky, 'Thomas Keneally: My Part in His Downfall', *Quadrant*, October 1995, pp. 23–6: p. 23). This is partly a political issue, as Keneally's republican sympathies have not endeared him to all. Salusinzky arraigns Keneally for a decline in the quality of his prose, which, he claims, began 'around the time of *Schindler's Ark*' with 'the advent of the word-processor' (ibid., p. 24). Christopher Pearson, in similar vein, refers to Keneally's penchant for 'warm, fuzzy holocaust novels' (quoted by Peter Pierce, ' "The Critics Made Me": The Receptions of Thomas Keneally and Australian Literary Culture', *Australian Literary Studies* 17 (1), May 1995, pp. 99–103; he describes Pearson, editor of the *Adelaide Review*, as a 'pro-monarchist', p. 100). Salusinzky is equally caustic in his estimate of *Schindler's List*: he claims that 'a search for ever more worthy subjects was bound to bring Keneally, eventually, to the Holocaust. *Schindler's Ark* [*sic*] is the schlockmeister's greatest schlockfest. By now the wordiness, the moralising, the tendency to didacticism: they are all out of jail, as safely nestled under Tom's wing as the poor Jewish workers were under Oskar's' ('Thomas Keneally', p. 25): this must be the *reductio ad absurdum* of a slide from an apparently moral to a stylistic charge. Some details of Keneally's stylistic solecisms in *Schindler's List* are cited, not without reason, by Salusinzky, who concludes, 'Thomas Keneally … must be stopped. He is without a doubt one of the two or three most over-rated writers in the world today, and if an increasing number of Australian critics realise this, it is not a sign of a culture of envy. It is a sign of culture' (ibid., p. 26). Pierce takes an opposite, more measured view: 'One wonders whether critics have made of Keneally the scapegoat for their own distaste for, or lack of confidence in, Australian culture, so that attacks on his art, subjects, politics signify a cultural death-wish?' (' "The Critics Made Me" ', p. 103).

2 Omer Bartov, discussing Spielberg's film, 'Spielberg's Oskar: Hollywood Tries Evil', in Loshitzky, *Spielberg's Holocaust*, p. 49.

3 Thomas Keneally, *Schindler's List* (London: Sceptre, 1986); all further references, cited in brackets in the text, are to this edition. It was first published as *Schindler's Ark* (London: Hodder and Stoughton, 1982; and New York: Simon and Schuster, 1983). See Loshitzky, *Spielberg's Holocaust*, which consists of chapters on the reception of the film in countries ranging from Germany and Israel to France and the United States.

4 Worldwide sales of *Schindler's List* had exceeded 2 million by 1994 (Peter Pierce, *Australian Melodramas: Thomas Keneally's Fiction*, St Lucia, Queensland: University of Queensland Press, 1995, p. 18). Loshitzky, 'Introduction', *Spielberg's Holocaust*, p. 3; Jeffrey Shandler, 'Schindler's Discourse: America Discusses the Holocaust and its Mediation, for NBC's Miniseries to Spielberg's Film', in Loshitzky, *Spielberg's Holocaust*, p. 164.

5 See Loshitzky's argument that the film represented an ' "epistemological break" in Holocaust cinematography through its introduction of the Holocaust into mainstream cinema' ('Introduction', *Spielberg's Holocaust*, p. 3).

6 Laurie Hergenhan, 'Interview with Thomas Keneally', *Australian Literary Studies* 12, 1986, pp. 453–7: p. 456.

7 D.J. Enright concludes his review by declaring that '*Schindler's Ark* deserves to have won the Booker Prize – as long as it isn't *really* a novel', suggesting that the story itself needs the canonization of a public award ('Fouling up the System', *Times Literary Supplement*, 29 October 1982, p. 1189). By contrast, Byron Rogers in the *Spectator* laments that 'it was Thomas Keneally and not a humble news reporter who one afternoon walked into that leathergoods store in Los Angeles' where Leopold Pfefferberg worked ('Bulletin', 8 March 1994, p. 37).

8 Geoffrey Hartman, 'The Cinema Animal', in Loshitzky, *Spielberg's Holocaust*, p. 75. Hartman has in mind daily life in the ghettos, an element which is missing from Spielberg's film and replaced by the 'privileged' viewpoint of the perpetrators. Hartman's essay is the site of more double-bind criticism: Spielberg is taken to task simultaneously for avoiding private memory and for giving 'the private story ... more weight than public history' (Yosefa Loshitzky, 'Holocaust Others: Spielberg's *Schindler's List* versus Lanzmann's *Shoah*, in ibid., p. 107). The film may omit the gas chambers but it does represent the otherwise unseen: the liquidation of the Cracow ghetto, the deportation of children from Plaszów, selections of Plaszów inmates, the exhumation and burning of bodies, and people hiding in the ghetto.

9 Michael Hulse, 'Virtue and the Philosophic Innocent: The British Reception of *Schindler's Ark*', *Critical Quarterly* 25 (4), 1983, pp. 45ff.; *pace* the Textplus edition of *Schindler's Ark*, ed. Terry Downie (London: Hodder and Stoughton, 1989), which says it was first advertised as 'fiction' (p. 343), an error repeated by Peter Quartermaine in his *Thomas Keneally* (London: Arnold, 1991), p. 62. On the thirtieth anniversary of the inception of the Booker Prize, its administrator Martyn Goff is quoted as saying the following about the panel's decision to award the prize to Keneally despite its hybrid status: 'The year *Schindler's Ark* won (1982) John Carey was chairman. The judges (Frank Delaney, Lorna Sage, Janet Morgan and Paul Bailey) were split very much between Keneally and William Boyd. [According to Goff] The chairman said, "Well, of course the Keneally isn't really a novel." I cited the fact that the novel was a novel because by shortlisting it they had made a decision, and the publisher was publishing it as fiction.... The more the controversy raged, the more it sold' (Ion Trewin, 'Winners and walkouts', *Daily Telegraph*, 5 September 1998, p. A5).

10 *Bookseller*, 5 March 1983.

11 The current American edition has 'A Novel' after the book's title, which the British edition does not, and 'Fiction/Judaica' as the subject categorization on the backcover; it also includes the Author's Note; while the current UK edition says it used to be *Schindler's Ark*.

12 Two rather mythical reasons are offered for the change: Irmtraud Petersson claims that it was the result of 'Jewish wishes' (' "White Ravens" in a World of Violence: German Connections in Thomas Keneally's Fiction', *Australian Literary Studies* 14 (2), October 1989, p. 166, n. 22) but Keneally, in personal correspondence, denies that this was the case; Simon Louvish argues that the title was changed because mass American audiences would have problems with the word 'Ark' ('Is Spielberg's *Schindler's List* More than a Ride in a Holocaust Theme Park? And How Has the Film Imagined the Unimaginable?', in Thomas Fensch (ed.), *Oskar Schindler and His List: The Man, the Book, the Film, the Holocaust and its Survivors*, Forest Dale, Vt: Paul S. Eriksson, 1995, p. 76).

13 Keneally saw the Ark as that of the Covenant (the container of the tablets of the law, described in Exodus 25–35), according to Valerie Takahama, '*Schindler's* Author Gives Film a Standing Ovation', in Fensch, *Oskar Schindler and His List*, p. 47.

14 See, for instance, 'Poldek did not want to share a profession with grey-shirted Spira or with Spitz and Zellinger, the makers of lists' (p. 110; and pp. 159, 247).

15 In the text Goldberg is described as an ex-OD member: of the *Ordnungdienst*, or Jewish Police.

16 This is not in the film; Goldberg is interesting as perhaps the only representative of Primo Levi's 'gray zone' of 'agonizing choices and ethically intolerable alternatives' faced by the Jews during the Holocaust years. The present textual world, however, adopts a 'terrible but decipherable' Manichaeanism, with perpetrators who are evil and victims who are 'completely pure' which 'fatally undermines [the film's] docu-

mentary realism' (see Zygmunt Bauman, *Modernity and the Holocaust*, Cambridge: Polity Press, 1989, p. 122; Michael André Bernstein, 'The *Schindler's List* Effect', *The American Scholar* 63 (3), Summer 1994, pp. 429–32: p. 430; and Bryan Cheyette, 'The Uncertain Certainty of *Schindler's List*', in Loshitzky, *Spielberg's Holocaust*, p. 232). Equally, in Keneally's novel we read of neither the dehumanization nor complicity that would make the reader 'emerge shaking in horror' at him- or herself, in Gillian Rose's phrase on reading Tadeusz Borowski's *This Way for the Gas, Ladies and Gentlemen* ('Beginnings of the Day: Fascism and Representation', in Bryan Cheyette and Laura Marcus (eds), *Modernity, Culture, and 'the Jew'*, Cambridge: Polity Press, 1998, p. 248).

17 See Tim O'Hearn's argument: the original British title depicts Schindler as 'the more concerned, the more godlike, the more heroic "character" than that of *Schindler's List*' ('Schindler's Ark and Schindler's List: One for the Price of Two', *Commonwealth Novel in English* (52), Fall 1992, pp. 9–15: p. 10).

18 Mikhail Bakhtin, 'Discourse in the Novel', *The Dialogic Imagination: Four Essays*, trans. Caryl Emerson and Michael Holquist, ed. Michael Holquist (Austin, Tex.: University of Texas Press, 1981), p. 261.

19 Fiona Fullerton, *Bookseller*, 21 August 1982; Enright, 'Fouling up the System', p. 1189; Marion Glastonbury, review in the *New Statesman*, quoted in Hulse, 'Virtue and the Philosophic Innocent', p. 50.

20 Lorna Sage, the *Observer*, 17 October 1982; Enright, 'Fouling up the System', p. 1189; and Robert Taubman, 'Holocaust Art', *London Review of Books*, 20 January–3 February 1983, p. 23; Paul Bailey, *Evening Standard*, 20 October 1982; Gay Firth, *Financial Times*, 23 October 1982; Hulse, 'Virtue and the Philosophic Innocent', p. 48; David Lodge, *Sunday Times*, 24 October 1982.

21 In his 'Introduction' to the Textplus edition of *Schindler's Ark*, Keneally says of the Holocaust itself: 'I suppose you could call it real science fiction which happened in the past; history's most astounding and compelling science fiction' (p. v): a comment which raises important issues of narratability and time. As Quartermaine points out, this remark brings together 'the imaginative possibilities of the future and the historical parable – as Keneally would see it – of the past' (*Thomas Keneally*, p. 68).

22 Paula Rabinowitz, 'Wreckage upon Wreckage: History, Documentary and the Ruins of Memory', *History and Theory* (2), 1993, p. 121.

23 See, for instance, Barbara Foley, *Telling the Truth: The Theory and Practice of Documentary Fiction* (Ithaca and London: Cornell University Press, 1986).

24 Michael Hollington, 'The Ned Kelly of Cracow: Keneally's *Schindler's Ark*', *Meanjin* 42 (3), March 1983, p. 46; Petersson notes that 'The European world of violence in Keneally's writing could be read as a reversal of an "antipodean" myth, implying that hell is over there' (' "White Ravens" ', p. 172). Salusinzky takes a negative view of this phenomenon, and criticizes what he sees as the repeated 'cliché' in Keneally's novels, almost all of which 'are about vital, life-affirming Irishmen (who are sometimes Aboriginal Irishmen, sometimes German industrialist Irishmen) coming into conflict with repressed, repressive, propertied types' ('Thomas Keneally', p. 24).

25 Laurie Hergenhan, 'Interview with Thomas Keneally', pp. 453–7. As various critics have pointed out (e.g. Petersson, ' "White Ravens" ', p. 167), this faith in the individual battling against the system means that Keneally's view of history and political institutions is a negative one, which it is important to bear in mind alongside the accusations of his choosing a positive story in which 'Survival seems a matter not of chance, but of the consequences of a good deed', as Simon Louvish puts it ('Is Spielberg's *Schindler's List* More than a Ride in a Holocaust Theme Park?', p. 82). Loshitzky argues that the film shifted 'Holocaust consciousness' from the 'old' to the 'new' world ('Introduction', p. 4).

26 Quartermaine, *Thomas Keneally*, pp. 62, 66. Steven G. Kellman likens the tale rather to Homer's *Iliad*, in his '*Schindler's List* – Spielberg's Homecoming', *Midstream* 40 (2), February/March 1994, pp. 9–12: p. 12.

27 Rather like seeing *Schindler's List* as Christian allegory, François Mauriac's introduction to Elie Wiesel's *Night* (London: Fontana, 1972 [1958]) compares the survivor to Christ; and the play version of *The Diary of Anne Frank*, by Frances Goodrich and Albert Hackett, was widely criticized for emphasizing what critics have seen as a Christian view of humanity. The last words of the play's Anne Frank are spoken disembodiedly: ' "In spite of everything, I still believe that people are really good at heart" ' (Rosenfeld, 'The Americanization of the Holocaust', in Alvin H. Rosenfeld (ed.), *Thinking About the Holocaust: After Half a Century*, Bloomington: Indiana University Press, 1997, p. 126). Bruno Bettelheim, 'The Ignored Lesson of Anne Frank', in *Surviving and Other Essays* (New York: Alfred A. Knopf, 1979), argues that 'the fictitious declaration of faith in the goodness of all men which ends the play falsely reassures us since it impresses on us that in the combat between Nazi terror and continuance of intimate family living the latter wins out, since Anne has the last word. This is simply contrary to fact, because it was she who got killed.'

28 Bernstein, 'The *Schindler's List* Effect', p. 431.

29 Gillian Rose points out that not only does Keneally quote the epigram '*facetiously*' in its new context, it is also ironized in the Talmud itself, 'for no human being can save the world' ('Beginnings of the Day', pp. 244–5).

30 Hergenhan, 'Interview', p. 453; Spielberg quoted by Shandler, 'Schindler's Discourse', p. 164.

31 For instance, the narrator describes the bombing of the SS-only Cyganeria café in Cracow (pp. 158–9) as an action of resistance carried out by members of the Zionist youth movement Halutz which they feared would be forgotten.

32 The last line of the novel, in contrast to the 'Zionist closure' of the film (Bartov, 'Spielberg's Oskar', p. 45), is 'He was mourned in every continent'; David English discusses Keneally's view that the past is 'safe', known and populated by people just like us ('History and the Refuge of Art: Thomas Keneally's Sense of the Past', *Meridian* 6, 10 May 1987, pp. 23–9: pp. 24–5).

33 See the Introduction to this volume for a discussion of the support for uncertainty; it underlies Gillian Rose's discussion of the 'fascism of representation' of Spielberg's *Schindler's List*, in contrast to the radical uncertainty into which she argues spectators of Merchant and Ivory's *The Remains of the Day* are thrown (Cheyette and Marcus, *Modernity, Culture, and 'the Jew'*, p. 251). Ilan Avisar speaks of 'the restraints, hesitations, or stammers that have become characteristic of authentic artistic responses to the Holocaust' ('Holocaust Movies and the Politics of Collective Memory', in Rosenfeld (ed.), *Thinking About the Holocaust*, p. 50); David Lowenthal argues that ' "This is how it was" heralds faction', in contrast to ' "It may have happened something like this" ' (*The Past is a Foreign Country*, Cambridge: Cambridge University Press, 1985, p. 230), a tone familiar from testimony and witness.

34 The figures are in themselves interesting; their meaning is layered, concealing for instance a further fifty years' history of Jewish life in and emigration from Poland, and containing for Polish spectators an implicit criticism of their behaviour during the war. Nor do they appear in the book.

35 Quoted by Jerrold Kessel, 'Focus on secret wedding helps allay fears of hyperbole', *Guardian*, 2 March 1994, p. 24.

36 See Geoff Andrew's phrase in a preview of the film: 'the humanity it witnesses (or, to be more accurate, recalls and recreates)' ('Saving Graces', *Time Out*, 16–24 February 1994, p. 57).

37 Mikhail Bakhtin, 'Discourse in the Novel', p. 272.

38 Cf. Quartermaine, *Thomas Keneally*, p. 65; and Cheyette discusses some examples in 'The Uncertain Certainty' which show how Keneally's text 'self-consciously provides itself with a few moments of artifice to detract from its more ubiquitous rhetorical designs' (p. 230).

39 In his 'Report', the real-life Schindler mentions his 'gratitude for the help and services of that unfortunately small number of Germans who, despite their uniform, had the courage to stand up for a humane treatment of the Jews. ... Men who again and again granted me and my Jews protection and help directly or indirectly, never making this dependent on receiving anything in return. They are: General Schindler, Chief of the Armaments Inspectorate in Cracow, the lieutenant colonels Ott, Plathe, Süssmuth, Building Inspector Steinhäuser, Dieter Reeder and Hermann Toffel from the headquarters of the Security Police in Cracow, Major Franz von Korab, engineer Erich Lange from the Army High Command in Berlin' (p. 15).
    This list is partly the origin of Keneally's fictional party, attended by Toffel, Reeder, Steinhauser, Gebauer and Plathe. See also Quartermaine, *Thomas Keneally*, p. 65, and Enright, 'Fouling up the System', on plausible reconstruction.

40 Shlomith Rimmon-Kenan, *Narrative Fiction: Contemporary Poetics* (London: Methuen, 1983), p. 110; in the US version most instances of free indirect discourse are supplied with inverted commas, ostensibly to ensure that readers can tell when someone is speaking. However, this is a misleading intervention as the point of Keneally's omission of punctuation in the British edition is that *no* direct speech is taking place.

41 Quartermaine, *Thomas Keneally*, p. 64; according to Fritz Lanham, '*Schindler* Author Wins Attention for Rest of His Respected Oeuvre', in Fensch, *Oskar Schindler and His List*, 'What dialogue there is in the book is based on survivors' recollections of what was said, or what they were told was said': in itself a significant difference (p. 43). Petersson argues that the form Keneally has chosen makes it hard to know who is ' "construing" ' events: those who told the story from memory, or the person who wove them into narrative form (' "White Ravens" ', p. 162).

42 See, for instance, Sara Horowitz, 'But is it Good for the Jews? Spielberg's Schindler and the Aesthetics of Atrocity', in Loshitzky, *Spielberg's Holocaust*, p. 119.

43 English, 'Thomas Keneally's Sense of the Past', p. 27.

44 'To write these things now is to state the commonplaces of history. But to find them out in 1942 ...' (p. 152); the film follows this method of attempting to recreate the past, or, more controversially, to 'fabricate archives', in Claude Lanzmann's phrase ('Why Spielberg Has Distorted the Truth', *Guardian Weekly*, 3 April 1994, p. 14).

45 Keneally, *Schindler's Ark*, Textplus edition, p. iv.

46 Michael André Bernstein, *Foregone Conclusions: Against Apocalyptic History* (Berkeley, Calif., and London: University of California Press, 1994), p. 16.

47 The narrator says this presumably because although Keneally had access to Schindler's 'Report' in which he claims, 'The memory of a happy childhood spent with many Jewish friends and schoolmates, was for me a moral obligation that drove me on' (quoted in Ernie Meyer, ' "Saving Jewish lives was a moral obligation" ', *Jerusalem Post*, 29 October 1974), he must have been unable to locate any such Jewish friend.

48 Habitual aspect and predictive function are defined formally thus: 'Aspectual distinctions commonly refer to the distribution of an event over time. The main aspectual distinctions usually identified in English are "progressive" (indicating that an action is, or was, etc. in progress: *the cat is/was biting the dog*), and "perfective", indicating that an action has been completed (*the dog has bitten the cat*). Other aspectual distinctions often referred to in English include "habitual" (*I drive to work*) and "stative" (*I am clever*)' (E.K. Brown and J.E. Miller, *Syntax: A Linguistic Introduction to Sentence Structure*, London: Hutchinson, 1980, p. 105, n. 1). 'Predictive' means the action is in the future.

49 Petersson, ' "White Ravens" ', p. 168.
50 Rimmon-Kenan, *Narrative Fiction*, p. 111.
51 Quartermaine, *Thomas Keneally*, p. 68; he adds, 'The imbalance in Keneally's view of history is that while he promises unremittingly truthful access to a particular period we sometimes come away with little more than tourist curios – such disappointment is the price we pay for the Faustian excitement of witnessing history "in the flesh"' (this insight seems to rely on Hollington's comment on the flaming heart on Emilie's wall: 'a little something Dame Edna brought back from Cracow for the mantel-piece', 'The Ned Kelly of Cracow', p. 46). Less kindly, English calls this view of history 'voyeuristic fetishism', and to this condition he ascribes the list of SS ranks and their army equivalents (see also n. 56).
52 Avisar, 'Holocaust Movies and the Politics of Collective Memory', p. 53; this is clearer in the text. Patricia Waugh, *Metafiction*, London: Methuen, 1984, p. 92.
53 This is harder to argue of the film, whose roots in individual testimony are not perceptible, and in which there is 'a backdrop of "dwarfed" (literally and narra-tively) Jewish slaves', and no gentile Polish character of any significance (Loshitzky, 'Holocaust Others', p. 114). Spielberg claims he wanted the film to be 'more of a horizontal approach [than Steve Zaillian's original script], taking in the Holocaust as the raison d'être of the whole project' (quoted by Stephen Schiff, 'Seriously Spielberg', in Fensch, *Oskar Schindler and His List*, p. 153). See also Keneally's intro-duction to Brecher, *Schindler's Legacy*: 'Here … we have the memories of the Schin-dler survivors in their own right' (p. xiv).
54 Rosenfeld feels they 'marry' him, suggesting a rather different Oedipal relation ('The Americanization of the Holocaust', p. 142).
55 Herbert Steinhouse notes that Stern, whom he met in Schindler's company, had a 'fabulous' memory and would provide prompts for Schindler's reminiscences ('The Journalist Who Knew Oskar Schindler: An Interview with Herbert Steinhouse by Thomas Fensch', in Fensch, *Oskar Schindler and His List*, p. 16). Wundheiler empha-sizes the bond between the two men, which both Keneally and Spielberg seem to have wanted to portray but which gets overshadowed by the Schindler–Goeth relationship. In contrast to the latter, Stern 'brought out the best in [Schindler who] thanked him by loving him' (Luitgard Wundheiler, 'Oskar Schindler's Moral De-velopment During the Holocaust', *Humboldt Journal of Social Relations* 13 (1–2), 1985–6, pp. 333–56: p. 340).
56 Quartermaine points out that the Author's Note avoids any idea of 'imaginative' inspiration for the text, ascribing its genesis instead to the 'zeal' of a Schindler survivor, Leopold Pfefferberg, who 'caused' it to come into existence (*Thomas Keneally*, pp. 62–3). This 'factual' bias is supported by the prefatory maps and, as if it were a history of the official war, a list of 'SS Ranks and their Army Equivalents' – the latter is, more appropriately, demoted to the back pages of the US edition. This list of SS ranks has been the object of satiric critical comment, for instance by Sal-usinzky, who says its presence shows simply how 'keen' Keneally is to 'display his research' ('Thomas Keneally', p. 25). This is a strange instance to encounter even in a text named after lists. Peter Pierce argues that Keneally's insistence on the '*objet trouvé*' origins of his text is the result of over-anxiety after a plagiarism suit was brought against him for his novel *Season in Purgatory* (*Australian Melodramas*, p. 18).
57 In the Textplus edition there is an 'Introduction' before the Author's Note (*Schindler's Ark*, pp. iv–vi), signed, but not in facsimile, 'Thomas Keneally/ February 1989': this edition has two layers of authorial authentication, plus the efforts of an editor who has supplied historical and critical notes, to bolster up its historical appearance.
58 This information is presumably from a historical source. For this background 'Tom read as much about the Holocaust and Second World War as he could and relied

on no one particular source' (personal correspondence to the author from Keneally's assistant, March 1999).

59 See Bogumil Kosciesza's review of the first American edition, 'A Novel Informed by Prejudice', *Commonweal* X (9), 6 May 1983, pp. 284–5. Kosciesza sees Pfefferberg, and not a historical text, as the source here; and describes Keneally's detailed description of antisemitic Polish sentiment as 'equal to the best efforts of anti-Semitic libels' (p. 285).

60 Quartermaine, *Thomas Keneally*, p. 69.

61 English notes that a conflation takes place in the narrator's use of personal pronouns during this episode. The narrator announces, 'And from the hill you could see the oil on the machine pistol in his hand', of which English says, 'Of course Oskar could not have seen the oil, it is Keneally [*sic*] who imagines it' ('Thomas Keneally's Sense of the Past', p. 26). It seems rather that the second-person pronoun here interpellates the reader, who is made uncomfortably and filmically close to the action. Gillian Rose sees the dangers of this position as even more significant; she argues that the spectator of Spielberg's film, when watching the ghetto liquidation from Schindler's viewpoint, is constructed not as a survivor but as at best a bystander ('Beginnings of the Day', p. 245).

62 Although the exigencies of film make it necessary that the narrator's voice is replaced – see my *Introducing Bakhtin* (Manchester: Manchester University Press, 1997, pp. 139ff.) – it is interesting to note the occasions in the novel on which the narrator's voice is sufficiently double-voiced or personalized to be transferred directly to particular characters, e.g. Goeth (p. 191) and Stern (p. 314).

63 O'Hearn, 'Schindler's Ark and Schindler's List', p. 15; the US edition of *Schindler's List* (New York: Touchstone, 1993 [1983]), p. 216.

64 The narrator says 'this narrative has tried to avoid the canonisation of the Herr Direktor' but I think it does have a canonizing effect; for example, on p. 373, the narrator discusses an apocryphal story about an SS inspection at Brinnlitz thwarted, but even his reservations prop up the heroic image of Schindler: 'the anecdote is one of those stories that reflect people's picture of Oskar as a bounteous avatar, a provider who covers all eventualities', as does the phrase used elsewhere of Schindler as 'a minor god of rescue'.

65 On Schindler's opacity see, for example, p. 213; and several examples in Fensch, *Oskar Schindler and His List*, including: 'everyone … wondered, "Why?" Why did this unlikely hero do what he did? to save 1,100 lives' ('The Journalist Who Knew Oskar Schindler', p. 3). Richard Wolin says of the film: 'We see the Jews as tragic victims and servile accommodators.… They are the film's supernumeraries and huddled masses, waiting to be saved' ('*Schindler's List* and the Politics of Remembrance', in Fensch, *Oskar Schindler and His List*, p. 229). Michael André Bernstein puts it more strongly: the film follows 'the Hollywood convention of showing catastrophe primarily from the point of view of the perpetrators' and the Jews are depicted 'as a largely anonymous mass from whose midst an occasional figure emerges to show his individuality by the shuffling fervor of his gratitude for Schindler's aid' ('The *Schindler's List* Effect', p. 429). In a neat reversal, when Schindler becomes dependent on his rescuees after the war he is the one 'fervently stammering his thanks' at post-war reunions, according to Herbert Steinhouse ('The Man Who Saved a Thousand Lives', in Fensch, *Oskar Schindler and His List*, p. 30). In an argument on the film that would shock those who took exception to William Styron's analogy of plantation with Nazi slavery (see Chapter 5, this volume), Kirby Farrell sees a contemporary political motive behind our receptivity 'at this historical moment' to 'an account of a factory boss saving people from death by making them slave laborers' ('The Economies of *Schindler's List*', *Arizona Quarterly* 52 (1), Spring 1996, pp. 163–88: p. 166). In this view the film acts as a 'critique of acquisitive business that is implicit

throughout the story' (ibid., p. 180). In a letter to the *New York Review of Books* Harold Pinter takes an opposite view of the Holocaust as analogy in *Schindler's List*, and accuses the film of returning to a 'safe' historical event, to distract attention from the fact that 'The US has, I suggest, accepted that the death of millions is inevitable if its "national interests" are to be protected' (9 June 1994, p. 60).

66 Quoted in Berel Lang (ed.), *Writing and the Holocaust* (New York: Holmes and Meier, 1988), p. 188.

67 Of course Schindler's own freedoms were severely curtailed, and he had to make his own 'choice' of who to save and who not to. 'The names I know, that is, are the names I know' (p. 347), as he says in free direct discourse and in implicit answer both to the SS at Auschwitz who advise him, 'Don't get stuck on these particular names', and to the narrator, who asks of an SS officer who took the Pfefferbergs under his wing, 'It is a human puzzle why men like Schreiber didn't ask themselves, If this man and his wife were worth saving, why weren't the rest?' (p. 324). Schindler could not have saved 'the rest', and the comparative smallness of his rescue is not shied away from: Goeth 'would in a day abolish as many lives as Oskar Schindler was, by wit and hectic spending, harbouring in Emalia' (p. 281). Elsewhere, further to support the Schindler method, the narrator tells us that Oswald Bosko, the renegade SS officer, did want to save everyone, in fact saved no one and died in the process. In this respect Bosko is, in William Thornton's words, 'a more perfect hero', which is why he perishes within the Nazi system ('After the Carnival: The Filmic Prosaics of *Schindler's List*', *Canadian Review of Comparative Literature* 23 (3), September 1996, pp. 701–8: p. 703).

68 Hannah Arendt, *Eichmann in Jerusalem: A Report on the Banality of Evil* (Harmondsworth: Penguin, 1965), p. 111.

69 Ibid., pp. 48, 54.

70 Ibid., pp. 135, 276. For criticisms of Arendt's views, particularly her idea that European Judenräte did nothing to help their own cause, see, for instance, Gertrude Etorky, 'Hannah Arendt Against the Facts', *New Politics*, Fall 1963, pp. 53–73.

71 Arendt, *Eichmann in Jerusalem*, p. 19. The weight placed on 'brilliant' is complexly multi-accented: it resounds with the amoral way in which the Nazis themselves might have described their own strategy, as well as being the opposite adjective to one we might expect, such as 'grotesque' or 'breathtaking'; the same strategy is used in the far more obviously reversed phrase, 'the saving of Jews was not exactly what [the Security Police] had been trained for' (p. 192).

72 Ibid., p. 89, my italics.

73 Ibid., p. 45, my italics.

74 This phrase is taken from the book's blurb, credited to Frederic S. Burin, *Political Science Quarterly*.

75 Arendt, *Eichmann in Jerusalem*, p. 45.

76 Ibid., p. 154, my italics.

77 This is a constant theme of Arendt and other commentators (e.g. Christopher Browning; see his 'One Day in Józefów: Initiation to Mass Murder', *The Path to Genocide: Essays on Launching the Final Solution*, Cambridge: Cambridge University Press, 1992). It recurs in *Eichmann in Jerusalem* in such phrases as 'that put-upon way he found so hard to tolerate' (p. 241); and in Arendt's description of a German clergyman, Propst Grüber, who was asked in court if he had tried to influence Eichmann's conscience: 'Of course, the very courageous Propst had done nothing of the sort, and his answers now were highly embarrassing' (p. 131). Given the banality of the evil under discussion here, the sarcasm of 'very courageous' and the social discourse encoded in 'embarrassing' are absolutely apt.

78 Bakhtin, 'Discourse in the Novel', p. 363.

79 Arendt uses the same verb to equally double-voiced effect about the testimony given at a war crimes trial by Eichmann's friend and subordinate Dieter Wisliceny, who had elaborately prepared an alibi for himself 'to which he then *treated* the court at Nuremberg' (*Eichmann in Jerusalem*, p. 146, my italics).

80 Wundheiler, 'Oskar Schindler's Moral Development', p. 346; see also Wundheiler's flat, 'objective' description of Schindler's machinations in getting permission to move his workers to Brinnlitz, pp. 346–7, in contrast to that in Keneally's novel, pp. 299ff.

81 Peter Kemp in his *Listener* review praises Keneally for substituting 'tough delicacy for the pitfalls of sensationalism' (1982, p. 14): in other words, double-voiced for monologic discourse.

82 Arendt, *Eichmann in Jerusalem*, pp. 276, 287.

83 Hollington proleptically (his article was written in 1983, 10 years before Spielberg's Oscar-winning film) questions what he calls 'the highly emotional, moralistic ironies that dispense grace and damnation' ('The Ned Kelly of Cracow', p. 44), on the grounds that they emphasize the Holocaust's horrors yet again in order, perhaps, 'to catch that fat film contract' (ibid., p. 45) (MGM bought Schindler's story for $50,000 in the 1960s and Anthony Quinn was to have played Schindler).

84 Taubman compares Goeth to Eichmann, claiming both displayed the same 'indistinguishable ordinariness', but this seems to be a misreading ('Holocaust Art'); Richard Wolin's remark that the (filmic) Goeth is too easy to dismiss as a psychopath (*'Schindler's List* and the Politics of Remembrance', p. 229) is nearer the mark. However, Taubman's analysis of Schindler as an 'inverted Eichmann' whose concerns – 'the conscientious self-interest, the pride in professional skills, the "business as usual" mentality' – resemble 'the prototype of the banality of evil' is very perceptive, and Schindler is represented in Keneally's novel as 'incomprehensibly good' as Goeth is 'incomprehensibly evil' (Horowitz, 'But is it Good for the Jews?', p. 137). One recalls Arendt's remark that Eichmann 'had no motives at all' (see n. 82 above).

85 As Richard Johnstone declares, using the example of Truman Capote's 'Handcarved Coffins', faction is a stylistic phenomenon, 'a mode of writing, a matter-of-factness' ('The Rise of Faction', *Quadrant*, April 1985, pp. 76–8: p. 78). Critics, such as Taubman, hailed *Schindler's List* as an example of faction where crime was not the subject, in contrast to Truman Capote's and Norman Mailer's work; but Keneally's work does stay in the same general ballpark of the unconsoling. Johnstone concludes his article on a negative note – faction suggests 'Nothing is real. It merely seems real. And if nothing is real, then nothing matters' ('The Rise of Faction', p. 78) – with which Carmel Gaffney rather unconvincingly takes issue ('Keneally's Faction: *Schindler's Ark*', *Quadrant* 213 (XXIX), July 1985, pp. 75–7).

86 Hulse, 'Virtue and the Philosophic Innocent', p. 50.

87 Steinhouse, 'The Man Who Saved a Thousand Lives', p. 35, quoting a survivor.

88 Textplus, *Schindler's Ark*, p. v; David Thomson, 'Presenting Enamelware', in Fensch, *Oskar Schindler and His List*, p. 95; Steinhouse, 'The Man Who Saved a Thousand Lives', p. 24.

89 Hergenhan, 'Interview with Thomas Keneally', p. 456.

90 Quartermaine, *Thomas Keneally*, pp. 71, 72.

91 As Hollington puts it, 'Keneally seems to imagine the issues at stake to be primarily personal and individual rather than social' (p. 42). English, 'Thomas Keneally's Sense of the Past'; Hollington, 'The Ned Kelly of Cracow', pp. 26, 44; Pierce, *Australian Melodramas*, p. 19.

92 See Hollington, 'The Ned Kelly of Cracow', p. 44.

93 Quoted in Thomson, 'Presenting Enamelware', p. 97; this dialogue is not in Keneally's book. Liliane Weissberg, in a discussion of the German reception of

Spielberg's film, notes a tendency to conflate Schindler with the actor who plays him, Liam Neeson: 'As Neeson-Schindler, Spielberg's hero was a rescuer, not a savior; a human, not a holy man; an actor par excellence' ('The Tale of a Good German: Reflections on the German Reception of *Schindler's List*', in Loshitzky, *Spielberg's Holocaust*, p. 181). Thomson discusses the metacinematic potential of the film in 'Presenting Enamelware'. The film critic Jonathan Romney quotes Spielberg's own comment that if Schindler were alive today, he would be a movie producer, perhaps Time-Warner head Mike Ovitz; and Horowitz cites Spielberg admitting that 'he modeled his Schindler on his mentor and father surrogate, Steve Ross, head of Warner studios. Liam Neeson, the actor who plays Schindler, studied home movies of Ross to learn his mannerisms' ('But is it Good for the Jews?', p. 135).

94 On the confusion or equation of Spielberg with Schindler see Loshitzky, 'Introduction', p. 12; she cites such titles of film reviews as 'Spielberg's List' or 'Steven's Choice', (p. 26); and in her article argues that 'as Schindler was trying to save life through his capital, so Spielberg is trying to resurrect destroyed life through his capital' (Loshitzky, 'Holocaust Others', p. 114).

95 Loshitzky, 'Introduction', p. 15; and see Miriam Bratu Hansen, '*Schindler's List* is not *Shoah*: Second Commandment, Popular Modernism, and Public Memory', in Loshitzky, *Spielberg's Holocaust*, p. 103, n. 37. Schindler also resembles Kane in the way he is represented, in Keneally's text rather than the film: through the words of others.

96 Christian Metz describes the realm of film as that of the 'imaginary signifier': film figures the apparent presence of an actually absent object with particular starkness (*The Imaginary Signifier*, Bloomington: Indiana University Press, 1981). Theories of lack and absence are usually linked to gender in film theory (see, for instance, Mary Ann Doane, *Femmes Fatales: Feminism, Film Theory, Psychoanalysis*, London: Routledge, 1991), but it seems that they can be applied equally aptly to narratives of loss and mourning.

97 Taubman, 'Holocaust Art', p. 23. 'Gloomy Sunday', a song written by a Hungarian Jew, Rezso Seress, who spent the war in a Ukrainian labour camp and committed suicide in Budapest in 1968, was the subject of Peter Muller's play *Gloomy Sunday*, produced in London at the Jermyn Street Theatre, autumn 1998.

98 Taubman, 'Holocaust Art'; Gaffney, 'Keneally's Faction'. Quartermaine opines: '*Schindler's Ark* avoids the mass slaughter of the concentration camps for the equally shocking, and shocking precisely because more mundane, minutiae of daily life' and 'the more intimate and apparently controllable dangers of the "factory family" whose fate the reader follows throughout' (*Thomas Keneally*, pp. 67, 68) – *pace* Hartman's argument in 'The Cinema Animal'. On the question of Schindler's profit motive, the narrator emphasizes that far from making money out of his rescuees, he spent money on them: indeed they were his 'profit'. Wundheiler points out that the two activities were 'ironically' inextricably linked: 'Schindler paid his workers with the profits of their own labor' ('Oskar Schindler's Moral Development', p. 337): he sold enamelware on the black market and bought food with the proceeds.

99 Wundheiler, 'Oskar Schindler's Moral Development', p. 343.

100 Ibid., pp. 352, 333.

101 Ibid., p. 340.

102 Wundheiler quotes Schindler's explanation: 'The German word he used to describe himself was "maßlos". Literally, "maßlos" means without moderation or restraint, but it has the additional connotation of the presence of an irresistible inner force that drives a person beyond what is considered acceptable behavior' ('Oskar Schindler's Moral Development', p. 340). See also Moshe Bejski's reminiscence of Schindler's remark, ' "If I'm walking in the street and I see a dog in danger of being crushed by a car, wouldn't I try to help him?" ' (in Eric Silver, *The Book of the Just:*

Unsung Heroes Who Rescued Jews from Hitler, London: Weidenfeld and Nicolson, 1992, p. 148); and the episode recounted by a post-war friend of Schindler's in which a motorcyclist fell into some water: 'Hardly a moment passed before Schindler jumped into the river to rescue the motorcyclist' (Wundheiler, ibid., p. 341). The opposite of this impulsiveness is suggested by Schindler's involvement with the Zionists in Budapest, which again does not figure especially prominently in either the book or film but which Wundheiler terms 'possibly the most important evidence for the [moral] development I am trying to sketch' (ibid., p. 348).

103 Elinor Brecher, *Schindler's Legacy: True Stories of the List Survivors* (London: Hodder and Stoughton, 1994), p. xx; Steinhouse, 'The Man Who Saved a Thousand Lives', p. 34. He speaks unhesitatingly of Schindler's 'more active anti-fascist role' after 1943 (p. 27); and refers to the 'true motives of Schindler's request' to move his Jewish workers to a sub-camp near the factory, which Goeth was never to discover – as if we, on the other hand, are quite clear what they were (p. 28).

104 Fensch says Steinhouse's contemporary corroborative records are valuable in deflecting revisionist views of Keneally's novel ('The Journalist Who Knew Oskar Schindler', p. 19); one such revisionist view is expressed in the risible website, 'The Facts Spielberg Suppressed in Schindler's List' (Michael A. Hoffman II, 1994, http://www.hoffman-info.com). Much concern was expressed over the 'water not gas' scene in the film that it might play into the hands of those who deny there ever was any gas used (the phrase is Rose's, from 'Beginnings of the Day', p. 246); see also Horowitz, 'But is it Good for the Jews?', pp. 128–9. Making Schindler's rescue the subject of a factional story means that such clear duplicity and distance from committed Nazis *must* be asserted. Indeed, the contrast between Goeth and Schindler, though the former is described as Schindler's 'dark brother', rests precisely on the commandant's murderous impulsiveness which Schindler as part of a long-term strategy urges him to curb.

105 Thomson, 'Presenting Enamelware', pp. 95, 97.

106 Steinhouse, 'The Man Who Saved a Thousand Lives', p. 27.

107 Bartov argues that narratives about the past aim for both 'conventionality' – a story of human choice and triumph – and 'authenticity'; in the case of the Holocaust this is usually a contradictory imperative, but not in the case of Schindler ('Spielberg's Oskar', pp. 46–7).

108 This is not the same as hindsight, because that involves staying put in one's own time, but what Lowenthal says of hindsight could also be said of foreshadowing: it 'paradoxically limits our ability to understand the past by giving us greater knowledge than people of the time could have had' (*The Past is a Foreign Country*, p. 217).

109 Ibid., p. 218; Lowenthal adds that the 'faction-writer' replaces the original's 'historian'. Lowenthal is quoting R.S. Humphreys, 'The rhetoric of history'.

110 Schindler is intentionalist rather than functionalist, to borrow terms used of Hitler's plans for the Final Solution; see, for instance, Christopher Browning, *The Path to Genocide*, pp. 3–5. Lowenthal raises the idea that the novelist may be able to avoid the historian's hindsight, because, as Keneally tries to do, fiction puts 'readers in the past like people of the time, who could not know what was coming next' (*The Past is a Foreign Country*, p. 226), but Keneally cannot avoid at least hinting at what is to come, and at the knowledge of his reader.

111 Omer Bartov, 'Spielberg's Oskar: Hollywood Tries Evil', in Loshitzky, *Spielberg's Holocaust*, pp. 42, 43; he is talking about the film.

112 Rosenfeld points out that Hilberg's triad has been expanded to include 'survivor' and 'rescuer', as well as 'liberator', 'resister', 'second generation survivor' ('The Americanization of the Holocaust', p. 135), and he discusses the rescuer as a theological issue (pp. 144–7). Natasha Lehrer claims in her discussion of the French reception of Spielberg's film that 'Oskar Schindler effects a sort of ambiguous

resolution between the antinomies of resistance and collaboration' by somehow doing both ('Between Obsession and Amnesia: Reflections on the French Reception of *Schindler's List*, in Loshitzky, *Spielberg's Holocaust*, p. 217).

113 This is to prevent their becoming, in Cheyette's words on the film, 'passive consumers of an already known ethic' ('Uncertain Certainty', p. 235). Thornton distinguishes between the novel and the film in this respect, arguing that the former 'keeps the problem of evil intact, leading one to ask how such a fine fellow as Schindler could bring himself to drink and carouse with SS thugs', while the film poses 'the most basic axiological question in reverse: not so much the problem of evil as the problem of good' ('After the Carnival', p. 703).

114 Keneally, quoted by Pedro Ponce, 'Making Novels of Life's Ethical Dilemmas', in Fensch, *Oskar Schindler and His List*, p. 39; Wundheiler, 'Oskar Schindler's Moral Development', p. 334; Hulse, 'Virtue and the Philosophic Innocent', p. 51; Wundheiler, ibid., p. 339; Emilie Schindler's oddly unilluminating memoir of her husband is titled *Where Light and Shadow Meet* (New York: W.W. Norton and Company, 1997).

115 Wolin, '*Schindler's List* and the Politics of Remembrance', pp. 228–9.

116 Hollington, 'The Ned Kelly of Cracow', p. 42; Cheyette, in 'The Uncertain Certainty', points out that the Christ-like Schindler tells Helen in Goeth's kitchens that he 'knows her suffering' (this is not in the book, although the preceding dialogue is followed closely by the screenplay, where Schindler more mundanely observes, ' "Your circumstances are appalling, Helen" ', p. 31) and at the film's end gives 'a final crypto-sermon on the mount in Brinnlitz' (pp. 236, 237). In the text the narrator observes that Schindler 'desired [the Jews] with some of the absolute passion that characterised the exposed and flaming heart of the Jesus that hung on Emilie's wall' (p. 302).

117 Schindler's 'Report', written in Konstanz, July 1945, is now held by the Special Collections of the Library at Yad Vashem, Jerusalem. It is 4,700 words long, and its full title is, 'Report on efforts expended and expenses incurred towards the saving of the Jews in the period 1939–45 by Oskar Schindler, director and owner of the enamelware factory in Cracow, subsequently relocated to Brünnlitz labour camp, Czechoslovakia'. Page numbers are those of the original German typescript; all translations by Moray McGowan; extracts of the 'Report' appeared in English in commemoration of Schindler's death in Meyer's 'Saving Jewish Lives was "a Moral Obligation" '.

118 Schindler, 'Report', p. 1.

119 Ibid., pp. 2, 9.

120 Ibid., p. 13.

121 Ibid., p. 14.

122 Ibid., p. 12.

123 Ibid., p. 7.

124 Ibid., p. 4.

125 Ibid., pp. 10, 8.

126 Avisar argues that 'Spielberg took a fairly marginal text on the history of the Holocaust and tried to elevate it to central canonical status' ('Holocaust Movies and the Politics of Collective Memory', p. 49).

127 Kellman, '*Schindler's List* – Spielberg's Homecoming', p. 9; Keneally quoted in Pedro E. Ponce, 'Making Novels of Life's Ethical Dilemmas', *Chronicle of Higher Education* XL (22), 2 February 1994, p. A5.

5 Melodrama: William Styron, *Sophie's Choice*

1 John Henrik Clarke (ed.), *William Styron's Nat Turner: Ten Black Writers Respond* (Boston: Beacon, 1968); Clarke's collection includes discussions of Styron's alleged

historical inaccuracy and perpetuation of racist stereotypes. Styron's remarks are from ' "A Wheel of Evil Come Full Circle": The Making of *Sophie's Choice*', *Sewanee Review* 1997, p. 397. One interviewer describes the debate over the later novel as if it were just as incendiary: '*Sophie's Choice* was sharply criticized as being anti-Jewish, antifeminist, and so on. It was almost like a replay of *Ten Black Writers Respond*' (Victor Strandberg and Balkrishna Buwa, 'An Interview with William Styron', *Sewanee Review* 99 (3), Summer 1991, pp. 463–77: p. 471).

2 James L.L. West (ed.), *Conversations with William Styron* (Jackson and London: University Press of Mississippi, 1985), p. 270. *Sophie's Choice* was number ninety-eight in the Modern Library-sponsored list of 100 'books of the century' – for which Styron was one of the judges – widely reported during July 1998, for example, 'Books of the century', *Daily Mail*, 21 July 1998, p. 8. William Styron, *Sophie's Choice* (London: Corgi, 1980 [1979]). All further page references are given in brackets in the text.

3 Andréa Bernard and Elzbieta H. Oleksy summarize Polish critics' objections to the novel: 'In *Sophie's Choice* Styron offends two deeply rooted Polish cultural constructs: that of the immaculate heroism of the Polish people during World War II ... and the symbol associated with the [pure, maternal, patriotic] Polish woman.' They quote Henryk Weber saying that someone of Professor Bieganski's background and membership of the National Democracy party would be, as well as antisemitic, anti-German; of his preference for speaking German at home they assert that 'Neither historical sources nor private communications with inhabitants of Kraków confirm such extreme cases of Germanophilia' ('*Sophie's Choice*: The Depiction of Poles in the American Popular Imagination', in Waldemar Zacharasiewicz (ed.), *Images of Central Europe in Travelogues and Fiction by North American Writers*, Tübingen: Stauffenberg Verlag, 1995, pp. 262, 267, n. 3).

4 Elie Wiesel was prompted by the appearance of the film *Sophie's Choice* to write, in an article 'Does the Holocaust Lie Beyond the Reach of Art?' published in the *New York Times*, that 'Only those who lived it in their flesh and in their minds can possibly transform their experience into knowledge. Others, despite their best intentions, can never do so' (quoted in Rhoda Sirlin, *William Styron's 'Sophie's Choice': Crime and Self-Punishment*, Ann Arbor: UMI Research Press, 1990, p. 9).

5 Barbara Foley, 'Fact, Fiction, Fascism: Testimony and Mimesis in Holocaust Narratives', *Comparative Literature* 34, 1982, pp. 330–60: pp. 357–8.

6 Other critics comment on the complexity and seamlessness of the text's narrative form, for instance, Richard Pearce, 'Sophie's Choices', in Robert K. Morris and Irving Malin (eds), *The Achievement of William Styron* (Athens, Ga: University of Georgia Press, 1981), p. 291. See the diagram of *Sophie's Choice*'s four time levels in John Kenny Crane, *The Root of All Evil: The Thematic Unity of William Styron's Fiction* (Columbia: University of South Carolina Press, 1984), pp. 136–41; Crane considers it 'Styron's most perfect work in structure as well as in thematic unity' (p. 136). Terry White says the novel is structured, à la Southern gothic, as a 'vortex' featuring 'interlocking cycles of repetition of character and event', citing critic J. Douglas Perry ('Jemand von Niemand, Death-Camp Doctor: Evil as Structuring Principle in the Later Fiction of William Styron', *The University of Mississippi Studies in English* 10, 1992, pp. 144–57: p. 149).

7 Foley, 'Fact, Fiction, Fascism', calls *Sophie's Choice* 'pseudofactual': according to her definition, this means it stylizes non-fictional discourse, in this case autobiography, but of course it also uses the content of that discourse (pp. 354–6).

8 Valarie Meliotes Arms, 'An Interview with William Styron', *Contemporary Literature* 20 (1), Winter 1979, p. 12. Styron adds: 'I wouldn't feel happy unless [readers] identified Stingo as a man who is masquerading as Bill Styron' (p. 1): not the other way round; Styron adds, 'that [Sophie] "spilled the beans" so explicitly to the

narrator means that when I go into the third person and start describing what happened to Sophie the reader will believe it' (ibid., p. 3). Benjamin DeMott wryly observes that our credulity is stretched in being asked to believe that a taste for American bourbon accounts for Sophie's garrulousness, 'rather than a spell of the novelistic clumsies' ('Styron's Survivor: An Honest Witness' in A.D. Casciato and J.L.W. West III (eds), *Critical Essays on William Styron*, Boston: G.K. Hall, 1982, p. 259).

9   Styron, 'The Seduction of Leslie', *Esquire*, September 1976. Joan Smith is reminded by this of the genesis of *The White Hotel* ('Holocaust Girls', *Misogynies*, London: Faber, 1990, pp. 94–5): D.M. Thomas had an erotic poem published before he read about Babi Yar and decided to combine the two in his novel in what Smith sees as an exploitative manner (see Chapter 2).

10   Styron says, 'Though her "choice" was an imagined one, the Sophie I knew had suffered cruelly and had been a Catholic' ('Foreword' to Sirlin, *William Styron's 'Sophie's Choice'*, p. x); and 'Therefore a certain deterministic logic helped prevent me in my fiction from converting her to a Jew' (ibid.). In another article Styron uses the same metaphor for novelizing this woman at all: 'What if I were to *convert* my brief encounter with Sophie in Brooklyn … into a fictional narrative in which I actually got to know this young woman over a long and turbulent summer?' ('A Wheel of Evil', p. 397, my italics).

11   Alvin H. Rosenfeld, 'The Holocaust According to William Styron', *Midstream* 25 (10), 1979, pp. 43–9: p. 49, an article which forms part of the chapter 'Exploiting Atrocity' in *A Double Dying: Reflections on Holocaust Literature* (Bloomington and London: Indiana University Press, 1980); see also Alan Berger, *Crisis and Covenant: The Holocaust in American Jewish Fiction* (Albany: SUNY Press, 1985), p. 33.

12   Quoted in Rosenfeld, *A Double Dying*, p. 159. In an energetic review of *Sophie's Choice*, Leslie Fiedler says he once vowed that he would never get involved in the argument over whether Hitler's extermination camps are 'best understood as a monstrous climax to the millennial war of paganism against Judaism, or an episode in the eternal human struggle between good and evil', which sums up the issue aptly ('Styron's Choice: A Novel About Auschwitz', *Psychology Today* XIII, July 1979, pp. 102–7: p. 102).

13   William Styron, 'The Message of Auschwitz', in Casciato and West, *Critical Essays on William Styron*, p. 286. By the time of Sirlin's *William Styron's 'Sophie's Choice'*, Styron sounds increasingly impatient with the argument for the uniqueness of the Jewish fate and calls it in his Foreword 'proprietary in the extreme' (p. xi); in his interview with Sirlin he refers to Jewish 'exclusivity' over the matter (p. 103).

14   Interview with Morris in Morris and Malin, *The Achievement of William Styron*, p. 59.

15   'L'univers concentrationnaire' is David Rousset's phrase from *The Other Kingdom*, trans. Ramon Guthrie (New York: Reynal and Hitchcock, 1947). In 'A Wheel of Evil' Styron claims that Hannah Arendt 'always used the word *camps*, or, occasionally, *Auschwitz*, as a generic term for the Nazi terror – never Holocaust, which doesn't appear in *Eichmann in Jerusalem*' (p. 395).

16   Cynthia Ozick, 'A Liberal's Auschwitz', *Confrontation* 10, Spring 1975 (one year after Styron's 'The Message of Auschwitz', see n. 13 above), pp. 125–9: p. 128. Ozick risks 'muddling' her own argument for remembering the specifics of victim and perpetrator by using a spurious analogy: she claims we must remember 'the Nazis as Germans; at Babi Yar the Nazi-helpers for being Ukrainians; at Maalot the terrorists for being Palestinians' (p. 128).

17   West, *Conversations*, p. 248.

18   Quoted in Rosenfeld, 'The Holocaust According to William Styron', p. 45.

19 See the narrator's list, *Sophie's Choice*, p. 292; and Styron's list in Arms, 'An Interview', p. 8: '[Bruno] Bettelheim, [*The Informed Heart*]; [William] Shirer's *The Rise and Fall of the Third Reich*; *This Way for the Gas, Ladies and Gentlemen*, by a Polish political prisoner, Tadeusz Borowski; Eugen Kogon's *The Theory and Practice of Hell*; Olga Lengyel's *Five Chimneys*; and ... *Amidst a Nightmare of Crime* and *Auschwitz as Seen through the Eyes of the SS*'.

20 Sirlin, *William Styron's 'Sophie's Choice'*, p. x.

21 The use of the colloquial word 'yanked' in the description of unloading cattle cars at the ramp adds to this distance.

22 For a fictional construction of the 'core' of Auschwitz, particularly the interior of gas chambers, see, for instance, André Schwarz-Bart's *The Last of the Just* (New York: Atheneum, 1960). Interview with Ray Ownbey, 'Discussions with William Styron', *Mississippi Quarterly* 30, Spring 1977, p. 288.

23 See, for instance, in interview with Styron by Robert K. Morris, in Morris and Malin, *The Achievement of William Styron*: 'I think the two are intertwined ... they represent variations of each other. Plainly there are very large differences' (p. 60). In Arms, 'An Interview', Styron claims: 'What I'm trying to say is that it's very dangerous to try and equate horrors in history' (p. 7). This is *pace* Sirlin, who claims throughout her monograph on *Sophie's Choice* that 'Styron links what are for him the two horrors of modern times – slavery and genocide in the American South, and slavery and genocide in Nazi Eastern Europe' (*William Styron's 'Sophie's Choice'*, p. 3). What Sirlin's evidence is for genocide among plantation slaves – she is not referring to native Americans – she does not say. Other critics seize on the implicit comparison as if it were a central tenet of the novel: Barbara Tepa Lupak claims Stingo and Sophie 'share a certain guilt over the genocidal past of their countries' (*Insanity and Redemption in Contemporary American Fiction*, Gainsville, Fla: University Press of Florida, 1995, p. 179), further disregarding accuracy or at least using the word 'genocide' loosely. According to Richard G. Law it is Poland and the South that are being compared, not Nazism and the South ('The Reach of Fiction: Narrative Technique in Styron's *Sophie's Choice*', *Southern Literary Journal* 23 (1), Fall 1990, p. 63); but Eva Hoffman denies this comparison: 'While Polish Jews experienced constraints imposed by prejudice and minority position, they were not burdened with the terrible legacy of slavery' ('Letters', *London Review of Books*, 30 July 1998, p. 4). Pearl K. Bell finds that Styron 'loses a sense of the full enormity of the Holocaust' through 'emphasizing not the end goal of the Nazi plan – mass murder – but rather the means of domination and enslavement which they settled on to effectuate that goal' ('Evil and William Styron', in Daniel W. Ross (ed.), *The Critical Response to William Styron*, Westport, Conn. and London: Greenwood Press, 1995, p. 186).

24 Rosenfeld 'The Holocaust According to William Styron', p. 44. Rosenfeld quotes Rubenstein from *The Cunning of History*: 'The most common view is that the camp was a place where Jews were exterminated by the millions in gas chambers – simply this and nothing more'; and he repeats incredulously, '*Simply this and nothing more?*' (ibid.).

25 Quoted in Samuel Coale, *William Styron Revisited* (Boston, Mass.: Twayne, 1991), p. 130.

26 See also Dawn Trouard, 'Styron's Historical Pre-Text: Nat Turner, Sophie, and the Beginnings of a Postmodern Career', *Papers on Language and Literature* XXIII, 1987, pp. 489–97: pp. 496–7.

27 Rosenfeld, *A Double Dying*, p. 161. Styron, in Arms, 'An Interview', p. 10, says he chose Höss particularly, rather than, say, Heinrich Himmler, as someone 'relatively unknown', thus heeding Georg Lukàcs's warning in *The Historical Novel* on the dangers of dealing with 'major' historical figures.

28 Styron's portrait of Höss certainly has this effect on Sirlin, who rather fantastically compares Höss with Sophie by suggesting that both are victims of matters they would rather forget (*William Styron's 'Sophie's Choice'*, p. 49). Other critics fall victim to the comparative urge. Michael Kreyling likens Höss to the irate taxi-driver who insults Stingo's father for not giving him enough of a tip ('Speaking the Unspeakable in Styron's *Sophie's Choice*', *Southern Review* XX, 1984, pp. 546–91: p. 555), while David Galloway moves straight from discussing the 'philosophical equivalence' of chattel slavery and concentration camp slavery to the 'degrading and destructive' capacity of the modern city ('Holocaust as Metaphor: William Styron and *Sophie's Choice*', *Anglistik and Englischunterricht* 13, 1981, pp. 57–69: p. 61. Judith Ruderman claims that as a 'victim of Höss and his regime, Sophie is no less a victim of her savior, Nathan Landau' (*William Styron*, New York: Ungar, 1987, p. 100).

Much more convincing is William Heath's discussion of the 'hopeless confusion' of Styron's voice with Stingo's. Rather than isolating unhelpful comparisons between Auschwitz and the present, Heath discusses a chain of metaphors which more subtly implicate Stingo in that other universe: at McGraw-Hill Stingo is involved in a 'selection process' of manuscripts which he describes as 'clubfooted' and 'helpless' and which he gleefully 'eviscerate[s]'. Heath argues that Stingo shows the same 'disdain' for people, particularly ' "inferiors" ' as he does for these typescripts (William Heath, 'I, Stingo: The Problem of Egotism in *Sophie's Choice*', *Southern Review* 20 (3), July 1984, pp. 528–45: pp. 532, 539). On the same passage, although not commenting on these particular words, Gavin Cologne-Brookes says that, 'The diction is often Stingo's, but the details enable the narrator to undermine Stingo's position through ironic imagery' (*The Novels of William Styron: From Harmony to History*, Baton Rouge: Louisiana State University Press, 1995, p. 166). This is not the only instance of 'concentration camp imagery' infiltrating later scenes, as both Joan Smith and Cologne-Brookes note of Stingo's description of Leslie Lapidus's breasts, 'imprisoned within the rim of a murderous brassiere made of wormwood and wire': Smith ascribes this lapse of taste to Styron ('Holocaust Girls', p. 88), while Cologne-Brookes credits it to the elder Stingo's ironic representation of his younger self (ibid., p. 175). Similarly, Stingo describes his mother's 'disgusting' death as a 'transport of pain': this example makes clear the 'trigger-troping' that all these examples constitute. Even when the Auschwitz material is not the subject of representation, its background presence is signalled in this way.

29 I should say ' "Styron" as implied author' whenever I am talking about such novelistic manifestations, but have assumed for the sake of brevity that the distinction between this Styron and the actual author may be taken as read.

30 *Pace*, for instance, John Kenny Crane who describes 'Styron-Stingo' focusing on Hannah Arendt, in 'The Root of All Evil: The Thematic Unity of William Styron's Fiction' in Daniel W. Ross (ed.), *The Critical Response to William Styron* (Westport, Conn. and London: Greenwood Press, 1995), p. 213; I prefer this way of describing what happens in the text to Gavin Cologne-Brooks's argument that there are 'passages [of dialogue with Holocaust literature] where the narrator moves beyond Stingo's discourse and in effect functions as Styron' (*The Novels of William Styron*, p. 157); and see also Rolf Hochhuth's *The Deputy*, which quotes from Höss's diary.

31 Cologne-Brookes, *The Novels of William Styron*, p. 160; Robert K. Morris mentions a critic who berated Styron for 'resorting' to the ' "literature of the Holocaust" ' because of a failure of imagination (and indeed DeMott points out that 'scarcely a word of what happens to [Sophie] is new to print', 'Styron's Survivor', p. 259), to which Styron replies that this is a very common tactic; which is a rather different point ('Interviews with William Styron', *The Achievement of William Styron*, pp. 66–7).

32 Rudolf Hoess, *Commandant of Auschwitz: The Autobiography of Rudolf Hoess*, trans. Constantine Fitzgibbon, with an introduction by Lord Russell of Liverpool

(London: Pan, 1961), p. 80; in *Sophie's Choice* the narrator notes, rather floridly, that Höss had been 'so successfully sucked clean of every molecule of real qualm or scruple that his own description of the unutterable crimes he perpetrated daily seemed often to float outside and apart from evil, phantasms of cretinous innocence' (*Sophie's Choice*, p. 201). Despite the anglicized spelling of Höss's name as it appears in Fitzgibbon's translation of the autobiography, I continue to refer to him as 'Höss'.

33 Höss, *Commandant of Auschwitz*, pp. 53, 80.

34 Ibid., pp. 36–7.

35 Sirlin's puffing study (*William Styron's 'Sophie's Choice'*) is keen to explain away all the slurs cast at *Sophie's Choice*, and she does this by a process of reductive analogy: plantation slavery and the Holocaust were equally genocidal; Höss is very like several of the novel's other characters. Kreyling says the Harlekin episode represents something far more sinister than Höss's wish to be taken away from all this, as 'a self-contradicting and ultimately perverting dream of pseudo-life without the flesh – a dream falsely accorded the status of the real and then used in the "monstrous", unspeakable foundation of the crematoria of Birkenau' ('Speaking the Unspeakable', p. 561).

36 Höss, *Commandant of Auschwitz*, pp. 68–76.

37 Styron draws upon both the extract from Höss's *Commandant of Auschwitz* reprinted in *KL Auschwitz* and its notes and appendices, as well as the full version of the autobiography (see n. 32 above), which is credited on the copyright page of *Sophie's Choice*.

38 Jerzy Rawicz, 'Foreword' to *KL Auschwitz Seen by the SS: Rudolf Höss, Pery Broad, Johann Paul Kremer*, footnotes and biographical notes ed. Jadwiga Bezwinska and Danuta Czech (Oswiecim: The Auschwitz-Birkenau State Museum, 1994 [1970]), pp. 14, 15, 17. In the Appendix, Dubiel testifies that the 'equipment and furniture of Höss's home' were the property of Jews sent to the gas chambers: 'The rooms were furnished with the most magnificent pieces, the desk drawers were lined with leather from the warehouses of the leather factory' (p. 222).

39 Rawicz, 'Foreword', p. 16; 'Canada' was the name given the warehouses full of goods stolen from prisoners and the dead.

40 In the Appendix to *KL Auschwitz Seen by the SS*, Stanislaw Dubiel notes that Frau Höss would also try to use the underwear destined for the women prisoners in the household as items of exchange in the camp black market (p. 222). See also Olga Lengyel: 'Only a few of the select were awarded underwear. The majority had to wear their dresses next to their skins' (*Five Chimneys*, London: Mayflower, 1972, p. 32).

41 Höss, *Commandant of Auschwitz*, p. 63; Wilhelmine is a substitute for Styron's original plan to have Frau Höss assault Sophie until he learned that Höss's wife was still alive and could charge Styron with libel (interview by Gavin Cologne-Brookes, in West, *Conversations*, p. 246).

42 Rawicz, 'Foreword', pp. 17, 15; Hodys was thought to be Italian.

43 Ibid., p. 19.

44 Höss, *Commandant of Auschwitz*, pp. 29, 32.

45 *KL Auschwitz Seen by the SS*, p. 40.

46 Rawicz, 'Foreword', p. 40, n. 38. Styron cites verbatim (the narrator also uses that term, although he means something different by it) the 'welcoming statement of SS Hauptsturmführer Fritzsch' (*Sophie's Choice*, p. 518); it was originally cited by Rawicz (*KL Auschwitz Seen by the SS*, p. 41, n. 40) to back up his estimate of prisoners' life-expectancies. I have italicized the words omitted by Styron from Rawicz's original – he presumably really is quoting verbatim: ' "You have come to a *German* concentration camp, not to a sanatorium, and there is only one way out – up [*through*] the

chimney.... Anyone who don't [*does not*] like this can try hanging himself on the wires. If there are Jews in this group, you [*they*] have no right to live more than two weeks [*a fortnight*].... Any nuns here? Like the priests, you have one month [*if there are priests*]. All the rest, three months.' Styron's changes are, apart from the omission of 'German' and addition of the nuns, for his own stylistic purposes – to make the speech sound idiomatic ('up the chimney') or to show it is narrated in Sophie's imperfect English ('don't').

47 Szczurek mentions a prisoner Bronek Jaron from Cracow who worked at Höss's home (*KL Auschwitz*, pp. 225, 219).

48 Ibid., p. 222, a detail Styron embellishes in an unpleasant manner: 'They were the special favorites of Frau Höss ... they had been in the house for many months and had grown complacent and plump, their sedentary labour allowing them to acquire a suetlike avoirdupois bizarre-looking amid this fellowship of emaciated flesh' (*Sophie's Choice*, p. 341).

49 *KL Auschwitz Seen by the SS*, p. 226. Styron also uses the incongruous nickname, 'Onkel Heini', by which, according to Dubiel, Höss's children knew Heinrich Himmler (*KL Auschwitz*, pp. 220–1).

50 Rawicz does not annotate this section of the autobiography; there seems to be no reason to doubt Höss's antipathy to Julius Streicher's brand of racism, especially as he goes on to emphasize, in dyed-in-the-wool Nazi style, his own 'fanatical' anti-semitic credentials.

51 Höss, *Commandant of Auschwitz*, p. 55.

52 Ibid.

53 In a letter home Stingo reports, ' "due purely to an alphabetical coincidence ... Pete Strohmyer and Chuckie Stutz are my roommates here" ' (p. 296).

54 West, *Conversations*, pp. 197–8.

55 Richard Pearce, 'Sophie's Choices', in Morris and Malin, *Achievement*, p. 294. He sees the Nazi doctor as a means of commenting obliquely on Stingo, but in fact the presentation of the doctor says more about the narrator than about the characters he is describing, including his younger self.

56 Rosenfeld, *A Double Dying*, p. 162. See the different estimate of Colville, who reads the state of being ' "someone from noone" ' as analogous to the position of the narrator, 'writing himself into being through Sophie's story' ('Killing the Dead Mother: Women in *Sophie's Choice*', *Delta* (Montpellier) XXIII, 1986, pp. 111–35: p. 116). Several critics see von Niemand as an Everyman figure, e.g. Lupak, *Insanity and Redemption*, p. 167; John Lang, 'God's Averted Face: Styron's *Sophie's Choice*', *American Literature* 55 (2), May 1983, pp. 215–32: p. 229, n. 18 – a startling interpretation the implications of which are not explored.

57 Hence the irony of the novel's title; although this is obviously the starkest instance of a choice which is no such thing, there are several other instances of choice made by Sophie which push her in one narrative direction and not another. Sophie has a choice to make at every level of horror in the plot: for or against Nazis; for or against antisemites; whether to be a member of the Resistance; to live or die; to be with Stingo or with Nathan. Carolyn A. Durham remarks upon the rhetorical force of the novel's title: 'Our limited, popular, and generally sensationalist knowledge of history prepares us to suspect Sophie's involvement in sexual crimes or experiments at Auschwitz, and the mysterious secret announced in the title encourages us to believe she participated more as collaborator than as victim' ('William Styron's *Sophie's Choice*: The Structure of Oppression', *Twentieth Century Literature* 30 (4), 1984, pp. 448–64: p. 456). As readers we are put off the right track because in Sophie's first narration of the attempt to seduce Höss, which she later represents as the effort to save her child, we do not even know she has children (p. 457). Durham notes that Sophie only tells her own story without Stingo's narratorial intervention when she is

'lying or confessing previous lies' (p. 461): such moments include the false portrait of her happy Cracow childhood; Nathan as a Prince Charming; Wanda as evil and malicious.

58 Pearce points out that 'though a reliable narrator, [Stingo] is not a reliable witness' ('Sophie's Choices', p. 296). However, Pearce is repeating his earlier conflation of the young character with the older narrator, as it is the latter who is responsible for von Niemand and whom as a result we may judge to be unreliable.

59 Jack Beatty describes the narrator's tone as one of 'moral tepidity' (*New Republic*, 30 June 1979, p. 40). Both Heath ('I, Stingo', p. 541) and Janssens (in Casciato and West, *Critical Essays on William Styron*, p. 280) call Stingo's analysis of von Niemand's motivation 'deflating'.

60 Such a phenomenon is of course not unheard of, see, for instance, Ford Madox Ford's novel *The Good Soldier* (1915).

61 Heath, 'I, Stingo', p. 542.

62 In interview with Michel Braudeau, Styron claims to have 'stolen' from Walker Percy the idea of 'making God real in a world He has deserted' by committing 'the most horrible sin conceivable', which is the reason he has the narrator point out that von Niemand was to have taken holy orders (like the real-life Höss, *Commandant of Auschwitz*, p. 27). Styron goes on to strain credulity by adding, 'Who knows whether to affirm one's capacity for sin is not as positive an act in the eyes of God as a supreme act of life – Albert Schweitzer's work, for instance' (Styron, in West, *Conversations*, p. 250).

63 Robert Franciosi, 'Perverse Medicine: Holocaust Doctoring in William Styron's *Sophie's Choice*', in Bruce Clark and Wendell Aycock (eds), *The Body and the Text: Comparative Essays in Literature and Medicine* (Lubbock: Texas Tech University Press, 1990), pp. 200–2.

64 Lengyel, *Five Chimneys*, pp. 72–3.

65 Ibid., p. 180.

66 Rawicz, 'Foreword', p. 23. Though see the view put forward by Mario Biagioli that Nazi science was based on the same principles as all modern science ('Science, Modernity, and the "Final Solution" ', in Saul Friedlander (ed.), *Probing the Limits of Representation: Nazism and the 'Final Solution'*, Cambridge, Mass.: Harvard University Press, 1992).

67 Franz Link says Styron's model is Mengele ('Auschwitz and the Literary Imagination: William Styron's *Sophie's Choice*', p. 138, n. 17), but this seems too obvious. Terry White also suggests Mengele, and names other defendants from the Doctors' Trials at Nuremberg, Werner Rhöde and Hans König, as elements of this 'historical composite' ('Jemand von Niemand, Death-Camp Doctor', p. 146).

68 Rawicz, 'Foreword', p. 21.

69 Franciosi, 'Perverse Medicine', p. 202.

70 Richard L. Rubenstein, *The Cunning of History: Mass Death and the American Future* (New York: Harper and Row, 1975; repr. 1978 with introduction by William Styron); see also Rubenstein's 'The South Encounters the Holocaust: William Styron's *Sophie's Choice*', *Michigan Quarterly Review* 20, 1981, pp. 425–42; and Franciosi, 'Perverse Medicine', p. 204.

71 Lang, 'God's Averted Face', p. 223.

72 Franciosi, 'Perverse Medicine', p. 205.

73 Styron, 'A Wheel of Evil', p. 396: 'Curiously enough, she does not identify herself as Jewish, although this would appear almost certain, given the chronology of the transports from Hungary.' The editors of *Different Voices: Women and the Holocaust* (New York: Paragon House, 1993), Carol Rittner and John K. Roth, make the same error (p. 73).

74 For instance, Lengyel identifies *others* as Jewish – 'Eva Weiss, one of the nurses, a young, pretty Jewish girl from Hungary' (*Five Chimneys*, p. 76) – as if this is a distinguishing mark, suggesting that she is not thus distinguished. Other elements of (Jewish) survivor testimonies are strikingly absent: Lengyel continues to pray to an unidentified God; she never muses on either the fate of the Jews as a whole or why she has been identified as one, whatever her own attitude to it. Lengyel's survivor guilt is also partly explained by her non-Jewishness, as she cannot only blame Nazi antisemitism for her family's journey to Auschwitz or their fate there. This also accounts for the great emphasis Styron places on slavery: as a non-Jewish woman, Sophie suffered enslavement rather than immediate extermination.

75 Styron, 'A Wheel of Evil', p. 398. Such confusion is echoed in the tautologous sentence about Sophie in the novel: 'Although she was not Jewish she had suffered as much as any Jew who had survived the same afflictions', followed by the coded idea that she actually suffered more than many Jews: '[she] had in certain profound ways suffered more than *most*' (my italics).

76 Rosenfeld, 'The Holocaust According to William Styron', p. 44.

77 Styron says he also used a scene of 'choice' offered to a gypsy woman cited in Hannah Arendt's *Eichmann in Jerusalem* (Harmondsworth: Penguin, 1965 [1963]).

78 Lengyel, *Five Chimneys*, p. 13.

79 Ibid.

80 Ibid., p. 27.

81 The fact that Sophie 'saves' Jan and lets Eva be killed has been the subject of much comment by, for instance, Ruderman: 'One may even go one step further, wondering if [Sophie's] utter quiescence of will is related to her femaleness, and whether it has led to her earmarking her daughter for extinction rather than her son' (*William Styron*, p. 105).

82 Lawrence Langer calls actions in such circumstances 'choiceless choices' which do not 'reflect options between life and death, but between one form of abnormal response and another, imposed by a situation that [is] not of the victim's own choosing' (quoted in Rittner and Roth, *Different Voices*, p. 70, to accompany an extract from *Five Chimneys*). This phrase is clearly appropriate to Sophie's choice since both of her children die anyway. As Franciosi points out, Sophie also makes wrong 'abnormal choices', as Lengyel did, in telling von Niemand facts which she thought would save her but which actually doom her daughter ('Perverse Medicine', p. 197); Styron then adds an element very different from the chilling indifference of Klein in Lengyel's testimony to make sure the reader gets the point.

83 Lengyel, *Five Chimneys*, pp. 102, 158, my italics.

84 Interview with Stephen Lewis, in West, *Conversations*, p. 258. In an interview with Michel Braudeau, Styron says, 'As Hannah Arendt wrote in *Eichmann in Jerusalem*, by putting you in such a position, the Nazis made you the executioner of your own children, which is perhaps the ultimate form of evil' (in West, *Conversations*, p. 249).

85 Styron describes Höss's 'confessions' as revelatory of 'the banality, the mediocrity, the true nature of evil' (interview with Braudeau, ibid., p. 249), although this quality is not wholly successfully transposed to the novel.

86 Kremer in *KL Auschwitz Seen by the SS*, pp. 158, 161, 163, 179–80, 162–5.

87 Lengyel, *Five Chimneys*, p. 30.

88 Ibid., pp. 31, 39; note also the irony that, according to Lengyel, Irma Griese had 'faultless, pearly teeth' (ibid., p. 101).

89 Ibid., p. 89.

90 Ibid., pp. 100–1.

91 Ibid., p. 155.

92 Ibid., p. 160. Kreyling describes Sophie's encounter with Dürrfeld as having 'the thin feel of "Great Coincidences in History" ' ('Speaking the Unspeakable', p. 559).

93 Von Niemand says to Sophie, ' "*Ich möchte mit dir schlafen*" ', ' "I'd like to get you into bed with me" ' (639).

94 Lengyel, *Five Chimneys*, p. 217.

95 Styron's widespread use of details from historical sources betrays a certain anxiety of invention. In interview with Braudeau, Styron is pleased that he has not been taken to task for any 'grave' or 'small' errors in his representation of the camp (in West, *Conversations*, p. 251), although such fidelity to detail coexists with a significant strand of inventiveness, for instance of Höss's behaviour and voice. In an interview Styron says that even in the case of the Flatbush sections of the novel he was sufficiently concerned with accuracy to rely on Leo Rosten's *The Joys of Yiddish* to get the Yiddish phrases right (Gideon Telpaz, 'An Interview with William Styron', *Partisan Review* 52 (3), 1985, pp. 252–63: p. 259). When Braudeau asks Styron about the amount of historical invention in his novel, the latter says he did not receive the proceeds of the sale of a slave, although his family did own them; however, he was in love with a young woman who committed suicide, and the episode of his mother's death and his guilt about it are also accurate (in West, *Conversations*, p. 244). The readers' reports, which appear in the imitation autobiography part of the novel, were invented, Styron reports to Arms ('An Interview', p. 3).

96 Lengyel, *Five Chimneys*, p. 79.

97 Lawrence L. Langer, *Holocaust Testimonies: The Ruins of Memory* (New Haven: Yale University Press, 1991), for instance, the testimony of William R. who persuaded his brother to accompany him on a selection for deportation, hoping they would both be sent to the left to work in the ghetto, but the Gestapo sent his brother to the right: ' "I'll never forgive myself.... I know it's not my fault, but my conscience is bothering me" ' (pp. 32–3).

98 See, for instance, Philip Caputo, 'Styron's Choices', *Esquire* CVI, December 1986, pp. 136–59: p. 152; and Styron, 'A Wheel of Evil', pp. 398–9.

99 The opposite movement also occurs when the narrator's voice speaks within as well as about Sophie's story: 'Sophie too – Sophie the stainless, the inaccessible, the uninvolved – was adventitiously ensnared' (p. 500).

100 Rosenfeld, *A Double Dying*, p. 164; with regard to the spoof, Rosenfeld finds the plot of *Sophie's Choice* hard to credit and summarizes it incredulously as a 'story of the Polish girl who stole a ham and forever after suffered sexual, moral, and psychological abuse'. The ham, which incidentally Sophie did not steal, appears to be a particularly farcical detail in Rosenfeld's eyes: he gives it an exclamation mark on p. 163. Sirlin, as ever, leaps to Styron's defence in claiming that the novel 'explores the evils of sexism, but is not sexist itself' (*William Styron's 'Sophie's Choice'*, p. 6). Durham, in a very nuanced discussion, proposes that in the novel 'the situation of women becomes the basic model through which a general concept of systematic oppression can be illustrated' ('William Styron's *Sophie's Choice*', p. 451).

101 Gloria Steinem, 'Night Thoughts of a Media Watcher', *Ms*, 1981, quoted in Sirlin, *William Styron's 'Sophie's Choice'*, pp. 27–8. Joan Smith goes further in arguing that 'the secret of the novel's popularity' is that 'the juxtaposition of sex and the Holocaust has been dressed up as art' ('Holocaust Girls', p. 88), in a manner she likens to D.M. Thomas's in *The White Hotel*. See also Kreyling, 'Speaking the Unspeakable', p. 549: 'we are alerted to Stingo's idée fixe: luxuriant seminal liquidity means verbal fluency', or vice versa. Even the brand of pencils he uses is pressed into this bodily service: he calls one of them 'a virginal Venus Velvet' (p. 51).

102 Colville, 'Killing the Dead Mother', p. 122 (of whose article Styron said in interview, 'I love that hysterical attack on me in *Delta*' – interview with Cologne-Brookes, in West, *Conversations*, p. 229). Julian Symons puts the distanced effect of

the scene down to novelistic misjudgement: the scene is 'described in as much detail as possible, and with as little emotional effect' as possible too ('The Penalties of Survival', *Times Literary Supplement*, 30 November 1979), while Cologne-Brookes says its discourse is 'more appropriate to a car enthusiast than to a passionate lover' (*The Novels of William Styron*, p. 178).

103 The artificiality ranges from the scene where Sophie meets again the Nazi industrialist Walter Dürrfeld in Auschwitz, where, as the head of I.G. Farben, 'the creature of [his] passion and desire' has become 'synthetic rubber', to Stingo's description of the 'sickish plasticity' of her 'reassembled' flesh; and, horrifyingly, his father mishearing Stingo's cry when asleep: 'soapy!' (p. 399); Kreyling finds a bathetic double meaning in Mary Alice Grimball's plea to Stingo, ' "I got burnt so badly." ' Bernard and Oleksy claim that through Sophie's trials Poland itself is implicitly condemned by Styron: 'Depicting the Pole as a woman "naturalizes" her cowardice, her passivity, her deceit, just as it naturalizes her lack of professional accomplishment or aspiration … her surface allure masks an irredeemably pathetic and morally flawed character – and a culturally inaccurate one at that' ('Sophie's Choice', p. 266).

104 In the Leslie Lapidus incident, Stingo takes Leslie's interest in talking about sexual activity as an expression of her desire to enact such things with him; and in the case of Mary Alice Grimball (*sic*), Stingo is disappointed that her willingness to have sex with him is decidedly non-penetrative.

105 See Durham's even more thoroughgoing version of this idea, that *Sophie's Choice* takes sexual oppression as its theme and shows how the other oppressions with which it is concerned – racism and antisemitism – arise from it ('William Styron's *Sophie's Choice*', *passim*).

106 Judith Fetterley, *The Resisting Reader: A Feminist Approach to American Fiction* (Bloomington: Indiana University Press, 1978). Leslie Fiedler, however, calls the Lapidus scenario 'the hilarious high point of the book' ('Styron's Choice', p. 104).

107 The older narrator signals his Southern credentials by announcing the supersession of precursors like Robert Penn Warren: 'Move over, Warren, this is Stingo arriving.'

108 In an ill-tempered outburst, Sophie elaborates: ' "These *Jews* with their psychoanalysis, always picking their little sores, worrying about their little brilliant brains and their analysts and everything" ' (p. 469).

109 The fruit image is discussed by Cologne-Brookes, *The Novels of William Styron*, pp. 173–4; Pearce, 'Sophie's Choices'; and Arms, 'An Interview', p. 4. Jules Chametzky argues that Styron is trying out some one-upmanship on the Jewish as well as the Southern competition ('Styron's *Sophie's Choice*, Jews and Other Marginals, and the Mainstream', in Jack Salzman (ed.), *Prospects: The Annual of American Cultural Studies*, Cambridge and New York: Cambridge University Press, 1984, p. 435); but a similar 'distance' applies to the representation of the potent, charismatic Jewish male character as it does to the Holocaust – Styron fictionalizes this distance, by making the Portnoy-with-extras Nathan merely a supporting actor alongside the protagonist, 'horny, Calvinist' Stingo. Ralph Tutt claims that Norman Mailer's 'egosphere of the Fifties and Sixties' is the model for Nathan, what with the latter's 'murderous rages, Harvard degree, and delusion of winning the Nobel Prize for a breakthrough in cancer research' ('Stingo's Complaint: Styron and the Politics of Self-Parody', *Modern Fiction Studies* 34 (4), Winter 1988, pp. 575–86: p. 582).

110 The older narrator also knows about later political events, such as the My Lai massacre; he imagines Leslie Lapidus as a mature wife; has written the novels which have made him a famous writer; refers to research on and responses to Auschwitz which were unavailable in 1947; allows Nathan to predict the coming of the Jewish

novel and LPs; and his own father 'prophetically' remarks upon the Civil Rights movement.

111 West, *Conversations*, p. 237. The narrator echoes this: 'If Sophie had been just a victim … she would have seemed merely pathetic'; as in the case of Höss's auto-biography, the narrator comments on 'facts' which are of course the result of careful construction.

112 This detail is taken from Jan Kott's introduction to Tadeusz Borowski's *This Way for the Gas, Ladies and Gentlemen*, trans. Barbara Vedder (Harmondsworth: Penguin, 1976 [1959]), a text Styron cites as one which influenced his portrayal of Auschwitz. Kott notes, 'At the end of April [1943 Borowski] was sent with a transport of prisoners to Auschwitz. [He and his fiancée] were both "lucky". Three weeks earlier "Aryans" had stopped being sent to the gas chambers – except for special cases. From then on only Jews were gassed en masse' (p. 15).

113 West, *Conversations*, p. 197.

114 Fiedler, 'Styron's Choice'; Symons, 'The Penalties of Survival'; Galloway, 'Holocaust as Metaphor', p. 66; John Gardner, 'A Novel of Evil', in Ross, *The Critical Response to William Styron*, p. 178; Colville, 'Killing the Dead Mother', p. 133; Ruderman, *William Styron*, p. 93.

115 As John Gardner says, 'Those who wish to can easily prove [Styron] anti-black, anti-white, anti-Southern, anti-Yankee, anti-Polish, anti-Semitic, anti-Christian, anti-German, anti-American, anti-Irish – the list could go on and on' ('A Novel of Evil', p. 177).

6 Historical polemic: Helen Darville, *The Hand that Signed the Paper*

1 Helen Demidenko, *The Hand that Signed the Paper* (Sydney: Allen and Unwin, 1994); reissued in 1995 under the name Helen Darville. All page references are in brackets in the text, and I will refer to the novel as *The Hand* for the sake of brevity. Helen Daniel, 'Editorial', *Australian Book Review*, February/March 1996, p. 2. Robert Manne, *The Culture of Forgetting: Helen Demidenko and the Holocaust* (Melbourne: Text Publishing, 1996) discusses the threat of legal action against Dershowitz (p. 85). On 11 July 1995 the leaders of the Jewish and Ukrainian communities issued a joint statement promising future co-operation.

2 Both appear in a symposium, 'The Demidenko Debate', *Australian Book Review*, February/March 1996, pp. 11–17: Ivor Indyk, 'Calling the Kettle Black', pp. 11–12: p. 12; Peter Craven, 'A Kind of Boswell' (review of Natalie Jane Prior, *The Demidenko Diary*, Port Melbourne, Victoria: Mandarin, 1996), pp. 14–17: p. 17. For a compendium of press coverage of the debate, see John Jost, Gianna Totaro and Christine Tyshing (eds), *The Demidenko File* (Ringwood, Victoria: Penguin Books Australia, 1996).

3 The cartoon, by Peter Wilkinson and originally published in *The Australian*, 22 January 1996, is reproduced in Manne, *The Culture of Forgetting*, p. 177. Quotation from Raymond Gaita's talk, 'Scepticism and Taboos: Reflections on the Demidenko Debate', delivered August 1996. Manne calls the same phenomenon 'intense Holocaust irritation' and 'general Holocaust jadedness' ('Reflections on the Demidenko Affair', *The Way We Live Now: The Controversies of the Nineties*, Melbourne, Victoria: Text Publishing, 1998, pp. 202, 203).

4 The awards were the Vogel Award in 1993, for an unpublished manuscript; the Miles Franklin Award, and the Australian Literature Society Gold Medal, both in 1995.

5 See also Andrew Riemer's remark in *The Demidenko Debate* (St Leonards, NSW: Allen and Unwin, 1996): 'most of those who objected to the novel's political and

ideological bias were also intent on emphasizing its poor literary quality' (p. 118). Interestingly, the grounds for 'ideological' disapproval shifted away from attention to the novel's alleged antisemitism to its receipt of three literary awards after Helen Demidenko was revealed to be Darville, as Riemer indicates: 'It became mandatory, therefore, for the novel's most passionate detractors to withdraw from their earlier position of regarding its author as the product and heir of Ukrainian anti-Semitic prejudices and to condemn both novel and writer on somewhat different grounds' (ibid., p. 174). In other words, in the eyes of some critics Darville had committed such a cardinal sin that her novel had to be rejected on any grounds; in Riemer's opinion, this sin was her refusal to accept 'as an article of faith that the so-called Holocaust was a uniquely momentous historical phenomenon' (p. 105) – a refusal Riemer shares. Manne's counter-argument to such a refusal is to observe that 'Even a dictionary will make clear that unique means singular not worse' ('Reflections on the Demidenko Affair', p. 203).

6 Ron Shapiro, 'Literary Representations of Ukrainian Anti-Semitism: Helen Demidenko and Aharon Appelfeld', *Southerly* 55, Spring 1995, pp. 174–82: p. 182.

7 Riemer, *The Demidenko Debate*, pp. 64–5; Jost *et al.*, *The Demidenko File*, pp. 62–8. In the later version of Darville's Author's Note, only the first two sentences remain.

8 Critics considered the Vogel Award, made for a first novel, appropriate, but balked at the Miles Franklin, awarded to a novel 'about Australian life in any of its phases', and at the ALS Gold Medal, usually awarded to an author for a lifetime's work.

9 Many of Demidenko's self-mythifications are set down in her article 'Writing After Winning' (*Southerly* 55, Spring 1995, pp. 155–60), the text of a talk given at the Sydney Writers' Festival in January 1995. This is a stylized piece purporting to be by an artless yet talented young Australian-Ukrainian woman attending her first writers' festival, full of such *faux-naïf* remarks as, 'For some reason our Sunday afternoon session was shaping up as the most popular of the Festival', and '[I was] delivering a paper to people who were … how do you say it … my betters' (p. 155). Other assertions construct an ersatz exoticism, both ethnic and class-based, such as, 'My Baba, despite her poor English, came to the session to provide "moral support" ' (p. 155), and, 'So my mother, who left school at the age of twelve to go out as a domestic (it was fashionable to have servants with Irish accents) read her first book' (p. 160). Darville's mother, as it turned out, was of neither working-class nor Irish origin. (Riemer speculates that the only contact Darville had with the Ukraine may have been 'the gardener at the Lutheran school she attended', *The Demidenko Debate*, p. 184). The essay also includes the kind of *bons mots* which came to be associated with Demidenko: 'Allen & Unwin were worried that my manuscript was politically explosive (i.e. the Zionists would blow [their] St Leonards office into the middle of next year)' (p. 158).

Demidenko also published some apparently factional short stories featuring mythified apologias for her novel and versions of her own past. 'Other Places' is about an invitation to a now-famous author to address her inner-city high school. It ends with an ex-pupil, also a fictional character's namesake, Vitaly, commenting on the privileged lifestyle of a woman who wrote a negative review of the alumna's book in the *Sun-Herald*: ' "I'd join the SS. Better than the fuckin' dole" ' (*RePublica* 3, 1995, pp. 94–7: p. 97). 'Pieces of the Puzzle', described by its author as a factional 'story/essay', was accepted and typeset by *Meanjin* before Darville's confession that Demidenko was a fabrication (an editorial note has it that, 'At the time of going to print we received no instruction from [the author] to modify the piece in any way', p. 429). In this story, the first-person narrator tells of a fight she witnessed among teenagers of different ethnic backgrounds – Croat, Ukrainian, Serbian and Jewish – at her high-school, and concludes, 'In the end, I found I could no more explain the puzzle [of interracial conflict] than solve it. So I simply told the story' (*Meanjin* 54

(3), 1995, pp. 430–7: p. 437). Peter Craven notes that at the height of her pre-unmasking fame, Darville created an identity for the city of Logan, where she claimed to have gone to school, as 'the site of impacted racial strife, often luridly and tastelessly presented'; he adds that 'no one' who reads the stories can fail to be struck by 'their sensationalism and their weird racial obsessiveness' ('A Kind of Boswell', p. 15).

10 Grace Darville, quoted in Jost *et al.*, *The Demidenko File*, p. 108. Robert Manne sarcastically notes, 'Even post-modernist geographers would, I imagine, be obliged to concede in the end that Scunthorpe is not in the Ukraine' ('The Strange Case of Helen Demidenko', *Quadrant* 39, September 1995, pp. 21–8: p. 21). Darville denied this particular detail, claiming that her father was from London – 'but of course the media would stop at nothing to blacken her name' (Riemer, *The Demidenko Debate*, p. 262). In his article, 'Demidenko – Questions Posed About the Author's Past' (19 August 1995), David Bentley of the Australian newspaper the *Courier-Mail* 'outed' Demidenko as Darville after talking to her former high school principal, and won the 1995 Walkley Award for 'Best Current Story' for this piece; see Jost *et al.*, *The Demidenko File*, pp. 98–111, 299.

11 As Thomas Keneally wisely said in an interview on the matter, 'It's happened before, that people have pretended to be someone they're not' (quoted in Kateryna Olijnyk Longley, 'Fabricating Otherness: Demidenko and Exoticism', *Westerly* 42 (1), Autumn 1997, pp. 29–45: p. 29). Such people include the infamously fabricated Australian poet Ern Malley; Paul Radley, whose uncle had actually written the novel which won him the 1980 Vogel Prize; an autobiography, *My Own Sweet Time*, published in 1992 by the award-winning Aboriginal writer Wanda Koolmatrie, turned out to be by a white, middle-aged male, Leon Carmen. A week earlier, Australia's leading Aboriginal painter Eddie Burrup was revealed to be Elizabeth Durack, a white artist. Nino Culotta's popular mid-1950s book *They're a Weird Mob*, a supposedly autobiographical account of Italian immigrants to Australia, was really by John O'Grady. The reasons for these impersonations are all different: in the Malley case, the invention was supposed to embarrass the literary establishment; in Carmen's, it was a bid to win fame despite the literary institution's alleged bias against middle-class white men. Bernard Cohen, however, objects to such comparisons as mitigations: 'I am angry at the move to recast the author in the great Australian "tradition" of literary hoaxes, as if a false and libellous claim that Demidenko's imaginary family was murdered by Jews is equivalent to a jape at the expense of a few modernists' ('The Quality of Anti-Semitism in *The Hand that Signed the Paper*', *Southerly* 56 (1), 1995, pp. 152–68: p. 168). See also Michael Heyward on literary hoaxes, 'Papers from the 1995 Melbourne Writers' Festival', *Australian Book Review*, December/January 1995/6, pp. 28–9.

The various phases of Darville's masquerade and the fortunes of her book have a complex relation, accompanied by a surprising stability of critical direction among her opponents. Manne concludes 'The Strange Case of Helen Demidenko' with the challenging remark: 'Thus far the supporters of this book have dismissed out of hand the charges of overt anti-Semitism, historical ignorance and moral weightlessness which its opponents have levelled against it. We have yet to learn how they will respond in detail when it becomes clear the author of *The Hand that Signed the Paper* is a teller of untruths who has assumed for herself a false ethnic identity and a psychological bond with war criminals' (p. 28), of which Riemer acutely observes: 'Manne's curious statement seems to imply that Darville's deception somehow confirms her anti-Semitic bias rather than rendering it less self-evident' (*The Demidenko Debate*, p. 175).

12 Martin Gilbert, *The Holocaust: The Jewish Tragedy* (London: HarperCollins, 1986); S.O. Pidhainy, I.I. Sandul, A.P. Stepovy (eds), *The Black Deeds of the Kremlin: A White*

Book. Volume I: Book of Testimonies, trans. Alexander Oreletsky and Olga Prychodko (Toronto: The Basilian Press, 1953).

13 As Morag Fraser pithily puts it, when details of Darville's 'finessing' her own background emerged, 'a bemused public didn't quite know whether it should be backing the underdog or clobbering an upstart' ('The Begetting of Violence', *Meanjin* 54 (3), 1995, pp. 419–29: p. 423).

14 Acknowledgement is given to the testimony of I. Mariupilisky from Pidhainy's *The Black Deeds*, and Alexander Donat from Gilbert's *The Holocaust* (p. vi).

15 Serge Liberman, quoted in Jost *et al.*, *The Demidenko File*, p. 87.

16 Manne, *The Culture of Forgetting*, p. 20. Allen and Unwin released a statement headed 'Helen Darville Apologises' which was signed by the author and appeared in most Australian newspapers on 25 August 1995 – the text of the letter is in Jost *et al.*, *The Demidenko File*, pp. 208–9.

17 Linda Hutcheon, 'Literary Borrowing … and Stealing: Plagiarism, Sources, Influences, and Intertexts', *English Studies in Canada* XII, 2 June 1986, p. 230. Riemer rightly says that all of Darville's 'dishonest practices', including plagiarism, were taken by her opponents as evidence of 'slanderous and partisan attitudes' in general (*The Demidenko Debate*, p. 206).

18 D.M. Thomas, *The White Hotel* (Harmondsworth: Penguin, 1981). (It is also the surname of a distinguished Russian pianist, Nikolai Demidenko.) The surname of the novel's Ukrainian family appears in a list of Ukrainian writers murdered by the Russians: Borys Kovalenko was a literary critic 'exiled to a concentration camp' (Pidhainy, *The Black Deeds of the Kremlin*, p. 398).

19 Serge Liberman, 'On Helen Demidenko's *The Hand that Signed the Paper*', *Southerly* 55 (3), 1995, pp. 161–74: p. 161, written before the August 1995 watershed when Demidenko was 'outed'.

20 A. Anatoli (Anatoly Kuznetsov), *Babi Yar* (London: Sphere Books, 1970), pp. 110–11; see also Manne, *The Culture of Forgetting*, pp. 17–19.

21 Demidenko said this in a radio interview with Terry Lane on 11 June 1995, quoted in Jost *et al.*, *The Demidenko File*, p. 49.

22 Susan Moore, 'Home Truths: A Reflection on the Demidenko Affair', *Quadrant*, October 1995, pp. 10–17: p. 13; Fraser, 'Begetting Violence', p. 424. Similarly, David Cesarani casts doubt on the historical value of Martin Amis's intertext in *Time's Arrow*, Robert Jay Lifton's *The Nazi Doctors*: 'the work has not fared well in the hands of fellow historians. I think Lifton himself now qualifies some of the points he makes' ('Writing the Unwritable: A Debate on Holocaust Fiction', *Jewish Quarterly* 170, Summer 1998, pp. 12–15: p. 15). However, value according to strict historical criteria is not the point of incorporating such texts into the novel.

23 Pidhainy, *The Black Deeds of the Kremlin*, p. 284; see also Manne, *The Culture of Forgetting*, p. 108.

24 On 17 September 1995, Allen and Unwin's lawyers, Minter Ellison, gave their verdict that 'allegations of plagiarism were unsustainable' (Jost *et al.*, *The Demidenko File*, p. 266).

25 Riemer, *The Demidenko Debate*, p. 206

26 Pidhainy, *The Black Deeds of the Kremlin*, *passim*, particularly pp. 12, 222, specifically in relation to the Famine.

27 See one such brief mention: a man is said to have used land taken from 'Jewish city-dwellers' (ibid., p. 141). Rosenberg is mentioned p. 115, Katsnelson p. 392.

28 Ibid., pp. 390, 413–34.

29 Ibid., p. 14.

30 Ibid., p. 354.

31 Ibid., p. 262; Manne, *The Culture of Forgetting*, p. 148.

32 Pidhainy, *The Black Deeds of the Kremlin*, p. 354.

33 The second volume shows as little evidence of antisemitic bias as the first: Arthur Koestler and the Yiddish newspaper *Forward* are quoted expressing horror at the Famine (S.O. Pidhainy, V.I. Hryshko and P.P. Pavlovych (eds), *The Black Deeds of the Kremlin: A White Book. Volume II: The Great Famine in Ukraine in 1932–3*, Detroit: Globe Press, 1955, pp. 90–1, 102, 110); and while it is noted that a group of 'atheists … among the Jewish population' voted to turn the synagogue into a community centre on that well-known 'Jewish feast day, "Yona Cooper's Day" ' – presumably Yom Kippur – this observation is followed by a detail about an analogous 'anti-Christmas campaign' (ibid., p. 208).

34 Ibid., p. 556.

35 Ibid., p. 575. Zolotarevich is presumably of Jewish origin.

36 As well as misquotations, the 'plagiarism' from some of these sources took the form of adaptation; for instance, the sentence from *The Hand*, 'The brothers Kovalenko and their comrades – Nikolai and Shura – did not kill Jews because they were poor and Ukrainian, and did not know any better. They killed Jews because they believed that they themselves were savages' (p. 77), sounds as if it is indebted to this sentence from Toni Morrison's *The Bluest Eye*: 'The Breedloves did not live in a store front because they were having temporary difficulty adjusting to the cut-backs at the plant. They lived there because they were poor and black, and they stayed there because they believed they were ugly' (quoted in Riemer, *The Demidenko Debate*, p. 209). It seems that the detail of the white scars on Vitaly's back, the result of a flogging by 'The Jewish and Russian Bolsheviks' (p. 117), is a similar transposition of the 'chokecherry tree' of scars on Sethe's back in Morrison's *Beloved*, the result of a beating by a white slave-owner. In the curious instance from *The Bluest Eye* it is the structure and balance of Morrison's sentence that has been borrowed, as well as its awareness of internalized racism – but transposed to a quite different context. It is revealing that the smaller borrowings from these assorted, non-Holocaust works (in *The Demidenko Debate* Riemer discusses phrases and styles borrowed from Graham Greene's *The Power and the Glory*, Robert Lowell's poetry, Alan Paton's *Cry, the Beloved Country*, Saul Bellow's *Mr Sammler's Planet*, and Thomas Keneally's *Gossip from the Forest*, p. 208) have not attracted accusations of plagiarism in the moralistic way that those from Martin Gilbert's *The Holocaust* or Pidhainy's *The Black Deeds of the Kremlin* have done. The content alters how the act of borrowing is seen; Manne is not at all concerned with material taken from novels or non-fiction sources other than those directly concerned with the Holocaust or antisemitism: and it is the historical texts that are now credited in all editions of *The Hand*.

37 Robin Morgan, 'Dear Helen, just give me back my words', *Sydney Morning Herald*, 23 March 1996, p. 11. These words were taken from Morgan's *The Demon Lover: On the Sexuality of Terrorism* (London: Methuen/Mandarin, 1993, p. 172), an analysis of women and terrorism: ' "I don't like what I – what we – what happens. I – I" … His dark eyes fill. "I – we do … bad things, lady", he whispers, "bad things. And we're – I'm scared. I'm scared all the time." ' In *The Hand*, this peerless prose appears in the scene where a young boy is troubled by the mass killing he is party to at Treblinka: ' "I don't like what I … what happens … what we do –" He looked up. His dark brown eyes filled. "I … we … do bad things, Pani. Bad things … and I'm scared. I'm scared all the time" ' (p. 114).

After her unmasking it emerged that Darville had been guilty of an earlier instance of large-scale plagiarism of a short story by the academic and writer Brian Matthews. In parts Helen Demidenko's story 'Other Places' used material almost verbatim from Matthews's story 'Pioneers', originally published in Andrew Sant (ed.), *Toads – Australian Writers; Other Work, Other Lives*. Matthews claimed to have received a letter from the author of 'Other Places', in which Demidenko explained that a friend had been reminded of one of Matthews's stories by Demidenko's.

Matthews's summary of the letter continues: 'Demidenko said that she had made unsuccessful efforts to find such a story and was now writing to me direct to check whether the text of "Other Places" included any unintentionally plagiarized passages. She added that she had occasional trouble with her intermittent capacity for uncontrollably photographical recall of unattributed material' (*Australian*, 10 October 1995).

Riemer is of the opinion that this sequel to the unmasking of Demidenko constitutes a 'warning about the possibly exceptional circumstances that may lie behind Darville's masquerade – circumstances that may require the competence of psychiatry to analyse and interpret' (*The Demidenko Debate*, p. 177). He points to the 'astonishing' nature of the 'passion and conviction with which she acted out her masquerade', leaving him in no doubt that she was part-Ukrainian when he visited her before August 1995 (p. 181). It was pointed out that many people in Brisbane, Darville's home town, must have known all along who Helen Demidenko was, and perhaps took pleasure in the thought that they had got the better of big-city critics and media personalities in Sydney and Melbourne (p. 269) (particularly the latter, for reasons Riemer speculates on, pp. 232–40).

38 Kuznetsov, *Babi Yar*, p. 253.

39 Manne, *The Culture of Forgetting*, p. 68 (two earlier copy-editors had refused to work on Darville's typescript).

40 Quoted in ibid., p. 45.

41 Ibid., p. 109; Riemer, *The Demidenko Debate*, p. 97.

42 Manne, *The Culture of Forgetting*, p. 125.

43 Ibid., pp. 44, 22.

44 Mikhail Bakhtin, *Problems of Dostoevsky's Poetics*, trans. and ed. Caryl Emerson (Minneapolis: University of Minnesota Press, 1984), p. 72. The critic Don Anderson uses the term 'polyphony' in an article on *The Hand* ('After Humanism, What Forgiveness?', *Australian Book Review*, February/March 1996, pp. 12–14: p. 13), although he does not mention Bakhtin. He also likens Darville's novel to Jerzy Kosinski's *The Painted Bird*, which is an interesting link not only stylistically – Anderson writes of the effective use in both cases of 'cold' prose against a background of 'sympathy' for the Jews – but also generically – see this volume, Chapter 4.

45 Manne, *The Culture of Forgetting*, p. 121; Kaganovich's name does, however, crop up in Pidhainy, *The Black Deeds* volume II. Bernard Cohen speculates that the 'unattributed narrations' could be those of 'a Fiona who through her research has gained objectivity to the point of omniscience' (p. 153), but, as Cohen is aware, it is hard to use such an idea to explain the 'documentary' evidence of the letter sent by Judit the commissar's wife to her mother, and the access we gain to private conversations between all manner of characters, including Judit and her husband Vanya. Even more speculatively, he hazards that 'Fiona narrates the entire book', including all utterances attributed to other characters; however, the only concrete evidence given for this is Wilhelm Hasse's anachronistic use of the phrase 'politically correct' (p. 154). At least Cohen is conducting this debate using the narrator and not the author as a point of reference (although another way to put his second theory would be to say that *Darville* is responsible for the entire narration, including all other characters' utterances).

46 Bakhtin describes *skaz* as, 'Stylization of the various forms of oral everyday narration' (*The Dialogic Imagination: Four Essays*, trans. Caryl Emerson and Michael Holquist, ed. Michael Holquist, Austin, Tex.: University of Texas Press, 1981, p. 262).

47 Manne reminds us that, of course, the equation of Jews with Bolsheviks had its roots in propaganda and not history; an illustration from *Der Stürmer* of July 1941, reproduced in his book, shows 'Jewish Bolshevik' Karl Radek's grinning face superim-

posed on images of children dying in the Ukrainian Famine, under the caption: 'Soviet Judea: where Jews govern over non-Jews there is hunger, miscegenation and mass murder' (*The Culture of Forgetting*, p. 160). The illustration was part of the Nazis' propaganda campaign during the summer of 1941 in preparation for genocide on Russian territory by blaming the Jews for Soviet-inflicted malaise.

48 Bakhtin, *The Dialogic Imagination*, pp. 300, 278. In a review of Andrew Riemer's *The Demidenko Debate*, Ron Shapiro questions the (polyphonic) irony and detachment Riemer finds in Darville's novel on the grounds of what he sees as its *lack* of detachment, due to a 'morbid fascination with violence', a 'narratorial zest' in describing 'military uniforms and paraphernalia' as well as the depiction of 'human brutality' (*Westerly* 41 (4), Summer 1996, pp. 138–42: pp. 140–1). One could counter this by arguing, as Adorno does, that any representation of extreme violence runs the risk of appearing 'morbid' and 'fascinated', and in Darville's case it seems that lapses of novelistic control rather than voyeurism are to blame. This is Fraser's argument: she avers that the text's 'confident naïveté' can look like the author's 'tribal strut' (p. 424); and it is John Hughes's, in a review of the novel written before the scandal: 'apart from the graphic nature of the killing, most of the scenes lack substance' (*Meanjin* 53 (4), 1994, pp. 765–7: p. 766). In other words, what appears to be a moral failing in the novel may simply be an aesthetic one.

49 See Howard Aster and Peter J. Potichnyj, *Jewish–Ukrainian Relations: Two Solitudes* (Oakville, Ontario: Mosaic Press, 1987), p. 19, on the debate over Petlyura's role in Jewish–Ukrainian relations between 1917 and 1921; and Manne, *The Culture of Forgetting*, p. 150.

50 Manne, *The Culture of Forgetting*, pp. 52, 152.

51 Fraser, 'The Begetting of Violence', p. 421. As she says of a passage in which Kateryna is not narrating events but giving her own account, the force of such moments 'is dramatic, not persuasive' (p. 424): that is, polyphonic, not monologic.

52 Quoted in ibid., p. 422.

53 Manne, 'Strange Case', p. 24.

54 Fraser, 'The Begetting of Violence', p. 425. See also David Marr, quoted in Riemer, *The Demidenko Debate*, p. 158: '*The Hand that Signed the Paper* makes me feel rage for [the Jews'] fate. And I can't believe Helen D. didn't mean me to feel this.'

55 Peter Singer's letter to the *Sydney Morning Herald* is quoted in Jost *et al.*, *The Demidenko File*, p. 278.

56 Riemer adds that this logic of revenge has a structural role in the text. The actions of Ukrainians, and Ivan the Terrible, need to be given some 'plausibility of motivation' for the novel to be readable (*The Demidenko Debate*, pp. 55, 74). There is something of a contradiction in the novel's construction of this motivation, as on the one hand the murderous Ukrainians are supposed to have suffered famine and death at the hands of Jewish Bolsheviks, but on the other hand, they are just 'ordinary men' drawn willy-nilly into genocidal mass murder. Darville is not concerned with the really 'ordinary men' of, for instance, the historian Christopher Browning's study of depositions by members of the German Reserve Police Battalion 101. These men shot at point-blank range 1,500 Jews from the Polish town of Józefów on a single day in July 1942. They were, Browning is at pains to point out, mostly apolitical, middle-aged blue-collar men, certainly not devoted Nazis ('One Day in Józefów: Initiation to Mass Murder', *The Path to Genocide: Essays on Launching the Final Solution*, Cambridge: Cambridge University Press, p. 181; see also his full-length study *Ordinary Men: Reserve Police Battalion 101 and the Final Solution in Poland*, New York: HarperCollins, 1992). Browning's summary of the motives of these men sounds rather like Hannah Arendt's analysis of Adolf Eichmann's motives (see Chapter 5): 'Crushing conformity and blind, unthinking acceptance of the political norms of the time on the one hand, careerism on the other' (p. 183). Indeed, Browning notes that

the really ' "dirty work"' of mass murder was left to the "Hiwis" (Hilfswilligen or volunteers)' (p. 178), trained at the Trawnicki SS camp as death-camp staff and 'itinerant ghetto clearers' (p. 170): it is these rather less obviously ordinary men with whom Darville's novel is concerned and their motives were rather different.

57 Manne, *The Culture of Forgetting*, p. 12. Cohen declares that Vitaly's 'explanation' for Ivan's behaviour can only be one of two things: ' "fiction" or an anti-Semitic lie' ('The Quality of Anti-Semitism', p. 157). Elsewhere Cohen is revealingly unable to recognize free indirect discourse. Of the narrator's comment on Wilhelm Hasse that 'He felt that Jews were dark and dirty', Cohen asks, 'who is speaking here?' (p. 160). As is the case in free indirect discourse, there are two voices present: the narrator's, as it is in the third person, and the character's. Cohen values the narrator's word over the character's as he does in the case of Vitaly's words on Ivan the Terrible, and reads this moment as one of endorsement. In a collection of his essays, Manne presents the contested idea of Ivan's motivation as if it were fact: 'We learn that [Ivan the Terrible] is mad because of an incident in his childhood' ('Reflections on the Demidenko Affair', p. 199).

58 Sneja Gunew, 'Performing Ethnicity: The Demidenko Show and its Gratifying Pathologies', *Australian Feminist Studies* 11 (23), 1996, pp. 53–63. See also Longley, 'Fabricating Otherness: Demidenko and Exoticism'. An article in the *Australian Independent Monthly* purporting to be the diary of Helen Demidenko's visit to the Ukraine, that is, hoaxing the hoaxer, emphasized the un-ethnic nature of Anglo-Saxon identity in the following entry, where the italics represent 'editorial comment' ('My Ukrainian Christmas', *Independent Monthly*, December 1995/January 1996, p. 37): 'Jeeze, I'm glad I'm Ukrainian. Who'd be a Skippy? Rape of the land, extermination of the Aborigines, utter boredom of Anglo culture, Menzies years, philistinism, Christian Brothers … Thank God I'm Ukrainian. At least we can blame the Jews. (*I'm not terribly happy about that last bit.*) (*I think it's a typo, the "J" should be "N", as in Rupert Murdoch.*).'

59 Riemer, *The Demidenko Debate*, p. 30. However, he also sees the local focus of Darville's and other contemporary writing as a matter of regret: 'the tone … is banal, commonplace, domestic in an infernal and diabolic way' (p. 49); it is 'undernourished' at times, 'admirably icy and restrained' at others (p. 79).

60 Manne, 'Strange Case', p. 23. He may of course also have in mind the self-mythifying remark the six-foot tall Darville made before being outed as Demidenko: 'In the Ukrainian community I'm just average. Ukrainians are really tall' (in Jost *et al.*, *The Demidenko File*, p. 50). In 'Strange Case' Manne asserts that 'Kaganovich-obsession has always been a reliable indicator of anti-Semitism' (p. 23).

61 Manne, 'Strange Case', p. 24. He adds: 'Demidenko's wartime Poland is a kind of contemporary Queensland with death camps' (p. 25), which continues his lament at a contemporary postmodern sensibility levelling out all temporal, aesthetic and moral distinctions.

62 Moore, 'Home Truths', p. 13. She uses the Demidenko affair as the springboard for a generally conservative fulmination against changed times: she sees the publication of the novel as part of the same phenomenon as the 'shocking increase in the number of broken homes and broken lives'. Riemer's book expresses a more liberal and academic regret, at 'contemporary culture, its lack of ability to perceive almost any values, its flirtation with modish relativism' (*The Demidenko Debate*, p. 95). He adds that an immoderate interest in contemporary literary theory may have laid the groundwork for the form of Darville's novel (ibid., p. 198).

63 Gaita, 'Remembering the Holocaust', *Quadrant*, December 1995, pp. 7–15: p. 15.

64 Fraser, 'The Begetting of Violence', p. 423; Moore, 'Home Truths', p. 15.

65 Bakhtin, *Problems of Dostoevsky's Poetics*, p. 182.

66 Demidenko, 'Writing After Winning', p. 157; Donald Richie (ed.), *Focus on 'Rashomon'* (New York: Prentice-Hall, 1972), p. 6. Darville wrote this essay in her Demidenko persona, but this need not mean we must dismiss her account of *Rashomon*'s influence (four different versions of events are given in the film, not eight).

67 Moore, 'Home Truths', p. 15; William Schaffer, 'The Book that Evaded the Question', *Southerly* 55 (1), Spring 1995, pp. 175–84: p. 183.

68 Bakhtin, *The Dialogic Imagination*, p. 401.

69 Serge Liberman, 'On Helen Demidenko's *The Hand that Signed the Paper*', *Southerly* 55, Spring 1995, pp. 175–84. However, Liberman does qualify his position, adding that, 'Ms Demidenko may profess that she deliberately chose not to make moral judgements. Given her material, however, such a statement is, *of itself*, already a moral judgement, while the very tone of her narrative, her selection of material, the way she presents it, her character portrayals and her own studied pose of being *non-engagé*, betray a position as clearly as any direct manifesto she might make' (p. 167).

70 Liberman, 'On Helen Demidenko's *The Hand that Signed the Paper*', p. 169.

71 Ibid., p. 169.

72 See, for instance, Bakhtin, *The Dialogic Imagination*, p. 292.

73 Riemer also seems to be groping for a word like 'dialogic' in his description of Darville's text, in which 'voices slide over each other, merge and clash' (p. 45).

74 Liberman, 'On Helen Demidenko's *The Hand that Signed the Paper*', p. 170. In *The Hand* Barsek takes the place of Dina Pronicheva in Kuznetsov's account of the Babi Yar massacre: 'Barsek alone somehow managed to escape from the pit' (70).

75 Liberman, 'On Helen Demidenko's *The Hand that Signed the Paper*', p. 172.

76 Ibid., p. 173.

77 Cohen, 'The Quality of Anti-Semitism', p. 155, my italics. This view is shared by several others, including Paul Redding, 'Truth in Fiction – Fiction as Truth', *Southerly* 56 (1), Spring 1996, pp. 169–73: p 172.

78 Schaffer, 'The Book that Evaded the Question', pp. 181–2. This is not how the matter is presented in the novel; Kateryna points out that within two years, all twelve of her young cousins were dead (p. 10).

79 Indeed, Schaffer's likening the novel's effect to skipping between TV channels make it sound like a kind of bad dialogism in which conflict between discourses has been replaced with amoral congruence: 'We are randomly switching channels between the Ukrainian famine and the Holocaust, only to find that the show looks pretty much the same; except for the uncanny way the actors keep changing roles' ('The Book that Evaded the Question', p. 183). He asserts that *The Hand* makes an 'attempt to expunge the stain of anti-semitism from the memory of the Holocaust, to make everything fade into one great, familiar wound across the suffering face of humanity' (p. 184). A counterview to this is Barry Joseph's: in relation to Spielberg's film he claims that part of the 'cursed legacy' of the Holocaust has been the Jewish habit of 'rabidly defending [Judaism's] victim status to the exclusion of other marginalized groups' ('Comforting Nightmares: A Meditation on *Schindler's List*, Holocaust Memories and Jewish Liberation', *Response* 62, 1994, pp. 4–14: p. 5).

80 Pamela Bone, *The Age*, 9 June 1995, p. 15. Other critics, including Raymond Gaita, have asserted that the kinds of discourse that Darville's novel released were retrograde. Gaita cites Peter Wilkinson's cartoon as an instance – see n. 3, above – in 'Scepticism and Taboos: Reflections on the Demidenko Debate'. He makes the point that it also brought to the surface 'long-standing resentment of Jews and of what they had made of the Holocaust', and unhelpfully polarized other debates, such as that over war crimes legislation (p. 9).

81 At the beginning of 'Scepticism and Taboos', Gaita observes that some critics of Darville's novel 'are accused of having succumbed to a form of moralism that

distorted their understanding of the standards that are appropriate when judging a novel. David Marr, Andrew Riemer and Dame Leonie Kramer have said that such critics do not know how to read fiction' – then proceeds not to mention anything novelistic in the rest of the half-hour talk.

82   Riemer says: 'I, for one, am not entirely convinced that blaming the Jews for the Ukrainian famine is no more than the beliefs or prejudices of the characters in the novel: on the few occasions that an authorial voice intrudes into the structure of *The Hand that Signed the Paper*, it, too, seems to subscribe to such a view' (*The Demidenko Debate*, p. 159). This analysis seems correct, except that it is not an authorial but a *narratorial* voice that we hear; and while it does seem that 'Demidenko', if not Darville, was also of this opinion, that must remain irrelevant as it is not possible to detect traces of it *in the novel*.

83   Even in the 'reconciliation' scene at the novel's end, in which Fiona visits Treblinka and meets the nephew of a woman who died there, that victim was not Jewish but a Quaker who sheltered Jews (p. 157).

84   Manne produces evidence to the effect that many instances of the epithet 'Jewish Bolshevik' were editorial replacements for the unadorned 'Jew' in Demidenko's manuscript (*The Culture of Forgetting*, p. 30).

Conclusion

1   Aviva Kipen, *Jewish Quarterly* 165, Summer 1997, p. 78.

2   Binjamin Wilkomirski, *Fragments: Memories of a Childhood, 1939–1948*, trans. Carol Brown Janeway (London: Picador, 1996). See also Binjamin Wilkomirski in interview with Anne Karpf, 'Child of the Shoah', *Guardian*, section 2, 11 February 1998, p. 2.

3   Elena Lappin, 'The Man with Two Heads', *Granta* 66, Summer 1999, pp. 7–65; Philip Gourevitch, 'The Memory Thief', *New Yorker*, 14 June 1999, pp. 47–58. See also Christopher Olgiati's documentary, *Child of the Death Camps*, BBC1 1999.

4   *Fragments* has been translated into sixteen languages; it won the National Jewish Book Award, the *Jewish Quarterly* non-fiction prize and the Prix de la Mémoire de la Shoah. Silvia Rodgers (*Sunday Times*, 15 December 1996, p. 6) wrote: 'I was in shock but also entranced by this extraordinary book', while Karpf ('Child of the Shoah') declares that the memoir 'ranks with Primo Levi'.

      However, in October 1999 the hardback version of the book was pulled by its German publishers, and in November 1999 the Bristish publishers of the book, Picador, suspended publication.

5   See William Langley and Nick Fielding, 'The victim who never was', *Mail on Sunday*, 18 October 1998, pp. 30–1; and an article by Philipp Blom, *Independent*, Review, 30 September 1998, p. 1. Thanks to J.M. Ritchie and Lesley-Anne Heap for these references. Ganzfried claims he was made suspicious of Wilkomirski's credentials by his text: ' "I didn't like his obsession with brutality, and the confusion between a child's view and that of a grown man" ' (quoted in Lappin, 'The Man with Two Heads', p. 23). Gourevitch notes that Wilkomirski is 'in every way' the opposite of a memoirist like Primo Levi, who 'never draws attention to himself; he detests his victimization; he knows irony' ('The Memory Thief', p. 68).

6   Roger Boyes, 'Testimony of Holocaust "survivor" denounced as fiction', *The Times*, 8 September 1998, p. 2.

7   Andrew Riemer, *The Demidenko Debate* (St Leonards, NSW: Allen and Unwin, 1996), p. 206.

8   Boyes, 'Testimony of Holocaust "survivor" denounced as fiction'. He adds that the real problem is that the man now known as Wilkomirski has been touring widely

and giving lectures on the 'fate of anonymous children from the camps as if he were one of them' (p. 2).

9 See the Introduction to this volume.

10 Elie Wiesel, *Night* (New York: Hill and Wang, 1960).

11 Wilkomirski, *Fragments*, p. 87. Gourevitch quotes the writer Norman Manea's suggestion of a non-fictional generic identity for *Fragments*: 'if Wilkomirski had called his book "fragments from a therapy" he would have avoided the current controversy' ('The Memory Thief', p. 54).

12 This is a paraphrase of Berel Lang's phrase (*Act and Idea in the Nazi Genocide*, Chicago: University of Chicago Press, 1990, p. 133) on Rolf Hochhuth's play *The Deputy*. See Philip Roberts, *The Royal Court Theatre and the Modern Stage* (Cambridge: Cambridge University Press, 1999) for an account of Max Stafford-Clark's decision to withdraw the play.

13 Arnold Wesker, *Guardian*, 26 April 1999, p. 17, my italics. The play was shown at the Gate Theatre, London, using an amended script.

14 See David Cesarani's analysis of the trial and *Perdition* itself, 'Israel on trial', *Times Higher Education Supplement*, 3 March 1987, p. 10. Allen's tactic for avoiding libel did not entirely succeed. In some editions of the play it is noted that sections have had to be removed pending the outcome of a libel action; these sections, pp. 62–3 and 77 in the play and 119 and 152 in the appendices, concern a letter written during the war by the Swiss Zionist Nathan Schwalb, allegedly urging the abandonment of doomed Jews in order to make the case for a Jewish homeland as strong as possible.

15 Jim Allen, *Perdition: A Play in Two Acts* (London and Atlantic Highlands: Ithaca Press, 1987), pp. 15, vii, vi. See *To Stage or Not to Stage: The Case of 'Perdition'* (Britain/Israel Public Affairs Committee, March 1987).

16 Quoted in the 'Appendix', *Perdition*, p. 111.

17 David Cesarani identifies the published script as a fourth 'drastically revised' version; he points to elements which were added to the published script of the play apparently as a result of critical reviews (in 'Appendix', *Perdition*, pp. 112–14). Allen hotly denies this idea, and claims instead that his critics are taking credit for the natural process of script revision: 'To watch Zionists in retreat is to observe the intellectual and moral bankruptcy of its apologists' ('Appendix', *Perdition*, p. 114). However, it is clear in at least one incident that the play is archly referring to its own earlier reception by Martin Gilbert: Lawson, counsel for the prosecution, observes, 'I know of at least one eminent historian, an Oxford don no less, who would offer a different version of what happened at the Skalat ghetto' (p. 52). The placing of this caveat – which Allen refuted – in the mouth of the prosecution, who are doomed to fail, is as revelatory of the play's agenda as the witness's retort which makes Lawson, according to the stage direction, 'sorry he asked'.

18 Allen, *Perdition*, p. viii.

19 Ibid., p. 70.

20 Ibid., p. 67. David Pryce-Jones adds that the idea of Nazi–Zionist collaboration was common in Soviet Russia from the early 1950s onwards as part of a pro-Arab policy: 'If it could be shown that contacts between Jews and Nazis had not been acts of despairing expediency but positive collaboration, then clearly Israel could not be a legitimate refuge for Holocaust survivors' (*Times Literary Supplement*, 30 January 1987, p. 112).

21 Both witnesses leave the court 'angrily', according to the stage directions (ibid., pp. 25, 32), to signal awareness of their defeat. Within the play, the possibility of anti-Zionism acting as a front for antisemitism is discussed by the characters (p. 7). However, in his defence of *Perdition* Allen revealed his tendency to blur the difference between the adjectives 'Zionist' and 'Jewish', as is shown by his many references to 'Zionist critics', 'Zionist academics' and to Martin Gilbert as 'the oiler and

greaser of this Zionist juggernaut' (interview with Jim Allen by Ray Comiskey, *Irish Times*, 6 February 1987). David Cesarani, referred to as a 'Zionist historian', drily observes in a letter to *The Times*, 'I doubt whether Mr Allen has any idea what my views on Israel happen to be and if he did, would it matter?' (7 February 1987, p. 9).

22 See, for instance, Allen, *Perdition*, pp. 7, 33, 42. The *Evening Standard* ('Hot tickets', 2–8 July 1999, p. 22) referred to the counsel's 'ranting diatribes' in the 1999 London production of the play, which it judged to be a 'travesty of English courtroom procedures'.

23 See Mikhail Bakhtin, *Problems of Dostoevsky's Poetics*, trans. and ed. Caryl Emerson (Minneapolis: University of Minnesota Press, 1984), pp. 17–18.

24 Jim Allen in interview with Steve Grant, *Time Out*, 21–8 January 1987.

25 Opposition to banning the play was shared by a pair of unlikely bedfellows, Bernard Levin and Noam Chomsky. The former wrote in *The Times* (2 February 1987, p. 16) that not only would banning *Perdition* allow it to be assumed that the play was 'uncommonly fine and well-written', but, more fundamentally, that a democracy 'must … tolerate the activities of those who wish to destroy it'. Chomsky expressed a similar view in a letter to Allen's press agent; he would not be concerned with the accuracy of the play's content since 'it is the refusal to allow such material to be expressed that is, in my view the crucial issue' (Allen, *Perdition*, p. 107).

26 It is this anti-Israeli stance rather than an antisemitic agenda which is the play's thesis, although the potential by-product of anti-Jewish feeling was a worry in some critics' minds. In a resonant phrase quoted by Victoria Radin, ' "British antisemitism … is a can of worms. *Perdition* provided the can-opener" ' (*New Statesman*, 6 February 1987).

27 See, for instance, two articles by Robert Cunliffe: 'The Architectonics of Carnival and Drama in Bakhtin, Artaud, and Brecht', in David Shepherd (ed.), *Bakhtin, Carnival and Other Subjects, Critical Studies* 3–4 (1–2), 1993; and 'Monologism, Drama: Bakhtin, Derrida', in Carol Adlam, Rachel Falconer, Vitalii Makhlin and Alastair Renfrew (eds), *Face to Face: Bakhtin in Russia and the West* (Sheffield: Sheffield Academic Press, 1997).

Bibliography

Primary and historical texts

Arendt, Hannah, *Eichmann in Jerusalem: A Report on the Banality of Evil*, Harmondsworth: Penguin, 1965.

Freud, Sigmund, *The Standard Edition of the Complete Psychological Works of Sigmund Freud*, London: Hogarth, 1953.

Gilbert, Martin, *The Holocaust: The Jewish Tragedy*, London: HarperCollins, 1986.

Gilman, Sander L., *The Case of Sigmund Freud*, Baltimore: Johns Hopkins University Press, 1993.

—— *Jewish Self-Hatred: Anti-Semitism and the Hidden Language of the Jews*, Baltimore and London: Johns Hopkins University Press, 1986.

KL Auschwitz Seen by the SS: Rudolf Höss, Pery Broad, Johann Paul Kremer, footnotes and biographical notes ed. Jadwiga Bezwinska and Danuta Czech, Oswiecim: The Auschwitz-Birkenau State Museum, 1994.

Kuznetsov, Anatoly [A. Anatoli], *Babi Yar*, trans. David Floyd, London: Sphere Books, 1970.

Lifton, Robert Jay, *The Nazi Doctors: Medical Killing and the Psychology of Genocide*, New York: Basic Books, 1986.

Schoenberner, Gerhard, *The Yellow Star*, New York and London: Bantam, 1969.

Thomas, D.M., *Memories and Hallucinations*, London: Abacus, 1989.

Imaginative works

Allen, Jim, *Perdition: A Play in Two Acts*, London and Atlantic Highlands: Ithaca Press, 1987.

Amis, Martin, *Time's Arrow*, Harmondsworth: Penguin, 1991.

Begley, Louis, *Wartime Lies*, London: Picador, 1991.

Borowski, Tadeusz, *This Way for the Gas, Ladies and Gentlemen*, New York: Penguin Books, 1976.

Bukiet, Melvin Jules, *After*, New York: St Martin's Press, 1996.

Darville, Helen, *The Hand that Signed the Paper*, Sydney: Allen and Unwin, 1995.

Demidenko, Helen, *The Hand that Signed the Paper*, Sydney: Allen and Unwin, 1994 (see Darville).

Ellman, Lucy, *Man or Mango?*, London: Headline, 1998.

Fink, Ida, *A Scrap of Time*, Harmondsworth: Penguin, 1989.

Green, Gerald, *Holocaust*, London: Corgi, 1978.
Hartnett, David, *Black Milk*, London: Jonathan Cape, 1994.
Hersey, John, *The Wall*, New York: Alfred A. Knopf, 1950.
Hochhuth, Rolf, *The Deputy*, New York: Grove Press, 1964.
Kenneally, Thomas, *Schindler's List*, London: Sceptre, 1986 (first published 1982).
Kosinski, Jerzy, *The Painted Bird*, New York: Bantam, 1978 (first published 1965).
Michaels, Anne, *Fugitive Pieces*, London: Bloomsbury, 1997.
Ozick, Cynthia, *The Shawl*, London: Jonathan Cape, 1991.
Roth, Philip, *The Ghost Writer*, London: Jonathan Cape, 1979.
Skibell, Joseph, *A Blessing on the Moon*, London: Little, Brown and Company, 1997.
Spiegelman, Art, *Maus I*, New York: Pantheon Books, 1986.
—— *Maus II*, New York: Pantheon Books, 1991.
Styron, William, *Sophie's Choice*, London: Corgi, 1980 (first published 1979).
Thomas, D.M., *The White Hotel*, Harmondsworth: Penguin, 1981.
—— 'The Woman to Sigmund Freud', *New Worlds*, 1979.
Wilkomirski, Binjamin, *Fragments: Memories of a Childhood, 1939–1948*, trans. Carol Brown
    Janeway, London: Picador, 1996.

Critical works

Adorno, Theodor, *Negative Dialectics*, trans. E.B. Ashton, New York: Seabury, 1973.
Amis, Martin, 'The D.M. Thomas Phenomenon', *Atlantic Monthly*, April 1983, pp. 124–6.
Auerbach, Erich, *Mimesis: The Representation of Reality in Western Literature*, New York:
    Doubleday, 1957.
Bentley, Eric, *The Storm Over the Deputy: Essays and Articles about Hochhuth's Explosive Drama*,
    New York: Grove Press, 1964.
Berger, Alan L., *Children of Job: American Second-Generation Witnesses to the Holocaust*, Albany,
    N.Y.: State University of New York Press, 1997.
Bernard, Catherine, 'A Certain Hermeneutic Slant: Allegories in Contemporary English
    Fiction', *Contemporary Literature* 38 (1), Spring 1997, pp. 164–84.
Bernstein, Michael André, *Foregone Conclusions: Against Apocalyptic History*, Berkeley and
    London: University of California Press, 1994.
—— 'Homage to the Extreme: The Shoah and the Rhetoric of Catastrophe', *Times
    Literary Supplement*, 6 March 1998, pp. 6–8.
Brooks, Peter, *Reading for the Plot*, New York: Columbia University Press, 1984.
Cahill, Daniel J., 'Kosinski and His Critics', *North American Review*, Spring 1980, pp. 66–8.
Clendinnen, Inga, *Reading the Holocaust*, Melbourne, Victoria: Text Publishing, 1998.
Cowart, David, 'Being and Seeming: *The White Hotel*', *Novel* 19, Spring 1986, pp. 216–31.
Easterbrook, Neil, ' "I know that it is to do with trash and shit": Narrative reversal in
    Martin Amis's *Time's Arrow*', *Conference of College Teachers in English Studies* 55, 1995, pp.
    52–61.
Felder, Lynn. 'D.M. Thomas: The Plagiarism Controversy', in Richard Ziegfeld (ed.),
    Dictionary of Literary Biography Yearbook 1982, Detroit: Gale Research, 1983, pp. 79–82.
Foley, Barbara, 'Fact, Fiction, Fascism: Testimony and Mimesis in Holocaust Narratives',
    Comparative Literature 34 (4), Fall 1982, pp. 330–60.
Foster, John Burt, 'Magic Realism in *The White Hotel*: Compensatory Vision and the
    Transformation of Classic Realism', *Southern Humanities Review* 20, 1986, pp. 205–19.

Friedlander, Saul (ed.), *Probing the Limits of Representation: Nazism and the 'Final Solution'*, Cambridge, Mass.: Harvard University Press, 1992.

Granofsky, Ronald, 'Holocaust as Symbol in *Riddley Walker* and *The White Hotel*', *Modern Language Studies* (16) 3, 1986, pp. 172–82.

Hansen, Miriam Bratu, '*Schindler's List* is not *Shoah*: Second Commandment, Popular Modernism, and Public Memory', in Yosefa Loshitzky (ed.), *Spielberg's Holocaust: Critical Perspectives on Schindler's List*, Bloomington and Indianapolis: Indiana University Press, 1997.

Hirschkop, Ken, and David Shepherd (eds), *Bakhtin and Cultural Theory*, Manchester: Manchester University Press, 1989.

Horowitz, Sara, 'Auto/Biography and Fiction after Auschwitz: Probing the Boundaries of Second-Generation Aesthetics', in Efraim Sicher (ed.), *Breaking the Crystal: Writing and Memory after Auschwitz*, Urbana and Chicago: University of Illinois Press, 1998.

Howe, Irving, 'Writing the Holocaust', in Berel Lang (ed.), *Writing and the Holocaust*, New York: Homes and Meier, 1988.

Hutcheon, Linda, 'Literary Borrowing ... and Stealing: Plagiarism, Sources, Influences, and Intertexts', *English Studies in Canada* XII, 2 June 1986, pp. 229–39.

—— 'Subject In/Of/To History and His Story', *Diacritics* 16 (1), Spring 1986, pp. 78–91.

Kappeler, Susanne, *The Pornography of Representation*, Cambridge: Polity Press, 1986.

Kauvar, Elaine M., *Cynthia Ozick's Fiction*, Bloomington and Indianapolis: Indiana University Press, 1993.

Lang, Berel (ed.), *Writing and the Holocaust*, New York: Holmes and Meier, 1988.

Langer, Lawrence, *Admitting the Holocaust: Collected Essays*, Oxford and New York: Oxford University Press, 1995.

—— *Pre-empting the Holocaust*, New Haven: Yale University Press, 1998.

Laplanche, J. and J.B. Pontalis, *The Language of Psychoanalysis*, trans. D. Nicholson-Smith, London: Karnac Books, 1988.

Leak, Andrew, and Paizis, George (eds), *The Holocaust as Text: Speaking the Unspeakable*, Basingstoke: Macmillan Press, 1999.

Loshitzky, Yosefa (ed.), *Spielberg's Holocaust: Critical Perspectives on 'Schindler's List'*, Bloomington and Indianapolis: Indiana University Press, 1997.

Lougy, Robert E., 'The Wolf-Man, Freud, and D.M. Thomas: Intertextuality, Interpretation, and Narration in *The White Hotel*', *Modern Language Studies*, 23 (3) 1991, pp. 91–106.

Miller, Emily Budick, 'Acknowledging the Holocaust in Contemporary American Fiction and Criticism', in Efraim Sicher (ed.), *Breaking the Crystal: Writing and Memory after Auschwitz*, Urbana and Chicago: University of Illinois Press, 1998.

Ozsvath, Zsuzsanna, and Martha Satz, 'The Audacity of Expressing the Inexpressible: The Relation Between Moral and Aesthetic Considerations in Holocaust Literature', *Judaism* 34 (2), 1985, pp. 197–210.

Parry, Ann, 'Idioms for the Unrepresentable: Post-war Fiction and the Shoah', *Journal of European Studies* 27 (4), 108, pp. 417–32.

Phillips, K.J., 'The Phalaris Syndrome: Alain Robbe-Grillet vs. D.M. Thomas', in Katherine Anne Ackley (ed.), *Women and Violence in Literature: An Essay Collection*, New York and London: Garland Publishing, 1990.

Robertson, Mary F., 'Hystery, Herstory, History: "Imagining the Real" in Thomas's *The White Hotel*', *Contemporary Literature* 25, 1984, pp. 452–77.

Shatzky, Joel, 'Creating an Aesthetic for Holocaust Literature', *Studies in Jewish American Literature* 10 (1), 1994, pp. 104–14.

Sicher, Efraim (ed.), *Breaking the Crystal: Writing and Memory after Auschwitz*, Urbana and Chicago: University of Illinois Press, 1998.

Soltan, Margaret, 'From Black Magic to White Noise: Malcolm Lowry and Don DeLillo', in Frederick Asals and Paul Tiessen (eds), *A Darkness that Murmured: Essays on Malcolm Lowry*, Toronto: University of Toronto Press, 2000.

Steiner, George, *Language and Silence*, Harmondsworth: Penguin, 1979.

Swinden, Patrick, 'D.M. Thomas and *The White Hotel*', *Critical Quarterly* 24 (4), 1986, pp. 71–82.

Tanner, Laura E., 'Sweet Pain and Charred Bodies: Figuring Violence in *The White Hotel*', *Intimate Violence*, Bloomington and Indianapolis: Indiana University Press, 1994.

Vice, Sue, *Introducing Bakhtin*, Manchester: Manchester University Press, 1997.

Wiesel, Elie, 'The Holocaust as Literary Inspiration', in Elie Wiesel, Lucy S. Dawidowicz, Dorothy Rabinowicz and Robert McAfee Brown, *Dimensions of the Holocaust by Elie Wiesel, Lucy S. Dawidowicz, Dorothy Rabinowicz, Robert McAfee Brown*, Evanston, Ill.: Northwestern University Press, 1977.

Wingrove, David/D.M.Thomas, 'Different Voices', *London Magazine*, February 1982, pp. 27–43.

Wirth-Nesher, Hana, 'The Ethics of Narration in D.M. Thomas's *The White Hotel*', *The Journal of Narrative Technique* 15, 1985, pp. 15–28.

'Writing the Unwritable: A Debate on Holocaust Fiction. Martin Amis, Bryan Cheyette, Lucy Ellmann, Joseph Skibell', *Jewish Quarterly* 170, Summer 1998, pp. 12–15.

Young, James E., 'Holocaust Documentary Fiction: The Novelist as Eyewitness', in Berel Lang (ed.), *Writing and the Holocaust*, New York: Holmes and Meier, 1988.

—— *Writing and Rewriting the Holocaust: Narrative and the Consequences of Interpretation*, Bloomington and Indianapolis: Indiana University Press, 1990.

Index

abjection 86–9, 194 n. 123, 194 n. 125, 194 n. 127
Adorno, Theodor 5, 20
Alkana, Joseph 72, 89, 188 n. 32
allegory 1, 68, 70, 81, 94
Allen, Jim, *Perdition* 1, 162, 164–7
Amis, Martin 177 n. 4; *Time's Arrow* 2, 3, 4, 6, 11–37 *passim*, 38, 43, 47, 59, 64, 67, 112, 116, 120, 123, 130, 145, 161, 162, 220 n. 22
Anatoli, A. *see* Kuznetsov, Anatoli
antisemitism 12, 52, 53, 58, 61–2, 75–6, 78, 119, 126–7, 134, 135, 140, 141, 143, 144, 148–55, 157–9, 192 n. 78, 201 n. 59, 207 n. 1, 217 n. 115, 218 n. 5, 219 n. 11, 224 n. 60, 227 n. 21
Appelfeld, Aharon, *Badenheim 1939* 19, 20
Arendt, Hannah, *Eichmann in Jerusalem* 7, 106–9, 122, 133, 202 n. 71, 202 n. 77, 208 n. 15
Auerbach, Erich, *Mimesis* 4, 6, 8, 72,188 n. 32
Auschwitz, Auschwitz-Birkenau 5, 13, 14, 15, 17–21, 23, 25, 27–37, 95, 105, 117, 118–36 *passim*, 147, 163, 210 n. 28
authenticity 1, 78, 143, 161, 162, 163–4, 205 n. 107
autobiography 2, 67–89 *passim*, 118
Avisar, Ilan 101, 198 n. 33, 206 n. 126

Babi Yar 5, 38, 41, 44, 46, 48, 50, 54–6, 57, 58–65, 142, 144–5, 156, 157, 179 n. 35, 182 n. 75, 182 n. 81, 184 n. 100, 184 n. 106, 185 n. 119; *see also* Kuznetsov, Anatoli
backshadowing 3, 18–24, 38, 44, 47, 51, 53, 58, 82, 97–9, 101, 111–12, 116, 122, 123

Bailey, Paul 93
Bakhtin, Mikhail 9, 48, 51, 72, 80, 82, 85, 92, 93, 96, 105, 108, 151, 152, 155–6, 167; *see also* dialogism, dialogized heteroglossia, double-voiced discourse, epic, heteroglossia, monologism, polyphony, *skaz*, Volosinov
Bartov, Omer 90, 198 n. 32, 205 n. 107
Begley, Louis, *Wartime Lies* 14, 70, 78, 80, 173 n. 14
Beijski, Moshe 204 n. 102
Bellow, Saul, *Dangling Man* 138
Belzec 5, 103, 107
Benigni, Roberto, *Life is Beautiful* 4, 168 n. 3, 169 n. 10
Benjamin, Walter 6
Bentley, David 143, 219 n. 10
Bergen-Belsen 147
Berger, Alan L. 169 n. 12
Bernard, Andréa, and Elzbieta H. Oleksy 207 n. 3, 216 n. 103
Bernard, Catherine 182 n. 78
Bernstein, Michael André 3, 7, 8, 18, 19, 23, 29, 51, 58, 94, 97–8, 112, 173 n. 25, 173 n. 31, 174 n. 53, 201 n. 65; *see also* backshadowing, foreshadowing, sideshadowing
Bersani, Leo 20
Bettelheim, Bruno 121, 198 n. 27
Birkenau 24
Black Deeds of the Kremlin, The see Pidhainy, S.O.
Bone, Pamela 159
Booker Prize 12, 14, 38, 90, 91
Borowski, Tadeusz 197 n. 16, 217 n. 112
Bosko, Oswald 112, 202 n. 7
Boyes, Roger 163, 164
Brecher, Elinor 112
Breuer, Josef 45

Brinnlitz, Moravia 91, 99, 105, 114, 201 n. 64, 203 n. 80
Brooks, Peter 60
Browning, Christopher, 'One Day in Józefów', 202 n. 77, 223 n. 56
Brzczinski, Zbigniew 188 n. 35
Buchenwald 147
Budapest 32, 99, 103, 165–7, 205 n. 102
Bukiet, Melvin Jules, *After* 4
Burroughs, William 32

Cahill, Daniel J. 190 n. 59
Cesarani, David 165, 220 n. 22, 227 n. 17, 228 n. 21
Cheyette, Bryan 6, 36, 199 n. 38, 206 n. 113, 206 n. 116
Chomsky, Noam 118 n. 25
Clendinnen, Inga 171 n. 29
Cluj 131, 132
Coale, Samuel 71
Cohen, Bernard 158, 219 n. 11, 222 n. 45
Cohn, Dorrit 190 n. 54, 193 n. 97
Cologne-Brookes, Gavin 210 n. 28
Colville, Georgiana 138, 212 n. 56
Compton, Neil 71
Corngold, Stanley 83, 186 n. 9, 187 n. 19, 188 n. 26, 193 n. 103
Cracow 90, 97, 99, 100, 102, 103, 104, 107, 117, 196 n. 8, 198 n. 31; *see also* Plaszów
Crane, John Kenny 207 n. 6, 210 n. 30
Craven, Peter 141, 219 n. 9

Dachau 126, 147
Daniel, Helen 141
Darville, Helen, *The Hand that Signed the Paper* 2, 3, 6, 8, 33, 36, 109, 120, 141–60 *passim*, 161, 162, 164, 166; 'Other Places', 218 n. 9, 221 n. 37; 'Writing after Winning', 218 n. 9
Delbo, Charlotte 6, 191, n. 75
Demidenko, Helen *see* Darville, Helen
Denby, David 169 n. 10
Dershowitz, Alan 141, 154
dialogism 9, 91, 152, 155, 158, 167
dialogized heteroglossia 9, 157, 158, 160, 166, 185 n. 123
Dick, Philip K. 14; 'Your Appointment Will be Yesterday', 26–7
Dickens, Charles, *David Copperfield* 80
doctors, Nazi 11, 14, 24, 26, 30–7, 127–8, 129, 130; *see also* Lifton, Robert Jay

documentary fiction 40, 81, 93–4, 103, 122, 127, 144, 181 n. 55, 192 n. 94
Donat, Alexander 149
Dostoevsky, Fyodor, Crime and Punishment 21, 130
double-voiced discourse 9, 10, 63, 82–3, 85, 88, 96, 106, 107–8, 129, 158–9, 201 n. 62, 203 n. 81
'doubling', 24–30, 34, 35, 129; *see also* Lifton, Robert Jay
Douglas, Mary 88, 193 n. 119
Dresden 27, 30
Durham, Carolyn A. 212 n. 57, 215 n. 100, 216 n. 105

Easterbrook, Neil 17, 20, 24, 25–6, 27, 31, 47, 176 n. 103
Eichmann, Adolf 23, 203 n. 84; *see also* Arendt, Hannah
Einsatzgruppen 33–4, 106, 156
Eliot, George, *The Mill on the Floss* 37
Ellmann, Lucy 8; *Man or Mango?*, 7, 153
English, David 97, 198 n. 32, 201 n. 61
Enright, D.J. 92, 93, 195 n. 7
epic 72, 188 n. 30
Epstein, Leslie 70, 71–2, 88
euthanasia 31, 33; *see also* Schloss Hartheim
Everman, Welch D. 82
Ezrahi, Sidra DeKoven 55–6, 68

faction 9, 91–4, 141, 142, 203 n. 85
Faulkner, Peter 21
Fenton, James 178 n. 11
Ferenczi, Sandor 58
Fiedler, Leslie 208 n. 12
Field, Andrew 191 n. 78
Fink, Ida, *A Scrap of Time* 14, 22–3; *The Journey* 22, 70, 78
First World War 7, 8, 21
Firth, Gay 93
Foley, Barbara 80, 81, 93, 118, 181 n. 55, 185 n. 123
foreshadowing 19, 20, 29, 59, 97–8, 112–13, 122, 123; pseudo-foreshadowing 29, 59–60
Foster, John Burt 56
Franciosi, Robert 130, 214 n. 82
Frank, Anne 94, 156, 198 n. 27
Fraser, Morag 146, 154, 155
free direct discourse 96–7, 100, 101–2, 104

free indirect discourse 82, 83–5, 86, 101,
104, 107, 112–13, 136–7, 159, 193 n.
107, 199 n. 40, 224 n. 57
Fremont-Smith, Eliot 73, 74, 188 n. 36,
189 n. 42
Friedlander, Saul 170 n. 23
Freud, Sigmund 38, 40, 44, 46, 49, 52,
55–6, 58, 61–3, 93, 176 n. 1, 177 n. 4,
178 n. 15, 179 n. 34, 181 n. 69, 184 n.
100; case history of Anna G. 48; case
history of Dora 39, 45, 57; case history
of Little Hans 86; case history of
Schreber 52–3; case history of Wolf
Man 60, 180 n. 41
Fullerton, Fiona 92

Gaffney, Carmel 111, 203 n. 85
Gaita, Raymond 155, 225 n. 80
Ganzfried, Daniel 163, 164, 226 n. 5
Gilbert, Martin, *The Holocaust: The Jewish
Tragedy* 143, 227–8 n. 17
Gilman, Sander L. 56–7, 174 n. 53, 183
n. 88
Glastonbury, Marion 92
Glendinning, Victoria 94
Goeth, Amon 96, 97, 101, 103, 104, 108,
109, 112, 202 n. 67, 203 n. 84, 205 n.
104
Goff, Martyn 196 n. 9
Golleschau 9, 115
Gourevitch, Philip 163, 226 n. 5
Grass, Günter, *The Tin Drum* 187 n. 22
Green, Gerald, *Holocaust* 1, 117
Griese, Irma 134
Guncw, Sncja 154
gypsies 67, 72, 75, 88, 123, 214 n. 77

Hall, Peter 4
Hansen, Miriam Bratu 110, 170 n. 21
Hartman, Geoffrey 196 n. 8
Hartnett, David 4
Heath, William 128–9, 210 n. 28
Hersey, John 4
heteroglossia 152
Hilberg, Raul 90, 205 n. 112
Himmler, Heinrich 105, 209 n. 27, 212 n.
49
Hirsch, Helen 101, 112
Hirschkop, Ken 174 n. 46
history, historical discourse 2, 6, 7, 9, 10,
31, 34, 43, 44–53 passim, 58, 59, 68,
72, 95, 116, 127, 145–6, 147, 164–7,

183 n. 81, 183 n. 87, 200 n. 58, 209 n.
23
Hitler, Adolf 23, 52
Hodys, Eleonore 124, 129
Hochhuth, Rolf, *The Deputy* 1, 130
Hollington, Michael 94, 114, 200 n. 51,
203 n. 83, 203 n. 91
Horowitz, Richard 101
Horowitz, Sara 169 n. 8, 169 n.14, 170 n.
24, 187 n. 16, 191 n. 76
Höss, Rudolf 93, 118, 120, 121, 129, 130,
136, 139, 209 n. 27, 210 n. 28, 211 n.
32, 212 n. 57; *Commandant of Auschwitz*
122–7, 140
Howe, Irving 105, 139, 169 n. 17, 170 n.
29
Hulse, Michael 93
Hutcheon, Linda 39, 144, 177 n. 5, 177
n. 10, 178 n. 15, 179 n. 20, 180 n. 39,
180 n. 53, 181 n. 58, 185 n. 110

Indyk, Ivor 141
intertextuality 2, 4, 25, 30–7, 130, 146,
153
Ivan the Terrible 154

Jerusalem 95, 102
Johns, Sally 73–4
Johnstone, Richard 109
Jung, Carl 58, 63

Kafka, Franz 23
Kaganovich, Lazar 147, 150, 151, 222 n.
45, 224 n. 60
Kalmanovich, Zelig 7
Kantaris, Sylvia 38, 177 n. 4, 182 n. 75,
183 n. 83, 184 n. 101
Kappeller, Susanne 39, 43–5, 46, 50, 54,
56
Kastner, Rudolf 165
Keneally, Thomas, *Schindler's Ark see*
Keneally, Thomas, *Schindler's List*
Keneally, Thomas 141, 219 n. 11; *A
Family Madness* 94; *Gossip from the
Forest* 148; *Schindler's List* 2, 3, 6,
36, 90–116 *passim*, 122, 137, 159,
161
Kenrick, D.A. 177 n. 5
Kermode, Frank 16, 17, 37
Kiev 38, 55, 59, 61, 64, 178 n.15
Kipen, Aviva 36–7, 176 n. 101
KL Auschwitz Seen by the SS 7, 123, 125,

127, 130, 211 n. 38, 211 n. 40; *see also* Rawicz, Jerzy
Klein, Fritz 130, 132, 133, 135, 136
Klinkowitz, Jerome 75, 187 n. 19, 191 n. 77
Koning, Hans 69
Kosciesza, Bogumil 201 n. 59
Kosinski, Henryk 191 n. 67
Kosinski, Jerzy 188 n. 26, 189 n. 42, 189 n. 46, 190 n. 64, 191 n. 66; *The Future is Ours, Comrade* 73; *The Hermit of 69th Street* 78; *No Third Path* 73, 191 n. 66; *The Painted Bird* 2, 3, 6, 67–89 passim, 161, 162, 222 n. 44; *Pinball* 73; *Steps* 73–4
Kremer, Johann Paul 130, 133
Kristeva, Julia 184 n. 94; , 86–9, 193 n. 115, 193 n. 119, 194 n. 123, 194 n. 124, 194 n. 125, 194 n. 129
Künstlerroman 80, 83, 85, 118
Kurosawa, Akira, *Rashomon* 156
Kuznetsov, Anatoli, *Babi Yar* 7, 38–9, 40–4, 49, 60, 61–2, 64, 69, 81, 93, 122, 127, 144–5, 178 n. 12, 178 n. 15, 180 n. 53, 181 n. 55, 181 n. 58, 182 n. 72, 182 n. 81, 184 n. 100, 185 n. 108

Lale, Meta, and John Williams 188 n. 26, 193 n. 104, 193 n. 113
Lang, John 130
Langer, Lawrence L. 12, 13, 16, 68, 69, 72, 136, 214 n. 82
Lanzmann, Claude 5, 170 n. 19, 199 n. 44; *Shoah* 27, 170 n. 21, 170 n. 29
Laplanche, J. and J.B. Pontalis 48
Lappin, Elena 163
Larsen, Eric 69, 186 n. 14
Lawson, Mark 11, 12, 36, 37
Lengyel, Olga, *Five Chimneys* 120, 126, 129, 130, 131–6, 140
Lenin, Vladimir Illych 85
Levi, Primo 6, 25, 139, 196 n. 16, 226 n. 5
Levin, Bernard 228 n. 25
Levin, Ira, *The Boys from Brazil* 130
Liberman, Serge 157–8
Lifton, Robert Jay 46; *The Nazi Doctors* 7, 11, 15, 25–6, 30–7, 129, 145, 174 n. 41, 176 n. 91, 220 n. 22
Lilly, Paul 74, 188 n. 39, 189 n. 46, 192 n. 92
Lodge, David 93

Loshitzky, Yosefa 195 n. 3, 194 n. 5, 197 n. 25, 204 n. 94
Lougy, Robert E. 180 n. 41, 180 n. 49, 181 n. 60, 183 n. 82, 185 n. 110
Louvish, Simon 11, 13, 14, 15, 37, 196 n. 12, 197 n. 25
Lowell, James 148
Lowenthal, David 198 n. 33, 205 n. 109, 205 n. 110
Lupak, Barbara Tepa 74, 189 n. 43, 209 n. 23

MacCannell, Juliet Flower 194 n. 129
McGowan, Moray 206 n. 117
Madritsch, Julius 98, 99, 112
Majdanek 76, 163
Manne, Robert 21, 109, 144, 145, 150, 152, 153, 154, 155, 159, 219 n. 10, 219 n. 11
Matthews, Brian 221 n. 37
Mengele, Josef 25, 32, 33, 175 n. 91, 213 n. 67
metaphor 10, 45, 46, 50, 70–1, 75, 91, 119, 133, 162, 193 n. 102
Metz, Christian 204 n. 96
Michaels, Anne, *Fugitive Pieces* 8, 9–10, 153, 161
Miller, Emily Budick 168 n. 6
Miller, Karl 12
Milton, John 94, 130
monologism 9, 96, 106, 108, 109, 158, 166–7, 203 n. 81
Montale, Eugenio 16
Moore, Susan 145–6, 155
morality, morals 29, 34, 67–8, 121, 133, 140, 142
Morgan, Robin, *The Demon Lover*, 148, 221 n. 37
Morrison, Toni 148, 221 n. 36
Morson, Gary Saul 18, 19, 22, 23, 175 n. 77
Moscow 85
Mosley, Nicholas 12
Müller, Filip, *Eyewitness Auschwitz* 170 n. 29
Muller, Peter, *Gloomy Sunday* 204 n. 97
Musil, Robert, *The Man Without Qualities* 20, 21

Nachträglichkeit 48, 98
narrator, narrative effects 3, 4, 12, 13, 15, 20–2, 24–30, 35, 43, 51, 60, 68, 84,

86, 91, 95–109 *passim*, , 110, 112, 120, 121–2, 127–9, 136, 138, 144, 150–5 *passim*, 162, 163–4, 176 n. 103, 193 n. 98, 201 n. 61, 207 n. 8, 213 n. 62; *see also* Bakhtin, Mikhail; free direct discourse; free indirect discourse
Nyiszli, Miklos, *Auschwitz: A Doctor's Eyewitness Account* 32

O'Hearn, Tim 104, 197 n. 17
Oleksy, Elzbieta H. *see* Bernard, Andréa
Ozick, Cynthia 4, 119, 208 n. 16; *The Shawl* 10, 72, 172 n. 46
Ozsvath, Zsuzsanna and Martha Satz 177 n. 4, 179 n. 34, 185 n. 119

Paulin, Tom 172 n. 11
Pawel, Ernst 23, 24
Pellegrini, Ann 57, 181 n. 68, 183 n. 88
Petersson, Irmtraud 99, 196 n. 12, 197 n. 24
Petlyura, Simon 152–3
Pfefferberg, Leopold 100, 107, 109, 200 n. 56
Phillips, K.J. 58, 182 n. 80, 184 n. 98, 184 n. 103
Pidhainy, S.O., ed., *The Black Deeds of the Kremlin, volumes I and II* 143, 145, 146, 148, 150, 153, 221 n. 33
Pierce, Peter 110, 195 n. 1, 200 n. 56
Pilger, John 159
Pinter, Harold 202 n. 65
plagiarism 2, 32, 34, 39, 40, 44, 65, 74, 142, 144, 146, 149, 153, 162, 163, 177 n. 11, 179 n. 16, 179 n. 20, 180 n. 53, 182 n. 72, 189 n. 43, 220 n. 17, 221 n. 36, 221 n. 37
Plaszów 95, 103, 104, 108, 111, 196 n. 8
Plath, Sylvia 4; *The Bell Jar* 80
poetry 7, 9, 44–53 *passim*
Poland 67–89 *passim*, 90–116 *passim*, 117–40 passim, 158, 186 n. 4, 190 n. 51, 191 n. 70, 198 n. 34, 209 n. 23, 224 n.61
polyphony 9, 21, 22, 59, 82, 105, 150–6, 159–60, 166, 184 n. 101, 223 n. 48, 223 n. 51
Ponar 5
Pontalis, J.B. *see* Laplanche, J.
pornography 39, 41, 43, 45, 54, 66, 69, 126, 156

Pronicheva, Dina 39, 40–3, 49, 50, 53, 57–8, 178 n. 12, 178 n. 15, 179 n. 19, 181 n. 58, 225 n. 74

Quartermaine, Peter 93, 94, 100, 103, 110, 196 n. 9, 197 n. 21, 200 n. 51

Rathenau, Walter 56
Rawicz, Jerzy 123–4, 125, 130, 211 n. 46
Rawicz, Piotr 191 n. 75, 191 n. 76
reader 12, 15, 20, 22, 24–5, 31, 36, 59, 65–6, 103, 159, 161, 162, 163, 180 n. 39, 185 n. 110, 187 n. 23
Redgrove, Peter 177 n. 4, 182 n. 72, 182 n. 80, 183 n. 83
Rendell, Ruth 194 n. 130
Richter, David H. 186 n. 4, 187 n. 23, 190 n. 59
Riemer, Andrew 150, 155, 159, 163, 218 n. 5, 219 n. 11, 222 n. 37, 223 n. 56, 226 n. 82
Rimmon-Kenan, Shlomith 84
Robertson, Mary F. 46, 55, 58, 63, 64–5, 182 n. 75, 183 n. 84, 183 n. 88, 185 n. 112, 185 n. 115
Rogers, Byron 195 n. 7
Rose, Gillian 197 n. 16, 198 n. 29, 198 n. 33, 201 n. 61
Rosenfeld, Alvin 119, 120, 122, 123, 128, 131, 136, 137, 198 n. 27, 209 n. 24, 215 n. 100
Roth, Philip 118; *The Ghost Writer* 4; *Portnoy's Complaint* 138–9, 216 n. 109
Rousset, David 208 n. 15
Rubenstein, Richard 121, 130
Rubinstein, W.D. 141

Sachsenhausen 119
Sage, Lorna 93
Salusinzky, Imre 195 n. 1, 197 n. 24
Samuels, Diane 4
Sanders, Ivan 186 n. 10, 192 n. 89
Santner, Eric 52
Satz, Martha *see* Ozsvath, Zsuzsanna
Schaeffer, Susan Fromberg 4, 177 n. 4
Schaffer, William 156, 158, 225 n. 79
Schindler, Emilie 100, 206 n. 114
Schindler, Oskar 90–116 *passim*; 'Report', 103, 111, 113–16, 199 n. 39, 199 n. 47, 206 n. 117
Schlink, Bernhard, *The Reader* 194 n. 130

Schloss Hartheim 20
Schwarz-Bart, André, *The Last of the Just*
209 n. 22
Schwarzbard, Shalom 152–3
science fiction 14
Shakespeare, William, *King Lear* 87
Shatzky, Joel 169 n. 13, 171 n. 38
Sicher, Efraim 169 n. 12
sideshadowing 18, 19, 21, 98, 101, 111,
112–13
Siedlecka, Joanna 75, 77
Singer, Peter 141, 154
Sirlin, Rhoda 209 n. 23, 210 n. 28, 211 n.
35
skaz 151–2, 222 n. 46
Skibell, Joseph, *A Blessing on the Moon* 7
Slater, Maya 15, 16–17, 18
Sloan, James Park 68–9, 74, 75, 77–8, 80,
186 n. 8, 187 n. 21, ,188 n. 36, 189 n.
42, 189 n. 43, 189 n. 48, 190 n. 50,
191 n. 68, 192 n. 80, 193 n. 96, 193 n.
101
Smith, Joan 138, 208 n. 9, 210 n. 28, 215
n. 101
Soltan, Margaret 177 n. 9
Spender, Dale 141
Spielberg, Steven, *Schindler's List* 1, 5, 36,
90, 91, 95, 101, 131, 170 n. 19, 200 n.
53, 201 n. 61, 203 n. 83, 204 n. 93,
204 n. 94, 206 n. 113
Stalin, Josef 84–5, 147, 150, 151
Steinem, Gloria 138
Steiner, George 4, 121, 122
Steinhouse, Herbert 112, 200 n. 55, 205
n. 103
Stern, Itzhak 102, 109, 110, 114, 200 n.
55
Stokes, Geoffrey 73, 74, 189 n. 42
Stone, Dan 173 n. 33
Streicher, Julius 126, 212 n. 50
Styron, William, *The Confessions of Nat
Turner* 117; *Sophie's Choice* 2, 3, 6, 93,
94, 105, 117–40 passim, 159, 161,
164, 201 n. 63
survivor testimony, testimony
Swift, Jonathan, *A Modest Proposal* 14
Swinden, Patrick 178 n. 14, 178 n.
15

Talmud 95
Tanner, Laura E. 44–6, 49, 50, 51, 55,
58, 63, 64, 179 n. 35

Taubman, Robert 93, 111
Tel Aviv 102
Tennant, Emma 185 n. 122
Terezin 23
testimony 2, 3, 5, 6, 7, 8, 31, 74, 79, 100,
102, 111, 112, 131, 137, 161, 163–4,
178 n. 12, 191 n. 70, 215 n. 97; *see also
KL Auschwitz Seen by the SS*; Müller,
Filip; Pronicheva, Dina; Schindler,
Oskar, 'Report'
Theweleit, Klaus 55
Thomas, D.M. 176 n. 101, 182 n. 72, 182
n. 80, 185 n. 107, 185 n. 123; *Memories
and Hallucinations* 39, 63, 176 n. 1, 177
n. 11, 178 n. 15; *Pictures at an Exhibition*
53, *The White Hotel* 2, 3, 4, 6, 8, 22,
39–66 *passim*, 67, 81, 93, 94, 127, 144,
162, 189 n. 43
Thomson, David 112, 203 n. 93
Thornton, William 202 n. 67, 206 n. 113
time, temporal effects 2, 18–19, 28–9, 48,
59–65, 83, 96–102, 105, 132, 137, 184
n. 98, 199 n. 48
Tolstoy, Leo, *War and Peace* 18, 23
Treblinka 4, 5, 6, 142, 143
Trocmé, André 114

Ukraine 39–66 *passim*, 141–60 *passim*;
Ukrainian Famine 142, 148, 152, 153,
223 n. 47, 225 n. 79
Updike, John 64, 173 n. 20, 174 n. 58,
175 n. 86

Vienna 55, 106, 107
Vietnam 30
Vilna 7
Vinnitsa 142, 147
Volosinov, V.N. 15
Vonnegut, Kurt 30; *Slaughterhouse 5*,
27–30, 62, 175 n. 80

Wallenberg, Raoul 113
Walter, Natasha 10
Warsaw, Warsaw Ghetto 142, 149–50,
156
Webber, Jonathan 174 n. 55
Weil, Simone 122
Weiss, Peter, *The Investigation* 1
Welles, Orson, *Citizen Kane*, 111, 204 n.
95
Wesker, Arnold 165
White, Patrick 148

Whitrow, G.J. 16, 22, 51
Wiesel, Elie 5, 7, 78, 173 n. 18, 207 n. 4; *Night* 14, 164, 198 n. 27
Wilkomirski, Binjamin, *Fragments*, 1, 76, 162, 163–4, 167
Williams, John *see* Lale, Meta
Wingrove, David 46
Wirth-Nesher, Hana 43, 56, 65, 176 n. 2, 179 n. 23, 181 n. 55, 181 n. 69, 183 n. 87, 184 n. 101

Wood, James 17, 35–6, 175 n. 85, 176 n. 101
Wundheiler, Luitgard 108, 111, 114, 200 n. 55, 204 n. 98, 204 n. 102

Yad Vashem 102
Young, James E. 49–50, 181 n. 55, 184 n. 106

Zelizer, Barbie 115